MW00800507

ITALIAN HEAVY CRUISERS

ITALIAN HEAVY CRUISERS

From Trento to Bolzano

Maurizio Brescia and Augusto de Toro

Naval Institute Press
Annapolis, Maryland

Frontispiece: The forward 203/50 turrets and the bridge tower of *Trento* with the original tripod, before the two forward struts were added to stiffen the structure and limit vibration at high speeds. On the tripod platforms there were also positions for the anti-torpedo and anti-aircraft fire control. The photo was taken shortly after the commissioning of the ship. (Augusto de Toro collection)

Copyright © 2018 & 2020 Edizione Storia Militare s.r.l, Parma
Translation © 2022 Seaforth Publishing

Translated from the Italian *Incrociatori Pesanti Classe 'Zara'* and *Incrociatori Pesanti Trento, Trieste e Bolzano* and edited into this single volume by Maurizio Brescia

First published in Great Britain in 2022 by
Seaforth Publishing
An imprint of Pen & Sword Books Ltd
47 Church Street,
Barnsley
S Yorkshire S70 2AS

www.seaforthpublishing.com
Email info@seaforthpublishing.com

Published and distributed in the United States of America and Canada by the Naval Institute Press,
291 Wood Road, Annapolis, Maryland 21402
www.usni.org

Library of Congress Cataloging Number: 2022946289

ISBN 978 1 68247 871 4

This edition is authorized for sale only in the United States of America, its territories and possessions, and Canada

All rights reserved. No part of this publication may be reproduced or transmitted in any form or by any means, electronic or mechanical, including photocopying, recording, or any information storage and retrieval system, without prior permission in writing of both the copyright owner and the above publisher.

The right of Maurizio Brescia and Augusto De Toro to be identified as the authors of this work has been asserted in accordance with the Copyright, Designs and Patents Act 1988

Typeset and designed by Stephen Dent
Printed and bound by Printworks Global Ltd, London/Hong Kong

CONTENTS

INTRODUCTION

Ever since they were conceived in the wake of the 1922 Washington Treaty which set the qualitative limits, 10,000-ton cruisers have occupied a prominent place in all the major navies. From the outset they were also controversial ships, so much so that their fortunes depended more on international constraints on naval armament than on any firm belief in their validity as a tool of maritime warfare. The '10,000s', as they were referred to in Italy, remained tied to these agreements and until the Treaty of London in 1936 they became a substitute for battleships in international competition, so much so that for over a decade they were the focus of the major-ship construction programmes of all the great naval powers.

In Italy, these ships formed the backbone of the fleet throughout the 1930s, even after the commissioning of the two

Heavy cruiser *Trieste* soon after commissioning. The high freeboard of her flush deck configuration gives a rather imposing aspect to the ship. (E. Bagnasco collection)

rebuilt battleships of the *Conte di Cavour* class in 1937, for which, according to the thinking of the time, the cruisers had to partially compensate for the battleships' inferiority to potential adversaries. They maintained an important role even with the entry into service of the fast and powerful *Littorio* class battleships, as they were considered more suitable than the rebuilt battleships to cooperate with them due to their greater speed and operational flexibility.

For these reasons, too, the heavy cruisers, as they would eventually be called, contained technical solutions of great interest, and naval historiography has rightly devoted numerous publications to them. There has been no lack of literature in Italy either; indeed, in some ways the subject has been a trailblazer. However, after Franco Gay's and Elio Andò's monographs and Franco Bargoni's photographs – still essential today, although dating back 40 years – the topic has not been taken up again in Italy, while abroad it has undergone a very different development.

The brass memento that was presented to distinguished visitors on board the *Trento*: it depicts an eagle of St Wenceslas, the symbol of the city of Trento, surmounting a stylised trident (from *Tridentum*, the city's Latin name). This coat of arms also adorned the brass tompions of the 203/50 guns. (G. Ercole collection)

This book about the seven Italian heavy cruisers, like the previous *Italian Battleships: Conte di Cavour and Duilio Classes 1911–1956*, by Erminio Bagnasco and Augusto de Toro (Seaforth Publishing, 2021), originates from two separate studies published in Italy between 2018 and 2020 in the series *STORIA militare Briefing* and in general follows the same mainly technical approach that aimed at providing the most comprehensive coverage in both text and illustration so far published.

We would like to thank in particular the Gruppo di Cultura Navale (Naval Culture Group) in the person of its president, Prof. Mario Sannino, who generously provided a large number of original building plans from the Ansaldo, CRDA. and Orlando shipyards, as well as other drawings expressly created by Giancarlo Barbieri. The presence of the original plans (reproduced here at the maximum size allowed by the format of this book) is real added value; also from an academic point of view, the use of primary documentary sources is intended to increase the general value of a study that we have tried to devise in graphically up-to-date and innovative terms, within the existing tradition of Italian naval publishing.

Thanks go also to the Ufficio Storico della Marina Militare (USMM), from whose archives the impressive documentation consulted and summarised in the Bibliography is taken; a number of photographs also come from the USMM's Photo Archives. The authors would also like to thank the State Archives and the Civico Museo del Mare in Trieste, the Ansaldo Foundation in Genoa, the Naval History Museum in Venice and our friends Mario Cicogna, Federico Fontana, Marco Gueli, Ermanno Martino, Francesco Mattesini, Fulvio Petronio, Nicola Siracusano and others who more or less recently passed away: Elio Andò, Franco Bargoni, Giorgio Bignozzi, Gino Chesi, Giuliano Colliva, Franco Gay, Renato Mancini and Aureliano Molinari for the documentary material made available over the years from their respective archives and collections, but also for the many in-depth discussions and valuable suggestions that have made it possible to produce this work.

A heartfelt and special thanks – although unfortunately posthumously – goes to our friend Lt. Cdr Erminio Bagnasco, who recently passed away in January 2022. He was the leading exponent of Italian naval history after the Second World War and, for both of us, a true 'Maestro' and friend who always provided effective, fundamental and selfless help for all the work we have carried out in this sector over the years and from whose archives a good part of the photographs accompanying this book come.

We therefore thought it right to dedicate this book to Erminio Bagnasco, in memory of the person who, more than anyone else, positively influenced our activity in the complex and fascinating world of Italian naval historiography of the Second World War.

M. Brescia and A. de Toro
Genoa – Udine, spring 2022

Chapter 1

ITALIAN NAVAL POLICY AND THE 10,000-ton CRUISER

During the First World War, the development of cruisers varied significantly, determined by the theatres of war in which individual powers found themselves engaged, the interests and aspirations of some of them for the post-war period (above all the United States and Japan) and the overall armaments policy pursued by each of them. The most striking case was France, which almost gave up the construction of combat vessels, including small ships and submarines, in order to devote the maximum productive resources and manpower to the service of the *Armee*, ending the conflict with the same ships that it had started with, minus losses. The United States gave the greatest impetus to the construction of large battleships, fleet destroyers and, last but not least, light cruisers (the *Omaha* class). The Italian navy and, to a lesser extent, the Austro-Hungarian navy, developed torpedo boats, the most suitable ship-type for a sea war in the Adriatic, made up of ambushes and rapid raids. In terms of doctrine and employment criteria, the United Kingdom and Germany developed cruisers along two distinct lines: battlecruisers, with the task of forming an armoured scouting force and a fast division of the battle fleet; and light cruisers with multiple fleet (scouting, flotilla leaders) or autonomous duties (mine warfare, escort for smaller ships and naval warfare against enemy communication lines). Finally, Japan and Russia turned to battlecruisers (even if Russia was unable to complete any, due to the course of the conflict and the outbreak of revolution) and, to a lesser extent, to light cruisers.

The end of the war led to the extinction of three great naval powers (temporarily for Germany and Russia), to the emergence of new enmities or rivalries between the victorious powers, including a renewed conflict between France and Italy. There were also doubts of a doctrinal and operational nature about what were now the best weapons for maritime warfare, given the advent of the submarine and the aircraft, as well as an awareness of the vulnerability of large ships. As for cruisers, the only common feature was the demise of the armoured cruiser, which all the powers had abandoned. Battlecruisers were destined to merge with battleships, like the British *Hood*, but, in effect, already the emphasis in German wartime battlecruisers. Such ships remained the sole prerogative of the three so-called 'oceanic powers' (the United Kingdom, the United States and

The British cruiser *Frobisher*, of the *Hawkins* class in the mid-1920s.

The cruiser USS *Omaha*, commissioned on 24 February 1923.

Japan), while in the field of light cruisers and scouts different tendencies emerged, as there was not even a universally accepted terminology.

At the end of the conflict, France had a marked superiority over Italy in terms of battleships but lacked light cruisers and scouts and was inferior in terms of torpedo boats and submarines. The gap had widened during the course of the conflict, as Italy had lined up some 70,000 tons of ships, almost all of which fell into these categories, while France stood at only 28,000 tons. Therefore it is not surprising that, as early as February 1919, the General Staff of the Marine Nationale had set its construction priorities for future naval programmes as: first, torpedo boats and submarines; second, scouts or light cruisers; third and last, large ships. This orientation was mainly influenced by concerns about escorting merchant ships between North Africa and southern France along the western Mediterranean routes, exposed to the threat of superior Italian light forces. The gap was increased by the Italian post-war naval programmes (1919/1920 to 1921/1922), that authorised the completion of all the small naval vessels laid down during the war, even if for cost reasons no new construction was included. By contrast, political difficulties in France delayed the first (impressive) programme for the renewal of the fleet until parliamentary approval in April 1922.

This gave the Regia Marina an appreciable, albeit temporary, advantage over the Marine Nationale, precisely in those ship types then most in demand. These ships were still effective, but of an outdated conception, and in part compromised by wear and poor maintenance due to the budgetary difficulties linked to demobilisation. In terms of light cruisers or large scouts, at the end of 1922 neither of the two navies had any under construction – Italy through financial constraints, France due to military policy disputes – and the only contributions were made by former war-prize German and Austrian warships of limited value.

Meanwhile, the United States and Japan were in the midst of a naval arms race which, if realised, would have taken the US Navy from 1.5 to 2.5 million tons and the Imperial Navy from 0.7 to 1.6 million within a few years. The competition also involved the United Kingdom, which had actually begun to scrap 300,000 tons of ships out of the 2.3 million existing at the end of 1918, but had to respond to the other two powers if it did not want to see its supremacy compromised. In order to put a stop to a race ruinous for public finances, towards the end of 1921 the American administration promoted a conference to reduce and limit naval armaments. The conference, attended by the five major naval powers, began in Washington on 12 November 1921 and ended with a treaty of the same name signed on 6 February 1922, which was valid until 31 December 1936 and shaped naval policies until the mid-1930s.

The treaty firstly established a proportionate reduction in the number of existing battleships and battlecruisers and, for the future, a 'holiday' in their construction until 1931 (1927 for France and Italy) and, then, a hierarchy between naval powers according to the ratio of 15, 15, 9, 5 and 5, resulting in the allocation of 525,000 tons of new battleships to the United Kingdom and the United States, 305,000 tons to Japan and 175,000 tons to both France and Italy as well as 135,000 tons, 81,000 tons and 60,000 tons, respectively, for aircraft carriers. On the qualitative side, the treaty set the standard displacement limit at 35,000 tons and the gun calibre at 16in (406mm) for battleships and 8in

The Japanese cruiser *Kako*, still equipped with single 200/50 guns, moored at Kure on 31 July 1926. (Kure Naval Museum)

The Japanese cruiser *Kinugasa* in 1929, following the refit during which the main armament was replaced; note, aft of the tripod, the catapult protected by canvas covers. (Kure Naval Museum)

(203mm) for aircraft carriers. Britain lost its worldwide primacy, having now to share it with the United States; but, in turn, the treaty guaranteed the Anglo-Saxon powers absolute naval supremacy in the world in every single theatre and in both categories of ship, so much so as to configure a real peace between them. In Europe, London could enjoy a ratio of 3 to 2 with respect to the sum of France and Italy, with a safety margin of 1/3 in the event that a third naval power of equal weight to the two Latin powers were to emerge. Italy almost unexpectedly achieved parity with France that, for her part, felt downgraded and humiliated and therefore wanted to keep itself free of quantitative restrictions on cruisers and destroyers for the future.

No agreement was reached, however, on the quantitative and qualitative limitation of the remaining ships – cruisers, destroyers and submarines – due to the resolute opposition of France, backed by Italy and Japan, and the irreconcilable relativity of the five powers. The only exception was the quality limits for cruisers, which were set at 10,000 standard tons and 8in (203mm) guns. The proposal had been formulated by the US delegation, at the suggestion of the British, who would have modelled it on the *Hawkins* class cruisers, ships of almost 9750 tons displacement at normal load, armed with 7.5in (190mm) guns and 30-knot speed. These were warships designed to hunt German light cruisers in the oceans but had been completed just after the First World War due to the Royal Navy's lack of interest in them. By contrast, they aroused great interest in the US Navy which in 1920 started studies for ships of a similar type (the future *Omaha*), and even more so in Japan, where in 1920/1921 a 'large fast scout' of 7500 tons displacement at normal load, six 200mm (7.9in) guns and a maximum speed of 35 knots was designed. This was the *Kako* class: two ships were laid down at the end of 1922 followed by two similar vessels of the *Aoba* class, expressly conceived to oppose the *Hawkins* and *Omaha* class ships, of 7050 tons displacement at normal load, armed with ten 152mm (6in) guns, 34 knots of speed and large radius of action.

At Washington, qualitative agreement on cruisers was easily reached, having found favour with Japan for the firepower and range offered by this new type of ship and for its substantial correspondence to the *Kako* class. France and Italy also joined in, but with less enthusiasm. Thus the 'Washington' or 'Treaty' type cruiser – known simply as the '10,000' in Italy – was born. It was the brainchild of the oceanic powers but was almost immediately imitated by the two Latin powers. Not derived from any of its predecessors, it was the result of diplomatic negotiations rather than technical and operational assessments. It gave rise to lively discussions everywhere because of the obvious impossibility of enclosing within those dimensions ships balanced in terms of armament, protection and speed, with the consequent need to sacrifice one of the three. But in spite of the doubts and criticisms, often sarcastic, as a result of the concomitant 'holiday' imposed on the battle line, a new season of naval construction and competition opened up from which no power was able to escape, even those not a signatory to the treaty, such as Spain or Argentina (or later Germany and Russia).

The 1923/1924 Naval Programme and the first '10,000-ton' cruisers: *Trento* and *Trieste*

Since the end of the First World War, the Regia Marina had identified France as the main enemy on which to predicate its budgets and war plans: the former were affected by the country's financial straits; the latter by the geopolitical situation, marked by the economy's dependence on sea lanes, but also influenced by still-relevant pre-war doctrines about seizing control of the sea through a decisive battle between fleets, which had emerged shaken from the experiences of the conflict, but not completely discredited. In the thinking of Vice Admirals Alfredo Acton and Giuseppe De Lorenzi, who succeeded each other as Chiefs of Staff of the Navy in those years, this duality became clear. If on the one hand the need to ensure vital maritime communications in the Mediterranean, especially in the central-eastern part of this world, was pre-eminent, on the other hand the possibility of a decisive clash of battle forces could not be ruled out, either as a consequence of naval operations or attacks on trade, or to counter enemy invasion attempts from the sea. In all these hypotheses it would have been necessary to have an appreciable armoured nucleus, as well as light and stealthy vessels, which would also have had the task of wearing down the French battle squadron in order to nullify its quantitative superiority.

But what worried De Lorenzi most, after he took over as head of the Navy on 11 February 1921, was that, without a systematic renewal of the fleet, in less than a decade it would find itself with only a few worn-out and outdated ships. In December 1921, with the Washington conference still in progress, he presented a proposal titled 'Studio di Programma Navale' to the Minister of the Navy, Hon. Eugenio Bergamasco. This was an organic programme of naval construction, openly inspired by Alfred von Tirpitz's naval laws, intended to renew and increase the fleet starting from 1922 by fixing its size and composition by law or other regulatory instrument that would ensure stability over time. Using the force of law, this would lay down the age limits of each category of ship as well as the schedule for replacement construction, and fix the number to be reached by 1935 on the basis of replacements and augmentations, subdivided for each main category of ship. De Lorenzi's programme can be summarised as follows:

Ship types	Maximum age (years)	Building period (Years)	Minimum age for ships to be replaced (years)	Final number (1935)
Fast battleships	20	5	15	6
Light cruisers	15	4	11	12
Scouts	12	4	8	21
Destroyers	12	3	9	90
Long range submarines	12	4	8	18
Smaller submarines	12	3	9	73

The programme added a further 36 anti-submarine gunboats, 80 minesweepers, 10 minelayers, 160 MAS (small MTBs), as well as auxiliary vessels to be determined separately. No aircraft carriers were envisaged.

The declared aim was to remove naval renewal from the oscillations of politics and to settle it in an automatic, stable and methodical manner. Financially speaking, the programme was divided into two parts: the first, including all naval vessels except battleships, envisaged an expenditure of 3551 million lire to be divided up over 14 years for an annual amount of approximately 254 million lire; the second, including only battleships, envisaged additional expenditure of between 1440 and 1680 million lire, to be divided up over 14 years for an amount of between 103 and 120 million lire per annum. The division seemed to be designed to make it easier to remove one or more battleships from the programme.

On 31 January 1922, at the end of the Washington conference and when the contents of the treaty were by then outlined, De Lorenzi presented Bergamasco with an update of his study. In this, noting the moratorium on battleships, he postponed consideration of their replacement until after the four-year period 1922–1926 and, given the lack of quantitative limits for light and underwater ships, concentrated all available resources in these categories. With this in mind and in light of the news of the French naval *tranche* being approved, he proposed as a minimum programme the construction of 3 light cruisers of 10,000 tons, to

The French cruiser *Primauguet* (*Duguay Trouin* class) in Toulon Bay on 15 April 1932. (Photo Marius Bar)

be completed by 1926; 10 destroyers of 1250 tons, of which 4 to be immediately laid down and 6 towards the end of the four-year period 1922–1925; 4 + 6 submarines to be completed by 1926. The '10,000s' made their first appearance here. They were to be financed with extraordinary funds, while spending for the remaining vessels would fall under the Navy's ordinary budgets.

Bergamasco did not like the project, judging it to be out of place and out of time. Hon. Roberto De Vito, who succeeded him as head of the department on 26 February 1922, more diplomatically, left the problem unsolved, but agreed with the arguments on the need to develop light warships and submarines, supported in this by the opinion expressed on 10 October 1922 by the Admirals' Committee, his advisory body. On that occasion, the Committee, chaired by Admiral Paolo Thaon di Revel, was called upon to express its opinion on the construction programme that should be adopted in light of De Lorenzi's study and two other parallel studies dedicated to the dislocation of naval forces in the event of war and Italy's future military maritime structure. Although with different emphases and nuances, the Committee shared the principles underlying De Lorenzi's studies and agreed, with the sole exception of Vice Admiral Enrico Millo, to proceed with the construction of three 10,000-ton light cruisers, in view of the vacancy in the fleet. Because no battleship would be started before 1927, without the '10,000s' in less than ten years the Regia Marina would have no major warship at all. Furthermore, France had announced the construction of three 7250-ton light cruisers, armed with eight 155mm guns (the *Duguay Trouin* class, financed in 1922).

With the advent of Fascism Thaon di Revel took over as Minister of the Navy. But the new government's naval policy did not deviate much from those of its liberal predecessors, continuing to be dominated by economy of expenditure. Thaon di Revel's first concern was to avoid the deterioration of the naval forces, starting with a restructuring of the Navy's budget, the reorganisation of the Armed Forces and, above all, the setting of multi-year spending plans, which, if they did not establish an organic development of the fleet, should at least free the Navy from the so-called 'one year budgets' that did not guarantee the stable renewal and strengthening of the fleet. This type of planning had already been implemented in 1923, as evidenced by the planned four-year programme for the financial years 1924/1925 to 1927/1928, which led to the construction of the first two 'Washington' cruisers, present in both the maximum and minimum programmes, as indicated below.

7 August 1923 programme

Type of ship	Budget (million lire)
Two 10,000-ton cruisers	280
Twelve 1300-ton destroyers	262
Ten 800-ton submarines	242
Six 500-ton minelayers	33
Six 40-knots MAS	11
Two 10,000-ton aircraft carriers*	300
Total (million lire)	1128

24 November 1923 reduced programme

Type of ship	Budget (million lire)
Two 10,000-ton cruisers	280
Ten 1300-ton destroyers	220
Eight 800-ton submarines	194
Six 500-ton minelayers	33
Six 40-knots Mas	11
One 10,000-ton aircraft carrier	150
Total (million lire)	880

* The displacement, not exceeding 10,000 tons, would have allowed these ships to avoid the category of aircraft carriers, which in the Washington treaty, by definition, was between 10,000 and 27,000 tons and, therefore, avoided inclusion in the 60,000 tons that the treaty allowed for Italy

Defined as (large) light cruisers, the '10,000s' became part of the 1923/1924 naval programme, but only two and not three due to budgetary constraints, and were partly financed with an extraordinary budget of 160 million lire spread over four years. They were given the names of the two most important cities assigned to Italy by the peace treaty, Trento and Trieste, and the

Trieste, 24 October 1926: launching of cruiser *Trieste* at the Stabilimento Tecnico Triestino yard. (E. Bagnasco collection)

construction was assigned in April 1924, respectively to the Cantiere Navale Fratelli Orlando & C. of Livorno (traditionally known as Leghorn to the British) and the Stabilimento Tecnico Triestino, San Marco shipyard in Trieste. In the final design, the standard displacement reached 10,500 tons, slightly over the prescribed limits, the main armament was eight 203mm (8in) guns and the speed was 35 knots; the protection was sacrificed in relation to the other requirements, but in terms of thickness of armour (belt and armoured deck) and extension it was equal or superior to that of the other 10,000-tonners of this first generation.

After the *Trento*s: large or small light cruisers?

Between the end of 1924 and early 1925, after the decision to lay down *Trento* and *Trieste*, the General Staff of the Regia Marina debated whether to build another pair of high-speed cruisers of the 'Washington' type or, alternatively, a larger number of much smaller cruisers of 4000 tons, armed with 152mm (6in) guns and similarly fast, for which plans had already been started. The decision came down in favour of the former, based on the following arguments developed in two memoranda from the 1st General Staff Department of December 1924 and January 1925:

- due to the progressive scrapping of battleships, which were of an outdated type, it would be necessary to have ships that combined the defensive and offensive qualities required to carry out 'those missions of a strategic and tactical nature that are not suitable for smaller vessels' and the 10,000-ton limit would have forced compromises that were difficult to resolve;
- it was not possible to give up a nucleus of ships with the same characteristics as those of the other powers, first and foremost France;
- war experience had highlighted the necessity of providing good protection for the main armament, which was feasible for ships armed with 203mm guns, but not convenient for smaller calibres;
- the totality of the protection (vertical, horizontal and underwater) had already undergone significant reductions in a displacement of 10,000 tons;
- the potential higher speed of smaller cruisers would not have been such an advantage as to allow them to be employed against more heavily armed and protected ships.

As for calibre, the 203mm gun presented decisive advantages over the 152mm in terms of hitting power, range, fire control and firing speed at greater distances, where even the smaller calibre could not be loaded at high angles of elevation. Finally, regarding numbers, the '10,000s' would have found taking on 4000-ton cruisers not unlike fighting against large destroyers, while the small cruisers would not have been able to face concentrations of 'Washington' type cruisers.

In this, the General Staff openly endorsed the opinion which appeared at the time in the *US Naval Institute Proceedings*, namely that 'no nation will be induced to build ships of less than standard displacement and armament (10,000 tons - 203mm guns) which would be a poor use of money in every respect'. As for the remaining characteristics, this is how they were conceived in the memoranda.

(a) **Protection**
- As a full 75mm armoured belt would not be sufficient to resist 203mm projectiles at the likely combat ranges, it would be extended with adequate thickness only at the 203mm turrets and associated ammunition stowage;
- the horizontal protection would consist of a single 60mm armoured deck, not too high, judged sufficient to withstand 203mm projectiles at a low angle of impact and the presumed air attack;
- given the impossibility of providing the ship with adequate protection against underwater attack, the longitudinal structure would have been strengthened according to the criteria already adopted by Lieutenant-Gen. Giuseppe Rota of the Construction Corps in the contemporary aircraft carrier-cruiser project, which would have offered good resistance against this type of attack; this latter solution could not be applied to cruisers of lesser displacement;
- adoption of forced ventilation systems against the possible enemy use of poison gas.

b) **Smaller guns and torpedo armament**
- for the ASW and AA armament, inspiration was still drawn from Rota's projected carrier-cruiser, that is, 102mm to 120mm (4in to 4.7in) guns to stop enemy destroyers at a distance of 15,000m, multiple machine-guns and a grouping of 102mm guns, respectively, for close and distant AA defence;
- torpedo armament confined to no more than four torpedo tubes on deck, the possibility of their use being only occasional.

c) **Machinery in order to gain the maximum speed of 36 knots and large range**
- Speed was considered a factor of paramount importance for ships of the type under consideration, in view of the theatre (the entire Mediterranean) and the variety of missions which they would be called upon to perform. High speed would have been decisive both in taking the initiative and in evading a superior enemy, given that financial resources would not allow the provision of more cruisers than the enemy could deploy. The same was true for long range in order to ensure rapid intervention throughout the Mediterranean basin, even in support of smaller forces.

d) **Aviation facilities**
- for 4 aircraft (2 reconnaissance and 2 fighter) with stowage inside the ship, launching by catapult, but without the possibility of recovery at sea.

e) **Habitability**
- taking into account the most up-to-date hygiene arrangements, already adopted in other navies.

The General Staff declared this type of ship to be 'the true surface combatant core of the future war', but this policy statement was not enough to overcome the resistance of those within the Navy who opposed the '10,000'.

On 9 May 1925, with the resignation of Thaon di Revel, who

Livorno, Orlando Shipyard, 4 September 1927: launching of the heavy cruiser *Trento*. In fact, probably due to sabotage (sand mixed with tallow used to lubricate the slipway) the ship's launch came to a halt after only 47 metres. After the necessary interventions, launching was only completed a month later, on 4 October 1927. (Cantiere Orlando Livorno, courtesy F. Fontana)

The *Trento* still stuck on the slipway due to sabotage in September 1927. (Cantiere Orlando Livorno, courtesy F. Fontana)

was a staunch supporter of the 'Washington' type, Mussolini took over as interim Minister of the Navy, while Admiral Giuseppe Sirianni became Undersecretary. A few days later, on 14 May, Alfredo Acton, now 'Ammiraglio d'Armata' (Regia Marina's highest rank), succeeded Admiral Gino Ducci as Chief of Staff, also taking over the chairmanship of the Admirals' Committee. With Sirianni's arrival at the top of the department, the line of thought favouring the 'preponderance of numbers' took over from the 'preponderance of displacement'. As individual losses would be of smaller size, this was considered more suitable to a war of rapid attacks against the potential French enemy in the central-western Mediterranean, leaving the eastern Mediterranean free for shipping to Italy. This line of thought was very much alive within the Navy and enjoyed the decisive support of Costanzo Ciano, who had already held the position of Undersecretary of State. If, since the end of the war, it had not been translated into concrete actions, it was only because of the stagnation of new construction dictated by the policies of demobilisation and cost saving.

From 11 to 13 August 1925, the Admirals' Committee held a series of meetings focused on new construction, attended by Sirianni, Acton and – for the only time during a twenty-year period – Mussolini. The meeting of 11 August is famous for the question posed by the Head of Government as to whether or not an aircraft carrier was necessary and the unanimous negative response given by the Committee. The Committee's unanimous negative response paved the way for Mussolini's alternative question as to whether, since two 10,000-ton cruisers were already under construction, it was necessary to build two more (which the King had already named *Zara* and *Fiume*) or as many 'Rota'-type aircraft carriers or six 4500-ton cruisers. This question intersected with another, arising from the interest just expressed by the Argentine Navy in purchasing one or two *Trento*s, as to whether or not the formal request should be granted and, if so, with which vessels to replace them. Without going into the details of the intense discussions of those days, the salient features and final consequences should at least be highlighted.

First of all, with various arguments, the Committee was largely in favour of transferring the two cruisers to Argentina and replacing them with similar ones, albeit with some improvements. Rota was very negative about them, as a type of ship and because of design flaws which would have led to a 260-ton increased displacement; he came to regard both the possible suspension of construction or their eventual surrender and replacement with other ships as a potential blessing.

Debate on further 10,000-ton cruisers

The construction of the *Trento*s proceeded slowly. They were commissioned between December 1928 (*Trieste*) and April 1929 (*Trento*) with a considerable delay and increased costs, due to the devaluation of the lira (before 'quota 90') and problems related to the new construction. The State did not apply penalties for delays, but did not recognise the increased costs. This resulted in a heavy loss for both companies, Stabilimento Tecnico Triestino and Cantiere Orlando, which would have led to the bankruptcy of the latter had it not been rescued by merging it with Odero-Terni s.a., already its majority shareholder and a major creditor.

As had been announced, Italy and France did not take part in the 1927 Geneva conference, which was supposed to complete the Washington treaty by setting limitations for the smaller ships (cruisers, destroyers and submarines) that had been excluded. Both sides wanted to keep their hands free on these categories of

The heavy cruiser *Trento* during sea trials, still painted in the dark grey colour in use up the end of the 1920s. (G. Ercole collection)

ships and on how to structure their defence at sea without falling foul of the proportionality-by-category constraints sought by the two Anglo-Saxon powers in order to strengthen their world supremacy. The Regia Marina, moreover, feared that the principle of parity with France would be called into question. The conference, attended by the three oceanic powers alone, ended in failure due to the lack of agreement between London and Washington on cruisers.

In the same year, Italy and France would have had the right to lay down a battleship each, within the limit of 35,000 tons of standard displacement, but neither was inclined to exercise this right for political – internal for Paris, international for Rome – and budgetary reasons. In Italy, apart from the always lively doctrinaire debate, there was not even any battleship project in hand, so much so that, paradoxically, they applied themselves more to studies of aircraft carriers. Thus, up to that moment, the two powers had developed the construction of smaller ships and submarines with only two '10,000s' for Italy, but five for France: the two *Duquesne* class and three more, later to become four, of the *Foch* class, similar in characteristics to the *Trento*, but, especially the first two, less protected. It should be noted that the first post-war French *tranche* (1922) did not include 'Washington' type cruisers, but 'only' the three *Duguay Trouin* class armed with 152mm guns. The *Duquesne*s were approved with the 1924 tranche, when the characteristics of the *Trento*s were not yet known, and only the *Foch* class, launched with the 1925 *tranche*, was conceived as an answer to the two Italian '10,000s'. Thus, France at the time had a considerable advantage in this category of ship.

In order not to fall too far behind the Marine Nationale, at the beginning of 1928 Admiral Ernesto Burzagli, Chief of Staff of the Regia Marina since 21 December 1927, was in favour of moving rapidly to the construction of medium displacement battleships (in this case 23,333 tons, a third of the 70,000 allowed), but felt the need for new larger ships as soon as possible. Taking his cue from one of the most debated questions of those years – whether existing and future battleships were suitable to serve as a support force for smaller vessels – he estimated that the *Trento*s were too vulnerable and that the Italian Navy, unable to achieve quantitative superiority over France, should pursue qualitative superiority, in order to have cruisers which, although derived from the 'Washington' type, possessed 'a combat resistance superior to that of light cruisers'. It must be said that this line of thought had been growing within the Navy since 1925; an example was the 'Bonfiglietti' project for new 10,000-ton cruisers approved by the 'Comitato Progetti Navi' in May 1927, derived from the *Trento*, but which contained all the elements that would soon distinguish the future *Zara*.

Based on these assumptions and the momentary decision not to build new battleships, at the end of the 1920s the decision was taken to build two new '10,000s' (*Zara* and *Fiume*) significantly different from the *Trento* and with a standard displacement of just under 12,000 tons. They became part of the 1928/1929 naval programme.

The French heavy cruiser *Duquesne* in the mid-1930s. (M Brescia collection)

28 January 1931: the French heavy cruiser *Tourville* at slow speed in Toulon harbour. (Photo Marius Bar)

May 1938: heavy cruisers *Trento* and *Trieste* at Genoa.

The *Trento* leaving Taranto's 'Canale Navigabile' and entering the Mar Grande in 1935. (M. Risolo collection)

The 1928/1929 Naval programme and the final design of the *Zara* class

At the beginning of 1928, on the basis of the above-mentioned appreciations, the General Staff of the Regia Marina came to even more extreme conclusions, namely:

- displacement should not be fixed *a priori* and therefore the 10,000 tons requirement of the Treaty of Washington should not to be taken into account;
- an extensive vertical protection of 200mm should be ensured together with a strong horizontal protection and a robust hull structure;
- the main armament was to be maintained at eight 203mm guns, as for large light cruisers;
- a few knots of speed could be given up compared to the *Trento*, ensuring a maximum speed in operational conditions of 32 knots instead of 35.

The General Staff estimated that the standard displacement would reach 12,500 tons, to which a margin for contingencies was added. By immediately fitting out two of these ships, in 1931 Italy would have been able to have ships capable of devaluing the 'Treaty' type cruisers, but also capable of operating alongside the *Trento*s, so as not to nullify the expense incurred in their construction. It is not clear, however, whether the General Staff planned to declare these ships as 'Washington' type cruisers, thus masking their greater displacement, or to make them fall into the category of battleships, as one might infer from some of Burzagli's statements.

The idea of breaching Washington's constraints was not shared by the Ministry of the Navy, for which the new cruisers would also have to fall under the 'Treaty' type, even if the ratios between the various components of armament, engine and protection were revised to the advantage of the latter. Thus, if the vertical armour thickness of 200mm had been accepted, it would have been necessary to reduce the main armament to six 203mm guns, while keeping the other main weight groups unchanged. This solution might have been acceptable to Sirianni if the available resources had made it possible to order three new large cruisers at the same time; but this would not have been financially possible in a single naval programme. As it was necessary to deploy a total of sixteen 203mm guns, not just twelve, the Navy Minister decided to reduce the armour belt to 150mm, having confirmed that such a thickness was adequate to withstand weapons of this calibre.

The main characteristics of the new ships would, therefore, be the following: standard displacement 10,000 tons (but when completed the ships would be between 11,500 and 11,900 tons), main armament eight 203mm (8in) guns, maximum speed

The *Fiume* on the slipway shortly before launching, with the stands for guests (partially visible on the right) already set up.

32 knots, vertical protection 150mm and horizontal protection 70mm. The reduction of 3 knots in speed with respect to the *Trento*s was not considered a disadvantage from a tactical point of view, as it could not be assumed that Italian ships would engage the enemy only if they had a higher speed than all ships they might encounter. Greater defensive qualities, therefore, and not a superior speed – as a young rising star of Italian naval thinking, Giuseppe Fioravanzo, would soon theorise in his major work *La guerra sul mare e la guerra integrale* – would actually imply a greater offensive attitude. With these first two ships, the Italian Navy adopted the criterion that, since quantitative superiority could not be achieved, qualitative superiority should be sought through the development of 'hidden qualities' capable of gaining the upper hand on the battlefield.

The two new cruisers, which were given the names of two other recently recovered cities very dear to the Italians, *Zara* and *Fiume*, became part of the 1928/1929 naval programme. Construction of the *Zara* was assigned to the Odero Terni Orlando shipyard in Muggiano (La Spezia), the *Fiume* to the Stabilimento Tecnico Triestino (San Marco shipyard) in Trieste.

The 1929/1930 naval programme: *Gorizia*, *Bolzano* and a never-ending controversy

The postponement of the construction of battleships also brought the construction of two more '10,000s'. If it had been possible to proceed with battleships, the General Staff of the Regia Marina would not have been too worried about the numerical inferiority to France in this category of cruiser. However, with the renouncement of new battleships at that time and the progressive withdrawal of the existing ones (in 1928 the *Dante Alighieri* was stricken, the *Conte di Cavour* was placed in reserve and the *Giulio Cesare* operated as a training ship), it 'resigned itself' to the construction of two more 'Treaty' type, bearing the names of another two irredentist cities: one of the *Zara* class, the *Gorizia*, and one of the *Trento* class, the *Bolzano*, in order to form two homogeneous Divisions, each of three ships. If France had decided to lay down a seventh 10,000-ton cruiser – which it did in 1930 with the *Algérie*, whose characteristics were close to those of the *Zara* – the squadron of six Italian major cruisers would have been sufficiently strong to face the equiva-

The cruiser *Zara* is launched at the Muggiano yard (La Spezia) on 27 April 1930. (G. Alfano collection)

Fiume fitting out at Trieste in late spring 1931. (G Alfano collection)

lent cruisers that the French Navy could deploy in the Mediterranean. The two new '10,000s' became part of the 1929/1930 naval programme. *Gorizia*'s construction was assigned to the Odero Terni Orlando shipyard in Livorno, the *Bolzano*, whose standard displacement was just over 11,000 tons, to the Ansaldo shipyard in Genoa Sestri.

For the General Staff of the Regia Marina approving the construction of two more 'Washingtons' did not imply that they were highly valued: they were still ships 'too vulnerable to form the backbone of the fleet' and, in essence, an unconvincing substitute for battleships.

All these considerations, as well as the previous ones which led to the construction of the first two *Zara*s, materialised in one of the most important documents of the General Staff of the Regia Marina, dating back to February 1929, enunciating criteria and guidelines for an organic and systematic renewal of the fleet and its complementary needs, including naval-air cooperation, the establishment of an auxiliary aviation component and the construction of an experimental aircraft carrier. The document drew inspiration from – but was not merely a repetition of – a September 1927 study by Rear Admiral Romeo Bernotti, at that time an acknowledged man of thought in the Navy. Even if it did not receive explicit political-legal sanction, it significantly influenced Italian naval policy at least until 1934, when new international events led to a shift towards large battleships. In any case,

Sea trials of *Fiume* off Trieste on 25 May 1931; the inclined funnel caps have still to be fitted.

Trieste, 5 May 1931: the heavy cruiser *Fiume* sets out for machinery trials, with the original funnel configuration and still without her main armament. (Studio C. Wernigg, Trieste)

the construction of a third *Trento*, explicitly set out in the document, opened up a controversy, still alive today in the debate between historians and scholars, as it appeared to be guilty of a step backwards compared to the *Zara*.

Late 1930: seen from the bridge *Fiume*'s forecastle while the ship was being fitted at the Stabilimento Tecnico Triestino; the temporary covers over the tops of the barbettes while waiting for the embarkation of the 203/53 turrets, the hangar doors and the bow catapult should be noted.

The main criticism was that Ansaldo s.a. of Genoa, which had been excluded from the contracts for the previous '10,000s', had no prospect of obtaining others, since none were currently planned. This would have had serious economic consequences for the company and social consequences because of the impact on employment. This would have led to local political pressure, which in conjunction with that of the company, would eventually have induced the Government to proceed with the construction of a third *Trento*.

It is sometimes forgotten that the *Bolzano* was the sixth and not the seventh of the Italian '10,000s' and that the extra cruiser compared to the original six was, if anything, the *Pola*, the last to be approved. The desire to create a third *Trento*, in order to have a division of at least two ships, in case the third was not serviceable or designated to tasks other than Fleet service, was a constant in the Regia Marina's thinking. It can be found, for example, in the studies on the multi-year naval programmes of the mid-1930s, when thought was given to rebuilding a single *Duilio* after the reconstruction of the two *Cavours*, and to building a third *Littorio* after laying down of the first two.

Nor can the pressure to award a large ship to Ansaldo be considered an anomaly, either at that time or in the years that preceded and followed it. The rivalry between Italy's major yards for orders for military vessels – although not always profitable, as in the cases of the *Trento* and *Trieste* – and the impetus it gave to military construction was a constant which would continue even after most of the Italian shipbuilding industry came under the control of the I.R.I. (Istituto Ricostruzione Industriale) and which was accentuated by a production overcapacity of about 40% compared to the needs of private armament and the Italian Navy. Indeed, economic interests and local social problems weighed heavily on the substantial abandonment of the I.R.I.'s restructuring plan for the shipbuilding industry in the

Right: Ansaldo shipyard, Genoa, 31 August 1932: the launching of *Bolzano*. Note, on the right, the numerous small fishermen's boats waiting to recover the precious tallow used to facilitate the sliding of the hull on the slipway. (Archivio Storico Ansaldo)

Left: Heavy cruiser *Fiume* on sea trials during summer 1931.

Right: The heavy cruiser *Gorizia* is laid down at the Odero-Terni-Orlando Yard at Leghorn (Livorno) on 17 March 1930. (Archivio di Stato di Livorno, courtesy F. Fontana)

mid-1930s. The case of the *Bolzano* appears to be of little importance compared to the disputes between Cantieri Riuniti dell'Adriatico, Odero Terni Orlando and Ansaldo over the two large battleships *Littorio* and *Vittorio Veneto*.

Finally, while each of these factors alone may have influenced the construction of the *Bolzano*, the most convincing remains the reason stated by the General Staff: that is, the desire to have a homogeneous division of three large fast cruisers. In other words, they wanted to build a third *Trento* in order to have a three-vessel division, even though they had no confidence in this type of ship. In this sense, some call the *Bolzano* a 'splendidly successful mistake'; but it remains to be seen what definition should be given to the reconstruction of the two *Duilio*s, which was an unforgivable waste of resources; or to the twelve magnificent scouts of the *Capitani Romani* class, conceived to conduct rapid raids against

(continued on page 28)

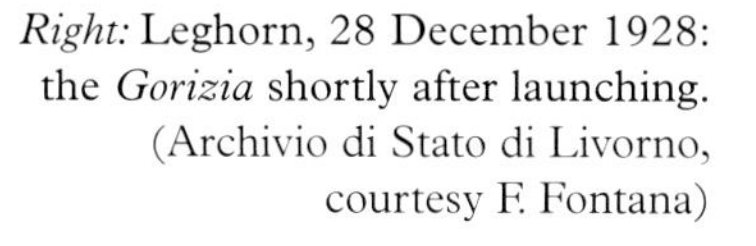

Right: Leghorn, 28 December 1928: the *Gorizia* shortly after launching. (Archivio di Stato di Livorno, courtesy F. Fontana)

Left: The *Fiume* at sea trials in summer 1931.

R.N. GORIZIA
MARZO 1930 VIII

1934: the French heavy cruiser *Suffren* leaving Toulon. (Photo Marius Bar)

The French cruiser *Foch* leaving Toulon on 21 August 1941. The red, white and blue bands painted on turrets 2 and 3 were typical of French ships in the period following the armistice with . (Photo Marius Bar)

Above: The *Gorizia* fitting out in Leghorn in late 1930. (Archivio di Stato di Livorno, courtesy F. Fontana)
Below: Heavy cruiser *Gorizia* steaming at full speed during sea trials in spring 1931: the 203mm main armament still has to be embarked. (Archivio di Stato di Livorno, courtesy F. Fontana)

French shipping between North Africa and France, which, once the war had started and this role vanished, the Navy hardly knew what to do with and which it would happily have cancelled if some of them had not been in an advanced stage of construction.

The 1930 London Conference and the construction of the *Pola*

The Washington conference had ended without any agreement being reached on smaller vessels and submarines. An initiative in this regard was taken again by the American administration in 1927 and led to a conference in Geneva between the three oceanic powers alone, Rome and Paris having declined the invitation due to the impossibility of reaching an agreement between them and in order not to aggravate the already rather delicate diplomatic relations between them. The conference ended in failure due to the irreconcilable divergence of views between the two Anglo-Saxon powers on the subject of cruisers.

In October 1929, the British government, having reached a preliminary understanding with the United States on the whole issue, called for a new conference to regulate the reduction of naval armaments not covered by the Washington Treaty until its expiry on 31 December 1936. All five major naval powers attended the conference, although the positions of Italy and France remained far apart: Rome, a supporter of the criterion of relativity, was determined, even at the cost of causing the conference to fail – as Mussolini instructed Foreign Minister Dino Grandi at the head of the Italian delegation – to obtain parity at the lowest levels of armaments, as long as they were not surpassed by any other European continental power; Paris, which formally did not reject the principle of parity, was a supporter of the theory of 'absolute needs', ready, that is, to make quantitative demands that were unattainable for Italy. These request, however, if accepted would in turn have forced Britain to renounce the 'two power standard' with respect to the two most heavily armed continental powers and to renegotiate the same relations with the other two oceanic powers.

The conference began on 22 January 1930 and ended three months later, without reaching a general agreement because of the unresolved disagreement between the two Latin powers.

Leghorn, 17 March 1931: the heavy cruiser *Pola* is laid down at the Odero-Terni-Orlando Yard. (Archivio di Stato di Livorno, courtesy F. Fontana)

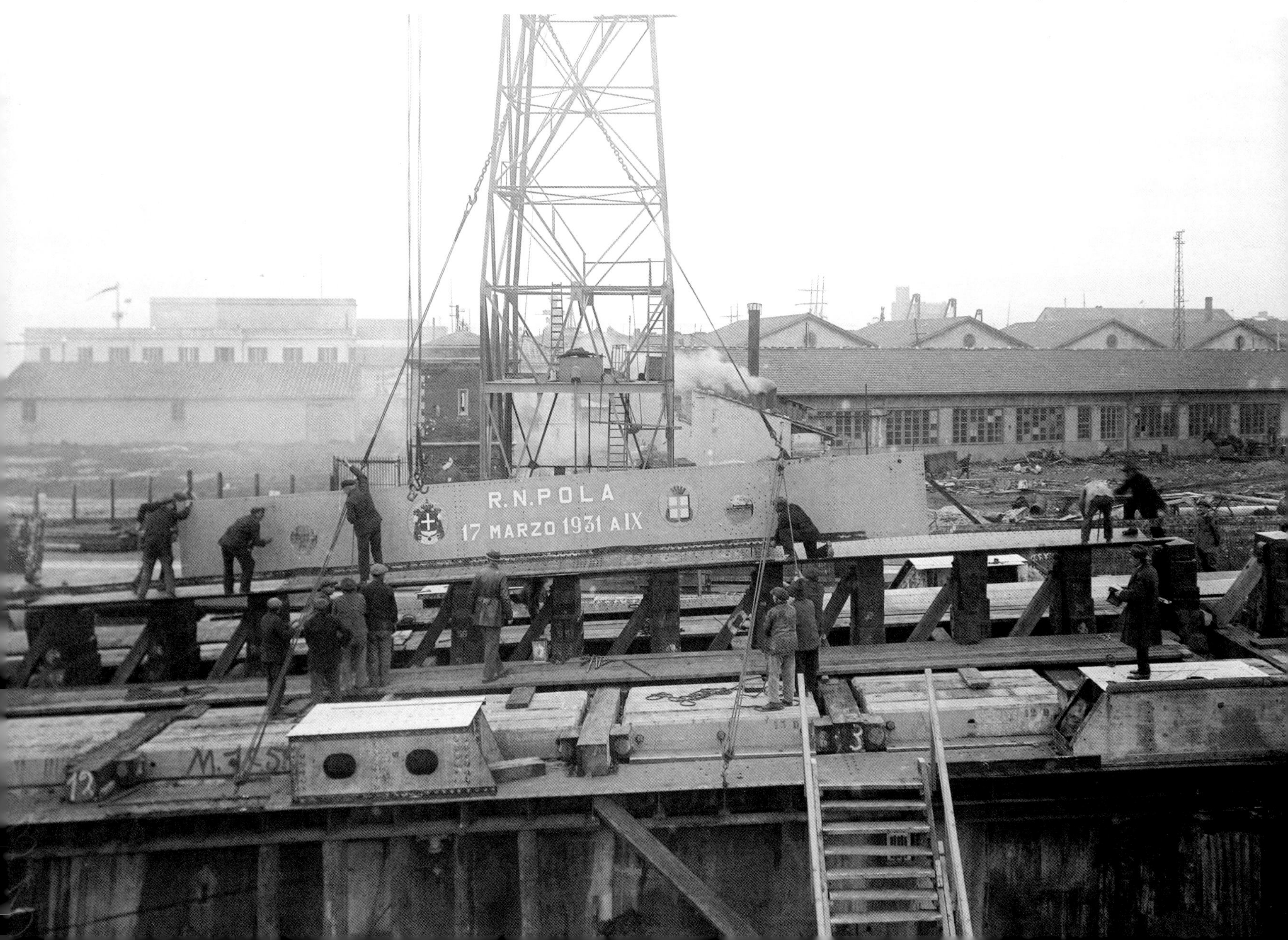

Above: The heavy cruiser *Pola* is launched at Leghorn on 5 December 1931. (Archivio di Stato di Livorno, courtesy F. Fontana)

Left: The *Pola* is launched at Leghorn on 17 March 1931. Of particular interest is the painting of the underwater hull, with the waterline set much lower than it would be when the ship was completely fitted out.

Above: Cruiser *Pola* fitting out at the end of 1932. (Archivio di Stato di Livorno, courtesy F. Fontana)

Left: Heavy cruiser *Zara* in 1934 with several small boats along her starboard side.

Fiume leaving the port of Genoa on 30 May 1938.

It was, however, agreed to sign a treaty on the points where an understanding had been reached and, on the Italian proposal, not to close but simply to adjourn the conference, in the hope of settling the Franco-Italian dispute in a more relaxed atmosphere and with British mediation, by means of a bilateral agreement regulating reciprocal construction until 31 December 1936. The treaty was signed on 22 April and Italy and France adhered to it, but with exceptions, the most important of which was Part III, which regulated the quantitative and qualitative limits on cruisers, destroyers and submarines.

It should be pointed out that even the parts of the treaty that the Latin powers had signed were not ratified by their respective parliaments, so that they were not legally bound by them either, remaining so only for the Treaty of Washington. For Rome and Paris, the conference ended as it had begun: the former was able to defend the position of parity it had acquired in Washington, and the latter was unable to obtain the quantitative limits that would have put its Mediterranean rival out of business.

By 1928 the general characteristics of the first two *Zara* class were known to the Marine Nationale, albeit by deduction. Although France was unaware that their displacement would be 1500/2000 tons more than Washington's limits, it was clearly perceived that they would undoubtedly devalue the *Tourville* and *Suffren* types and concluded that it would be necessary to counter

19 October 1937: *Algérie* (here in her original configuration) was the seventh and last heavy cruiser to be commissioned by the Marine Nationale. (Photo Marius Bar)

them with ships of an equivalent design. In that year, France approved a tiny naval programme because of delays in the implementation of the previous ones, and in the following year a programme was approved which included a fourth *Suffren* type cruiser, the *Dupleix*. It was only in the 1930 *tranche*, approved by Parliament at the opening of the London conference, that a new type of cruiser was included, the *Algérie*, close in concept to the *Zara*, but with a standard displacement of just over 10,000 tons.

On 30 April 1930, a few days after the close of the London conference, Italy announced its construction programme for the 1930/1931 fiscal year, which included a cruiser of '10,000' tons, the *Zara* class *Pola*, and two 7000-ton cruisers, the future *Raimondo Montecuccoli* class. No documentation has been found to explain the reasons behind the construction of the fourth *Zara*. She was entrusted to Odero Terni Orlando in Livorno, was the seventh '10,000' and was named after yet another irredentist city. She was the last to be built in Italy, as the *Algérie* was in France.

The end of the '10,000' in France and Italy

In the France of the Third Republic the development of the Navy depended heavily on public opinion, the mood of the parties and the parliament for the approval of the annual *tranches* and in all these circles there was widespread opposition to battleships. For this reason, in most of the 1920s the Marine Nationale did not concern itself with them any more than the Regia Marina did. Only in 1926/1927 did it study 17,500-ton battlecruisers (an equal division of the treaty 175,000 tons), armed with 305mm (12in) guns and with a speed of 35 knots, expressly conceived to oppose the *Trento*s in the western Mediterranean in defence of communications between France and North Africa. Nothing came of it, because towards the end of the decade the general characteristics of the first German battleship, the *Deutschland*, became known. This radical design was thought to be within the limits allowed by the Treaty of Versailles (10,000 tons displacement, six 280mm (11in) guns and 26 knots speed), so the General Staff of the French Navy opted for ships of 23,333 tons, in order to exceed her in speed (30 knots), armament (eight 305mm guns) and to be armoured to withstand the 280mm gun as well as adequate underwater protection, which could not be achieved in a ship of 17,500 tons. Construction was announced at the London conference of 1930 and the new ship was included in the 1931 *tranche*. This is not the place to follow the troubled events which led to her being laid down on 24 December 1932, but it must be said that the major financial commitment involved in constructing this and later capital ships destroyed any idea of building further cruisers armed with 203mm guns.

Shortly afterwards, the treaty of 25 March 1936, which crowned the second London Conference (1935–1936), prohibited the construction of smaller ships (surface ships other than aircraft carriers between 101 and 10,000 tons) with guns of over 155mm (6.1in) calibre, as well as warships between 8000 and 17,500 tons. The treaty was signed only by the Western powers, but through bilateral agreements with London in 1937, Rome, Berlin and Moscow also signed up to it, but not Tokyo. In fact, it legally put an end to 'Washington' type cruisers until the outbreak of war in Europe, when all powers regained freedom of action.

So, it was not until 1939/1940 that the French navy began to consider these ships again. It did so for the first time in the spring of 1939 following the development in Germany of five 'Washington' type cruisers (the *Admiral Hipper* and *Prinz Eugen* classes) between 1935 and 1936 – now allowed under the Anglo-German naval agreement of 18 June 1935 – whose effective standard displacement was already estimated at well over 10,000 tons. A first project, named 'C 5' of May 1939 revived a 1935 study directly developed from the *Algérie*, of which it was a substantial replica. There were two versions, both with a displacement of just over 10,000 tons: one without aviation facilities, the other equipped with two catapults and two seaplanes, but with both showing a marked increase in anti-aircraft armament.

With the outbreak of war in September 1939 all naval construction in France that could not be completed quickly was suspended. However, in January 1940 a study of a 13,000-ton cruiser was authorised and, with the first ambitious war programme, dated 27 May 1940, construction of three was approved, together with two 40,000-ton battleships, destroyers and submarines. Initial studies of the three large cruisers, the *Saint Louis* class, envisaged a standard displacement of about

CONSTRUCTION OF 'WASHINGTON' TYPE CRUISERS IN ITALY AND FRANCE

Italy					**France**				
Fiscal year	**Name**	**Laid down**	**Launched**	**Commissioned**	**Tranche**	**Name**	**Laid down**	**Launched**	**Commissioned**
1923/	*Trento*	08.02.1925	04.10.1927	03.04.1929	1924	*Duquesne*	30.10.1924	17.12.1925	25.01.1929
1924	*Trieste*	22.06.1925	21.10.1926	21.12.1928		*Tourville*	04.04.1925	24.08.1926	12.03.1929
					1925	*Suffren*	17.04.1926	03.05.1927	08.03.1930
					1926	*Colbert*	12.06.1927	20.04.1928	01.04.1931
					1927	*Foch*	21.06.1928	24.04.1929	20.12.1931
1928/	*Zara*	04.07.1929	27.04.1930	20.10.1931					
1929	*Fiume*	23.04.1929	27.04.1930	23.11.1931					
1929/	*Gorizia*	17.03.1930	28.12.1930	23.12.1931	1929	*Dupleix*	14.11.1929	09.10.1930	15.11.1933
1930	*Bolzano*	11.06.1930	31.08.1932	19.08.1932					
1930/	*Pola*	17.03.1931	05.02.1931	21.12.1932	1930	*Algérie*	19.03.1931	21.05.1932	19.10.1934
1931									

The heavy cruiser *Zara* leaving the port of Genoa at the end of May 1938. (G. Alfano collection)

14,500 tons, an armament of nine 203mm guns in three triple turrets, protection yet to be determined and a maximum speed of 33 knots. The entire programme vanished with the collapse of France, but it is just as well to note that, with the loss of any qualitative constraints, it was concluded that for ships armed with 203mm guns it would be necessary to reach a standard displacement well in excess of 10,000 tons in order to have ships balanced in their fundamental components.

After the *Pola*, there was no development of the '10,000'-type cruiser in Italy either. The last time the Regia Marina considered such a hypothesis was in 1932 during the discussions on what the response to the French fast battleship *Dunkerque* should be. The decisive session was held by the Admirals' Committee on 26 November 1932, in the presence of Giuseppe Sirianni, now a three-star admiral and since 15 September 1929 Minister of the Navy, and the new Chief of Staff, Admiral Gino Ducci. As an essentially pro forma exercise, Sirianni submitted an alternative to new ships or the radical modernisation of the two *Cavour*s, proposing the construction of three improved 'Washington' type cruisers, *ie* three ships of 12,000 tons, armed with 203mm guns or larger (defined as 'free tonnage' ships, but according to the Treaty of Washington falling into the category of battleships), in order to achieve superiority over France, at least in this type of ship. This alternative was undoubtedly discarded due to the unanimous desire to have sufficiently modern battleships available in the short term, and because the 12,000-ton ship, although already studied, would not have brought any real advantage even in the cruiser category. In the end, it was decided to rebuild the two *Cavour*s, renouncing both the construction of new battleships and large cruisers. From then on, the Italian Navy abandoned the '10,000' and statements to this effect were made in the Italian Chamber of Deputies during the discussion of the 1933/1934 budget. There was no mention of them, not even hypothetically, in the negotiations with Paris between 1930 and 1934 to reach a naval agreement valid until 1936 intended to crown the London treaty of 1930; nor did heavy cruisers, as they began to be called, appear in the impressive studies of multi-year programmes developed by the General Staff in the second half of the 1930s.

The *Pola* marked the end of the history of Italian heavy cruisers. This was a type of ship in which the Regia Marina did not have much belief, just as it was not enthusiastic about all intermediate vessels between scouts and battleships. It had built the *Trento*, to comply with the maximum limits set by the Treaty of Washington, and it built the *Zara* to replace the battleships that could not or would not be built. After the French decision to build two fast battleships of medium tonnage (*Dunkerque* and *Strasbourg*) and having been given the green light to rebuild the *Cavour*s and, in 1934, to build the *Littorio*, regardless of any other constraints or political factors, there was no reason to add to that category of ship.

Chapter 2

TECHNICAL DESCRIPTION

TRENTO CLASS AND *BOLZANO*

The rationale for the construction of the three cruisers *Trento*, *Trieste* and *Bolzano* have been described in detail in the previous chapter, with building divided between the three most important Italian shipyards of the time. Laid down between 1925 (*Trento* and *Trieste*) and 1930 (*Bolzano*), the three ships were launched and entered service, respectively, as shown in the table (right).

TRENTO CLASS BUILDING DATA

	Yard	Laid down	Launched	Commissioned
Trento	Orlando – Livorno	8 February 1925	4 October 1927	3 April 1929
Trieste	Stabilimento Tecnico Triestino – Trieste	22 June 1925	24 October 1926	21 December 1928*
Bolzano	Ansaldo – Genoa	11 June 1930	31 August 1932	19 August 1933

*Formally handed over though incomplete (see Chapter 6)

2A.1 Hull and superstructure

In pursuit of high speed the hull lines had been developed in a test tank, and the well-formed hull incorporated the first bulbous bow on Italian ships. In *Trento* and *Trieste* this was not very pronounced but on the *Bolzano* it would become more evident.

The hull appendages included bilge keels that extended the

The *Trieste* in the early 1930s; the starboard side lower 100/47 guns have been temporarily landed for improvements to be carried out. (E. Bagnasco collection)

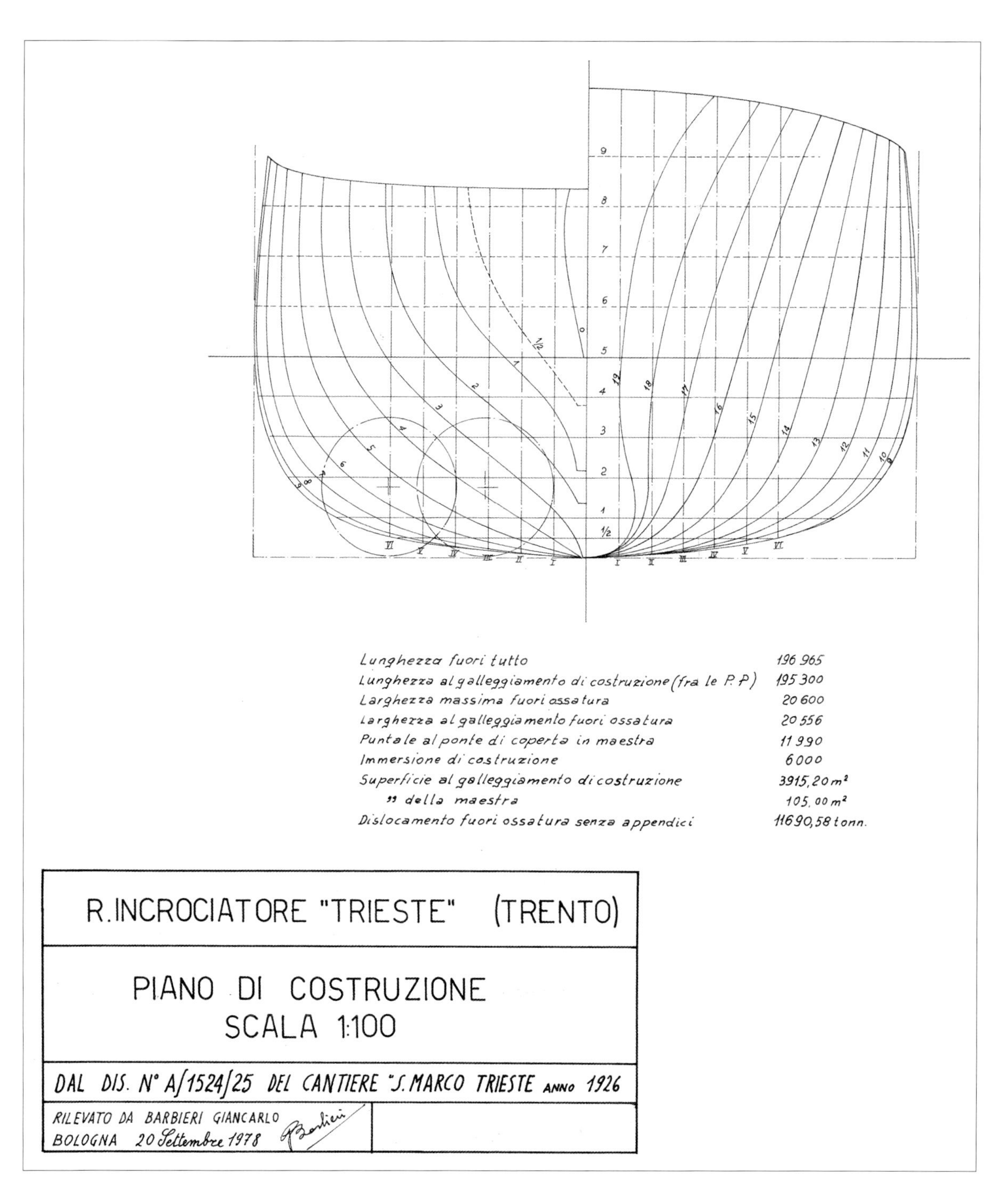

Body plan of cruiser *Trieste*. (Drawing by G. Barbieri from an original builder's plan, courtesy Gruppo di Cultura Navale)

length of the hull between the two funnels, a large single semi-balanced rudder (29.35m² with a maximum rudder angle of 35°) and the ends of the four propeller shafts, supported by V-shaped brackets.

The hull was of the flush-decked type and this made the whole construction rather massive, with a high freeboard and excessive height between decks, especially on the battery deck. In fact, if these proportions made it easier to use the hangar (see Chapter 4 Aviation Facilities) located forward of 'A' turret, where the deck-head height was 3.80m, towards the bow it increased to 4.40m, creating spaces that were too high for optimum use. In order to improve seaworthiness while not increasing displacement, the *Bolzano* design was therefore completed with a long forecastle extending almost to the level of the forward funnel, so that the height of the battery deck was kept constant at 2.30m, with similar values for the lower decks.

The three ships had a vertical stem which, at the top, raked forward, producing a gentle flare which extended aft to the level of the forward 203mm turret. The 'scallops' for the anchors were located on the gunwale: two on the starboard side and one on the port side on the *Trento*s and one on each side on the *Bolzano*, although the *Trento*s would often carry only one anchor on the starboard side. At the heel of the stem was a bracket to which chains for paravane gear were attached, paid out from deck fair-leads, and used for protective minesweeping while underway.

With the 'propensity for speed' in mind in their working out of the construction plans, the Regia Marina's designers turned to

(continued on page 40)

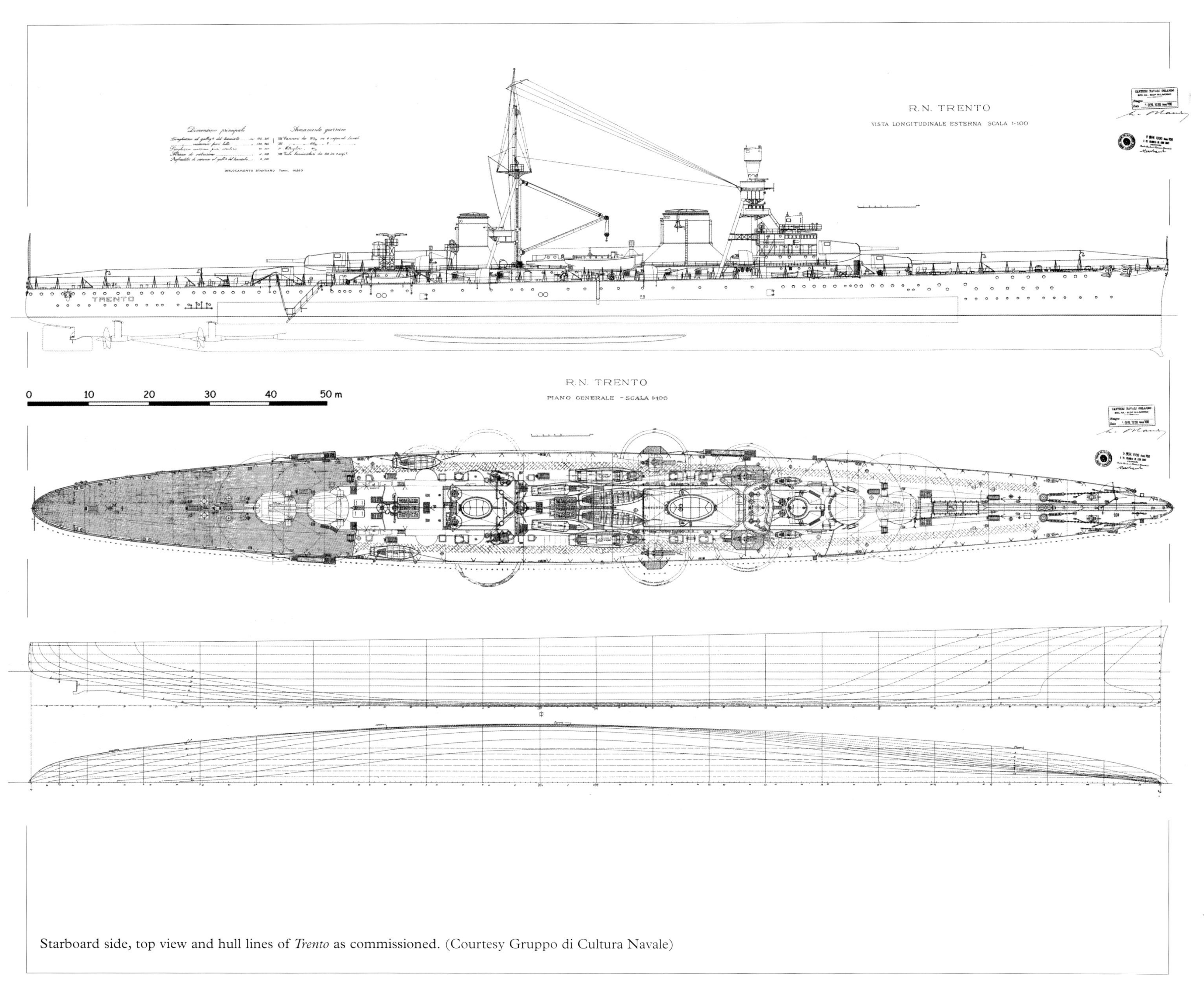

Starboard side, top view and hull lines of *Trento* as commissioned. (Courtesy Gruppo di Cultura Navale)

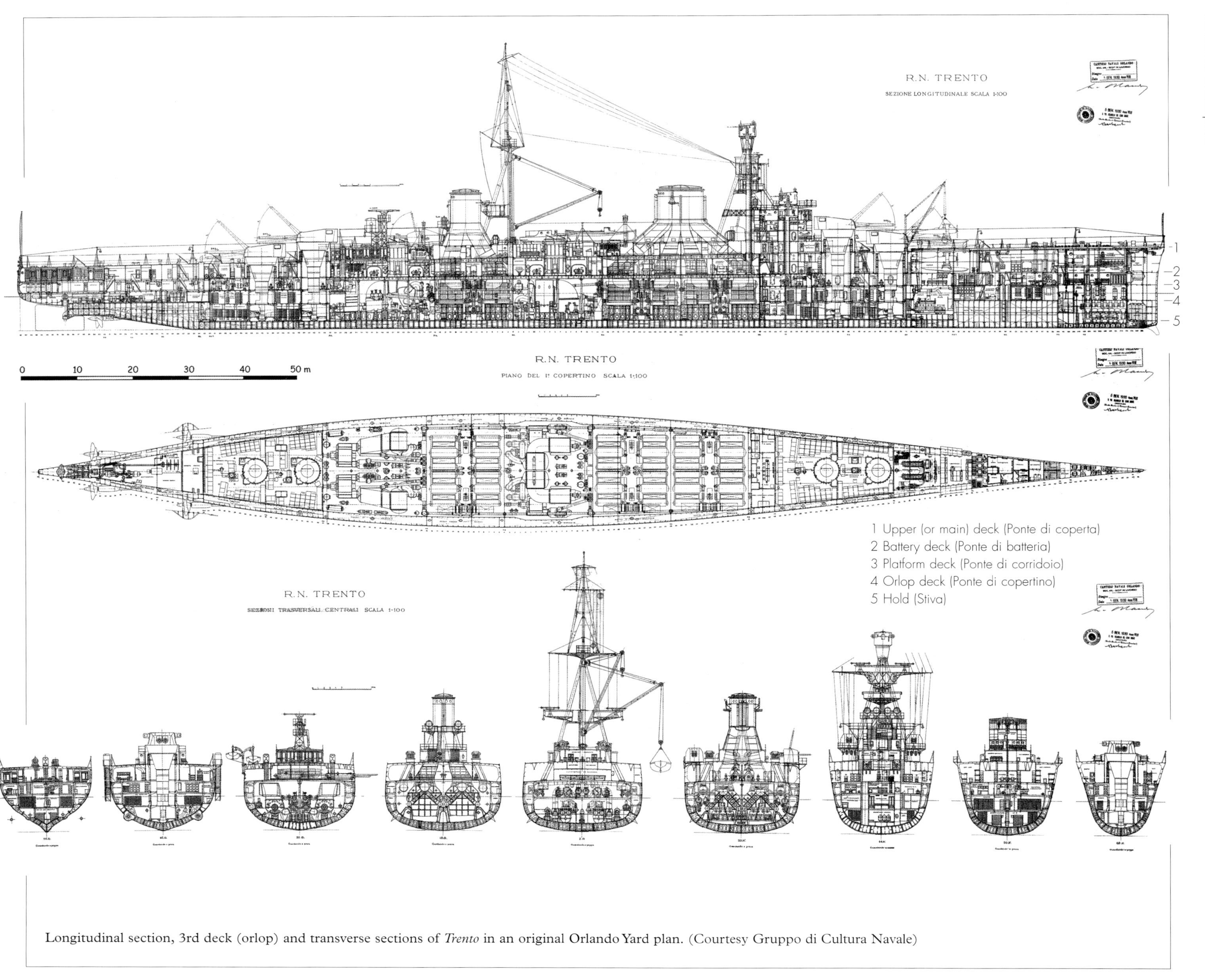

Longitudinal section, 3rd deck (orlop) and transverse sections of *Trento* in an original Orlando Yard plan. (Courtesy Gruppo di Cultura Navale)

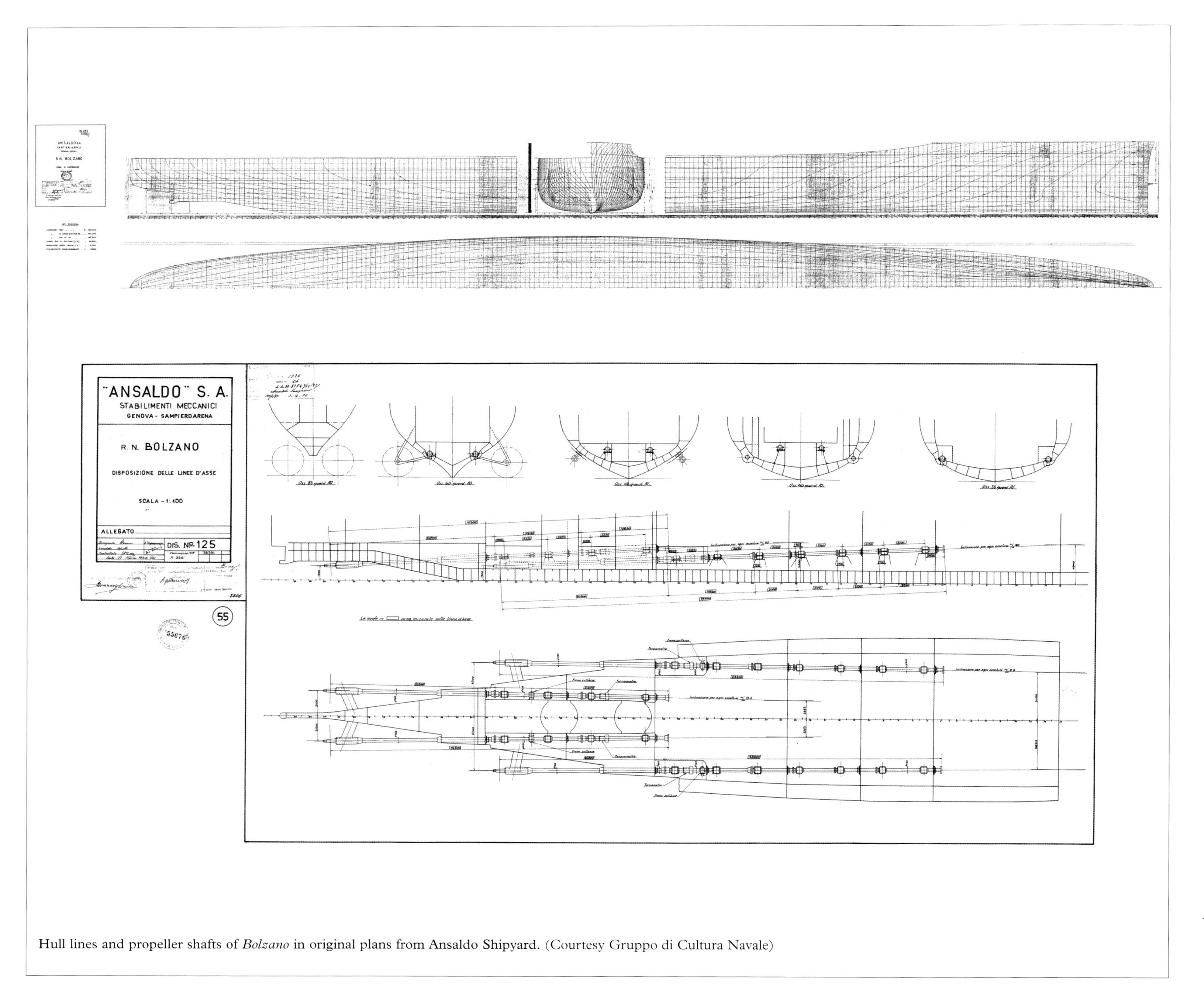

Hull lines and propeller shafts of *Bolzano* in original plans from Ansaldo Shipyard. (Courtesy Gruppo di Cultura Navale)

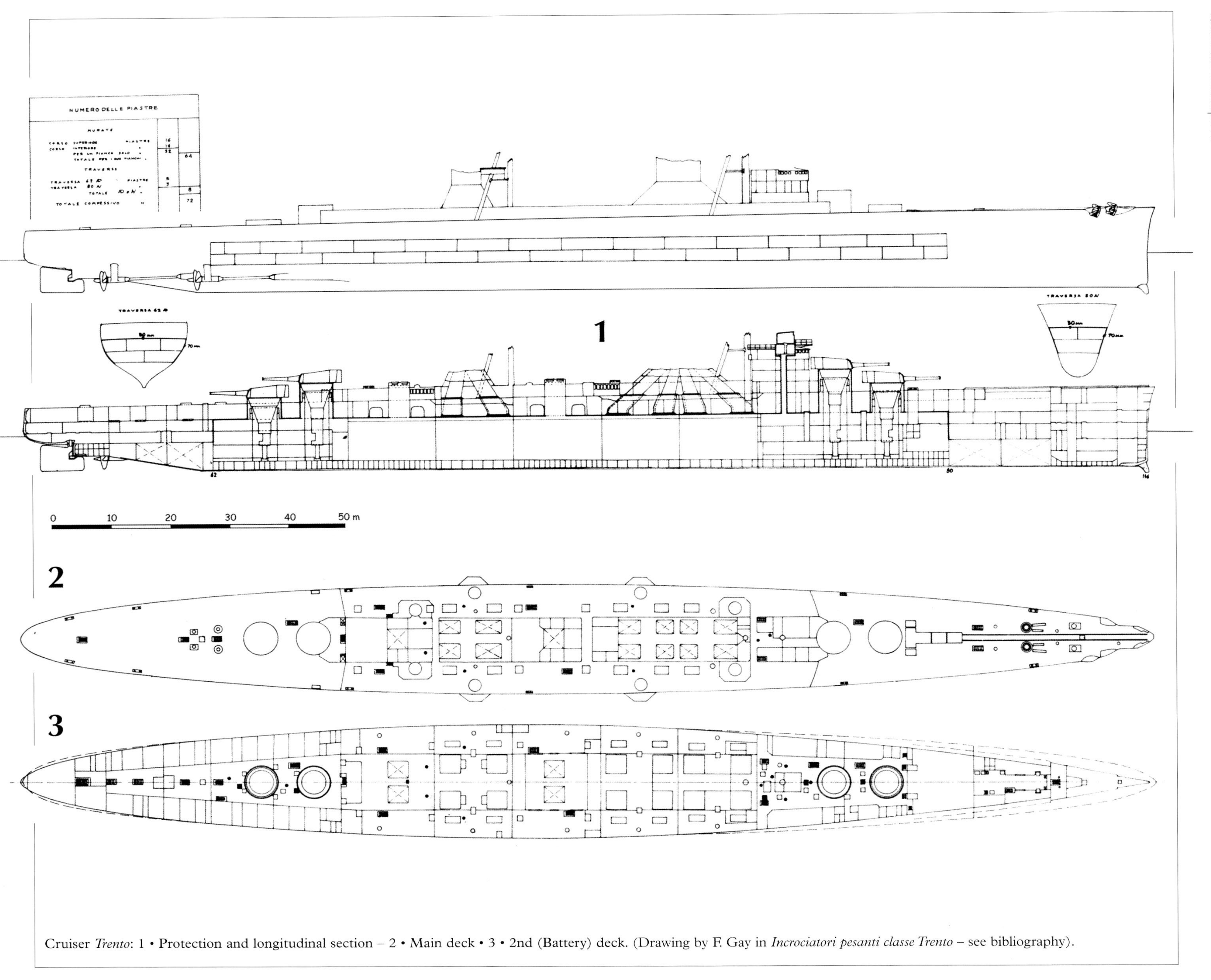

Cruiser *Trento*: 1 • Protection and longitudinal section – 2 • Main deck • 3 • 2nd (Battery) deck. (Drawing by F. Gay in *Incrociatori pesanti classe Trento* – see bibliography).

The stem of *Bolzano* drydocked at La Spezia on 28 January 1935. (M. Brescia collection)

lighter high strength steel for the hulls, except for the parts subject to high vibrations, for which 'Siemens-Martin' mild steel was used. The hull structure was mainly of longitudinal construction in the lower part and in the area between the battery deck and the weather deck, and of transverse construction in the intermediate area. It should be remembered that in longitudinal construction, the continuous elements consisted of the keel and frames, with the ribs subsequently placed on top of them; on the other hand, in a transverse hull, the ribs are the load-bearing element on which the longitudinal elements of the structure are subsequently placed. In addition to the weather deck, the battery deck and the double cellular bottom were continuous, while the 1st and 2nd platform decks and the hold deck extended forward and aft of the machinery rooms, which occupied a large portion of the hull between the bridge tower and the barbette of the after 203mm superfiring turret.

On the weather deck was a deckhouse which on the *Trento*s joined the barbette of the forward superfiring turret with the barbette of the after equivalent; on the *Bolzano*, the deckhouse was a continuation of the forecastle, meeting the barbette of the aft superfiring turret. The *Trento* and *Trieste* bridge towers, although similar in general design, showed some structural differences regarding the shape, dimensions and relative positions of the various decks and the command tower, with the whole being topped by a tripod mast whose main (vertical) trunk was stepped on the battery deck. This arrangement led to heavy vibrations and as early as the end of 1929, two additional struts were added towards the bow, transforming the mast into a pentapod.

The *Bolzano*'s bridge tower, although on a similar number of levels, was faired into the forward funnel, thus constituting a structure similar to that realised for the *Pola* of the *Zara* class, while the forward funnel of the first two ships was separated from the main body of the tower. For more details and comparisons of the three cruisers' towers and the modifications made over time, readers are referred to Appendix D where there are comparative tables and extensive descriptions of the various structures. Further aft were the tripod mainmast and after funnel, the base of the mast forming the step for a large cargo derrick used for launching and recovering service boats and, on the *Bolzano*, also for handling seaplanes, whose catapult was placed on the

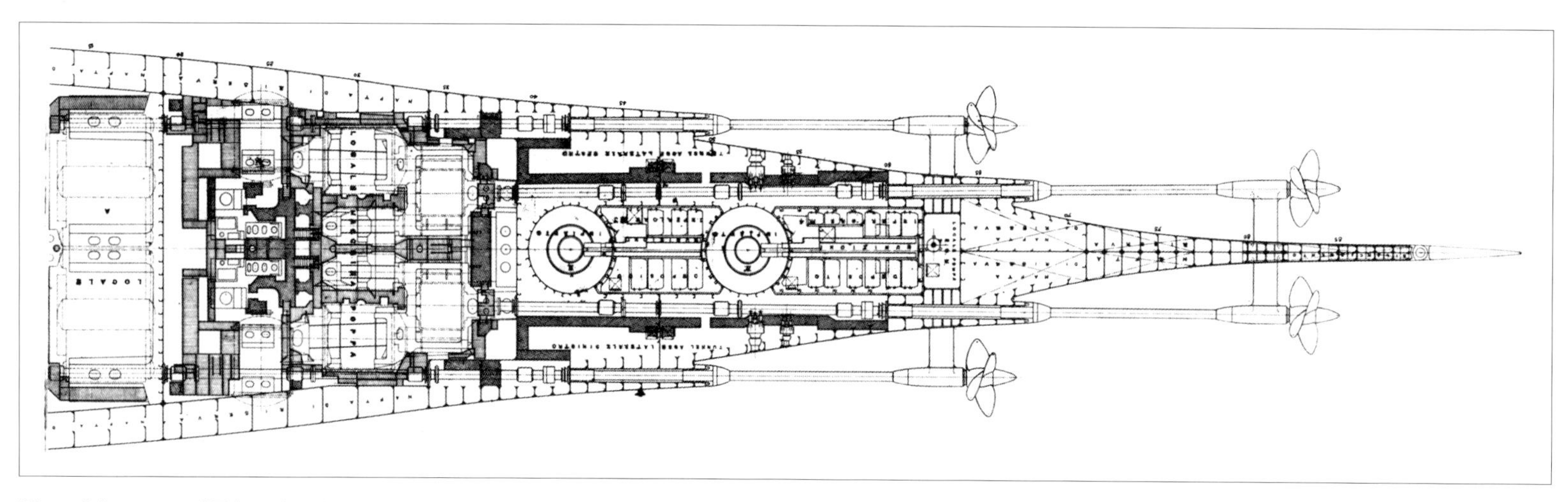
Plan of the stern of *Trieste* showing the run of the propeller shafts (the outer shafts continue towards the forward engine room). (Stabilimento Tecnico Triestino)

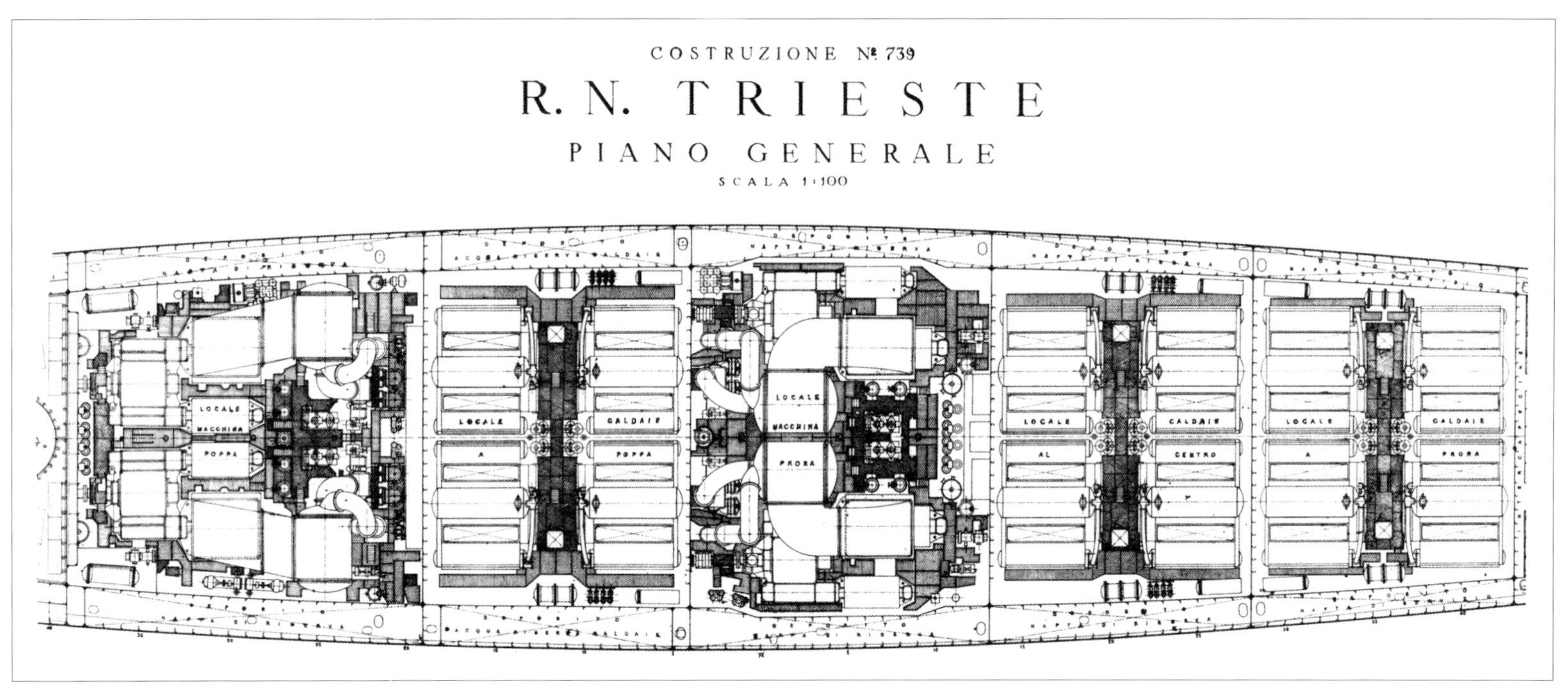

Trieste's machinery: note the division into five compartments (from right to left, *ie* from bow to stern: forward boiler room, centre boiler room, forward engine room, after boiler room, after engine room). (Stabilimento Tecnico Triestino)

deckhouse roof between the two funnels (see Chapter 4 Aviation Facilities).

On the whole, they were elegant ships, but with different distinctions: the *Trento* was more 'refined', but the *Bolzano* more massive (though retaining a certain elegance). In the context of a common design lineage for the seven Italian '10,000s', the *Trento*, *Trieste* and *Bolzano*, from a purely aesthetic point of view, were in the pre-eminent position with respect to the *Zara*s, whose appearance made them look more 'military' but also, due to their greater displacement and more adequate protection, indications

The heavy cruiser *Bolzano* moored in the port of Genoa in the mid-1930s. (E. Bagnasco collection)

of better general characteristics. In fact, it was not by chance (and not without a good dose of malice) that the *Bolzano* was defined by naval experts beyond the Alps as *un erreur magnifiquement exécuté:* a judgement which, while underlining the usual sterile French chauvinism, can at least in part be shared.

2A.2 Protection

The cellular subdivision rose up from the lower part of the light side armouring, linking downwards with the subdivision of the double bottom and thus creating a 'cofferdam' behind the armour. The somewhat fragmented internal subdivision included

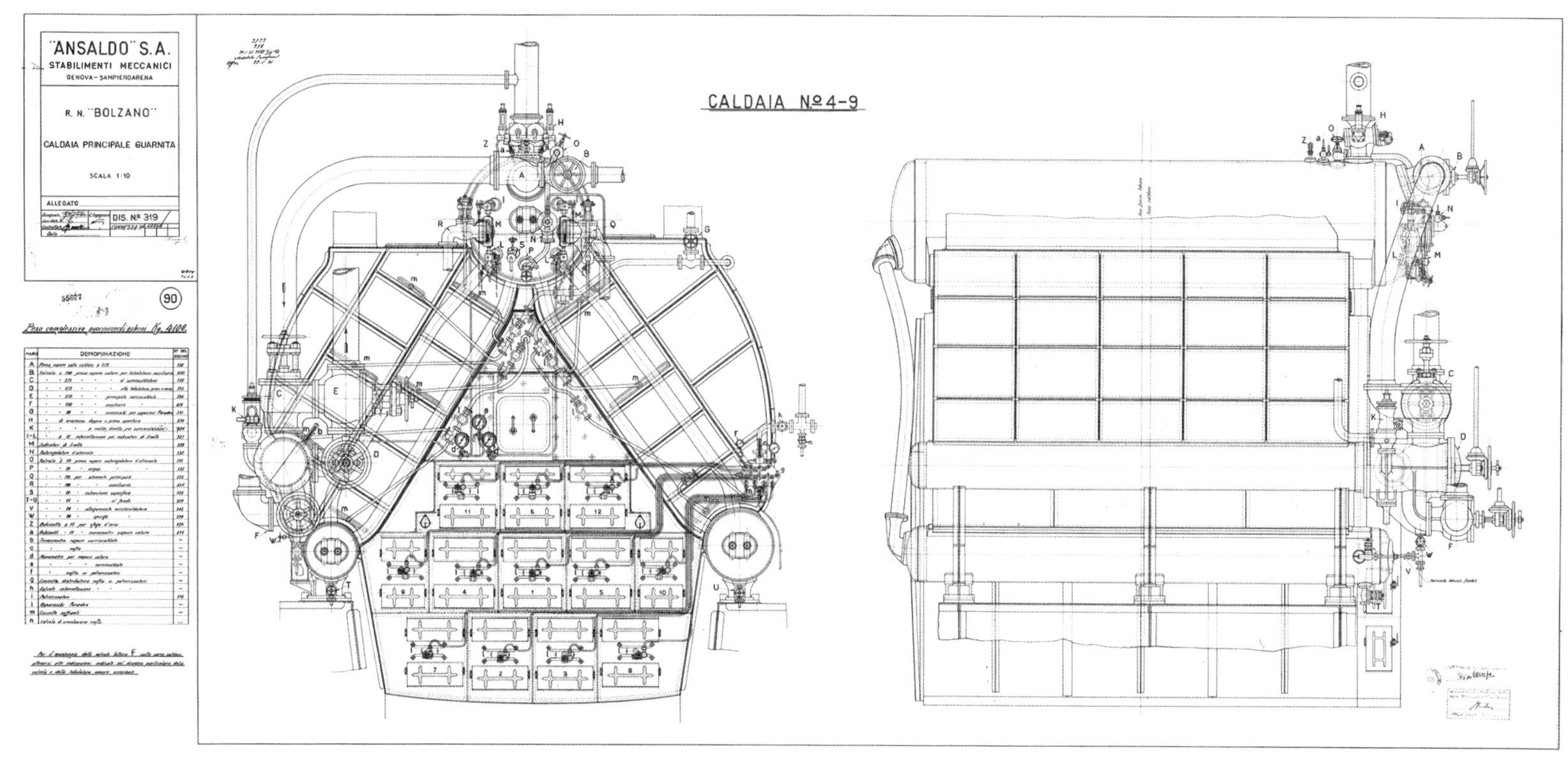

Front and side view of one of *Bolzano*'s boilers. (Courtesy Gruppo di Cultura Navale)

One of *Bolzano*'s geared steam turbines in the Ansaldo Stabilimento Meccanico in Genoa. (Courtesy Archivio Storico Ansaldo)

22 transverse bulkheads on the *Trento*s and 26 on the *Bolzano*, with those fore and aft rising up to the weather deck and the others up to the battery deck. The protected hull (including the engines and ammunition spaces, and, on the *Trento*s, also the diesel-dynamo room located ahead of the forward magazines) was formed by 70mm thick chrome-nickel steel plates on the sides; the corresponding thickness of the battery deck was 50mm. The thickness of the weather deck plating was 20mm, increased to 22mm on the *Bolzano*.

The curved plates which constituted the barbettes were 70mm thick on the *Trento*s and 60mm thick on the *Bolzano*, a reduction made necessary by the larger size of the 203/53 turrets embarked on the latter. The other elements of the protection were on a similar scale – 60mm for the armoured tube between the tower and the battery deck and 50mm for the main SDT (*Stazione di Direzione del Tiro*, fire control position), with the armoured command tower reaching 100mm in thickness. On the *Bolzano*, the ice room (over the rudder) was protected as much as possible, with 20mm thicknesses on the top and sides, with a 30mm sloping flap at the bottom to aft of the rudder head.

On the whole, the protection, if not entirely pro forma, was very limited, since, in particular, 70mm armour could not represent much defence against hypothetical 203mm projectiles. *Trento*, *Trieste* and *Bolzano* would therefore have had to rely on greater speed to avoid combat against similar enemy ships and on the main-calibre guns to engage smaller ships (which would normally have avoided combat in any case). With the illusory advantage of a few more knots of speed, much more valuable qualities were sacrificed, such as protection and a more general sturdiness of construction; among other things, the overall lightness of the hull and superstructure led to serious vibration at speeds in the order of 24 knots, making rangefinding impossible at that speed and sometimes even at higher speeds.

2A.3 Steering gear

There were three steering positions: one on the bridge, one in the armoured tower and one in the orderly room inside the hull; they were connected by a double system of pipes which, from the orderly room, reached the ice room. The pipes ran one on the starboard and one on the port side inside the cofferdam and were

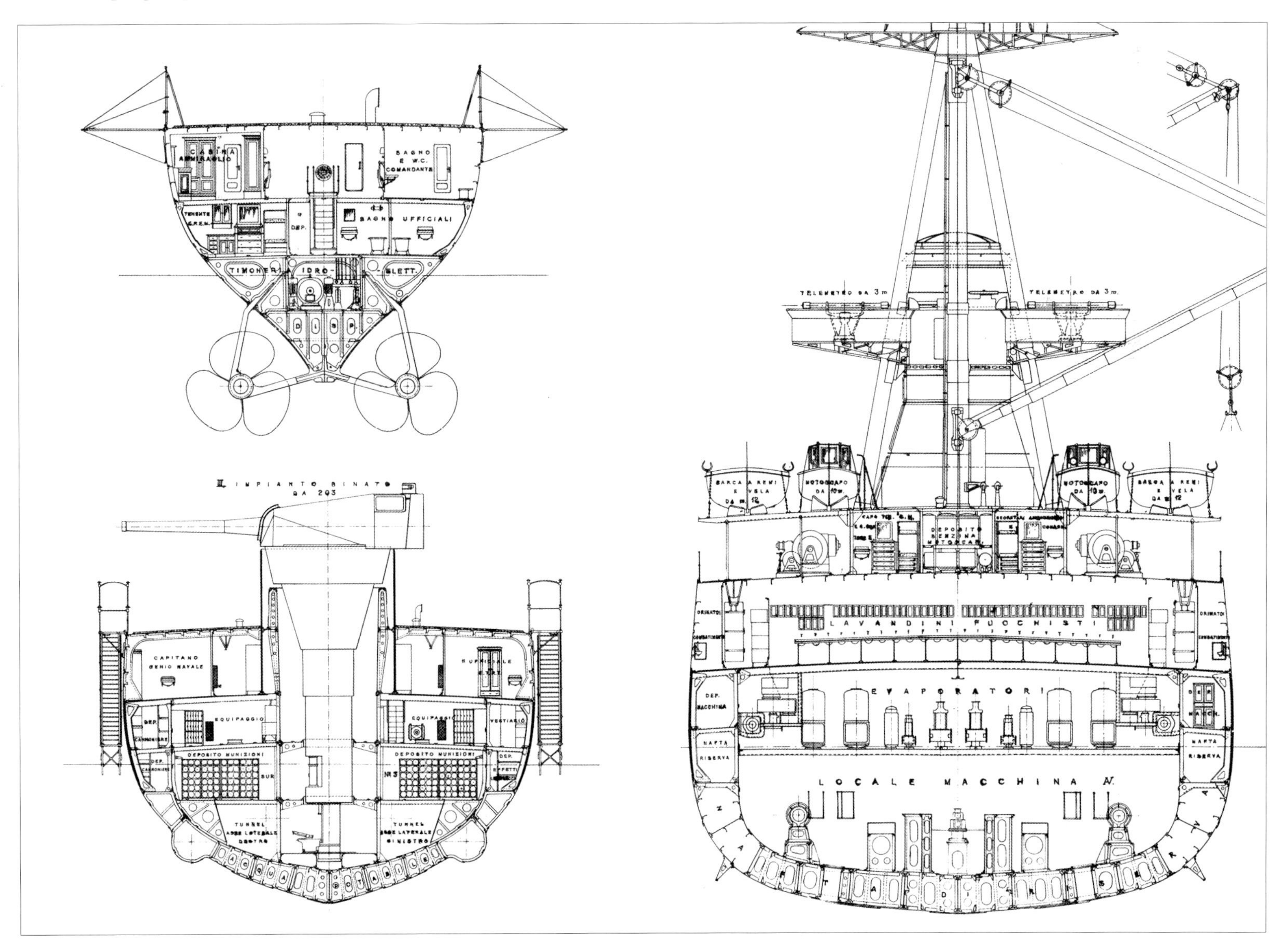

Cruiser *Trieste*: left, section at aft frame 81 (top) and 42 (bottom); right, section at aft frame 3. (Stabilimento Tecnico Triestino).

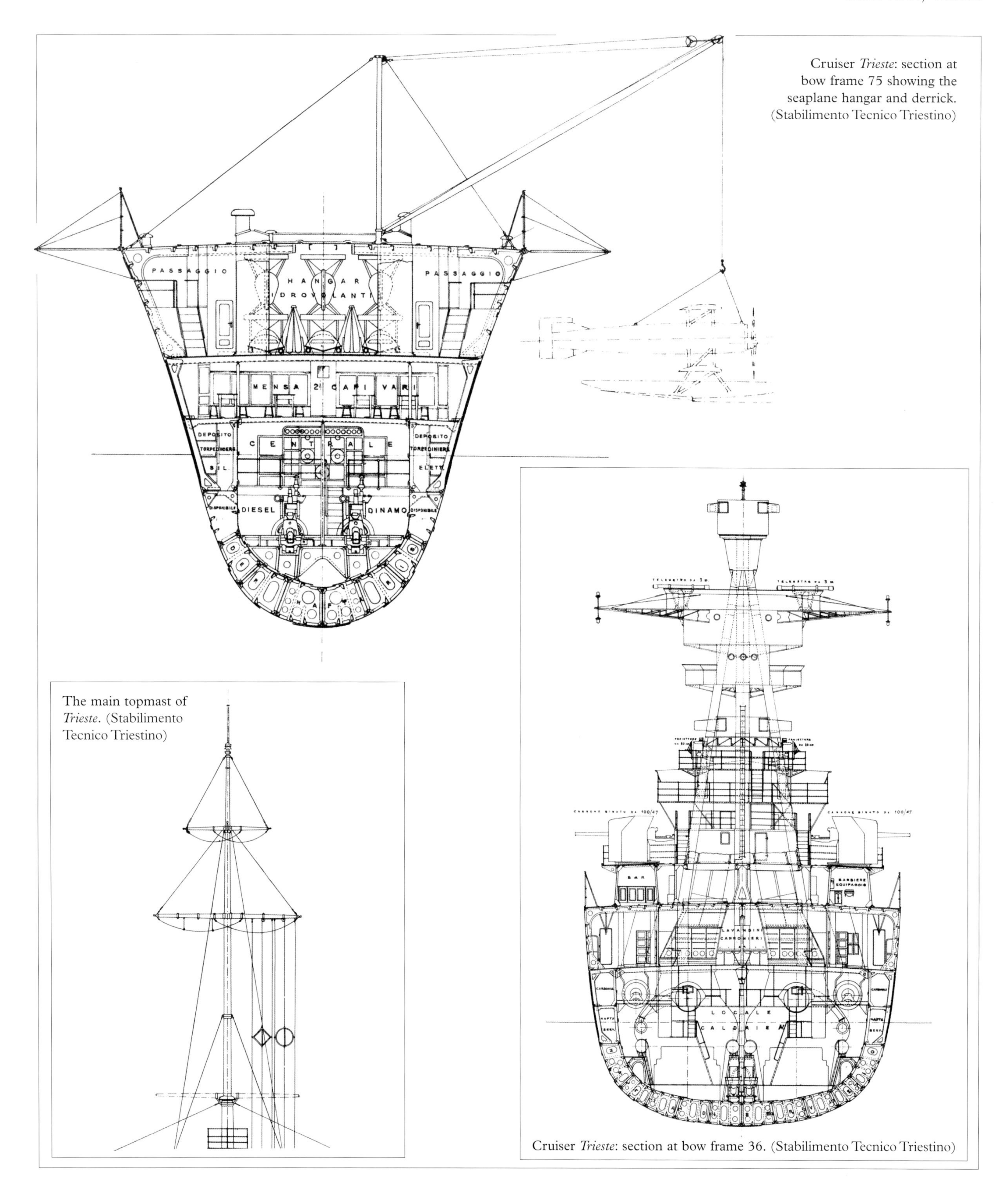

Cruiser *Trieste*: section at bow frame 75 showing the seaplane hangar and derrick. (Stabilimento Tecnico Triestino)

The main topmast of *Trieste*. (Stabilimento Tecnico Triestino)

Cruiser *Trieste*: section at bow frame 36. (Stabilimento Tecnico Triestino)

capable of operating independently in the event of damage or failure in one of them.

A hydraulic rudder angle repeater transmitted the data to two balloon and rhombus signals located to the left of the tripod, so that it was possible for other ships in the formation to visually follow the rudder angle of the preceding ship even before it began to turn.

2A.4 Ground tackle

The hawseholes were immediately below the gunwale and provided with a scallop towards the bow to house two 5600kg Hall type anchors, one each to port and starboard; as already mentioned, the two *Trento*s had a second anchor on the starboard side, but the after one was very rarely used. On the stern, rigged on deck, were a 2000kg Hall type anchor and a 1000kg Admiralty type kedge anchor.

The forward capstan winches were powered by two 70hp electric motors each with interchangeable action; for stern mooring

1936: cruiser *Trento* at slow speed in Taranto's Mar Piccolo. (M. Brescia collection)

The heavy cruiser *Trento* moored in the Bacino di San Marco in Venice on 29 June 1934, probably when *Bolzano* (in right background) received her 'Bandiera di Combattimento'. (Courtesy Museo Storico Navale di Venezia)

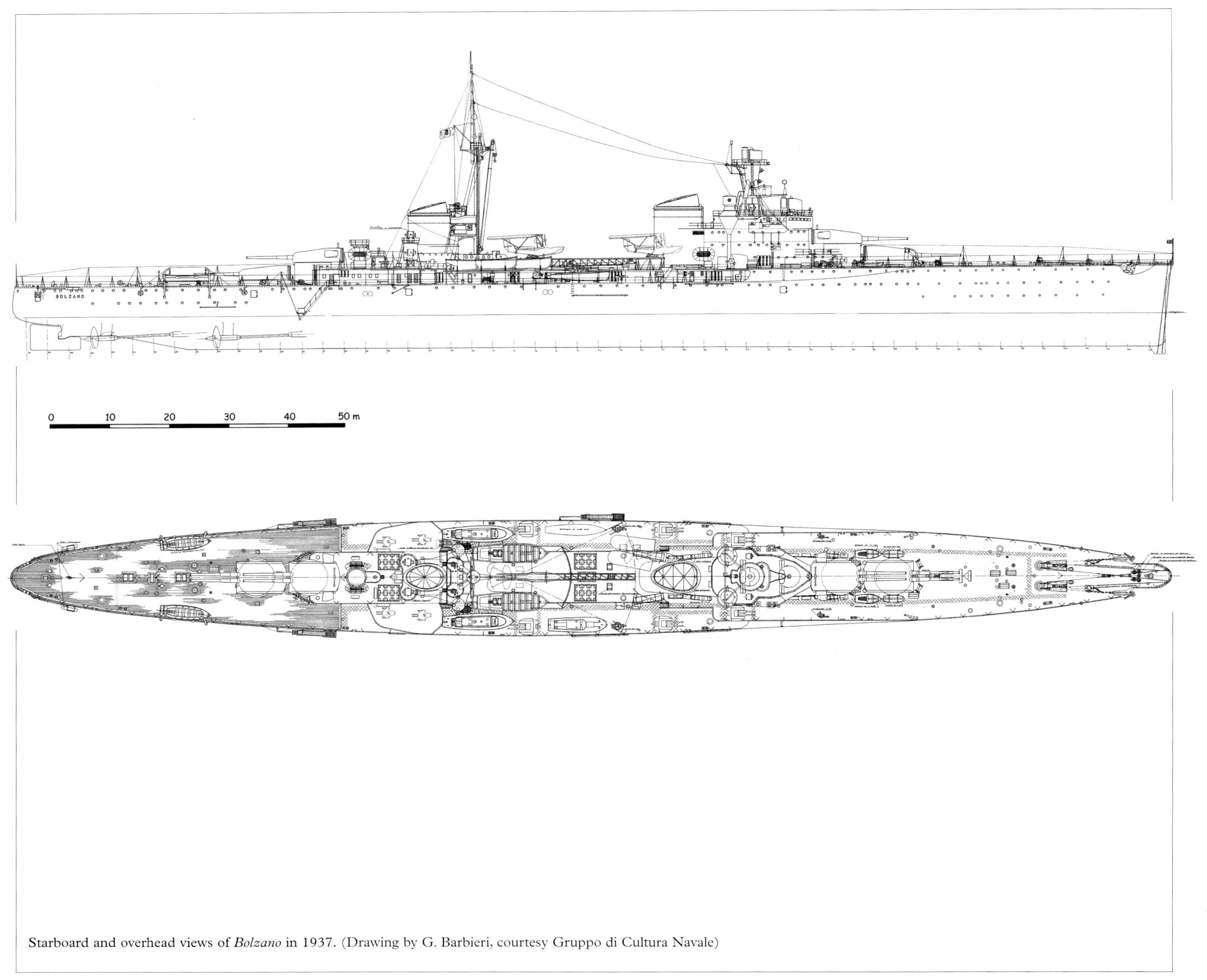

Starboard and overhead views of *Bolzano* in 1937. (Drawing by G. Barbieri, courtesy Gruppo di Cultura Navale)

there were two other winches at the stern, each powered by a 40hp electric motor. Chain cables for each of the two anchors measured 275m, or eleven lengths (1 length = 25m).

2A.5 machinery

The machinery of the three ships was made up of four units, each consisting of a high-pressure turbine, a low-pressure turbine (including the reverse turbine) and a gearbox. The high-pressure turbines discharged steam directly into the low-pressure turbines, which were of the double-outlet type, *ie* with the steam inlet in the middle and the outlet at the ends, finally discharging the steam into the main condenser.

Each group of turbines was coupled to a reduction gear consisting of two massive spools of nickel steel coupled, by means of a flexible joint, one to the high-pressure turbine and the other to the low-pressure turbine with a 'slow wheel' 2.70m in diameter attached to the shaft which, at the aft end drove a three-blade propeller. The propellers rotated outwards and each had a pitch of 4.40m and a developed surface area of 9.80m^2. On the *Trento* and *Trieste* steam was generated by twelve Yarrow type boilers divided, in groups of four, into three independent watertight compartments; the boilers operated at a pressure of 21kg/cm^2 (22kg/cm^2 for the *Bolzano*) and were each equipped with nine Mejani type oil-sprayers.

The maximum speed reached during the tests, with 150,000 horsepower, was 35.6 knots, with a maximum operating speed slightly lower (35 knots). The three ships carried 2252 tons of fuel oil, giving a range of 3190 miles at 25 knots.

The *Bolzano*'s engines, similar but technically more advanced, were powered by ten boilers (instead of twelve) arranged side by side in five watertight compartments, which improved the ship's ability to continue operating in the event of a hit in the engine room. Consequently, the subdivision and number of the various boiler and engine rooms – from bow to stern – differed between the first two cruisers and the *Bolzano*, as shown below.

Trento and *Trieste*:
1 - Compartment with 4 boilers
2 - Compartment with 4 boilers
3 - Forward engine room
4 - Compartment with 4 boilers
5 - After engine room

The heavy cruiser *Trento* in the 1930s with no funnel caps. (E. Bagnasco collection)

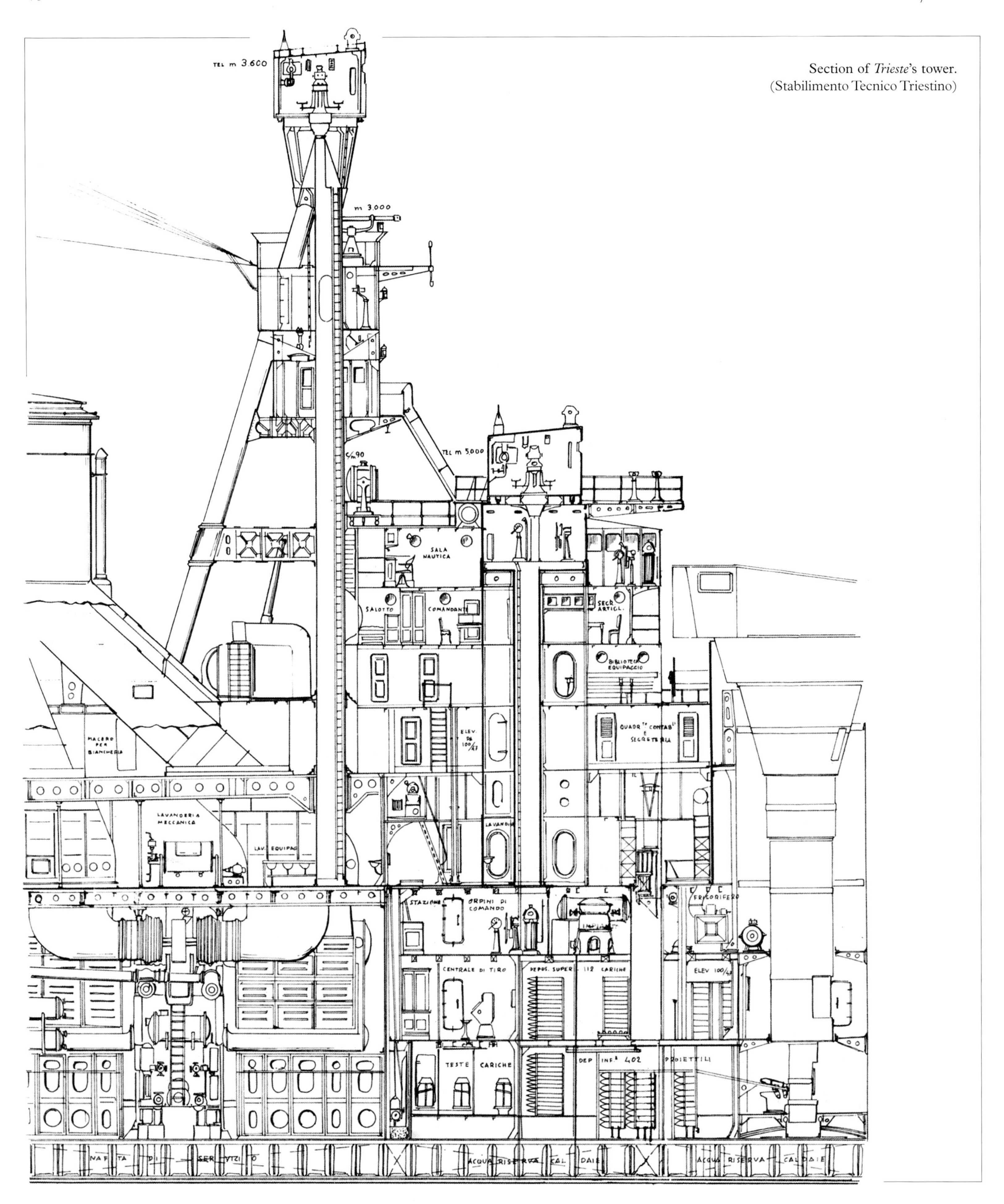

Section of *Trieste*'s tower.
(Stabilimento Tecnico Triestino)

Bolzano:
1 - Compartment with 2 boilers
2 - Compartment with 2 boilers
3 - Compartment with 2 boilers
4 - Forward engine room
5 - Compartment with 2 boilers
6 - Compartment with 2 boilers
7 - After engine room

While on the *Trento*s the condensers were located in their own room, on the *Bolzano* – in order to reduce the overall length of the spaces allocated to the machinery – they were located below the low-pressure turbines. This solution made it necessary to raise the position of the turbines, which resulted in a steeper angle of the propeller shafts compared with the *Trento* and *Trieste*.

2A.6 Auxiliary services

The fire-fighting service piping, from which water was also drawn for other services, consisted of a ring of pipes placed under the armoured battery deck; four pumps of 60-ton/h capacity and two 70-ton/h electric pumps placed in various positions in the engine rooms were connected to it. For pumping out large amounts of water from the hold spaces, four independent sections of piping were installed, which drew from the ammunition magazines, the boiler and machinery rooms and the shaft tunnels of the propellers; each collector was served by a 375-ton/h electric pump, while for the clearing the bilges there were two 25-ton/h capacity electric pumps, one forward and one aft.

Electricity, at 220 volts, was generated by two 150/160Kw turbo-dynamos located in the stern machinery compartment and driven by dedicated turbines. A diesel-dynamo power plant located in the hold forward of the first ammunition space (protected on the *Trento*s and unprotected on the *Bolzano*) produced direct current at 220 volts for 150Kw of power.

The interior of the ship was heated by steam heaters, which were fed by the auxiliary piping when at sea and by special boilers in port, and also by electric radiators. In the absence of air conditioning systems, mechanical ventilation was provided by the use of fans and extractors placed in positions so as not to cross the watertight bulkheads. For the refrigerated ventilation of the

The cruisers *Trento* (left) and *Trieste* moored in Naples in the spring of 1940. Note that the *Trento* has already been fitted with funnel caps, still absent on *Trieste*. (E. Bagnasco collection)

ammunition magazines and the command and fire-control rooms inside the hull, two main refrigeration systems with 60,000 refrigeration units per hour were used, while three smaller systems were used to refrigerate the galleys, other food storage areas and to produce ice.

Finally, the three ships were equipped with an evaporation and distillation plant for boiler feed-water, washing water and drinking water, as well as a mechanical laundry, a bread oven, six galleys for the various canteens and a mechanical workshop with a forge.

ZARA CLASS BUILDING DATA

	Yard	Laid down	Launched	Commissioned
Zara	Odero-Terni-Orlando, Muggiano (La Spezia)	4 July 1929	27 April 1930	20 October 1931
Fiume	Stabilimento Tecnico Triestino, Trieste	29 April 1929	27 April 1930	23 November 1931
Gorizia	Odero-Terni-Orlando, Livorno	17 March 1930	28 December 1930	23 December 1931
Pola	Odero-Terni-Orlando, Livorno	17 March 1931	5 December 1931	21 December 1932

ZARA CLASS

2B.1 Hull and superstructure

The hull and superstructure of the *Zara*s was more compact and better arranged than the earlier *Trento*s, due to a reduction in length of about 14 metres. The long forecastle, with flared sides and extending almost as far as the forward funnel, provided good seakeeping qualities and during trials, in force 8 conditions, a roll of no more than 25° was recorded. The stern was of the 'cruiser' type.

On *Zara*, *Fiume* and *Gorizia*, there were two long and pronounced 'scallops' in the deck-edge at the end of the forecastle designed to increase the forward firing arcs of the twin 100/47 mountings positioned immediately aft of the break of the forecastle. This feature was abandoned on the *Pola*, which had vertical hull sides in this area. The hull was constructed of high-strength steel, replaced by Siemens-Martin steel in the parts subject to high vibrations; the deck height of 2.20m was constant throughout the hull. The structure was longitudinal between the forecastle, battery deck and hold, and, for greater strength, transverse in the intermediate decks (1st and 2nd platforms and

The *Fiume* fitting out at Trieste in 1931. The forward 203mm twin turrets and all the 100/47 twin mountings have already been fitted, but the after 203mm turrets still have to be embarked. (E. Bagnasco collection)

The heavy cruiser *Zara* at slow speed in the first half of the 1930s, with its initial secondary armament consisting of eight twin 100/47 guns. (E. Bagnasco collection)

orlop). The nineteen main watertight bulkheads reached the battery deck amidships and rose up to the forecastle and quarter-deck fore and aft.

Underwater, the stem had a bulbous forefoot, and other hull appendages consisted of two bilge keels extending from the front of the bridge tower to the after funnel, two propeller shafts supported by V-shaped brackets and a large semi-balanced rudder on the centreline.

From the break of the forecastle, a long deckhouse extended aft to the barbette of the after superfiring 203/53 turret and on this, from bow to stern, was the bridge tower (different in each ship; for detail see Appendix D), the forward funnel, the boat deck, the tripod mainmast surmounted by a tall topmast, and the after funnel. The forward funnels, of elliptical section, were separated from the bridge tower, except in the case of the *Pola*; that of the *Gorizia* was slightly further away and with a much wider flared base, compared to the funnels of *Zara* and *Fiume*. The after funnels were also elliptical in cross-section, but smaller in size. When she first entered service, *Fiume*'s funnels were without caps, so very similar to those of the *Trento*s. However, her funnels were soon equipped with large hoods with a top elegantly raked aft, a modification made during the outfitting of *Zara* and *Gorizia*, while *Pola* was launched with the forward funnel already equipped with a cap, with the second funnel cap applied during outfitting.

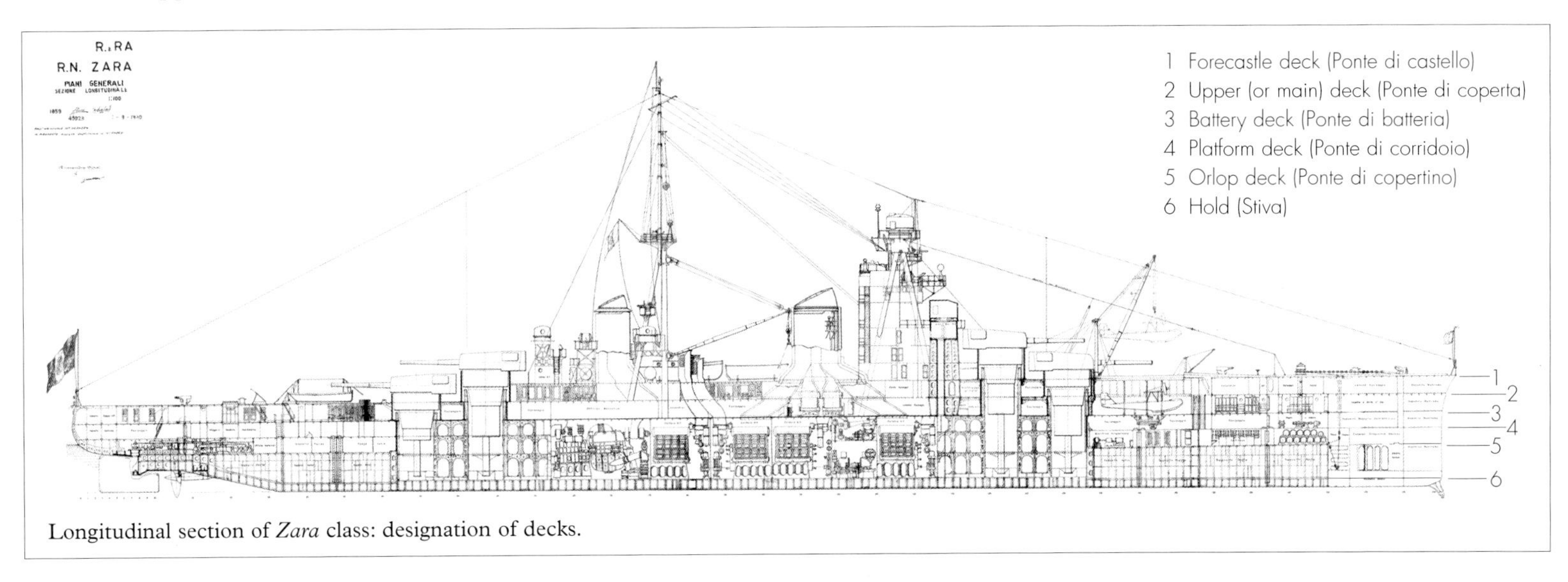

Longitudinal section of *Zara* class: designation of decks.

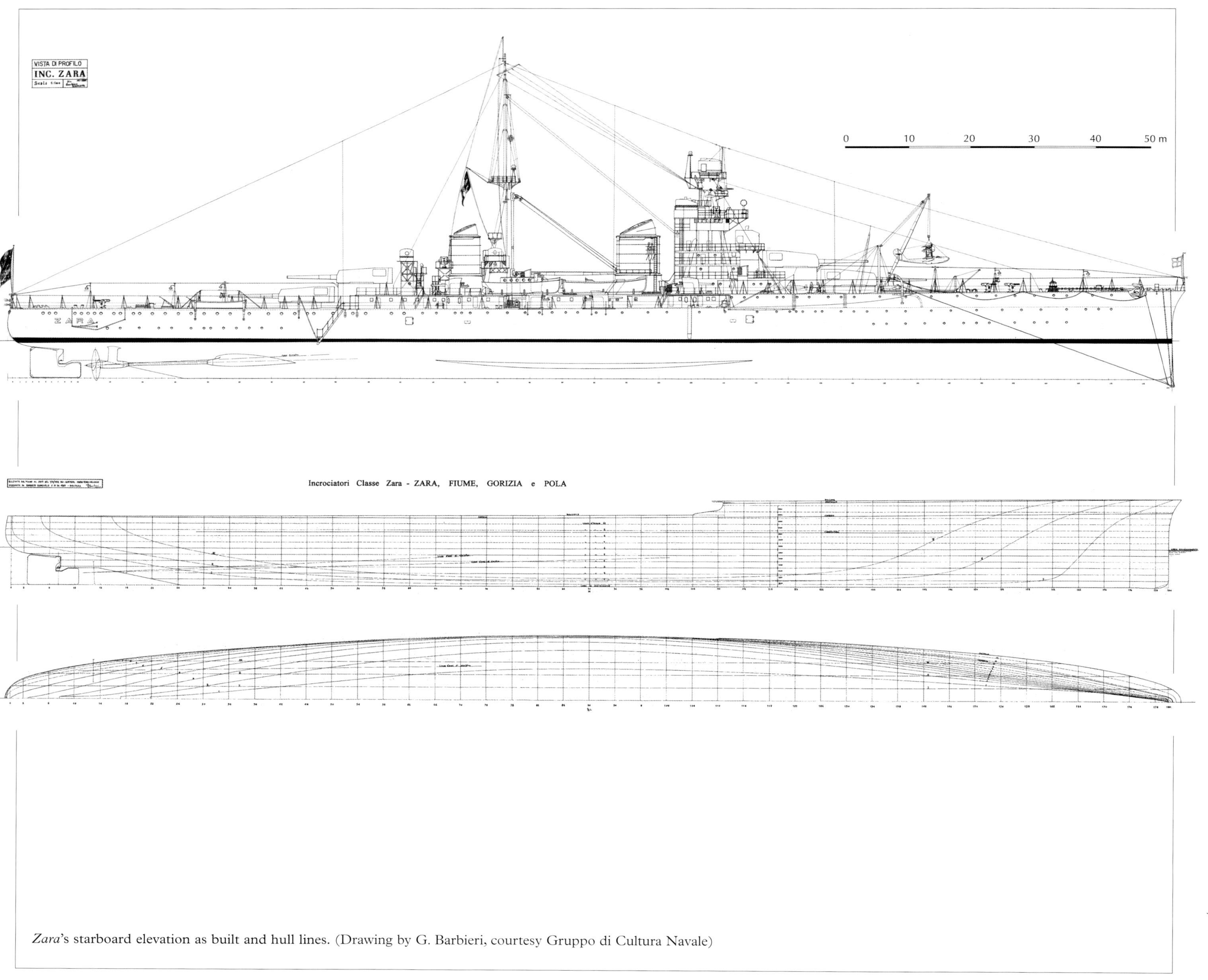

Zara's starboard elevation as built and hull lines. (Drawing by G. Barbieri, courtesy Gruppo di Cultura Navale)

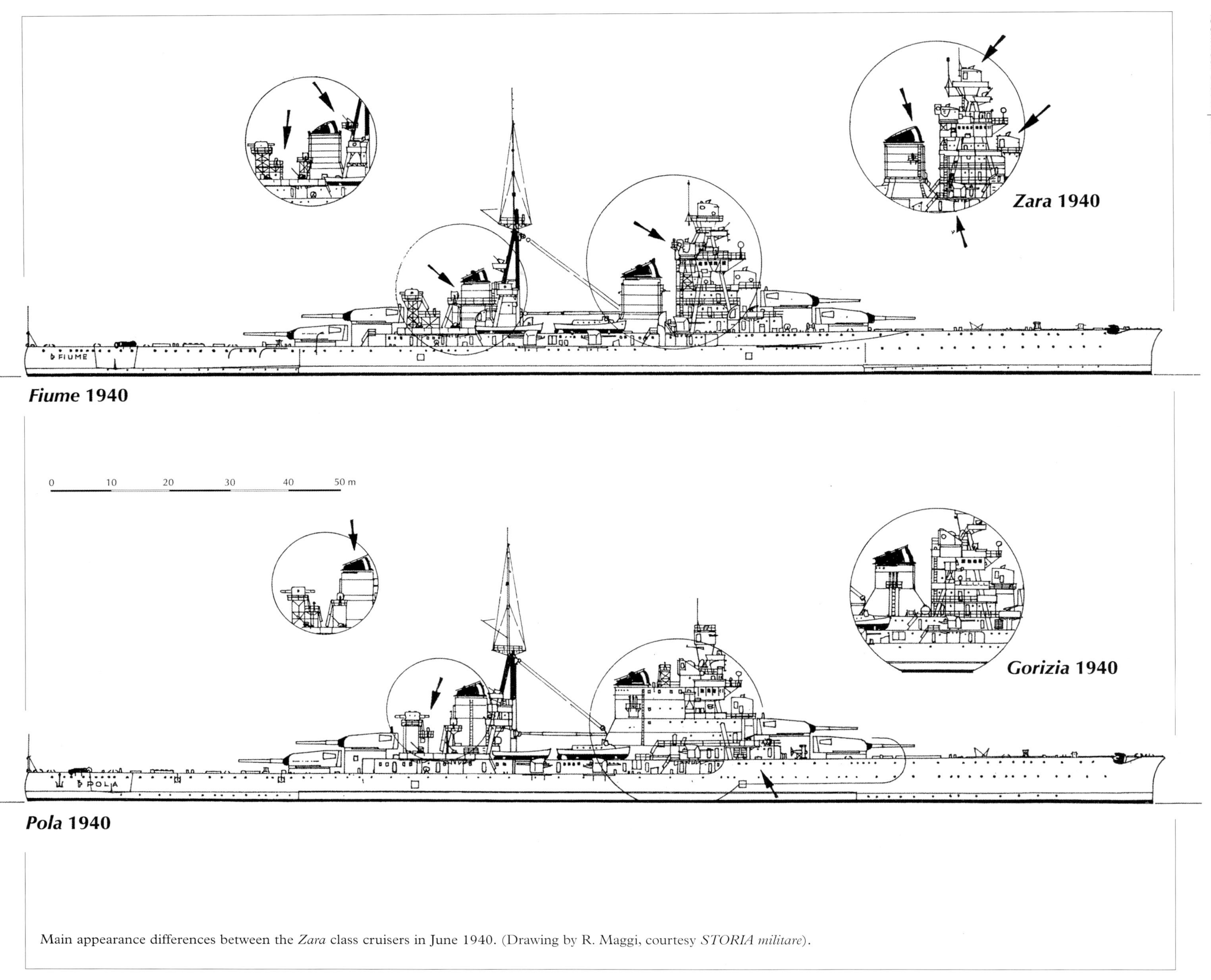

Main appearance differences between the *Zara* class cruisers in June 1940. (Drawing by R. Maggi, courtesy *STORIA militare*).

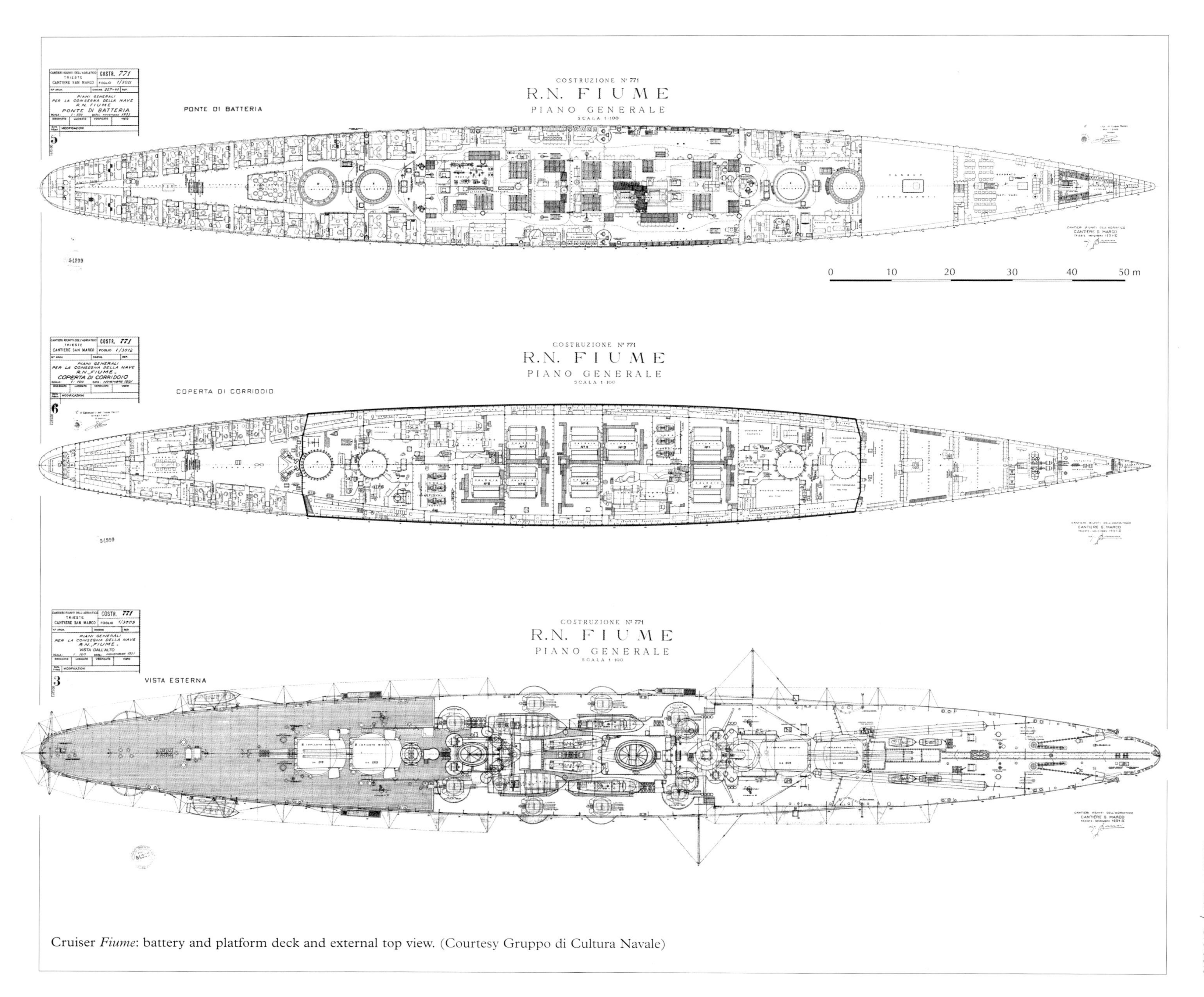

Cruiser *Fiume*: battery and platform deck and external top view. (Courtesy Gruppo di Cultura Navale)

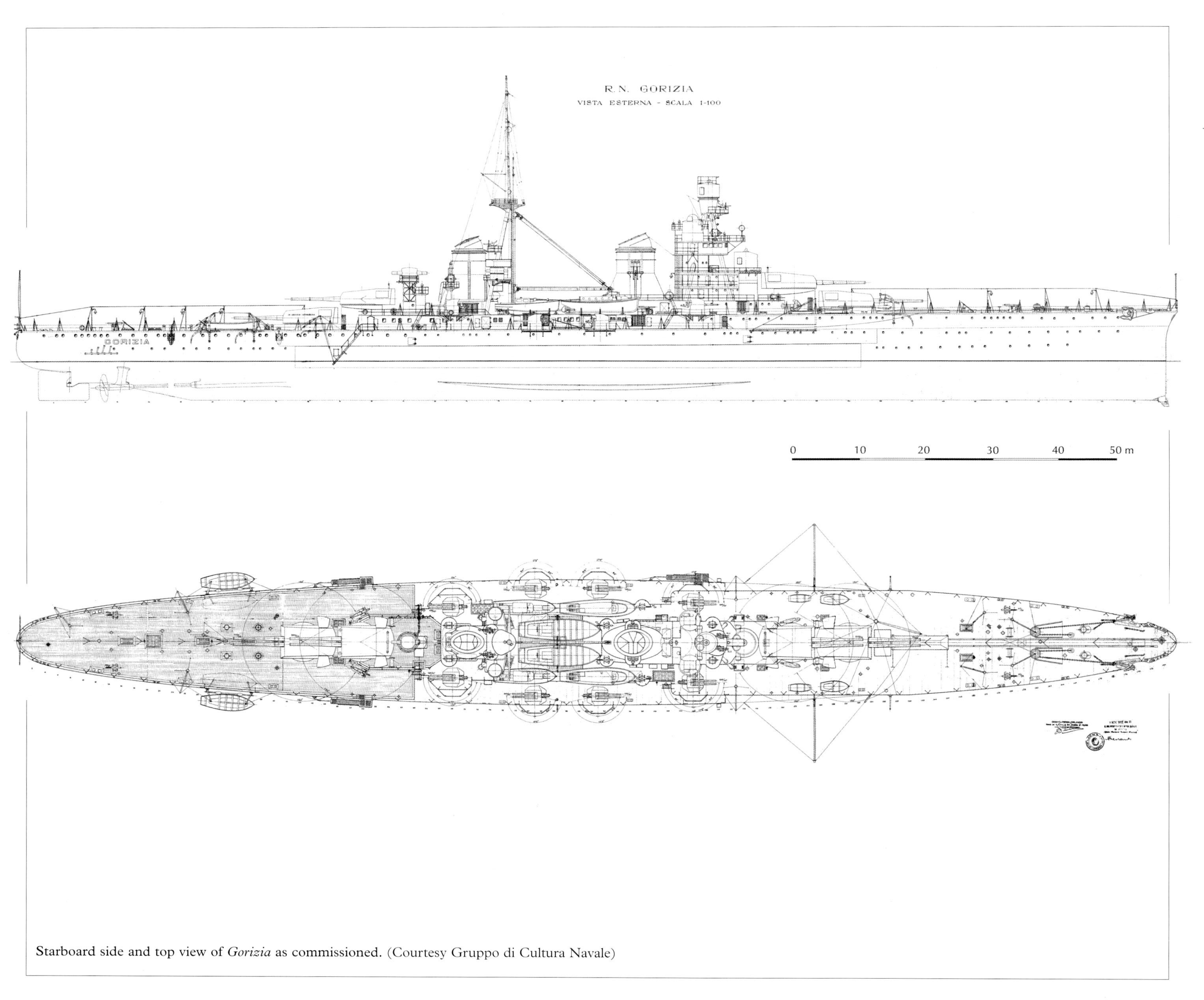

Starboard side and top view of *Gorizia* as commissioned. (Courtesy Gruppo di Cultura Navale)

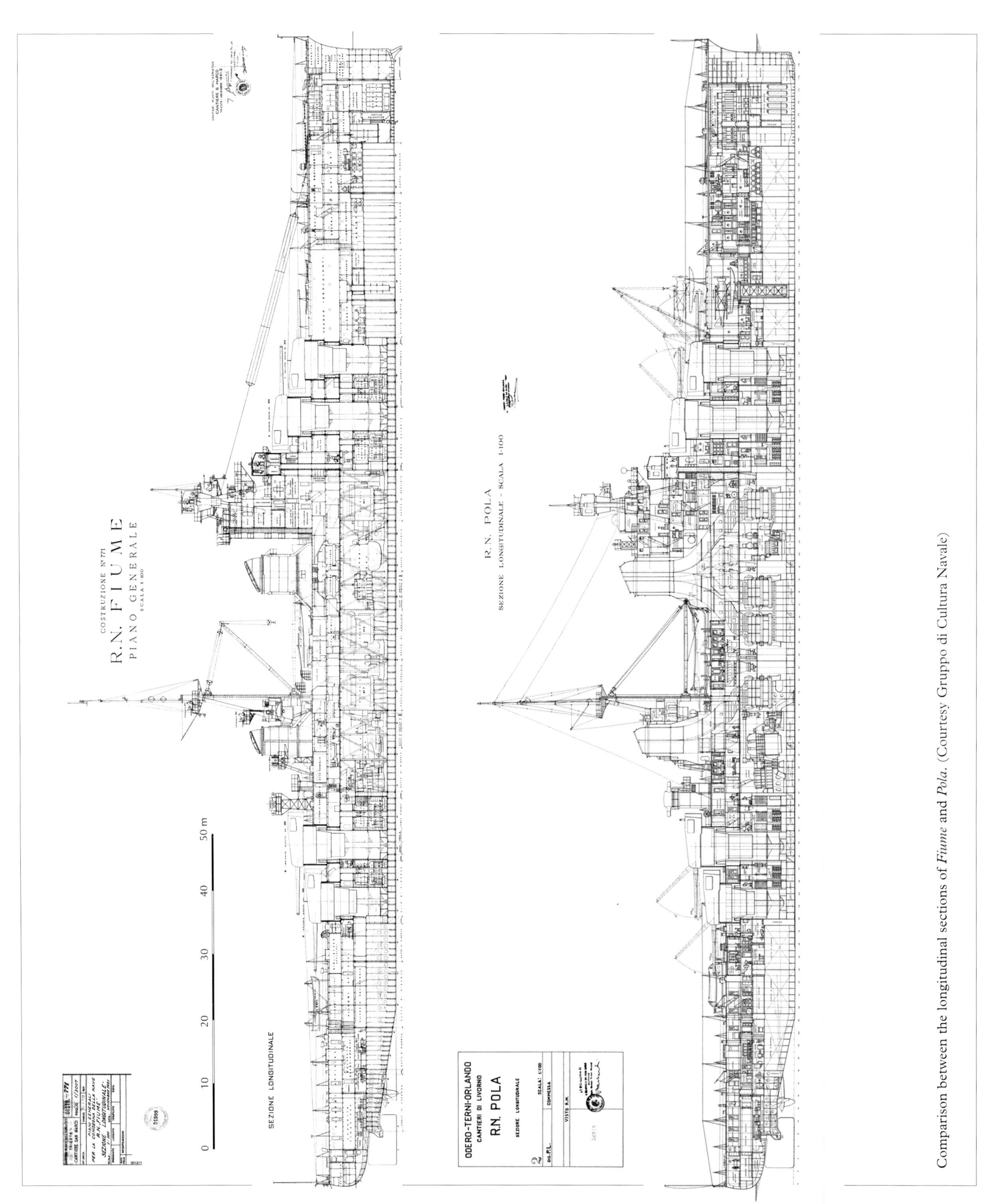

Comparison between the longitudinal sections of *Fiume* and *Pola*. (Courtesy Gruppo di Cultura Navale)

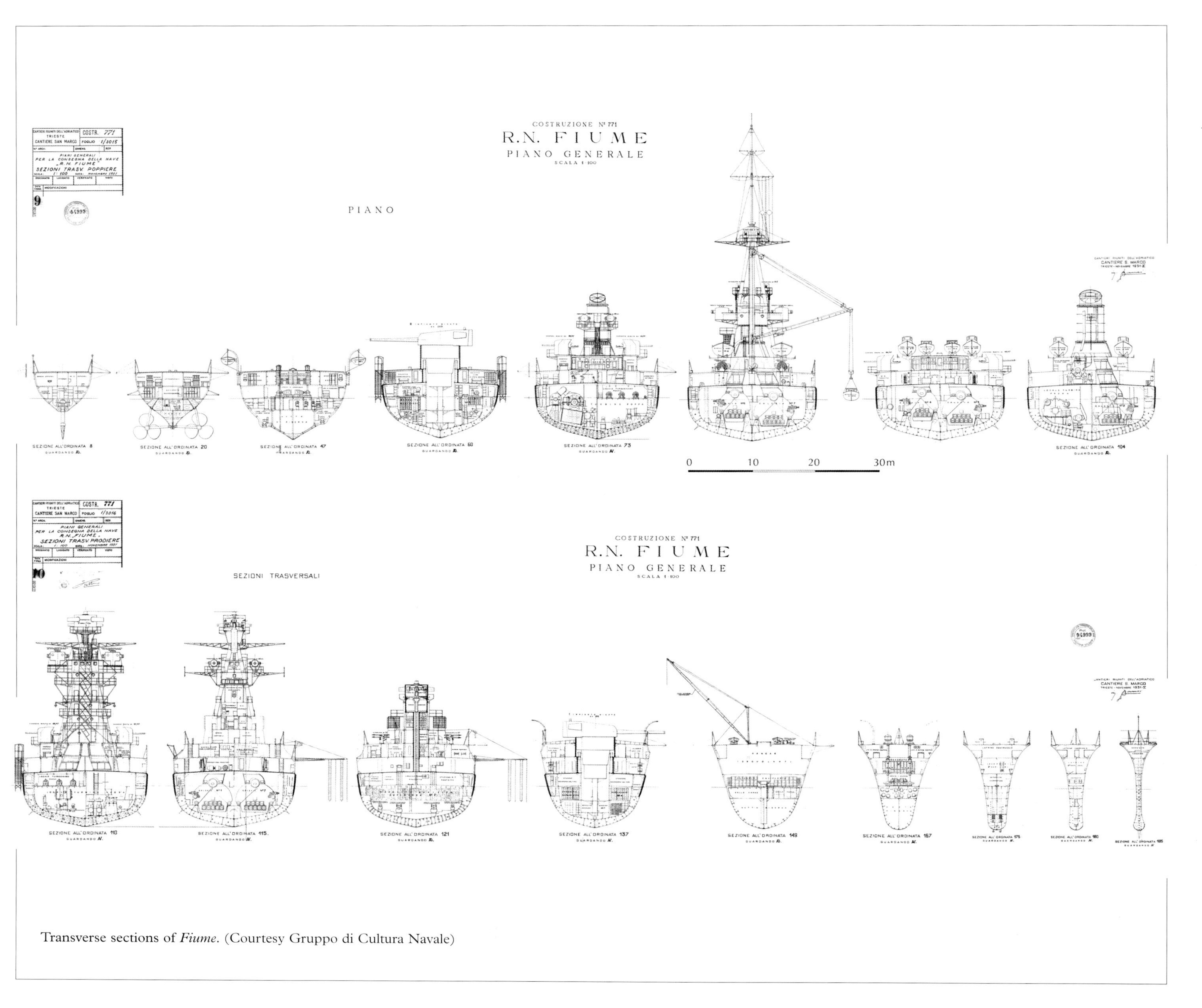

Transverse sections of *Fiume*. (Courtesy Gruppo di Cultura Navale)

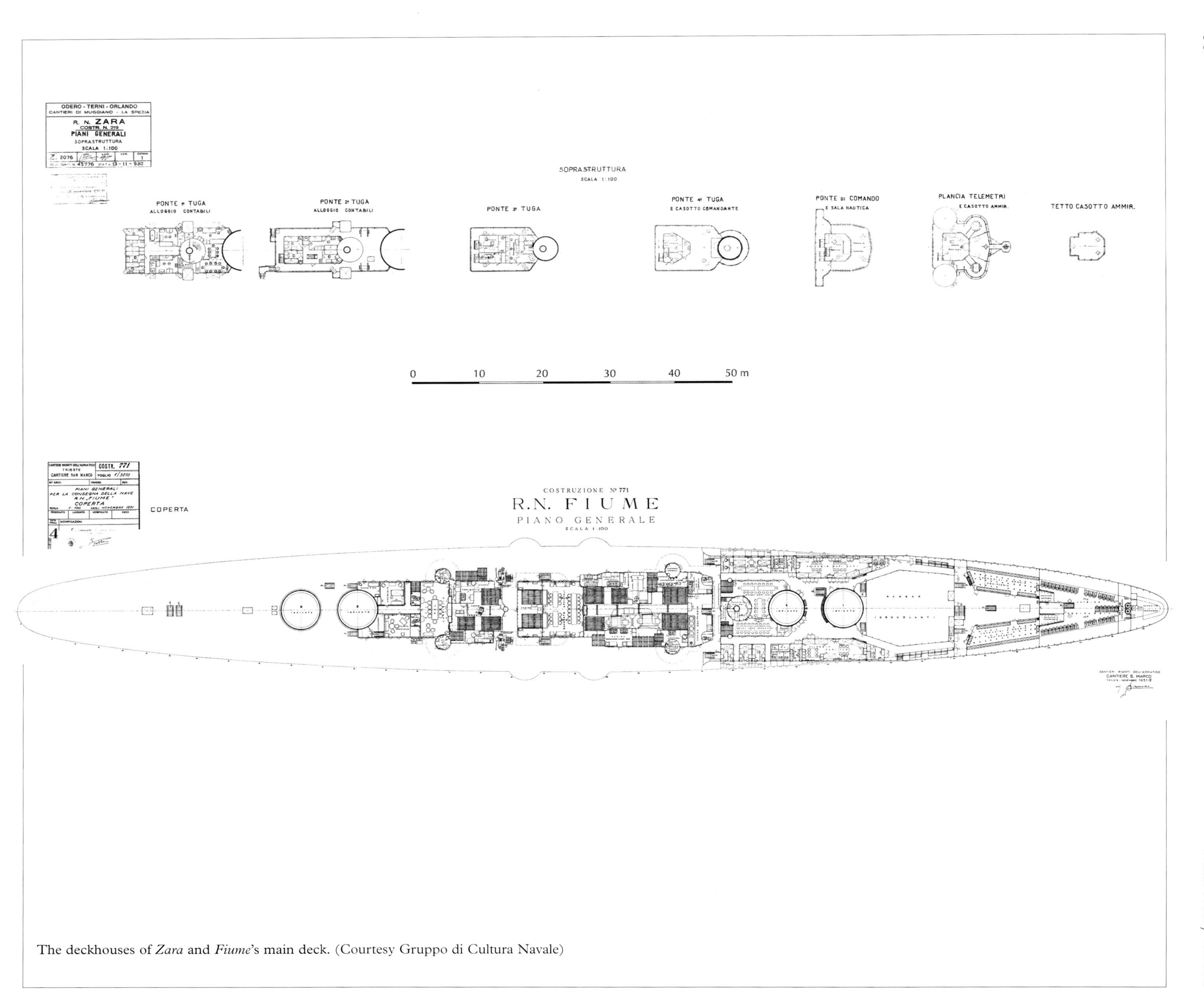

The deckhouses of *Zara* and *Fiume*'s main deck. (Courtesy Gruppo di Cultura Navale)

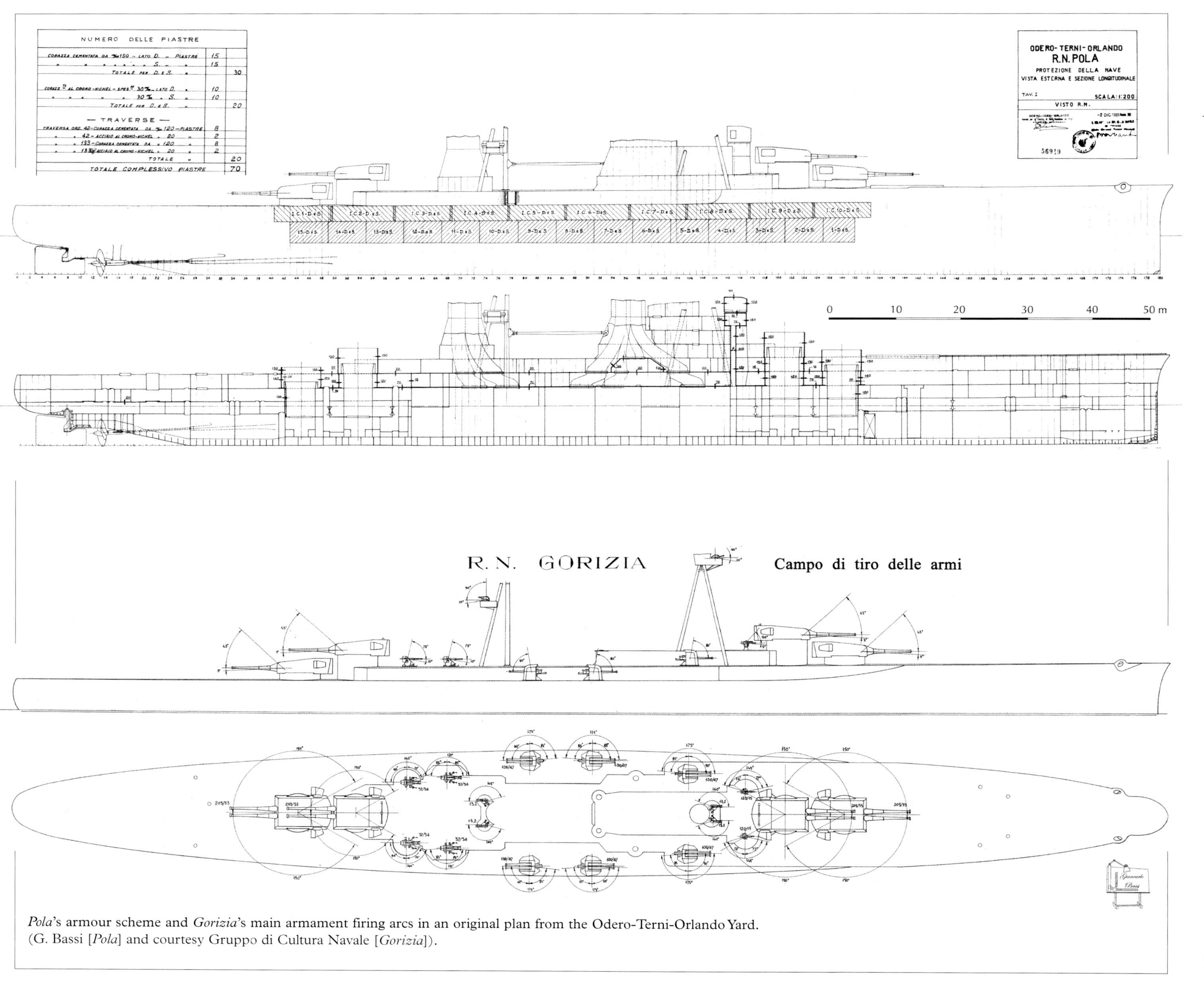

Pola's armour scheme and *Gorizia*'s main armament firing arcs in an original plan from the Odero-Terni-Orlando Yard. (G. Bassi [*Pola*] and courtesy Gruppo di Cultura Navale [*Gorizia*]).

The *Fiume* in the mid-1930s. (G. Alfano collection)

As mentioned above, the hull was stepped down aft of the forecastle, on which was mounted the catapult for launching the reconnaissance floatplanes. These were housed in a hangar that occupied a two-deck height between the battery deck and the forecastle just ahead of the forward 203mm turrets. The bases of the bridge tower tetrapod and the main mast itself of the after tripod were stepped on the battery deck.

2B.2 Protection

The hull armour was arranged around an armoured redoubt which included the centre of the ship with the machinery spaces and the magazines for the forward and aft main turrets, with a transverse armoured bulkhead at each end. It was made up, on each side, of a strake of ten 150mm thick case-hardened steel plates, each 6m long; beneath, covering the waterline and about one metre on the topsides, there was a second strake of fifteen 100mm thick plates, which gradually tapered downwards to 30mm. The thickness of the two armoured transoms forward of the fore magazine and abaft the after magazine was 120mm; the forecastle deck was protected horizontally by 20mm armour plates and the compartments below by 30mm plates on the hull sides. The battery deck, in turn, was 70mm thick and extended the full length of the armoured redoubt to protect the magazines and machinery rooms from above.

The plates that formed the barbettes of the 203mm turrets were 150mm thick at the top, which on the lower decks was reduced to between 140mm and 120mm. The armoured command tower was protected by plates 150mm thick on the sides and 80mm thick on the top, while the secondary SDT (see page 81) above was protected by plates of a lesser thickness (120mm and 95mm on the sides and top respectively). Finally, the cylindrical trunking leading down from the armoured tower to the decks below was also protected by 120mm thick steel elements, through which passed the hydraulic lines for the rudder, the electrical cables for the engine telegraph and other instruments, and the electrical lines and cables connecting the secondary SDT with the firing station. Other parts of the hull carried light armour of varying thickness and the double bottom was made up of a cellular structure in order to reduce damage from exploding underwater weapons.

Therefore, the protection, although extended only to vital areas (machinery, magazines, command and control areas, etc), was nevertheless more rational and complete than the *Trento*s. The armour scheme was designed to withstand the attack of 203mm shells, following the theories of the time which expected surface combat at great distances, relying on superior speed. As a result, the weight breakdown for the *Zara*s on the whole showed a much better balance (and more sensible emphases)

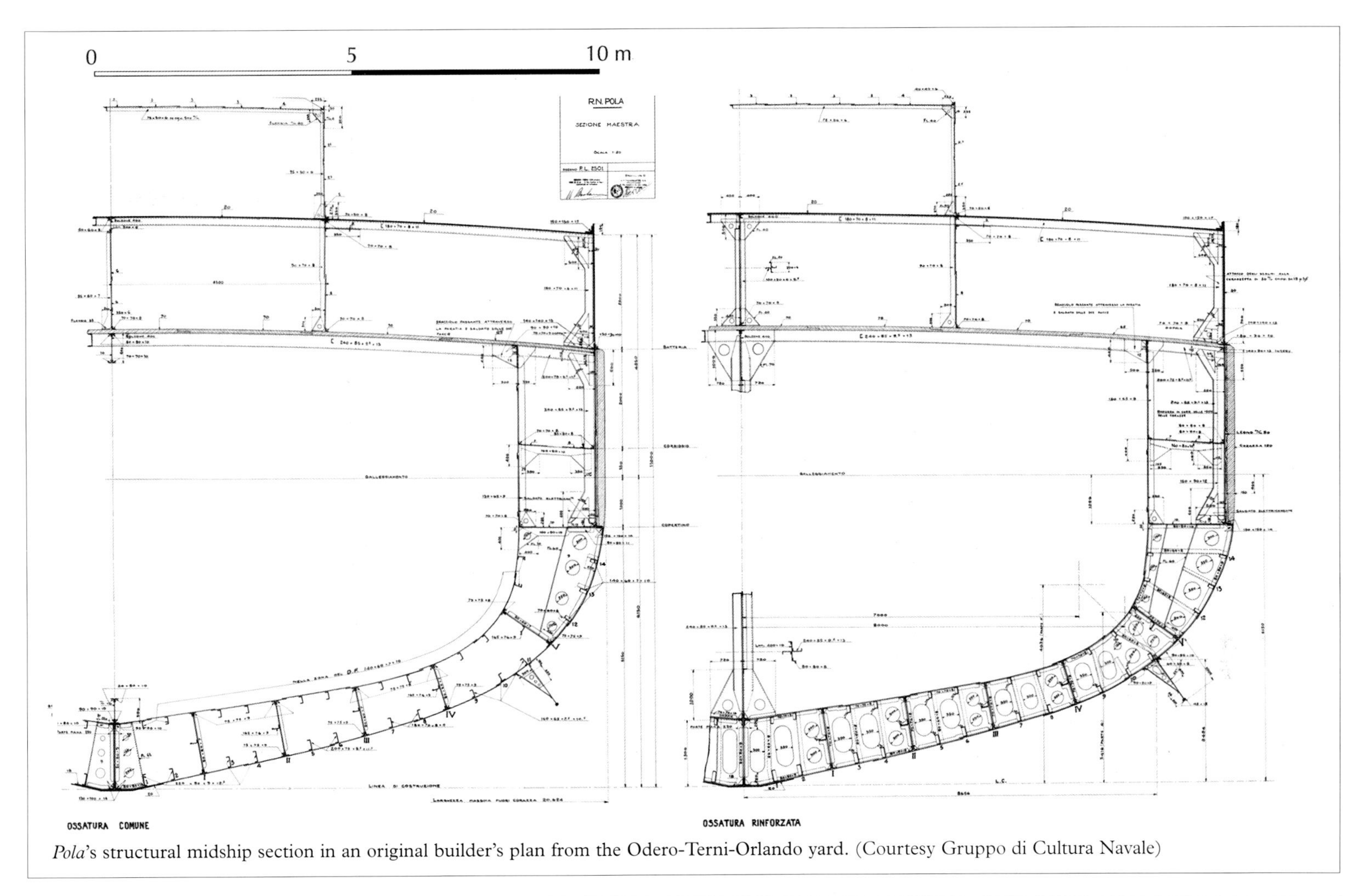

Pola's structural midship section in an original builder's plan from the Odero-Terni-Orlando yard. (Courtesy Gruppo di Cultura Navale)

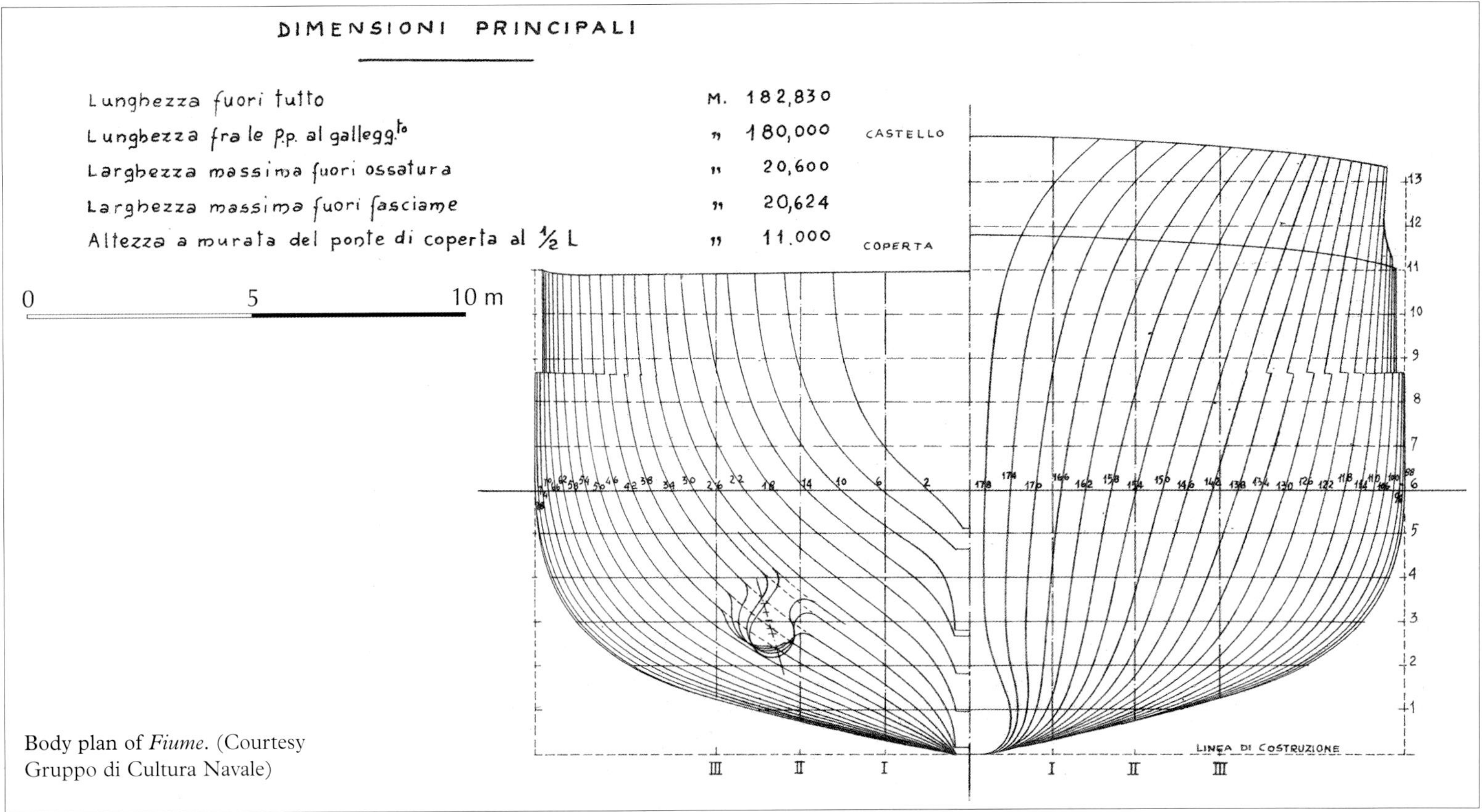

Body plan of *Fiume*. (Courtesy Gruppo di Cultura Navale)

when compared to the *Trento* and *Trieste*, as the following percentages indicate:

	Zara	*Trento*
- Hull	41.9	49.2
- Engine	13.1	22.4
- Protection	24.8	8.7
- Armament	12.2	10.0
- Outfitting etc.	8.0	9.7

2B.3 Steering gear

There were five steering stations on the *Zara* class: four of them were equipped with hydraulic transmitters and were located, respectively, in the main armoured tower, on the bridge, in the order room and in the stern gyrocompass room; a secondary position, with a mechanical transmitter, was located in the forward pump room.

The rudder, as mentioned, was of the semi-balanced type, and had a surface area of 29.37m^2 on *Zara* and *Fiume* and 29.74m^2 on *Gorizia* and *Pola*, with a rudder angle of 35 degrees on each side. As on all major Italian vessels of the time, the rudder angle was transmitted mechanically to two signals, one circular and the other rhomboidal, located on halliards on the port side yardarm of the tripod mainmast. From their position (horizontally aligned when the rudder was amidships and staggered when the ship was turning), it was possible for the other ships in the formation to visually follow the unit immediately ahead so as to manoeuvre without delay.

2B.4 Ground tackle

The hawseholes were placed immediately below the gunwale and the anchors were housed in a 'scallop' near the bow on the

Bow view of *Fiume* in drydock at Taranto: the bulbous bow can be clearly seen. (G. Alfano collection)

The rudder and the port propeller of *Fiume* in one of the drydocks of La Spezia Dockyard.

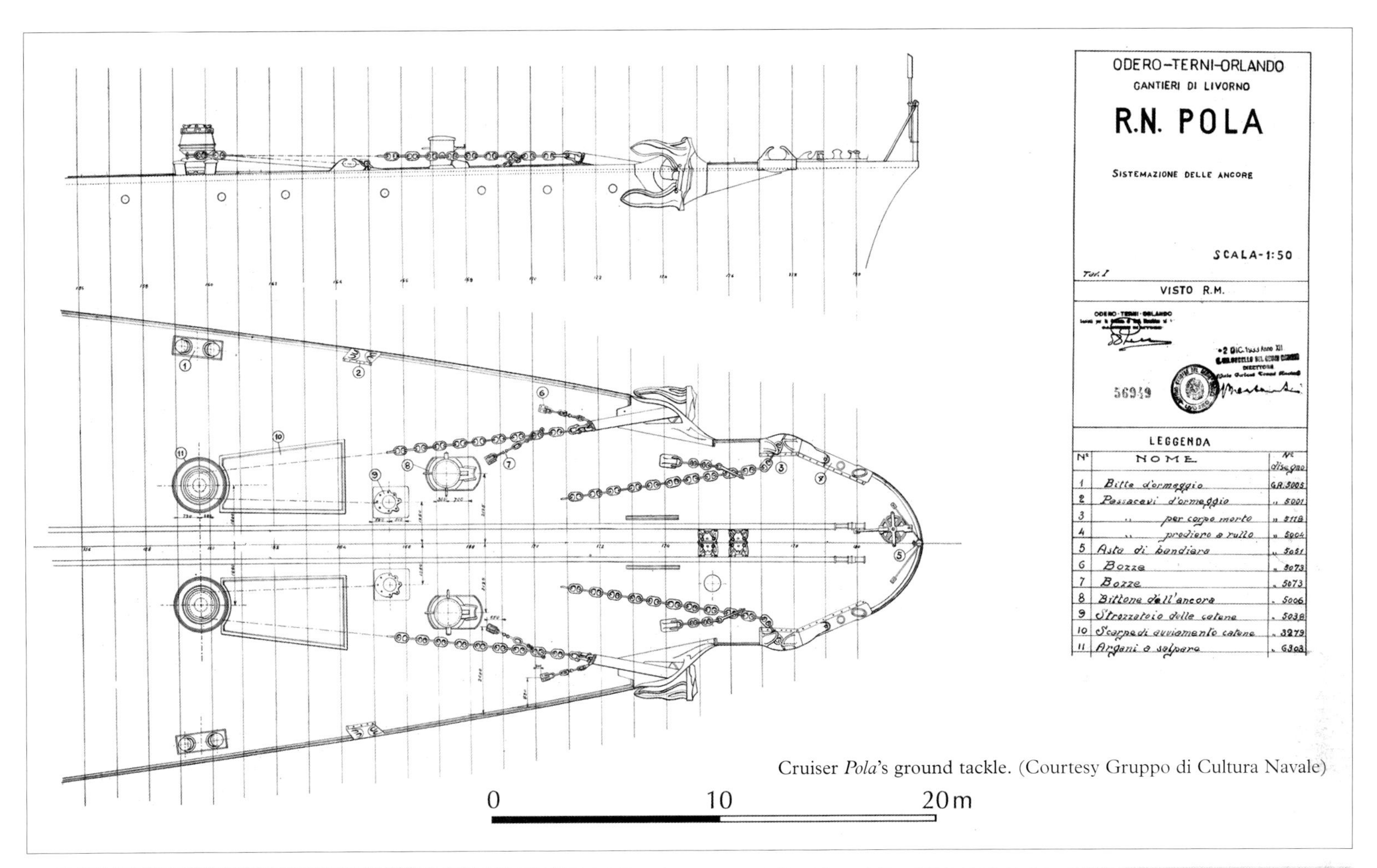

Cruiser *Pola*'s ground tackle. (Courtesy Gruppo di Cultura Navale)

The *Pola* in 1936: the port hawse's design may be clearly seen. (G. Alfano collection)

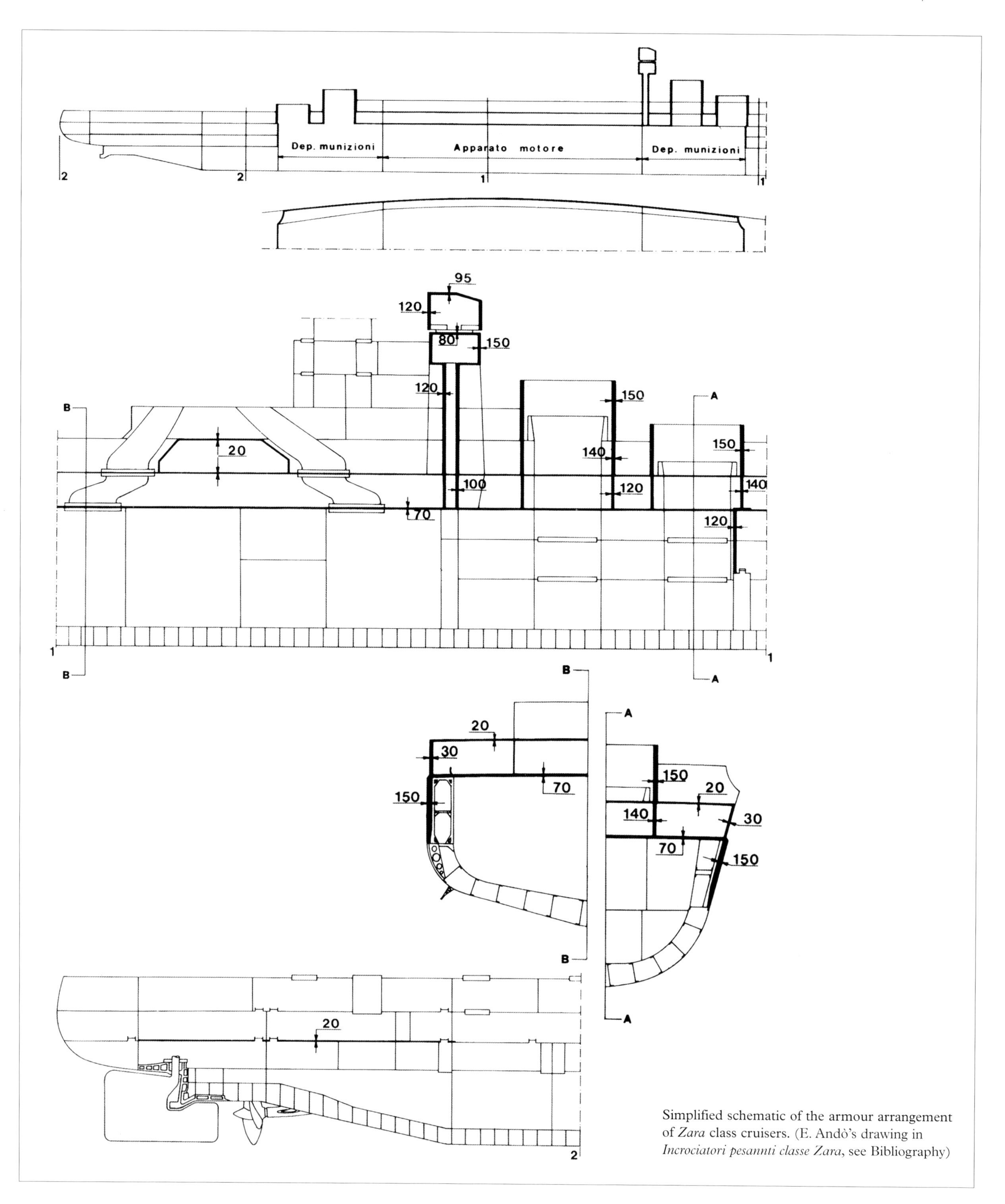

Simplified schematic of the armour arrangement of *Zara* class cruisers. (E. Andò's drawing in *Incrociatori pesannti classe Zara*, see Bibliography)

Trieste, 1931: two views of *Fiume* fitting out.

deck-edge, one each to port and starboard. These were Hall type of 6.5 tons on *Zara* and *Fiume* and FMA type of 6.7 tons on *Gorizia* and *Pola*; a third Hall type anchor of 1.8 tons was placed vertically on the stern, on the port side, but it was landed at the beginning of the conflict.

The forward capstans were powered by two 80hp electric motors each with interchangeable action; for stern mooring there were two more winches aft, each powered by a 40hp electric motor. Chain cables for each of the two anchors measured 275m, or eleven lengths (1 length = 25m).

2B.5 Machinery

The machinery of the *Zara* class was located in two separate rooms and consisted of a total of eight boilers and two turbine engines. The arrangement of the propulsion elements, from bow to stern, was subdivided longitudinally as shown below.

Port:
- one boiler
- one turbo-generator room
- three boilers
- the port engines

The horns for the sirens on either side of the forward funnel of the *Pola* (left); and the signal station at the rear of *Zara*'s bridge, visible immediately ahead of the funnel cap.

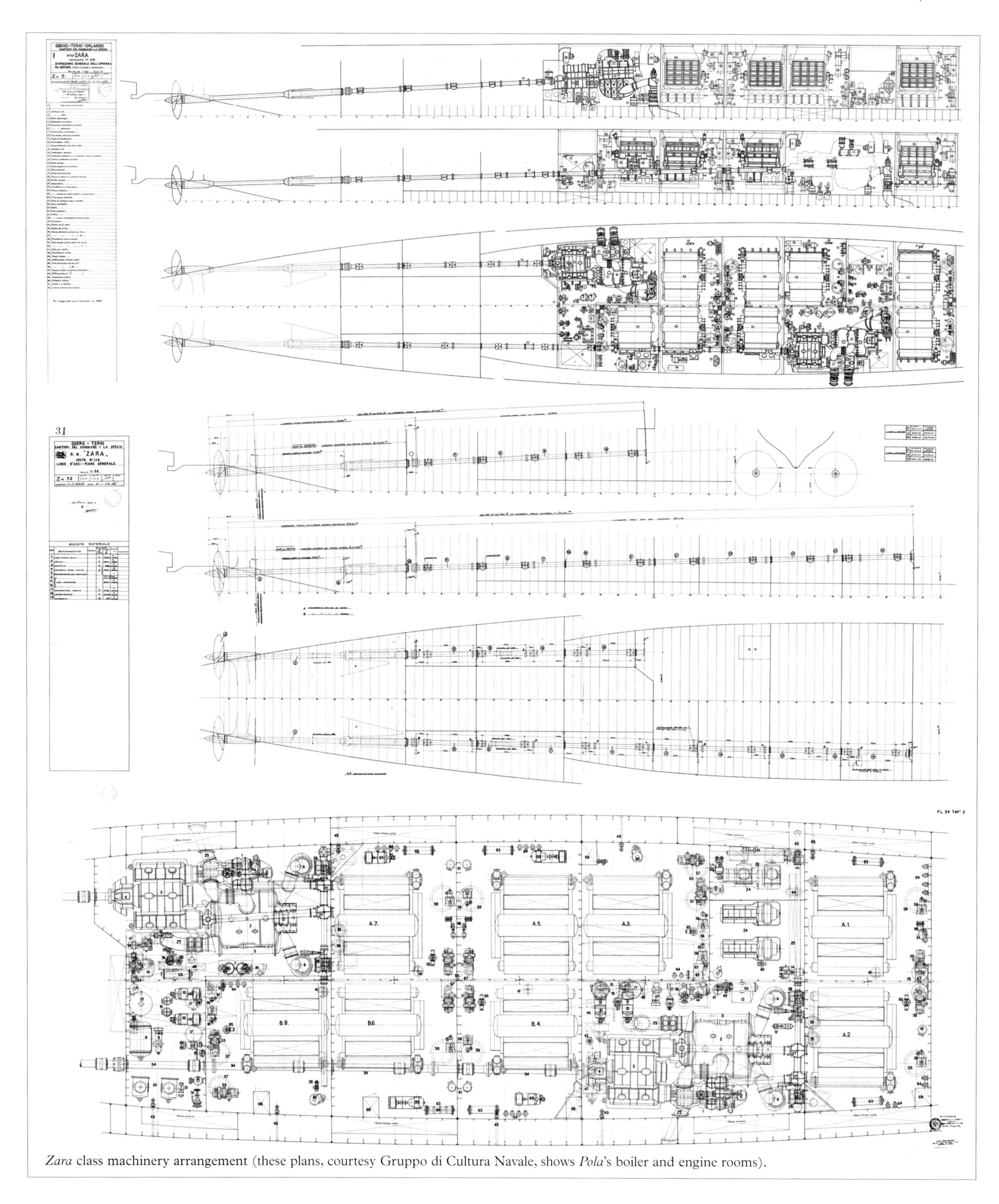

Zara class machinery arrangement (these plans, courtesy Gruppo di Cultura Navale, shows *Pola*'s boiler and engine rooms).

Starboard:
- one boiler
- the starboard engines
- three boilers
- an auxiliary machinery room

The water-tube boilers (Yarrow type on the *Fiume* and Thornycroft type on the others) provided steam at a pressure of 25kg/cm^2 and were arranged in five watertight compartments (containing, from bow to stern, two boilers side by side, one on the port side, two side by side, another two side by side, and one on the starboard side). These produced approximately 100,000hp/h of steam, which was piped to the two turbine units (Yarrow on the *Fiume* and Parsons on *Zara*, *Gorizia* and *Pola*), each comprising a high-pressure turbine (AP), a low-pressure turbine (BP) which in turn incorporated the astern turbine (AD) and a reduction gear with thrust bearing, main condenser and auxiliary condenser. The total design power (95,000hp) allowed for a maximum speed of 32 knots (30 under operating conditions). These values were lower than those of the *Trento*s, but certainly more than sufficient given the balanced general characteristics of the *Zara* class and the likely conditions in which they would have found themselves operating during the conflict.

Zara's after funnel. (Courtesy Gruppo di Cultura Navale)

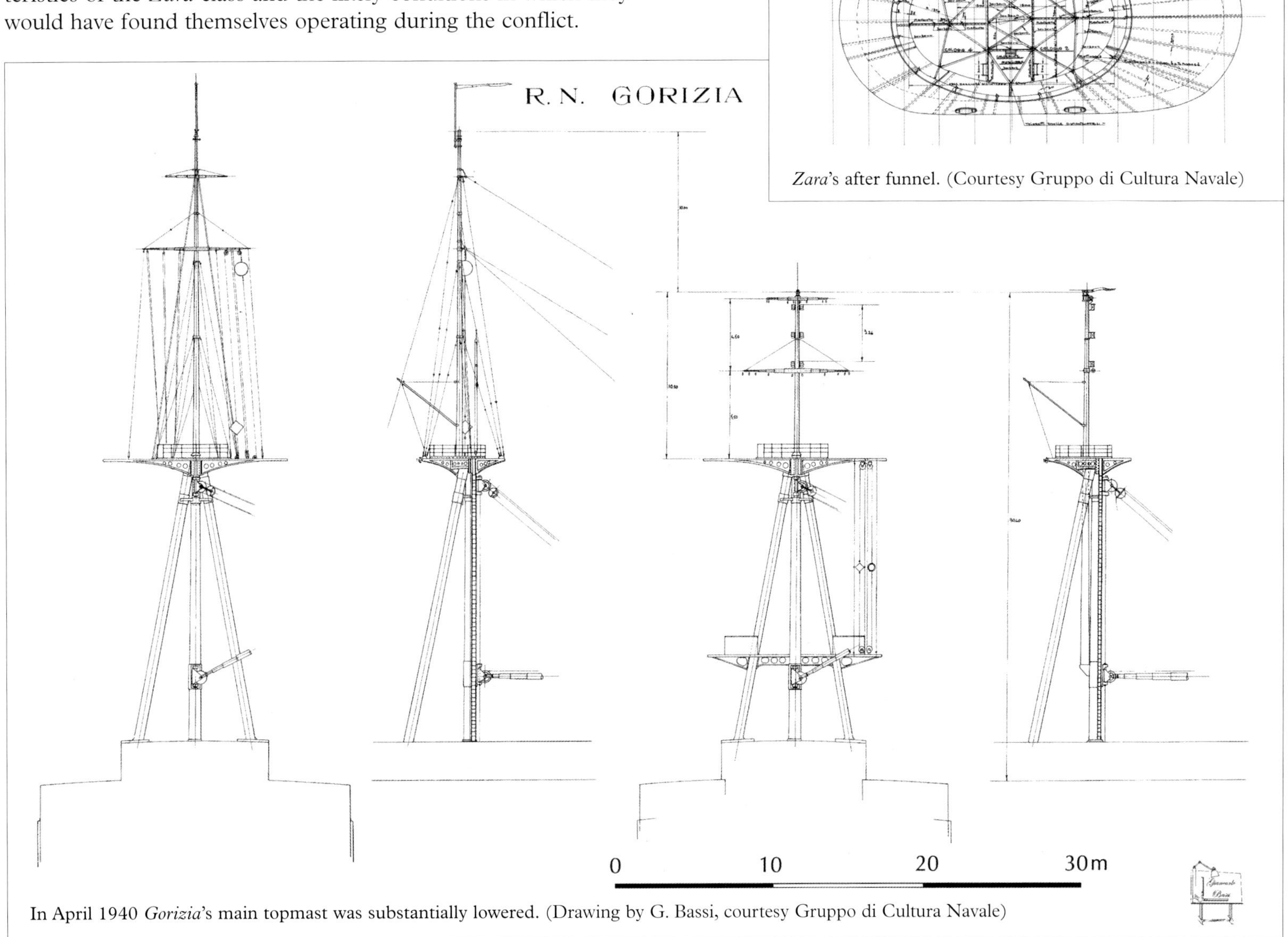

In April 1940 *Gorizia*'s main topmast was substantially lowered. (Drawing by G. Bassi, courtesy Gruppo di Cultura Navale)

Heavy cruiser *Fiume* at slow speed shortly after commissioning. (E. Bagnasco collection)

Cruiser *Fiume* (foreground) and battleship *Cesare* in the late 1930s. (E. Bagnasco collection)

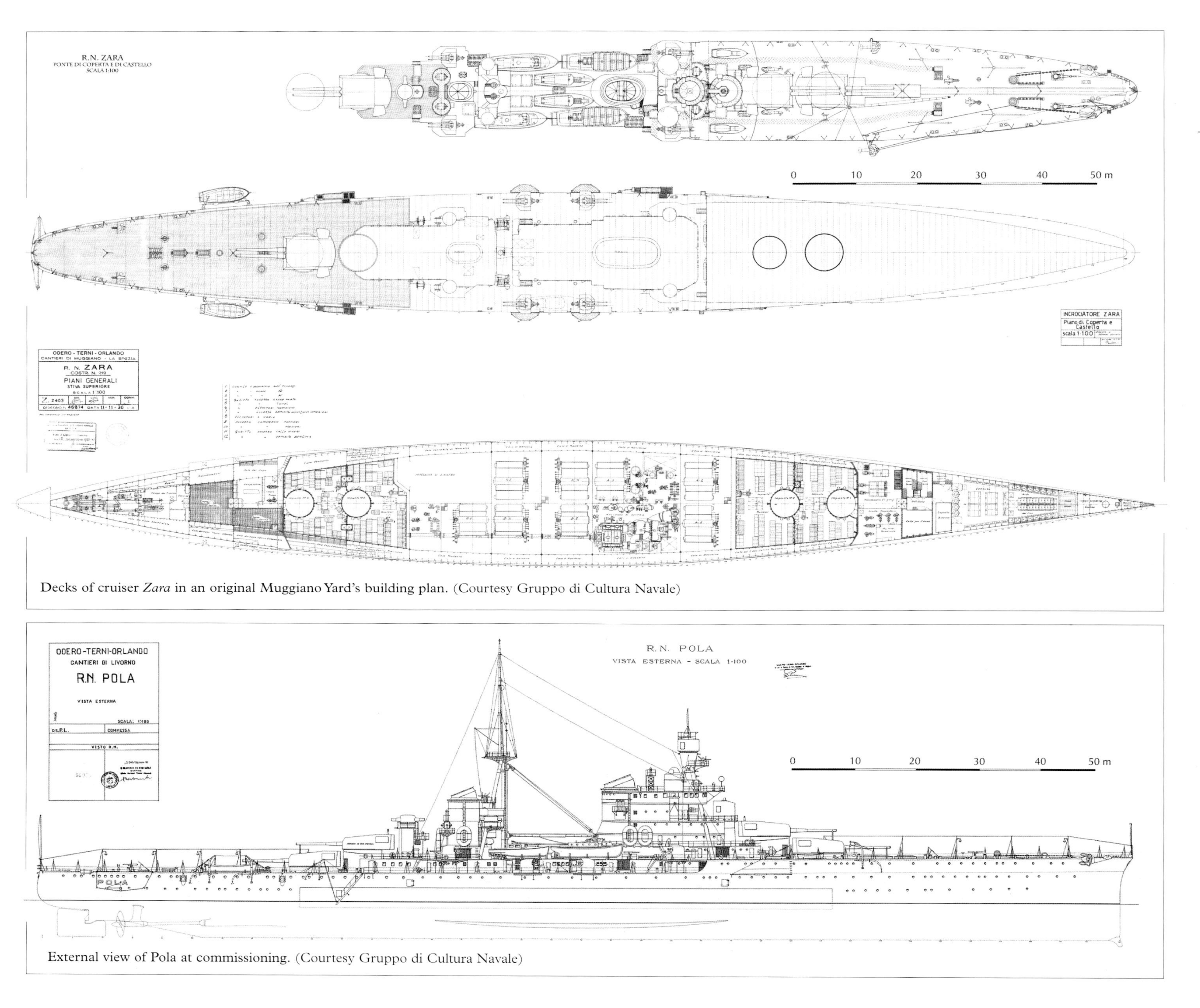

Decks of cruiser *Zara* in an original Muggiano Yard's building plan. (Courtesy Gruppo di Cultura Navale)

External view of Pola at commissioning. (Courtesy Gruppo di Cultura Navale)

The water supply for the boilers ranged from a minimum of 144.9 tons (*Fiume*) to a maximum of 183.8 tons for the *Pola*; total fuel oil bunkerage ranged from 2402 to 2528 tons and the corresponding tanks were served by two electric and two steam pumps for embarking/disembarking the fuel. Under normal conditions, preparation time for getting underway was about six hours (four and a half hours in an emergency), with the engines being warmed up periodically about every two hours.

The propellers, made of bronze, had a diameter of 4.85m and weighed 16.26 tons on *Zara* and *Fiume*; for *Pola* and *Gorizia* the measurements were 4.65m and 12.6 tons. In the special trial conditions of 'light' displacement and overload power of more than 110,000shp, the *Zara* and *Gorizia* reached 34 knots and the *Fiume* 32 knots; the *Pola* (with a displacement very similar to full load and with an overload power of 101,417shp) reached 30.85 knots, giving an indication of what would be the maximum effective speed of the *Zara*s during wartime service.

2B.6 Damage control, communication and auxiliary services

The damage control organisation was based at the main control centre, located in the order room and permanently manned, and was headed by the second-in-command with the cooperation of the officers in charge of the hull. The ship was divided into three zones and the second zone, which in turn comprised five subsections, was assigned to damage control and repair personnel.

Buoyancy was ensured by eighteen watertight compartments and, in the event of damage, in addition to closing the watertight doors, 375m³/h electric pumps were available, two of which were located in magazines 1 and 4. For fire-fighting, there was a ring main below the platform deck, the pressure of which was ensured by four turbo-pumps of 60m³/h plus another two reserve pumps of 25m³/h; in addition, about eighty portable fire extinguishers of various types were distributed through various compartments. In the event of fire, the magazines could be flooded and, at the same time, water sprinklers brought into action.

For radio communication, there was a main RT station in the bridge tower and five RDS (radio signalling) apparatuses in the aft deckhouse. For short distance visual communications, flags or groups of flags were hoisted from the signal station located on the aft side of the bridge tower, receiving orders directly from the admiral and command positions by telephone or pneumatic mail tube.

The *Zara*s were equipped with four searchlights located two on the bridge tower (one only on the *Pola* from the beginning of 1940) and two on a platform halfway up the after funnel. In this context it is worth quoting the comments made by Elio Andò in his book *Incrociatori pesanti classe 'Zara' Parte I* (see Bibliography):

> ... in this regard, it should be noted that the Regia Marina did not consider the possibility of a night battle between larger ships, so the use of searchlights for conducting the main fire was not envisaged. During the night of Matapan, for the first time, we realised how the British used searchlights with deadly precision. Although now equipped with radar, they had benefited from the experience of Jutland twenty-five years earlier, where they had the same bitter experience as we had: during the night phase of that battle, a cruiser and five destroyers of the Grand Fleet rearguard were sunk in a short time by precise German fire, directed by a skilful and then unknown use of searchlights.

Finally, on the *Zara*s electricity at 220 volts was produced by three 180Kw turbo-dynamos (Tosi on *Zara* and *Fiume* and Ansaldo on *Pola* and *Gorizia*). On board there was heating by means of steam radiators, cooling systems for the magazines, refrigerators for the food stores and two water distillation plants which ensured a daily production of 20 tons. The four *Zara*s were equipped with a laundry, a bakery and an infirmary (located at the extreme forward end of the battery deck, on the port side), with ten beds.

* * *

The *Zara*s were equipped to stream two 'C' type divergent paravanes for self-protective minesweeping which, towed from the bow by means of chains fixed to a bracket under the bulbous forefoot, each swept an area of 15 metres depth and maximum width. When not in use, the paravanes were stowed on the sides of the barbette of the forward superfiring turret, two on the starboard side and one on the port side (or vice versa, depending on the ship), the third paravane being a reserve.

The smoke apparatus comprised two naphtha smoke-generators inside each funnel, connected to the boiler uptakes. In port, when the boilers were cold, passive defence was provided by two chlorohydrin fog guns located on the stern, which could also be used while underway when necessary.

In normal service, the *Zara*s carried a motor launch, two motorboats, two diesel boats and two so-called 'unsinkable' launches on a boat deck over the amidships deckhouse. Two rafts for small outboard painting jobs and other uses were stowed on the forecastle deck. During the war, in order to reduce the fire risk and improve the firing arcs of anti-aircraft guns, most of these boats were landed; instead, life rafts of the 'Carley' type were embarked, which on the *Zara*s were usually stowed upright against the sides of the funnels or in similar positions on the superstructure.

Chapter 3

WEAPONS AND FIRE CONTROL

TRENTO CLASS AND *BOLZANO*

With the exception of the twin 203mm guns of *Trento* and *Trieste*, the secondary and anti-aircraft armament of the three ships (as well as the 203mm guns of the *Bolzano*) was the same in all respects as that of the *Zara* class. Consequently, in order to avoid repetition, this chapter will examine only those aspects that distinguished the armament of the first three Italian '10,000s' from the *Zara*s; the reader is referred to following sub-chapters for further details on the subject for the *Zara*s class.

Genoa, mid-May 1938: the forward 203mm guns and the tower of *Trieste*. (G. Parodi collection)

3A.1 203mm guns

Once the outline design of the *Trento* had been established, it was virtually compulsory to equip these ships with guns of the maximum calibre allowed by the Washington Treaty, *ie* 8 inches, or 203mm. In the political conditions of the time, there were pressures to ensure that new naval construction be equipped with weapons, fire control, ancillary systems and ammunition manufactured in Italy. For the main gun mountings this meant entrusting the production to the Ansaldo Company which – still linked by contractual and commercial interests to the French company Schneider – adopted for the two *Trento*s a twin mounting with guns of built-up construction with fixed liner and autofretted main components using a manufacturing process developed by its transalpine partner. This was not an optimal choice, but, like the single cradle arrangement of the twin barrels of each turret, it led to a considerable reduction in the overall weight of the system.

The *Trento*s were therefore equipped with eight 203mm 50-calibre Ansaldo 1924 model guns in four twin turrets, with turrets 2 and 3 superfiring over turrets 1 and 4. The firing arc was 300°, wide enough to allow the forward turrets to fire at 60° abaft the beam and those of the aft firing group at 60° forward of the beam.

A 203/50 mod. 1924 gun in the Ansaldo factory. (Courtesy Archivio Storico Ansaldo).

Left: One of the twin 203/50 turrets of *Trieste* being assembled in the Ansaldo factory, still without armour plates. (Courtesy Archivio Storico Ansaldo)

Below: Part of *Bolzano*'s crew manning the side. On the flank of 'Y' turret (known as 'Brennero' in the Italian Navy) is the ship's motto '*A magnanima impresa intenta ho l'alma*' and the Roman *fasces* symbol. (USMM, courtesy F. Fontana)

Above: The cruiser *Bolzano* fitting out in Genoa in 1933. The secondary fire director may be seen atop the superstructure. (E. Bagnasco collection)

Left: Trento's aft turrets in the mid-1930s. (E. Bagnasco collection)

The after 203mm gun turrets of *Bolzano* at the end of the 1930s. Note, on the side of 'Y' turret – known as 'Brennero' – the ship's motto '*A magnanima impresa ho intenta l'alma*'. Also visible on the left side of the tripod is one of the two directors for the torpedo launchers. (USMM via F. Fontana)

The main data relating to this gun were as follows:

- Total weapon weight: 20.8 tons
- Weight of the projectile: 118.5kg
- Weight of the firing charge: 47kg
- Initial velocity: 833m/sec.

The turret systems, thanks also to the adoption of the single cradle, were fairly light but had a single elevator that bound the operation of the two guns in each turret even more closely together. Furthermore, loading took place at a fixed angle, leading to a reduction in the rate of fire as the elevation increased. In fact, while the rate of fire was 20 seconds per round for low elevations, it could reach 40 seconds for increasingly higher elevations; and to all this must be added the notorious dispersion of salvoes, a problem that plagued Italian naval artillery for practically the entire duration of the conflict. For each turret, the revolving and elevating functions were carried out by means of electrical servo mechanisms contained within the turret trunk at the level of the platform deck;

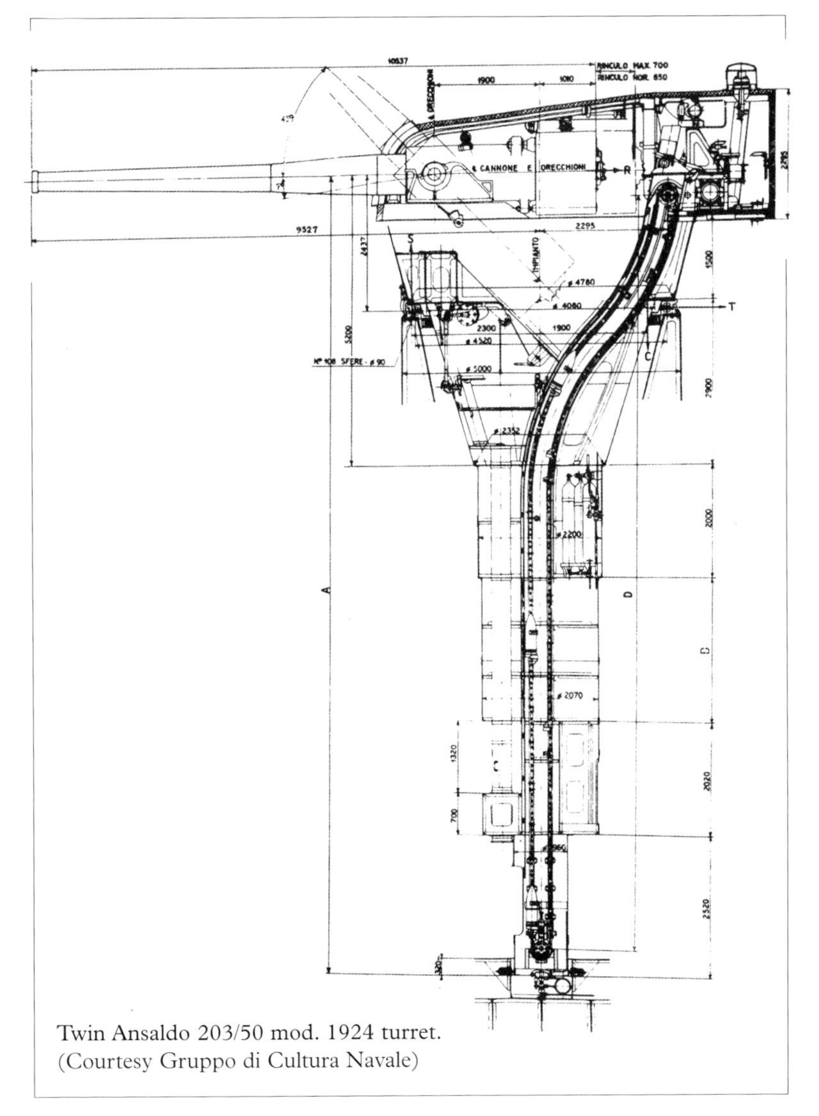

Twin Ansaldo 203/50 mod. 1924 turret. (Courtesy Gruppo di Cultura Navale)

Above: Trento's 203mm after gun turrets in a 'classic' propaganda image from the late 1930s. (M. Bresci collection)

Left: Trento's after 203mm turrets when she was open to the public during the visit to Genoa of the ships of the two Squadras, which took place in May 1938 following the 'Rivista H' held in the waters of the Gulf of Naples on 5 May. As for other Italian cruisers built before 1935, heavy and light, the main armament of the *Trento* suffered from the drawback of a single cradle installation of the twin guns. It was not just in Italy where this weight-saving measure was adopted, but it did have negative consequences on their performance. (G. Alfano collection)

there was also an electrically powered smoke extraction system.

A new version of the 203mm gun, 53 calibres long, was embarked on the *Bolzano*, a few years after the *Trento*s. This was the 203/53 model Ansaldo 1929, which was also to equip the *Zara* class as well. From the mid-1930s, the turrets were modernised and improved, with modifications and updates to overcome defects deriving from the single cradle arrangement (which, moreover, brought with it problems that were difficult to resolve) and from the complexity of the loading system which – by the standards of the time – was highly mechanised. These are the main characteristics of the gun:

- Total weight of the weapon: 19.5 tons
- Weight of projectile: 118.5kg
- Weight of the firing charge: 52kg
- Initial velocity: 900m/sec
- Maximum range: 30,000m approx.

3A.2 100/47 Guns

The three ships entered service equipped with eight twin 100/47 RM OTO mod. 1928 mountings. This 3.9in (100mm) 47-calibre weapon was a reproduction of the Skoda naval gun first embarked on the Austro-Hungarian scouts of the *Novara* class but modified to allow the barrels to be more easily re-tubed. Although still valid for anti-ship fire, by the second half of the 1930s it was an outdated weapon, particularly for anti-aircraft fire, because of its low maximum elevation and lack of an adequate fire control system); it was employed, at best, for barrage fire. The characteristics were as follows:

- Total weight with mounting: 20.02 tons
- Weight of the projectile: 13.8kg
- Weight of the launch charge: 4.7kg
- Initial velocity: 740m/sec.

The dimensions of *Trento*, *Trieste* and *Bolzano* allowed a rational arrangement of four twin installations on each side, which benefited from large firing arcs. On the first two ships, the forward mounts were placed on elevated platforms at the deckhouse level, on either side of the pentapod (further forward on the *Trieste*). The four amidships twins were mounted on the deck, two slightly aft of the forward funnel and two on either side of the aft one. Finally, the last two mounts were placed at the deckhouse level, on their own platforms aft of the second funnel. Initially, only the midships deck mounts were embarked on the *Bolzano*, which then proceeded to install two mounts on either side of the bridge

Twin Ansaldo 203/53 mod. 1929 turret. (Courtesy Gruppo di Cultura Navale)

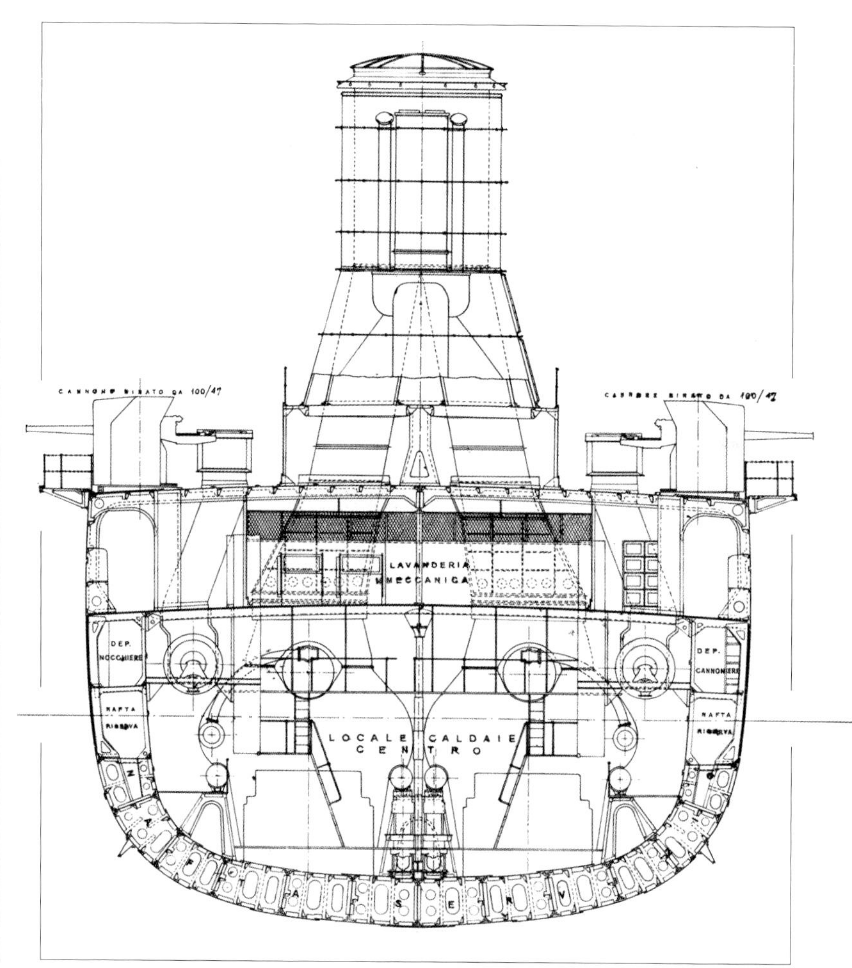

Cruiser *Trieste*: section at bow frame 21 showing two 100/47 guns on main deck. (Stabilimento Tecnico Triestino)

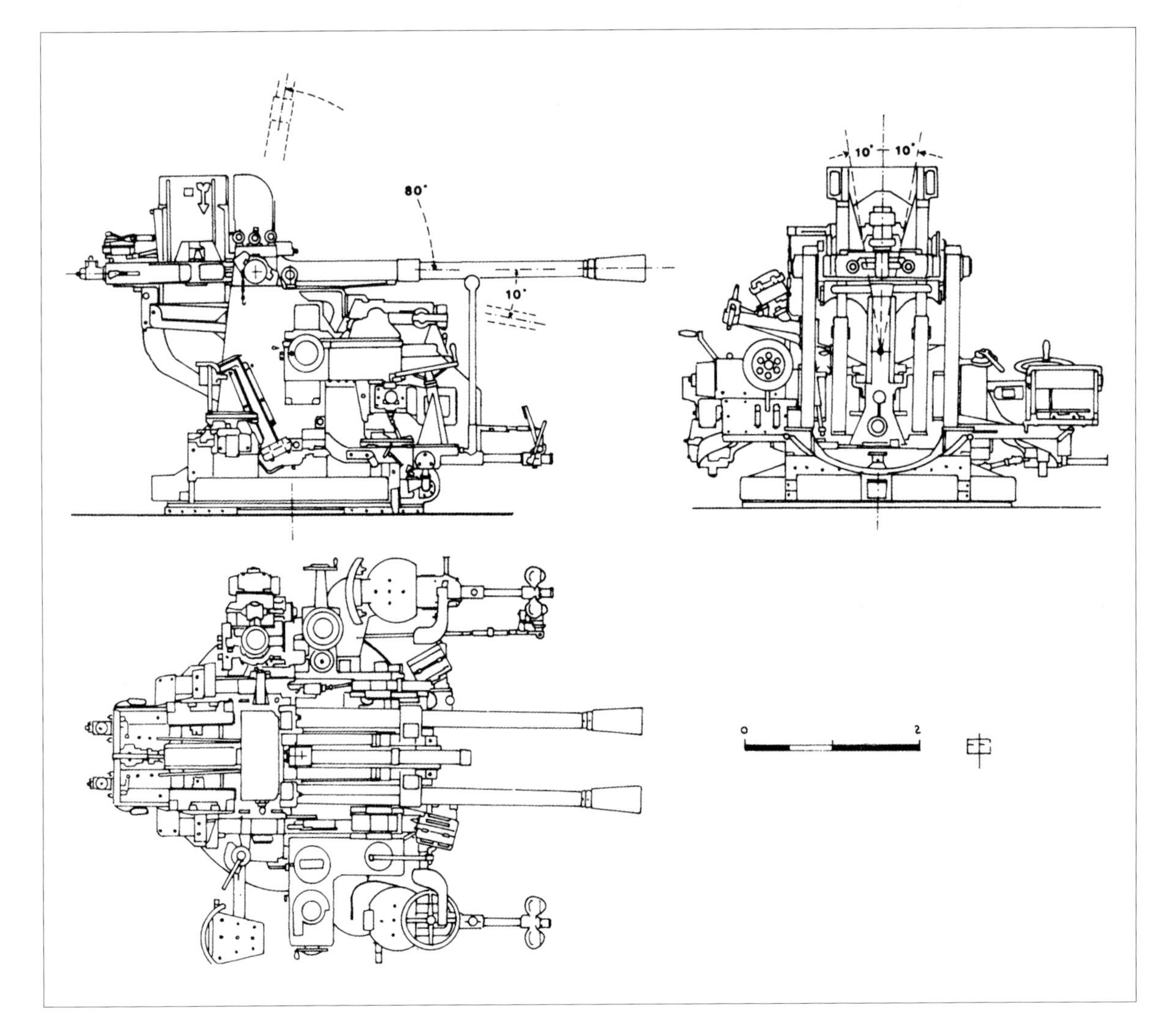

Air-cooled twin Breda 37/54 machine gun. (drawing by E. Baganasco)

tower at the aft end of the forecastle and another two port and starboard of the aft funnel. In 1937 the two aftermost mountings were removed from all ships and replaced with four mountings (two on each side) for Breda 37/54 machine guns.

Like many other Italian ships of the time, *Trento*, *Trieste* and *Bolzano* joined the fleet equipped with four Vickers-Terni 40/39 machine guns model 1916, which were then removed in the second half of the 1930s due to their obsolescence and low rate of fire.

The *Trieste* at Messina in early March 1941. (E. Bagnasco collection)

3A.3 Breda model 1932 37/54 machine guns

In 1937, the two aftermost 100/47 mounts were removed from the elevated platform on the deckhouse and each replaced by two twin 37/54 Breda machine guns. Designed around 1930, the 37mm 54-calibre gun was a gas-operated weapon with a recoiling bolt, fed by slab magazines and with a nominal rate of fire of about 200 rounds per minute which, however, was reduced to 140 due to the normal delays resulting from the manual loading system adopted. The maximum range was 6800m, with an effective range of 4800m; the cartridge had a total length of 38.4cm, with a 21cm long brass case and a bursting projectile with self-destruct.

The weight of each twin system was initially 5000kg, later reduced to 4300kg with the elimination of coolant pumps. On the whole, even the Breda 37/54 machine gun was of rather limited effectiveness due to a number of factors, from the complexity of the automation to its consequent and frequent failures.

3A.4 Machine guns of smaller calibres

The two *Trento*s initially embarked four twin 12.7mm calibre

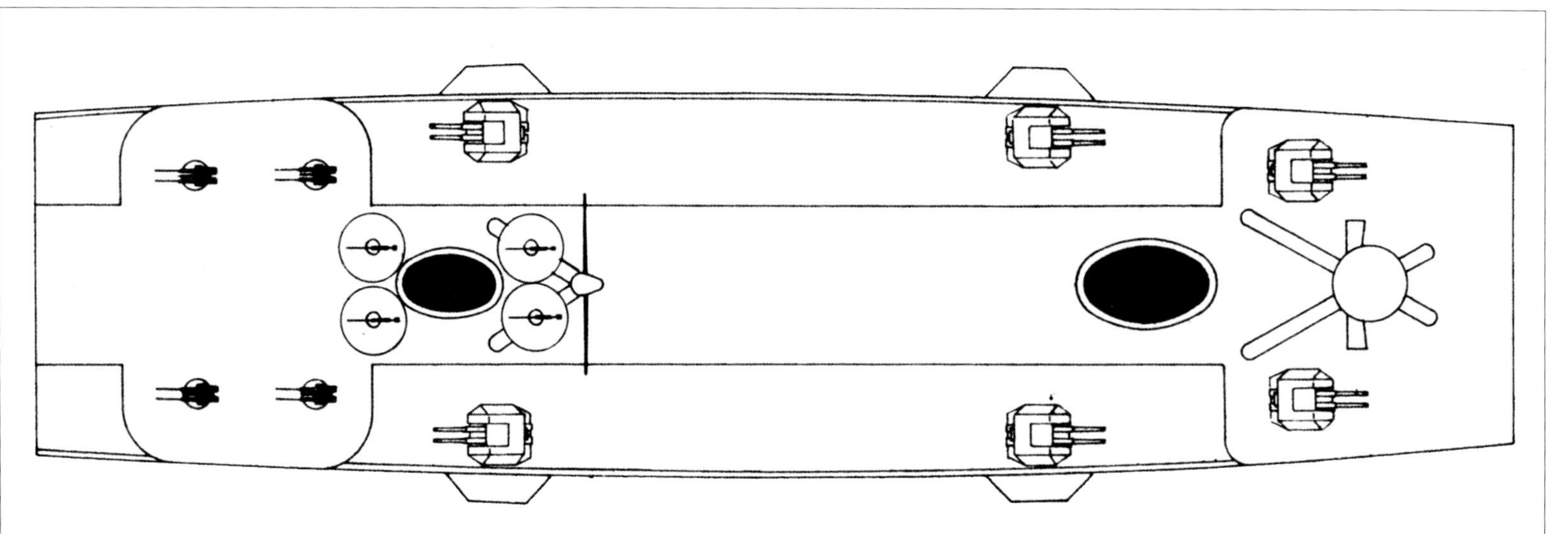

Bolzano – twelve 100/47 (6x2), eight 37/54 (4x2), four 20/65 (4 x 1)

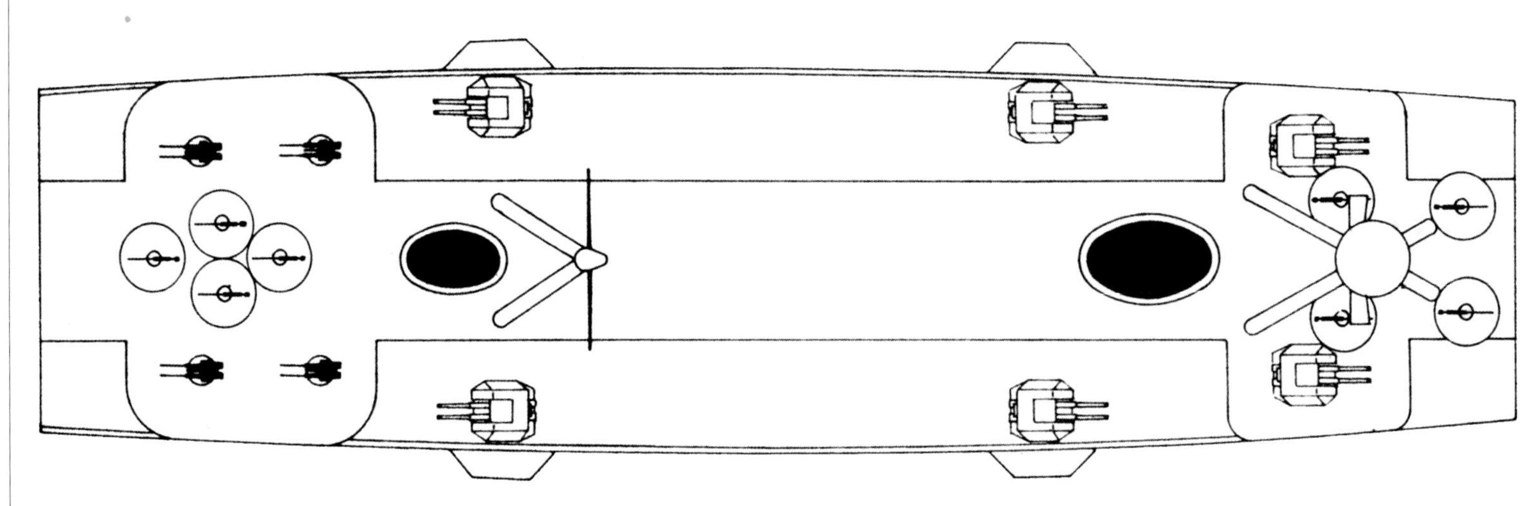

Trieste – twelve 100/47 (6x2), eight 37/54 (4x2), eight 20/65 (8 x 1)

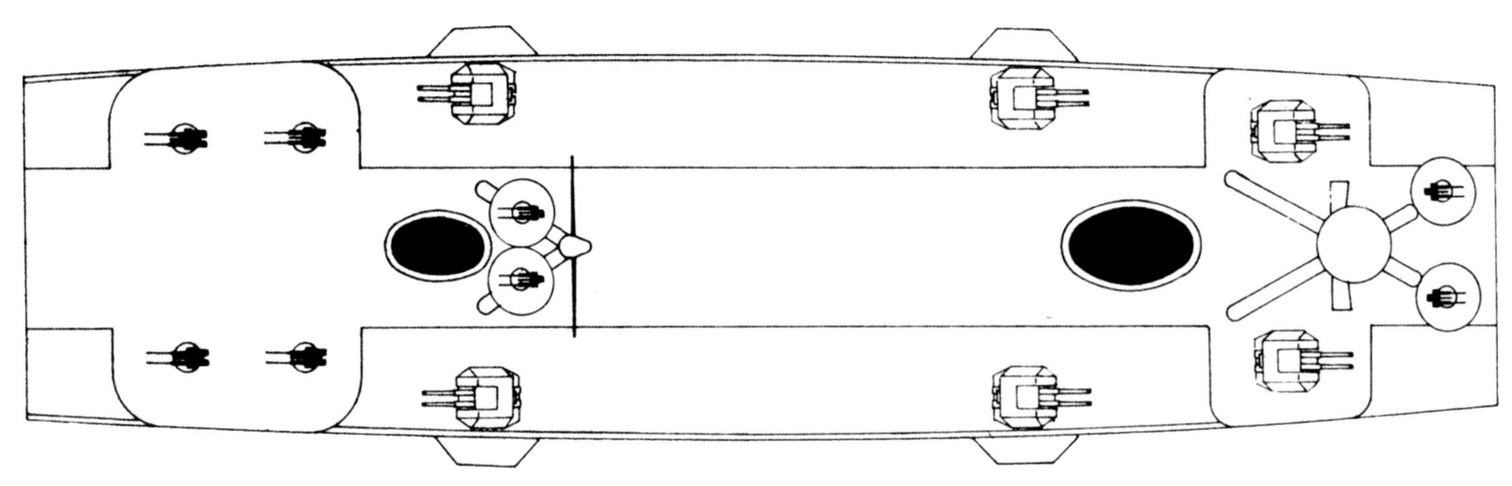

Trento – twelve 100/47 (6x2), eight 37/54 (4x2), eight 13.2mm (4 x 2)

Diagrams of *Trento*, *Trieste* and *Bolzano* showing AA weapons positions in 1942–1943.
(Drawing by F. Gay in *Incrociatori pesanti classe Trento* – see bibliography)

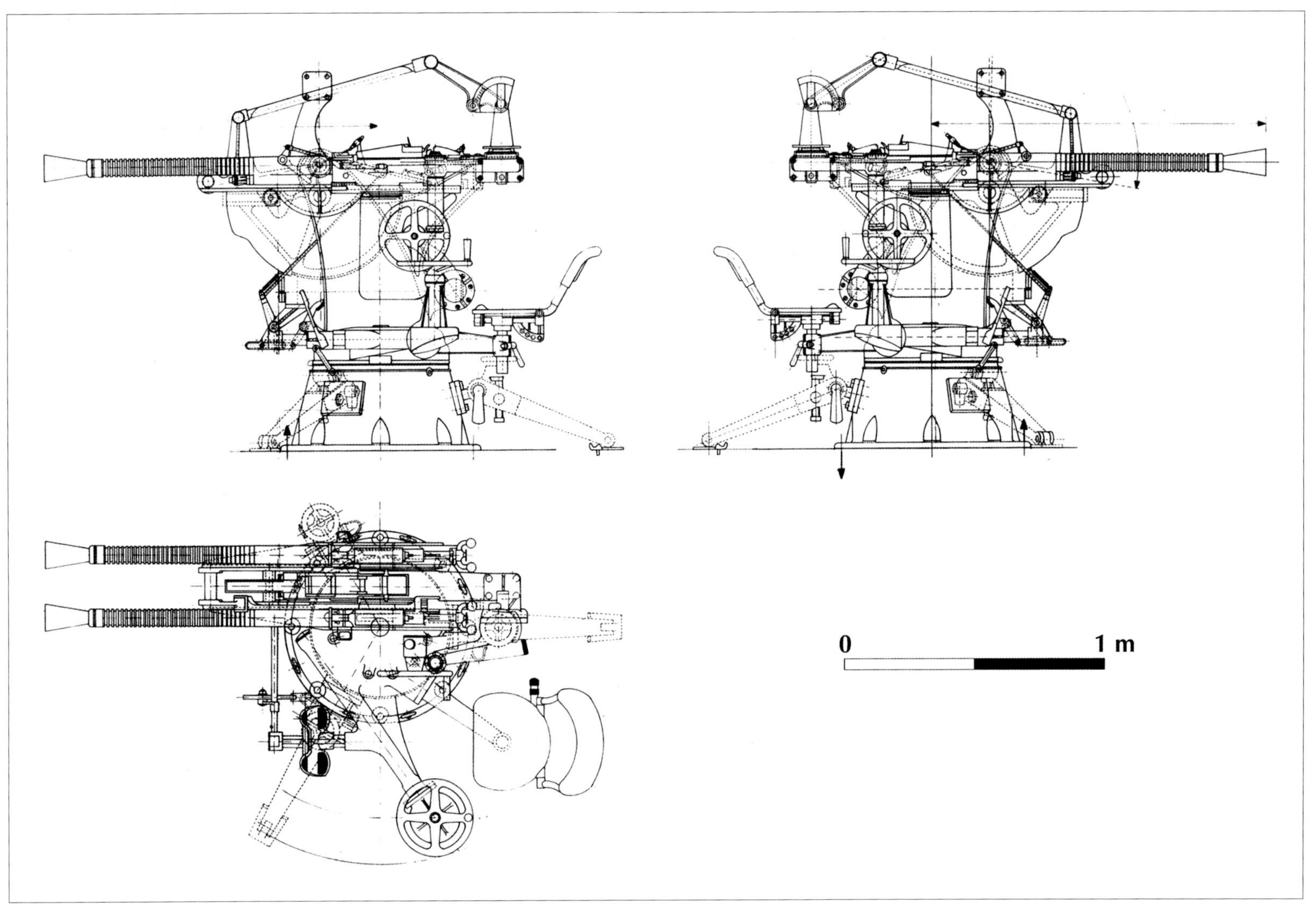

Three-view drawing of a twin Breda 13.2mm machine gun. (Courtesy Gruppo di Cultura Navale)

MGs on special platforms on either side of the pentapod and tripod, while the *Bolzano* had – on the forecastle and towards the stern – four twin 13.2mm calibre machine guns. Similarly, once the four Vickers-Terni 40/39 calibre machine guns had been disembarked, on the *Trento* and *Bolzano* they were replaced with four twin 13.2mm calibre MGs. In 1942, the *Trieste* landed all of the 13.2mm machine guns and replaced them with four single 20/65 guns, while the four twin 13.2mm guns of the *Bolzano* were eliminated, and at the same time four single 20/65 guns were installed on platforms in the upper part of the tripod and on the top of the deckhouse on either side of the funnel. In the last period of activity, the minor anti-aircraft armament of the three ships – further modified – for clarity and simplicity, is shown in the diagrams on page 78.

3A.5 Torpedo tubes

Unique among the Italian '10,000s', *Trento*, *Trieste* and *Bolzano* were equipped with eight 533mm torpedo tubes in four fixed twin installations arranged athwartships and sliding on rails; in the launch position, the tubes were slid outwards, through special hatches in the hull sides. The total number of torpedoes was sixteen: eight in the tubes and eight in reserve.

Loading a 533mm torpedo, without the warhead, on cruiser *Trieste*; note, on the right, the circular openings allowing the exit of two of the eight torpedo tubes with which the ship was equipped. (E. Bagnasco collection)

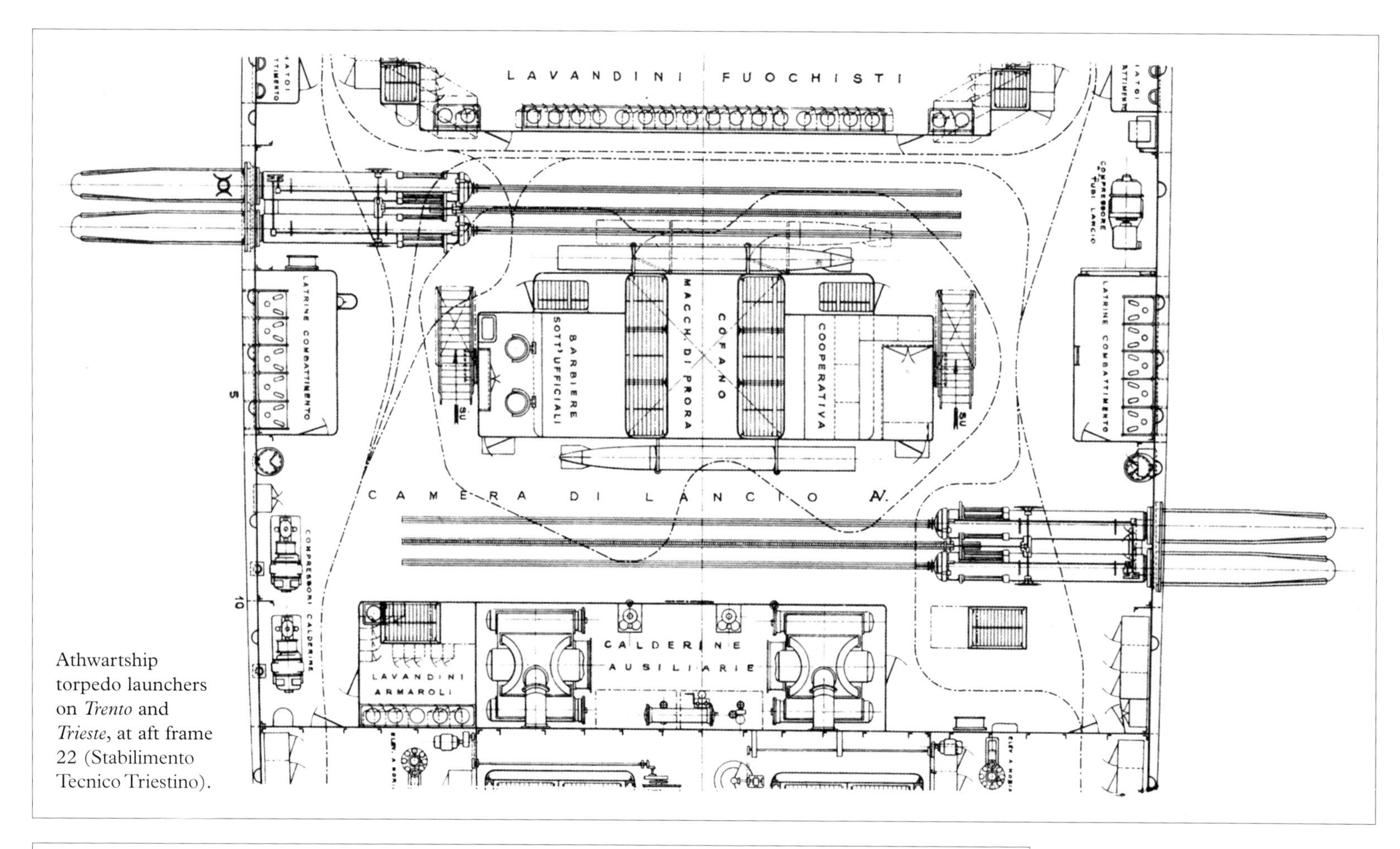

Athwartship torpedo launchers on *Trento* and *Trieste*, at aft frame 22 (Stabilimento Tecnico Triestino).

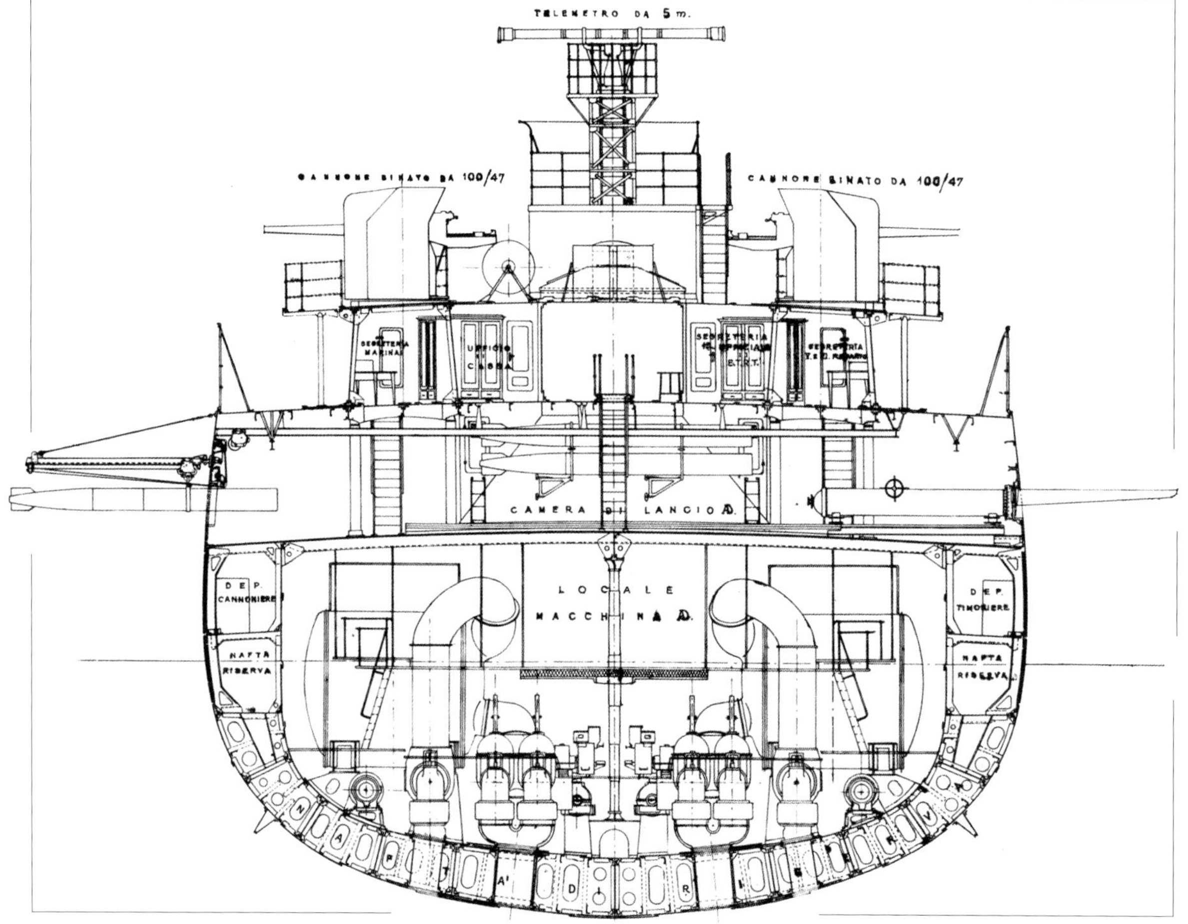

The torpedo tubes of *Trento* and *Trieste* at aft frame 22, with the stern torpedo room (right), torpedo magazine (centre) showing torpedoes without their warheads (which were stored in a protected magazine). Also visible is the loading derrick for embarking torpedoes, which were moved using an overhead rail. (Stabilimento Tecnico Triestino)

Equipping such large ships with torpedo launchers proved pointless, since the torpedo was not a defensive weapon and it was highly unlikely that a heavy cruiser would find itself engaged in close-range combat against destroyers or similar ships.

The *Trento*s and the *Bolzano* carried either W/270/533/7.2 torpedoes manufactured by Whitehead (Fiume) or SI/270/533/7.2 manufactured by Silurificio Italiano of Baia (Naples); the three numbers indicated, respectively, the weight in kilograms of the warhead, the calibre in millimetres and the length in metres of the weapons. Both torpedoes reached a speed of 48 knots with a range of approximately 4000m; at lower speeds, the range was obviously greater.

3A.6 Ammunition and magazines

Four magazines were located on the orlop underneath the platform deck and in the hold, with the shells stored in the upper section and the propellant charges stored in the lower section; the ammunition for the 100mm mountings and machine guns was located between the upper and lower portions of magazine, while the torpedo warheads were located in a magazine below the main firing station. The magazines contained a total of 1300 203mm shells with 2900 charges and 6150 100mm shells and casings.

The guns of the twin 203mm turrets were supplied by elevators inside the gunhouses, while the 100mm pieces received their ammunition by means of five elevators which arrived on the battery deck: from here, by means of special rail guides, the rounds were pushed towards eight other elevators which led to the main deck or shelter deck, near the various mountings.

All the magazines were equipped with sprinkler and flooding systems; these functions were driven by gravity – through the opening of special Kingston valves – for the section below the waterline or via pipework from the ring main of the fire-fighting system for the upper part. The Kingston valves were operated from the battery deck and allowed each magazine to be flooded in about 20 minutes; with sprinklers alone the time rose to 60 minutes while the simultaneous use of the two systems took only 15 minutes.

3A.7 Fire control

There were two Fire Direction Stations (SDT) for the main armament, equipped with 5-metre coincidence rangefinders: that of the 1st DT (Fire Director – at the top of the pentapod of the *Trento*s and the tetrapod of the *Bolzano*), and that of the 2nd DT, located on the top of the structure of the armoured command tower. Both SDTs were identical in shape, size and equipment, and were rotatable by hand. In 1940 the Galileo company converted the equipment from coincidence to steroscopic rangefinders.

Two secondary armament SDTs were located high up on the forward superstructure and two in the centre of the mainmast tripod; the two secondary SDTs forward were the main ones for the direction of anti-torpedo and anti-aircraft fire, while those aft were intended for directing the torpedo tubes. However, the presence of two SDTs for the direction of fire of the same 100mm battery did not prove to be functional as it created a complex situation in the case of combat against ships and aircraft at the same time, requiring shifts and variations in the passage of data with a consequent, inevitable reduction in the rate of fire. Consequently, in 1937, the two secondary aft SDTs were landed as it was understood that anti-aircraft fire would become the main function of medium calibre pieces. All machine guns, being intended for direct fire, received their data from the secondary SDTs forward.

The three cruisers were lost (*Trento* and *Trieste*) or were otherwise put out of action (*Bolzano*) before domestically produced radar sets were available in sufficient quantity to be added to these units. For the *Trieste*, however, provision had been made shortly before her loss for the installation of a radar, by installing a special half-height platform on the forward side of the pentapod.

ZARA CLASS

In terms of calibres and number of embarked weapons, the main and secondary armament of the *Zara*s followed that of the earlier *Trento*s, with four twin 203mm turrets and eight twin 100/47 mounts; but unlike the *Trento*s, they were not equipped with torpedo tubes.

The *Trento*s had been armed with the first 203mm guns produced in Italy, *ie* the 50-calibre model A 1924 made by Ansaldo and manufactured using the Schneider process. These were constructed with a single tube, full length jacket and breech ring and had a loose liner which could be changed on board, a single cradle in a twin turret, with a single elevator for the ammunition and restricted to loading at a specific predetermined angle; the most important defects were the low rate of fire and the considerable dispersion of the salvoes. The 203mm guns of the *Zara*s (the Ansaldo 1929 model with a length of 53 calibres) represented considerable improvement, including, while retaining the twin-barrel single-cradle arrangement, separate ammunition elevators for each gun and the possibility of loading at all angles. In addition, lowering the muzzle velocity from 930m/sec to 900m/sec resulted in less dispersion of the rounds.

3B.1 203/53 Ansaldo 1929 guns

The guns were mounted in twin turrets on the centreline, with turrets 2 and 3 superfiring over turrets 1 and 4, the two forward mountings on the forecastle deck and the after pair on the quarterdeck level. The firing arcs, totalling 300° for each turret (see the drawing on page 59), allowed ample opportunity for all turrets to engage targets both in pursuit and in retreat. During the 1930s, these guns were modernised and improved, with modifications and upgrades to overcome defects deriving from the single cradle arrangement, which brought with it problems that were difficult to solve, and from the complexity of the loading system which - for the time - was highly mechanised.

3B.2 100/47 RM OTO 1931 guns

At the time of their entry into service, the *Zara*s embarked eight twin mountings of this type for use in anti-ship and anti-aircraft roles. This 47-calibre 100mm (3.9in) piece was based on the design of the excellent Austrian naval gun of the same calibre,

Messina, spring 1942: the 203/53 after turrets of *Gorizia*; the inner lining of the gun barrels are being replaced. (E. Bagnasco collection)

with a barrel that could be easily re-tubed and automatically adjustable to be loaded at any elevation. As pointed out earlier in section 3A.2, by the second half of the 1930s it was an outdated weapon, particularly for anti-aircraft fire, although it remained effective for anti-ship fire.

The mountings were arranged four per side: one either side of the bridge tower on the forecastle deck, four (two per side) on the weather deck between the two funnels, and two on platforms on either side of the aft funnel. The firing arcs were approximately 87° forward and aft of the beam for each mounting.

3B.3 Vickers-Terni 40/39 machine guns

When first in service, the four *Zara*s were equipped with four single 40mm (2pdr) machine guns, a water-cooled recoilless barrel weapon which fired bursting projectiles, timed, with an effective range of only 4475m (with self-destruction of the projectile), and 7160m (maximum theoretical range). The ammunition feed system initially adopted did not allow a firing rate higher than 50 rounds per minute, at the same time causing frequent jamming. It was not until around 1930 that various improvements overcame the main defects of the weapon, thus reaching, in practice, the firing rate of 200 rounds per minute theoretically envisaged when first designed.

The *Zara* carried two mountings on the forecastle forward of turret 1 and two on the quarterdeck at the extreme stern; on the *Fiume* the positions of these guns were similar except that the two forward were located either side of the bridge tower. On *Gorizia* and *Pola*, all four guns were grouped together, two on either side of the aft funnel and two aft of it.

The Vickers-Terni 40/39 guns, by then obsolete and of little use, were landed in 1938–1939 or, at the latest, just before the outbreak of war.

3B.4 Breda 13.2mm machine guns

Towards the end of the 1920s Breda began production of its own 13.2mm machine gun, derived from a similar French gun designed by Hotchkiss; it was an automatic machine gun with a gas intake from the (fixed) barrel, with a piston-controlled lock; it was air-cooled, with finned sleeves placed along the entire length of the barrel. The cartridges, with non-explosive type projectiles, were 136.5mm long and were contained in magazines of 30 rounds each, weighing (loaded) 5.56kg. The weapon alone weighed 47.5kg, was 75.7 calibres long and had a maximum range of approximately 6000m.

The whole mounting weighed 695kg, of which 600kg was for the complete chassis and 95kg for the two guns. The Breda 13.2mm machine gun was, in the final analysis, a simple, reliable weapon with a good firing rate (over 400 rounds per minute), but during the course of the war its limitations became evident, due largely to the low weight of the projectile, which was now ineffective against the most modern aircraft.

Four twin mountings were mounted in the same locations on all four ships: two on a platform towards the top of the bridge tower (under the main SDT) and two on platforms located halfway up the tripod mainmasts

In the course of the work carried out on *Gorizia* at La Spezia in the summer of 1943, it was planned to remove the four twin 13.2mm guns and to instal fourteen 20/65 machine-guns (six twins and two single mounts) on the decks and superstructures, to improve the ships' close-in anti-aircraft defence.

3B.5 Breda 37/54 machine guns model 1932

In 1937, the two 100/47 guns in the elevated position on the after deckhouse were removed: each of them was replaced by two twin 37/54 Breda machine guns.

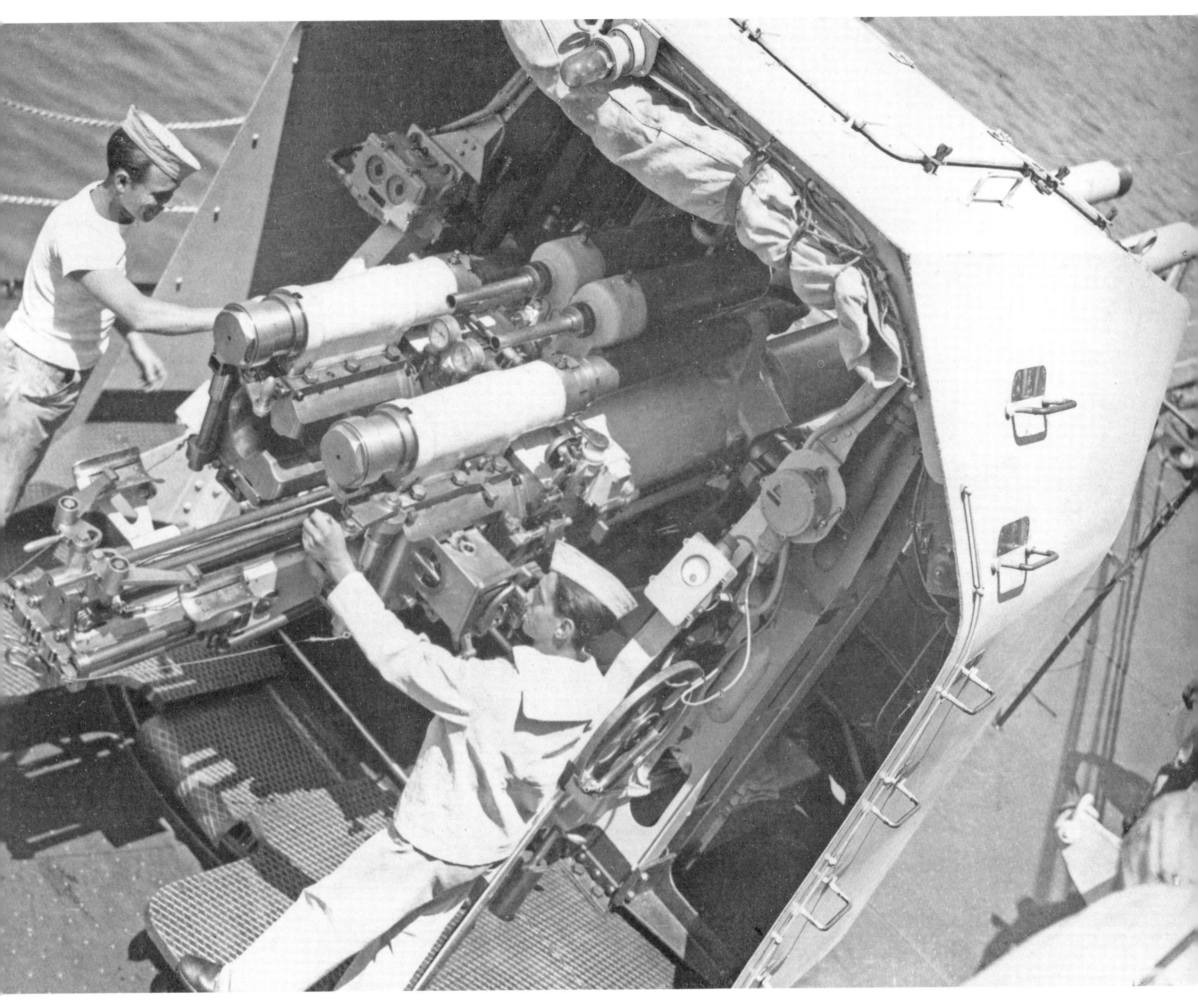

A twin 100/47 gun mod RM OTO 1931 aboard a *Zara* class cruiser.

Designed around 1930, the 37mm 54-calibre gun was a gas-operated weapon with a recoil-operated bolt, fed by slab magazines and with a nominal rate of fire of about 200 rounds per minute (in practice, reduced to 140 due to the customary delays imposed by the loading system). The maximum range was 6800m, with an effective range of 4800m; the cartridge was 38.4cm in total length, with a 21-gauge brass cartridge case and a bursting projectile with self-destruct feature.

The total weight of the twin mounting was almost 5000kg, but by eliminating the coolant pumps it was later reduced to about 4300kg, of which 554kg related to the guns and 3746kg to the gun carriage (platform type with a width of 1.2m). The recoil effort was 19 tonnes. As mentioned earlier, the Breda 37/54 machine guns were of fairly limited effectiveness mainly due to mechanical complexity and the consequent and frequent breakdowns.

3B.6 120/15 illuminating howitzers

Until just before the outbreak of war, the *Zara*s carried two 120/15 star-shell howitzers in gun tubs on either side, and just aft, of the forward superfiring 203mm turret. In 1942 the *Gorizia* was allocated two additional twin Breda 37/54 machine gun mountings for these positions

3B.7 Ammunition and ammunition magazines

There were four magazines, one for each of the main armament turrets, divided between two lowest deck levels. The 100mm and machine gun ammunition was divided between the two levels of each magazine.

The normal establishment for the 203mm guns was 100 rounds per barrel, including 440 armour-piercing and 360 explosive rounds with various types of fuses; for the secondary calibre, over 2300 anti-ship shells and 1200 anti-aircraft rounds were carried, again with various types of fuses; for the 37/54 machine guns, the supply totalled 6000 cartridges.

An endless-chain elevator moved the 203mm shells up to the transfer chamber, for a firing rate of four rounds per minute). The shell and propellant charges were then brought in line with the barrel via a secondary elevator in a position ready for ramming into the gun breech. There were no special arrangements for supply to the machine guns: the magazines were placed, as necessary, in ready-use reserves on the deck near the mountings, but the machine guns on platforms high in the superstructure were served by special elevators placed inside the uprights of the tetrapod and tripod.

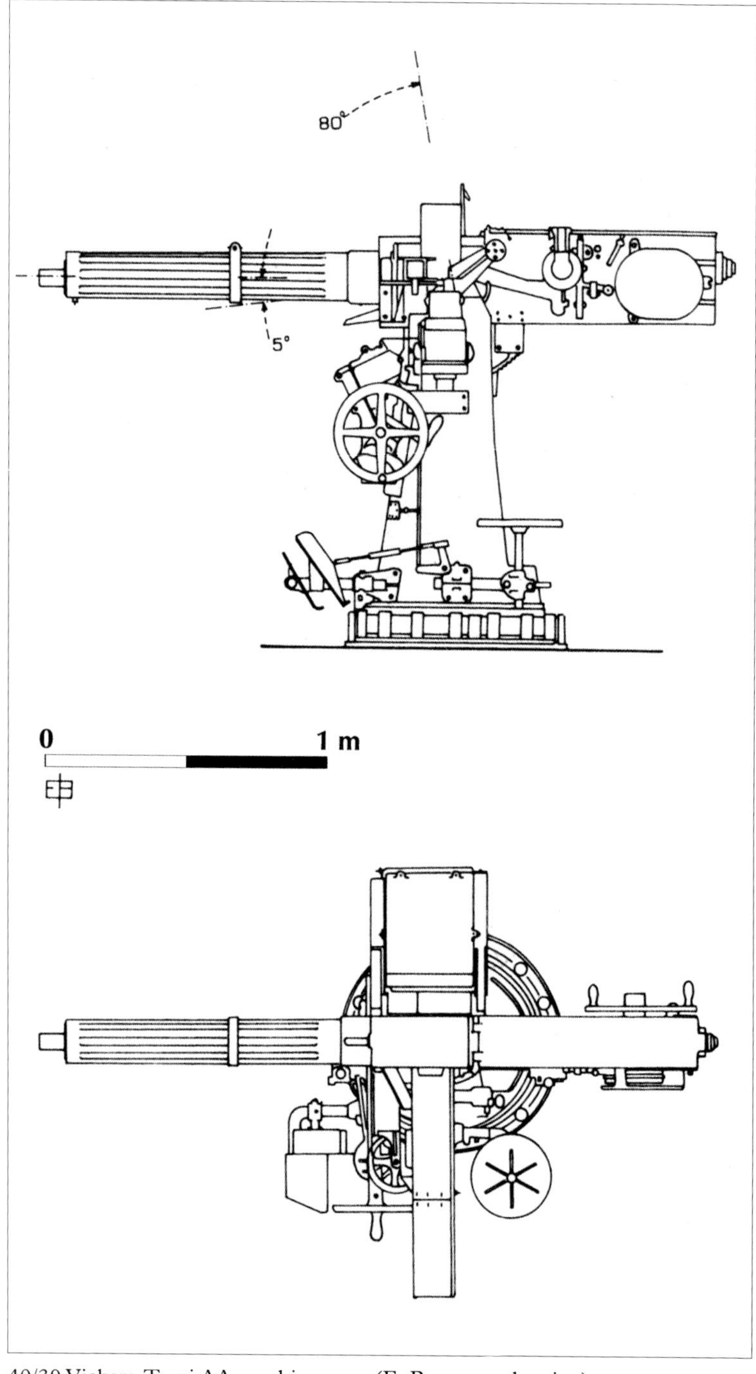

40/39 Vickers-Terni AA machine gun. (E. Bagnasco drawing)

3B.8 Fire control

The main SDT was located at the top of the tetrapod at a height of 18.3m on the bridge tower, while the secondary SDT was located lower down, on the top of the armoured command tower. Each was equipped with a San Giorgio-made APG (General Aiming Device), inclinometer and stereoscopic rangefinder with a 5-metre base. The data collected by the SDTs was conveyed to the firing station located inside the base of the tower, with the option of firing by groups of turrets or with all four turrets simultaneously.

The firing of the 100/47 mounts was directed by two secondary stations, one on each side of the bridge tower, each equipped with an APG for anti-aircraft fire and served by a rangefinder with a 3-metre base. For night firing, there were two gunnery pedestal sights positioned on either side of the bridge which simultaneously sent the elevation and bearing data to the searchlights on their own side.

Finally, anti-aircraft fire could also be directed by special pedestal sights equipped with graphic calculators, assisted by lookouts equipped with binoculars that, from the admiral's bridge, covered all sectors, allowing 360° surveillance.

3B.9 Radar

No cruiser of the *Trento* class received radars, but the *Trieste* was earmarked to receive an EC.3/ter 'Gufo' apparatus and the necessary support structure had been fitted by the end of March 1943. The subsequent loss of the cruiser on 10 April 1943 at La Maddalena evidently put an end to the whole scheme. As for the *Bolzano*, in the summer of 1943 she was lying in a state of near-abandonment at La Spezia, with all possible equipment and instruments removed for their better preservation or reuse; nevertheless, although the reconstruction of this ship was uncertain and problematic, a plan had been approved for the embarkation of a radar of the 'Gufo' type.

Not even the *Gorizia*, the last survivor of the *Zara* class, received radar equipment. During the repair at La Spezia after the bombing of 10 April 1943 at La Maddalena it was planned to embark an EC.3/ter 'Gufo' apparatus, but the project had only reached the approval stage at the time. It is difficult to foresee whether radar might have been fitted when the cruiser returned to service, as a few more months of work were still needed at the time of the Armistice on 8 September 1943.

* * *

By way of conclusion to the section on armament, below is shown a comparison between the performance of the guns arming the

Fiume's tower; in foreground a twin Breda 37/54 machine gun.

ARMOUR PENETRATION

KC type armour thickness [OD type, 'Omogeneo Duro' = Homogeneous Hard] penetrable by 203/50 and (203/53) guns with AP projectile as a function of distances and angles of impact

(Guidelines and rules for the employment of the Squadra Navale. Use of naval artillery, September 1942)

	Target bearing ('Beta') and vertical armour thickness (mm)					Horizontal armour thickness (mm)
Distance (m)	90°	80°	70°	60°	50°	
22,000	* (96)	* (94)	* (88)	* (79)	* (*)	(49)
20,000	100 (109)	* (107)	* (100)	* (89)	* (74)	(39)
18,000	117 (127)	115 (123)	107 (116)	* (100)	* (87)	(31)
16,000	137 (150)	135 (146)	127 (137)	112 (121)	* (102)	(25)

* *Does not pierce the minimum thickness of KC armour on enemy ships (vertical armour only).*

FIRING DISTANCES

Calibre	Maximum firing distance with good visibility (m)	Firing start distance in normal visibility conditions (m)	Average distance at which the action should take place (m)
203/50 – 203/53	22,000	20,000	17,000 – 20,000
100/47	14,000	12,000	9000 – 11,000

Trentos and *Zaras* as set out in official guidance drawn up by the Technical Organisations of the Regia Marina between 1940 and 1941.

Combat distances

The above-mentioned directives also indicated the most effective distances for good naval firing according to observation, range dispersion and other factors for almost all calibres in service (from the 381/50 of the *Littorios* to the 100/47 mounts in cruisers)

Summary collection of the main data from the firing exercises of the training years 1939–1940 and 1940–1941 by Stato Maggiore della Regia Marina, 25 November 1941 [excerpt]

At the end of the training year 1939 –1940, the General Staff of the Regia Marina's Artillery and Ammunition Inspectorate prepared the collection of statistical data concerning the firing exercises carried out independently by the 1st and 2nd Naval Squadrons, with the intention of developing and perfecting the collation of all firing data and results as far as possible. This data was indispensable for evaluating the progress achieved in the use of artillery with regard to material, personnel and, in particular, the working and capability of the firing directors. The data collection was intended to conclude with a final comparative report covering three successive training years. This was not compiled, as the data for the previous two years had not been collected, and the final report was replaced by a summary of the main data relating to the various calibres in service, from 381/50 to 90/50. Similar statistical work was carried out for the training year 1940–1941. Here too, the final report, which should have compared the exercises of a three-year period (at least 1938–1939 was missing), was not produced. The data collected did, however, make it possible to carry out a comparative examination of the results of the two-year period. The table above is taken from the two collections, which summarises the most immediately comprehensible and historically interesting statistical data regarding the artillery of Italian heavy cruisers. On the other hand, no similar data collection or final report of the subsequent training years has been found.

The problem of dispersion of fire on the eve of the war in a document of the Naval General Staff

The Ministerial Controlled Firing Exercises (ESCM) were held in the spring of 1940, for the third consecutive year, overseen by a single committee of the Ministry of the Navy, and governed by rules and procedures that differed from the exercises normally carried out by the two squadrons during their training years and

	Years 1939–1940						**Years 1940–1941**					
guns	203/50 Ansaldo			203/53 Ansaldo			203/50 Ansaldo			203/53 Ansaldo		
powder charge	I	III	III n	*I*	*III*	*III n*	I	III	III n	*I*	*III*	*III n*
distance (m)	19,900	7500	3300	*19,900*	*16,700*	-	21,300	8800	3500	*20,000*	*8200*	*4200*
useful salvoes[1] (%)	52	40	62.5	*21.2*	*43.6*	*45*	14.7	33.5	70	*27.5*	*40*	*45*
hits on target (%)	12	9.6	2	*1.3*	*14.8*	*2*	2.8	10.5	2	*3.6*	*12.7*	-
average rate of fire (seconds per round)	32.2	34.7	16.3	*39.8*	*32.6*	*17.3*	41.3	39.1	21.8	*49*	*29.6*	-
anomalous shots (%)	4.7	4.5	0	*3*	*3.4*	*0*	0	1.1	0	*3*	*3.1*	-
duds (%)	12,5	3,3	0	*7,4*	*11,2*	*10,4*	1,4	3,8	7,8	*8,1*	*14,0*	-
salvo dispersion[2] (m)	340	117	-	*195*	*108*	-	175	84	-	*210*	*126*	-
salvo width[3] (m)	276	151	-	*89*	*41*	-	265	98	-	-	-	-

1 Useful salvoes: salvoes within the dispersal limit of the regulations for each year shooting exercises. This limit was usually assumed to be 1% of the target distance.
2 Dispersion of a salvo: double the arithmetic average of the distances of the various shots from the centre of the salvo.
3 Longitudinal salvo width: distance measured from a line parallel to the firing line between the shortest and longest shot in the salvo.
n: night firing charge.

	Years 1939–1940				**Years 1940–1941**			
guns	100/47 OTO with electromechanical control				100/47 OTO with electromechanical control			
charge	I AA	II AA	II	II n	I AA	II AA	II	II n
distance (m)	-	3500	7100	3600	3600	4200	7100	3100
useful salvoes[1] (%)	-	55.7	24	41	80.5	66.6	29.5	50,5
hits on target (%)	-	-	5.7	2.6	-	-	4.8	2
average rate of fire (seconds per round)	-	14.1	14.5	14.4	10.8	13.2	14	16.4
anomalous shots (%)	-	0	3.7	0	0	0	2.1	0
duds (%)	-	12	4.9	3.3	2.8	5.8	2.6	0
salvo dispersion[2] (m)	-	-	19.6	-	-	-	214	-
salvo width[3] (m)	-	-	29.9	-	34	36	309	-

AA: anti-aircraft ('contraerei').

n: night firing charge.
See the table above for other notes.

included a wide selection of the ships of the two squadrons. The 1940 ESCM, in which five of the seven heavy cruisers took part, concluded with a detailed general report on the results obtained and with summary statistics comparing them with those of the 1939 and 1938 ESCMs. On the whole, the results were considered satisfactory with regard to the equipment, with the sole important exception of salvo dispersion, and somewhat less satisfactory with regard to the personnel.

The dispersion of salvoes – all calibres and models from 320/44 to 120/50 were included in the statistics (but not, therefore, the 381/50 of the brand new *Littorio*) – was considered worrying, also because the values had almost all deteriorated compared to the already unflattering results from 1939. This was particularly so for the 203/50 and 203/53 guns where dispersion had, respectively, increased from 188m to 311m and from 197m to 263m with firing opening at 20,000m in 1939 and 21,000m in 1940. This led to the establishment of a special commission, chaired by the Navy Chief of Staff, which at its meeting on 13 May 1940 reached the conclusions and proposals contained in the minutes given below. These are already partially known, but they are reproduced here in their entirety for the first time, as they are one of the most significant documents on how the problem was perceived at the time.

The report identifies the main causes of the phenomenon as being pivotal errors due to the dragging of the electric index of the tappet clocks and gaps in the transmission of the movement of the guns to the clocks themselves, confirming both the existence of the problem of dispersion and the perception of it at the time. However, like other contemporary documentation, while focusing attention on the worsening of the phenomenon from one year to the next, it does not mention, not even by implication, many of the causes raised by memoirs and post-war literature, such as the excessive weight tolerance allowed in the construction of the projectiles (until 1937, it was 0.4% or 0.5% and not 1% as generally claimed), the excessive initial speed of the projectiles, which was already partly reduced at the time, the vibrations of the gun ports due to their excessive size, the interference due to the air displacement of the opening rounds due to the excessive proximity of the gun barrels arranged in single cradles, and others. Naturally, for a balanced evaluation of the whole, these and other problems regarding the efficiency and effectiveness of the Regia Marina's weapons should be compared to those present in other navies at the same time, a comparison that has only recently been made by historians.

Minutes of the meeting held at Maristat on 13 May 1940-XVIIIth

On the afternoon of 13 May 1940-XVIII a Commission convened and chaired by Admiral Odoardo SOMIGLI, Sub-Chief of the Naval General Staff, and composed of:

Admiral Carlo BERGAMINI
Rear Adm. Antonio BOBBIESE, Weapons and Munitions Inspector

...

First of all, the conclusions and proposals reached by Rear Admiral Bobbiese regarding the causes of the still-problematic dispersions observed in 152/55, 203/53, and 320/44 are examined.

Having summarised these conclusions by E. Somigli, the phases through which the problem of tappet control has passed, and the harmful consequences of dispersions, the Commission, approving in principle the aforementioned conclusions and proposals, was unanimous in the following opinions:

1st - The system of enclosed relays (free relays) should be returned to as the only system capable of reducing losses due to tappet errors. Since the pre-existing arrangements for controlling these relays by means of fire contacts on the tappet clocks proved to be inadequate at the time, in that they caused the electrical index to drift and therefore significant tappet errors, the Commission is of the opinion that they should not be used for possible wartime use.

However, they will be restored and, at the beginning of the new training year, pointer training will be resumed with the relay system included, so that the personnel's mentality will already be oriented towards the use of this system when the more advanced devices that the D.G. A.A.N. is already studying will be implemented. The Directorate has been asked to complete these studies. As soon as the new devices are implemented and their absolute safety is established, they must always be used in peace and war.

For the two battleships CESARE and CAVOUR, in which the newer and more perfect signal clocks have shown fewer problems with fire contacts, training on the included relay system will be resumed immediately and the next Special Exercises will be carried out with this system.

2. It is necessary to be able to check the correct execution of the tappet by means of efficient tappet recorders. Such recorders also have the advantage of allowing good training of gunners through controlled daily cold pointing exercises. Since only the Olap type [Officine Lombarde Apparecchi di Precisione, n.d.a.] installed on some ships has demonstrated, when given a minimum of care, to respond well to the purpose, the D.G. A.A.N. has been instructed to abolish the other existing types of recorders and to order and install the Olap type on all ships.

3. It is necessary to reduce the slack in the transmissions that carry the movement of the guns to the target clocks. For this purpose, the D.G. A.A.N. will appoint a special Commission that will proceed, with the help of specialised personnel of the manufacturing companies, of the ship's Commands and of the various Marines, subdividing themselves appropriately in order to proceed as quickly as possible, to

- detect and eliminate existing gaps in the current transmissions,
- examine, for each type of installation, the possible mod-

ifications to be made to the transmission paths and ratios in order to reduce the constant occurrence of slack,
- examine the convenience of retaining all the existing correctors fitted to carry-over transmissions, comparing the amount of correction they make with the increase in inaccuracy they cause.

In the meantime, Marinarmi, in agreement with Maricominarmi, will examine the convenience of replacing the mechanical carry-over transmissions with electric transmissions on differential receivers, foreseeing their prompt experimental application on one of the ships.

Division Admiral Carlo BERGAMINI also pointed out the need for the problem of dispersion not to overlook the causes dependent on the calcification of the shell in storage and the accurate packaging of the ammunition, especially as regards 152/55. Marinarmi has been tasked with studying the details of cartridge packaging for this calibre and the correct adjustment of the scope.

Then the question of the high percentage (about 35%) of failed bursts when 0.Bo. fuzes hit the water is examined. [Borletti Fuzes, Authors' note, 1st type placed on 203 and 152 shells.] In this regard, the Commission is of the opinion that the phenomenon must depend on the particular arrangement of the nosepiece of these types of projectiles (severed nosepiece and fuze placed under the wind-cutter), since it does not occur on 120/50 shells in which similar fuzes are placed on normal nosepieces. It is acknowledged that this issue is only of concern with respect to observation of long range shooting, as recent experience with hard targets has proven the impact efficiency of the fuzes against such targets.

Since the ammunition cannot be radically changed, the Commission has examined the following two possible measures:

- lighten the wind-cutter in such a way as to ensure its immediate rupture at the impact in water,
- lengthen the piston in the concussion operation of the spools, carrying the head, with a specially guided rod, on the tip of the wind-cutter.

The Commission has noted that experiments with lightened wind-cutters have already been carried out by the Permanent Commission with poor results, having shown insufficient resistance to the strong initial forces. The Commission therefore considers that it will be difficult to find a solution to this problem. Maricominarmi was therefore invited to study the other measures as quickly as possible and, in agreement with Marinarmi, also making use of the trials carried out and the data collected in the first studies of 203 and 152 projectiles against the radio-controlled target.

Chapter 4

AVIATION FACILITIES

TRENTO CLASS and *BOLZANO*

Between 1928 and 1929, a catapult was tested aboard the cruiser *Ancona* (ex-German *Graudenz*) which, installed right forward on the forecastle deck, led to the creation of the 'Gagnotto' type catapult which, in this position, would become a distinguishing feature of the 'Condottieri' type cruisers of the first series (*Da Barbiano*, *Di Giussano*, *Colleoni* and *Bande* Nere), the two *Trento*s and the four *Zara*s.

In the case of the *Trento*s (but the arrangement was similar for all the other units mentioned above), the catapult consisted of a carriage propelled by compressed air which ran on a fixed structure along two guiderails pointing forward along the centreline. The aircraft were housed in a large hangar below the forecastle, ahead of the barbette of No 1 203mm turret. Because of the 'flush deck' configuration, the sheer of the upper deck produced a deckhead height of 3.80m on the battery deck, sufficient to allow easy handling and maintenance of the aircraft. These were hoisted into place on the catapult for launching with the use of a special 2-ton collapsible kingpost, equipped with derrick and hoist). The derrick was also used for the recovery and re-stowing of the seaplanes at the end of a mission.

The forward position of the catapult was certainly not an ideal solution: the presence of the aircraft on the foredeck (necessary for its immediate use in the tactical phases of an engagement) obstructed the field of fire of the forward guns and exposed the aircraft to the effects of blast, saline corrosion and decay, as well as the potential for damage from heavy seas.

Off the Island of Ventotene, a Piaggio P.6 ter floatplane is launched from *Bolzano*.

A partial solution was next tried aboard the light cruisers *Diaz* and *Cadorna* with the embarkation – at the aft end of the superstructure – of a fixed catapult, pointing to starboard: while reducing the risk of weather damage to the seaplanes this made it necessary to change course for their launch. A definitive arrangement was finally implemented on the *Bolzano* (as well as on the light cruisers of the *Montecuccoli*/*Duca d'Aosta* and *Abruzzi* classes) by installing a catapult between the two funnels. This was also of the 'Gagnotto' type but it could be swung out to starboard or port, with obvious advantages for its operation and that of the

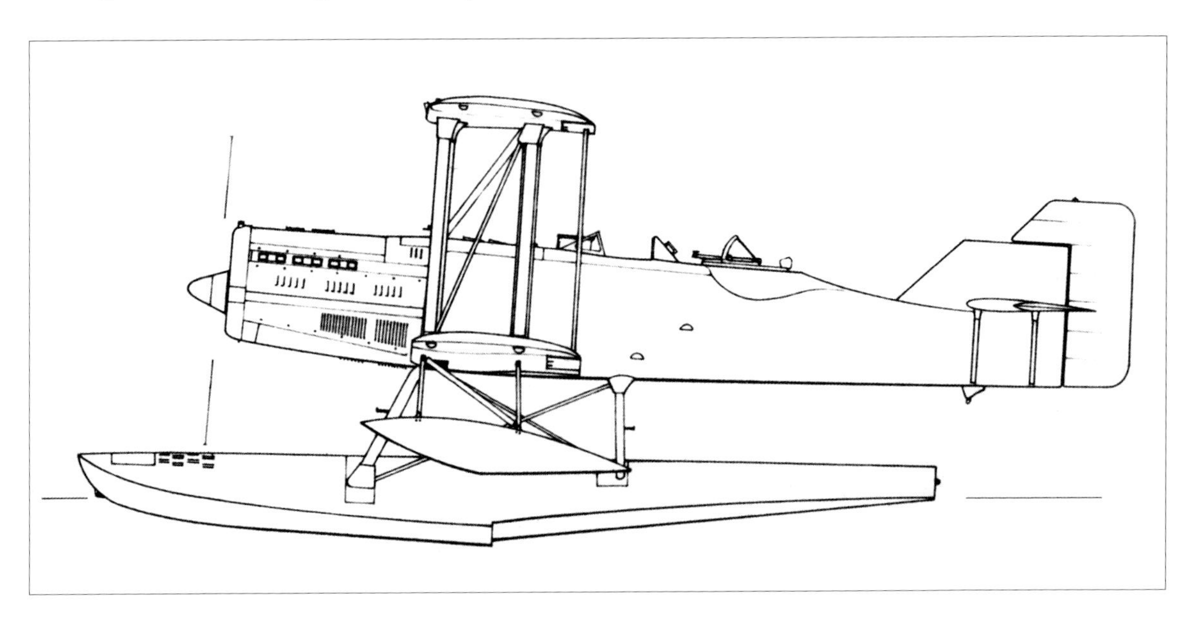

The Piaggio P.6 floatplane. (Drawing by G. Bignozzi via M. Gueli)

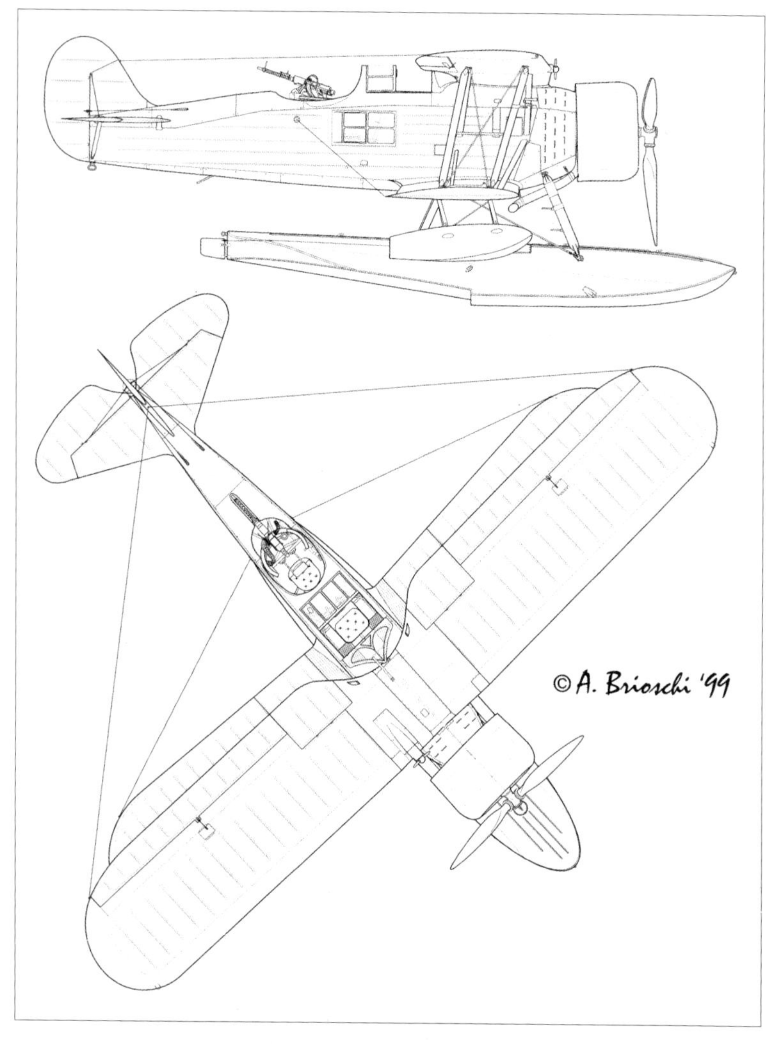

The IMAM Ro.43 floatplane. (Drawing by A. Brioschi)

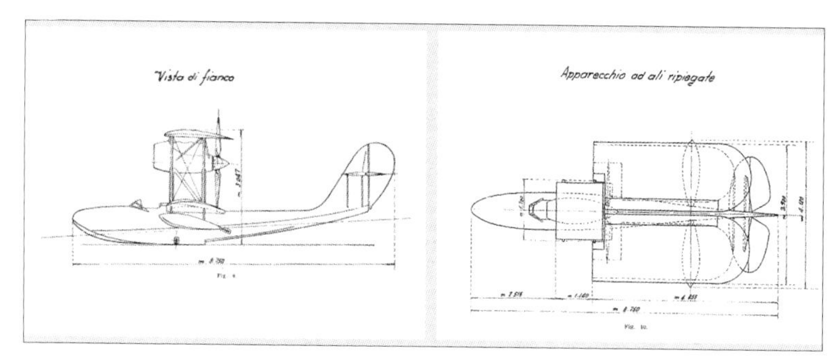

The CANT.25 AR (with wings folded in the plan view) from the original flight manual. (Courtesy CMPR)

aircraft; a second advantage was that these could be handled by the large cargo derrick hinged at the base of the mainmast that was also used for launching and recovering the ship's boats.

Three aircraft was the official establishment on these three cruisers, but in practice, two were always embarked, which on the *Trento* and *Trieste* were housed in the forward hangar, while on the *Bolzano*, which did not have a hangar, one was placed on the catapult and one on a special support on the left side of the forward funnel.

In the early years of operations, the *Trento*, *Trieste* and *Bolzano* carried the Piaggio P.6 seaplane, a biplane with a traditional structure with a central float, designed in 1927. It was 9.67m long and had a wingspan of 13.54m. It was equipped with folding wings and a 410hp FIAT A.20 inline engine. Two prototypes and ten production examples were built; contrary to what is reported by some sources, the later 'ter' version (fifteen aircraft produced), was actually embarked in the early 1930s on board the three cruisers, as can be seen from the photographs of the *Trento* and *Bolzano* in this chapter.

The next step, in the early 1930s, was the adoption of the

The *Trento* at Shanghai in 1932 with a Piaggio P.6 floatplane on the bow catapult. (US Navy, E. Bagnasco collection)

An IMAM Ro.43 floatplane aboard the *Bolzano*; note the latticework structure of the amidship rotating catapult. (USMM, courtesy F. Fontana)

CANT 25, which, in the 'AR' (folding wing) version, was to equip the three *Trento*s once the Piaggio P.6 was discontinued. This was a single-hull biplane flying boat, powered by the same FIAT A.20 engine as the Piaggio machine, which had a top speed of 245km/h; its dimensions were slightly smaller than those of the P.6 (length 8.75m and wingspan 10.40m).

Finally, between 1937 and 1938, like all other major ships of the Regia Marina equipped with aviation facilities, *Trento*, *Trieste* and *Bolzano* embarked the famous IMAM Ro.43 biplane reconnaissance floatplane which, although not exactly at the cutting edge of shipboard aircraft design, served with dignity until 1943. The only existing Ro.43, MM 27050, which was in service at the Orbetello Flying School, is now on display at the Air Force Historical Museum. With its traditional design of a central float with folding wings, the Ro.43 was powered by a nine-cylinder Piaggio P.X R radial engine of 700hp, giving a maximum speed of 303km/h at an altitude of 2000m (cruising speed 245 km/h). Maximum take-off weight was 2400kg, and its dimensions were similar to those of previous aircraft in the same role (length 9.71m and a wingspan of 11.57m); the armament consisted of a Breda-Safat 7.7mm machine gun operated by the observer, who had a square window on each side of the fuselage to facilitate his primary task. The use of the Ro.43, especially during the conflict, was mainly in the reconnaissance role, and only in rare cases was the aircraft used for anti-submarine escort and for observing the results of gunfire.

The cruiser *Trento* photographed from the *Trieste* in 1938. Note the IMAM Ro.43 floatplane on the catapult and in the foreground, below the 203/50 turrets, the sliding door under which the hangar for the aircraft was located. (E. Bagnasco collection)

After being torpedoed in August 1942 off the Aeolian Islands, the *Bolzano* was transferred first to Naples and then to La Spezia to undergo the necessary major repairs. At the Ligurian base, in response to the fleet's chronic lack of a necessary embarked air component, the idea matured of radically transforming the ship to adapt it to an aircraft launcher and fast transport. Obviously, this was merely a 'feasibility study', since a lack of materials prevented even the work of restoring the *Bolzano* to its original configuration. The study included the elimination of all superstructures and original armament, leaving the aft funnel and mast in place. It was planned to reduce the power of the engines (to create new space for liquid and solid loads) with the removal of some forward boilers and the consequent channelling of smoke from the remaining forward boilers into twin side-by-side funnels. This would have created a long continuous deck from the aft funnel to the extreme bow, which would have allowed the transportation of twelve Reggiane RE.2001 fighter aircraft, launched from two catapults forward, one each angled to port and starboard. The '2001' (which did not have folding wings), could not be recovered and would have had to land at shore bases, or ditch in the sea, after going into action. The armament would have consisted of ten 90/50 anti-aircraft guns in single stabilised mountings, five on each side (of the same model carried on the *Duilio* and *Littorio* class battleships), and twenty twin 37/54 machine guns.

The idea was clearly not followed up, but it is interesting because this rather desperate measure reflects a broader problem for the Italian Navy. The proposed solution was in any case original and, under different conditions, might have been feasible in practice.

The aircraft arrangements on the two *Trento*s, in addition to the drawbacks already outlined, proved to be unfortunate in other respects. The seaplane hangar, which occupied the height of two decks, sacrificed space that should have been devoted to accommodation for the petty officers and crew, which as a result were cramped, possibly even inadequate in terms of washing and sanitary facilities. In addition, the break in the continuity of the upper

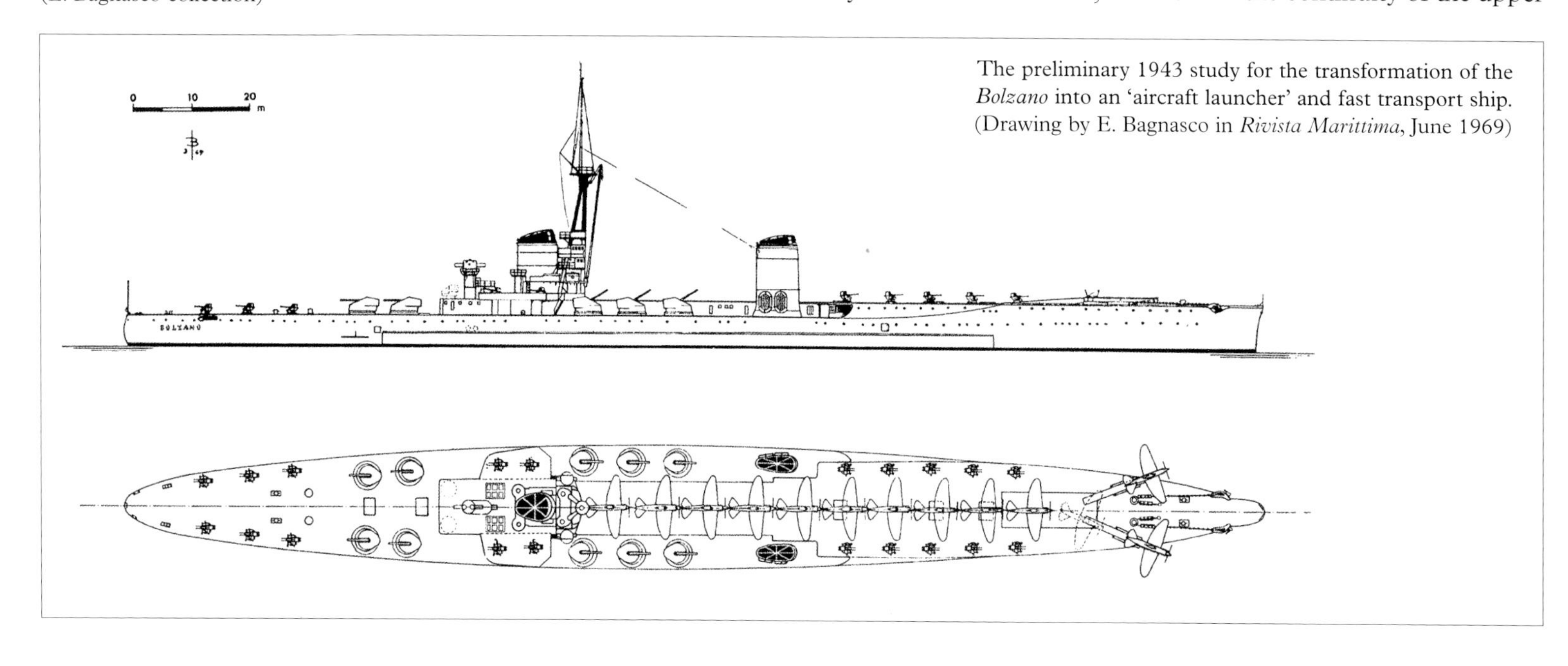

The preliminary 1943 study for the transformation of the *Bolzano* into an 'aircraft launcher' and fast transport ship. (Drawing by E. Bagnasco in *Rivista Marittima*, June 1969)

deck and battery deck reduced the girder strength of the hull forward, and affected the watertightness of the fore deck due to the hangar hatch.

For these reasons, in the second half of 1938, substantial modifications were made to the *Trento* and *Trieste*, with the transformation of the hangar into accommodation for non-commissioned officers and crew, through the elimination of the seaplane elevator and its trunking, as well as the embarkation hatch, and their replacement with two fixed sections of deck. As a result, the seaplane was permanently parked on the catapult on the deck forward of the 203mm turrets, which accentuated the damaging effects mentioned above and clearly seen in photographs from the war period. The *Bolzano* obviously did not need these alterations because of the different and more rational aeronautical systems with which she was equipped from the outset.

Above: An IMAM Ro.43 floatplane on the catapult of the heavy cruiser *Bolzano* in the late 1930s. The 'clocks' on the front of the structure located between the tripod's legs are instruments indicating wind speed and direction, the ship's speed and course and other elements useful to the aircraft pilot and crew members during the seaplane launch. (E. Bagnasco collection)

Fiume's pilots and airmen with the ship's second Ro.43 in background. (G. Apostolo Archive).

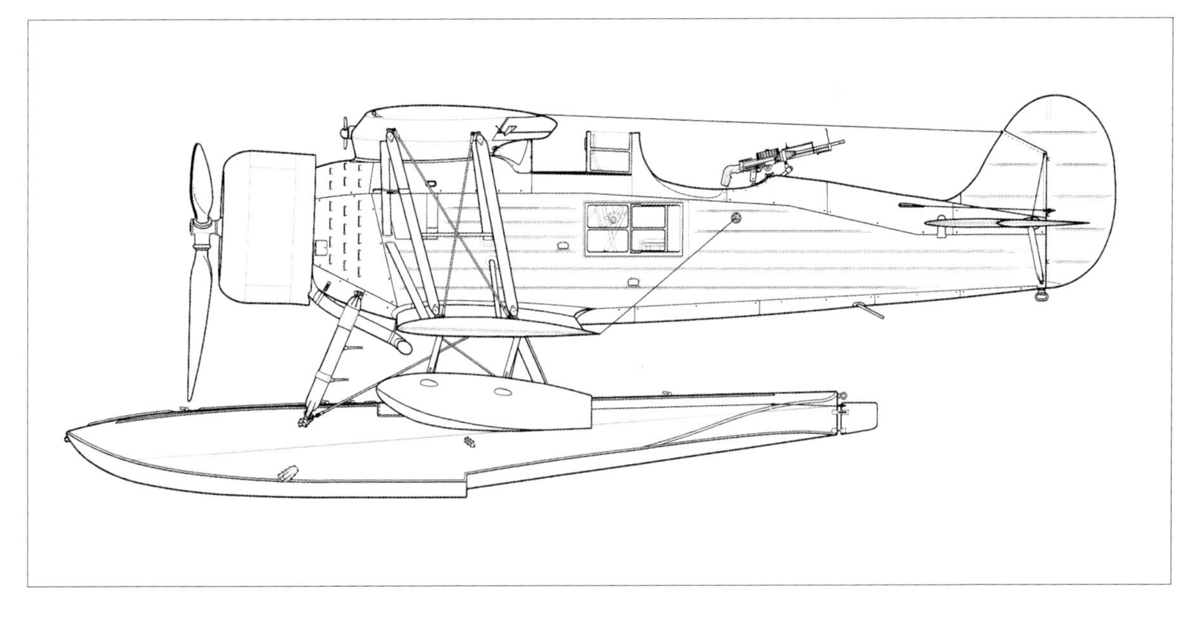

An IMAM Ro.43 floatplane. (G. Apostolo Archive)

Pola leaving Genoa on 30 May 1938 with an IMAM Ro.43 seaplane on the bow catapult.

Naples, 5 May 1938 ('H Review'): cruiser *Fiume* with an IMAM Ro.43 seaplane on the bow catapult.

ZARA CLASS

As in the *Trentos*, the *Zaras* were equipped with a fixed forward compressed air catapult of the 'Gagnotto' type, with a 16.2m stroke: an unfortunate arrangement in that the aircraft, which was always kept ready for launch during wartime missions, was subject to weather damage and corrosion by salt, while also obstructing the firing arcs of the forward turrets. Lifting the two aircraft and stowing them in the 13.7m long hangar, located immediately forward of the 203mm turret and closed by two sliding doors, was also very problematic. A 4-tonne cargo derrick, operated by one of the cargo winches, was used to move the aircraft.

On first entering service, the *Zaras* experimented with various types of seaplanes (including the Macchi M40 and M41), taking on the Cant 25 AR (AR = 'folding wings') in 1935. Between 1937 and 1938, the IMAM Ro.43 was finally adopted, and its use was standardised on board all cruisers and *Littorio* class battleships.

Lastly, it should be remembered that in 1935 a temporary flight deck was set up at the stern of the *Fiume* to test the take-off and landing of a 'La Cierva' autogyro, a rudimentary precursor to the helicopter. The experimental activity was successful, but the time was not yet ripe for the operational deployment of rotary-wing machines on warships, technology which – excluding a few small helicopters used by German submarines during the Second World War – would only find full application from the 1950s onwards.

The same applies to the aviation arrangements of the *Zaras* as to the two *Trentos*. Towards the end of the 1930s, the *Pola* and *Fiume* underwent similar alterations. It is not clear whether this also applied to *Zara*, but certainly not the *Gorizia*, whose modification was strongly urged by her last commander, Captain Paolo Melodia, but were only scheduled for June 1943. It should be noted that after the outbreak of the war, not even the hangar of the *Gorizia* was used and the aircraft remained parked on the catapult during sorties, as the operations of lifting and preparing the aircraft for launch were very cumbersome and slow and not compatible with wartime conditions. Moreover, the strong gale during the 2nd Sirte battle highlighted the structural deficiencies, although not particularly serious, resulting from the original hangar design.

La Spezia, 4 January 1935: a 'La Cierva' autogyro on a wooden flight deck temporarily fitted on *Fiume*'s quarterdeck.

Chapter 5

CAMOUFLAGE

For a short time after commissioning in the last years of the 1920s, the cruisers *Trento* and *Trieste* were painted dark grey overall, a colour that was applied to Italian naval vessels from the early 1920s until late 1929/early 1930.

Trento and *Trieste* were painted light grey in late 1930 (*Bolzano* was light grey from her launch); in the mid-1930s elegant raked caps were added to the funnels of both ships, painted dull black; *Bolzano* had black funnel caps from her commissioning.

The heavy cruiser *Trento* painted dark grey in the late 1920s. (E. Bagnasco collection)

This photograph, unfortunately of poor quality, shows the *Bolzano* moored at Messina probably in July 1941 with the funnel caps painted light grey to make the ship's silhouette less conspicuous. (E. Bagnasco collection)

Bolzano, with her crew manning the rails, during a naval review in the summer of 1937 in the Gulf of Naples. Note the mast in its original configuration; the colour scheme is light grey with black funnel caps. (E. Bagnaco collection)

The *Bolzano*, in two-tone grey camouflage with bow and stern painted white, at La Spezia in June 1942, at the end of the extensive repair following her torpedoing by HM S/m *Triumph* on 26 August 1941. (F. Bargoni collection)

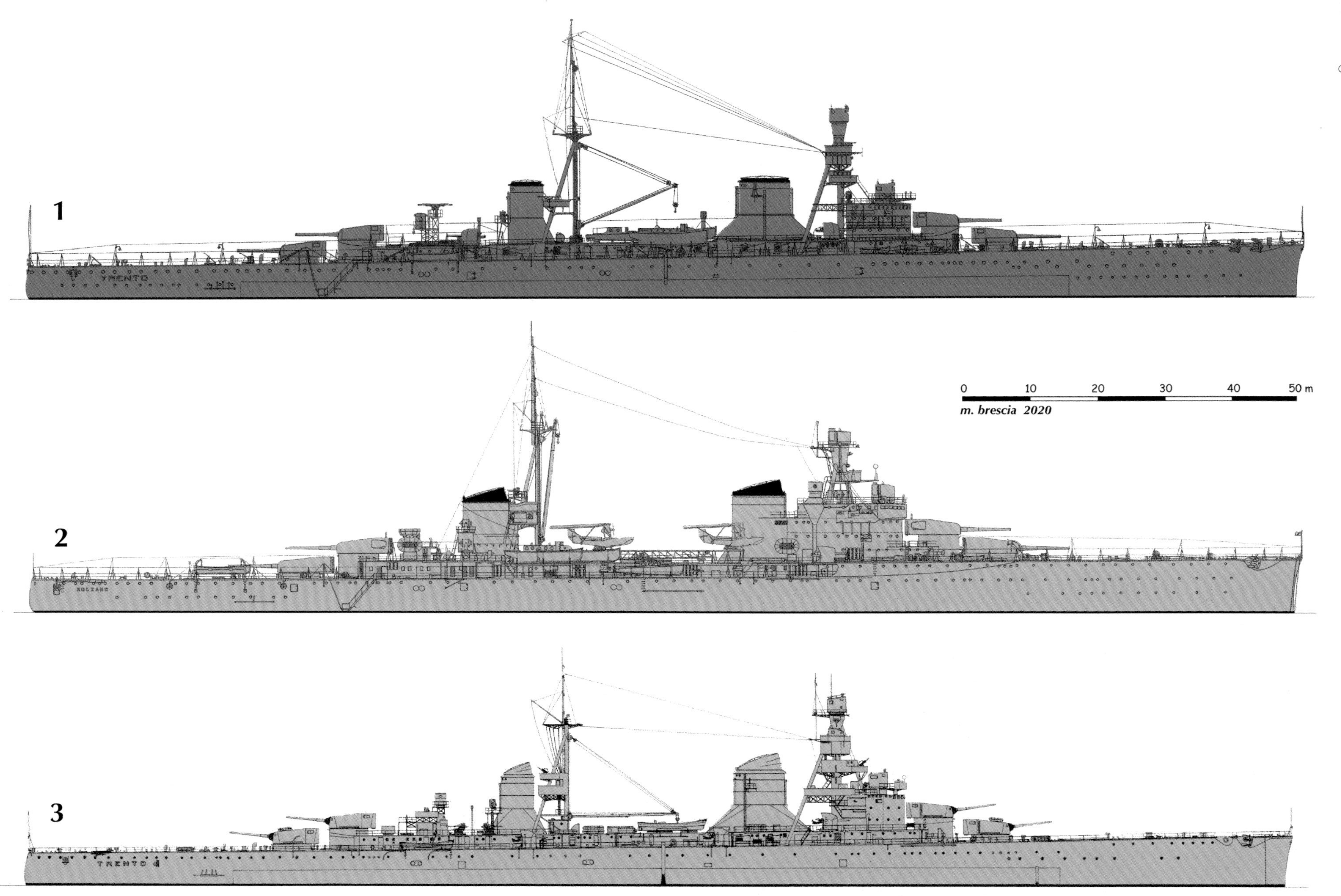

1: *Trento*, 1929 (dark grey overall at commissioning); *Trieste* scheme was similar.
2: *Bolzano*, late 1930s: light grey with black funnel caps (*Trento* and *Trieste* the same).
3: *Trento*, late 1940: light grey overall with light grey funnel caps to make the ship's silhouette less conspicuous. (Illustrations by M. Brescia)

Port and starboard side of *Trento* in spring 1942 with an experimental 'Claudus' type camouflage. (Illustrations by M. Brescia)

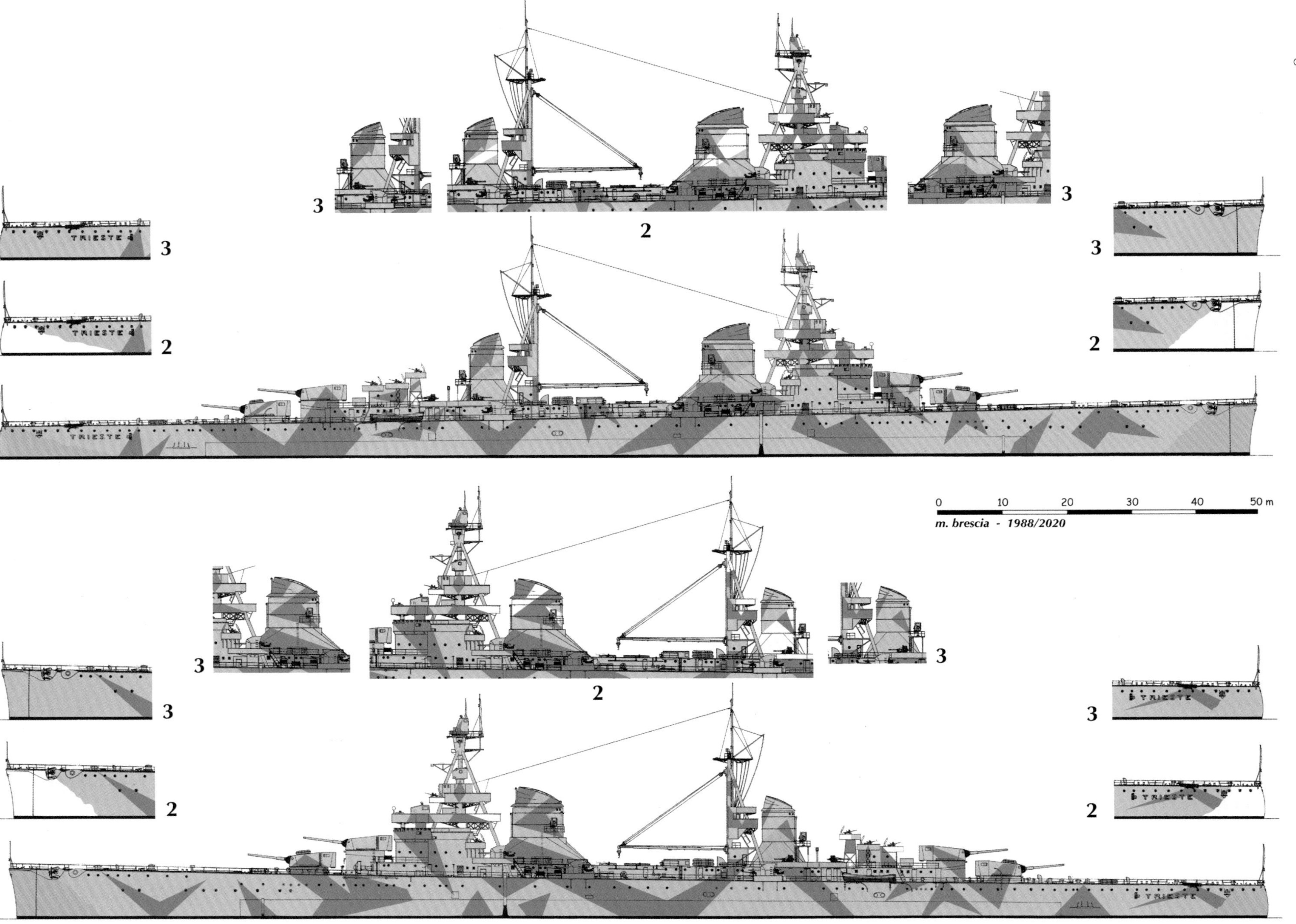

Heavy cruiser *Trieste*
1: May 1942 (two-tone 'standard' scheme in light and dark grey with light green areas fore, aft and on superstructures)
2: June 1942 (white replacing areas previously in light green)
3: Summer 1942 (light grey replacing white)
(Illustrations by M. Brescia)

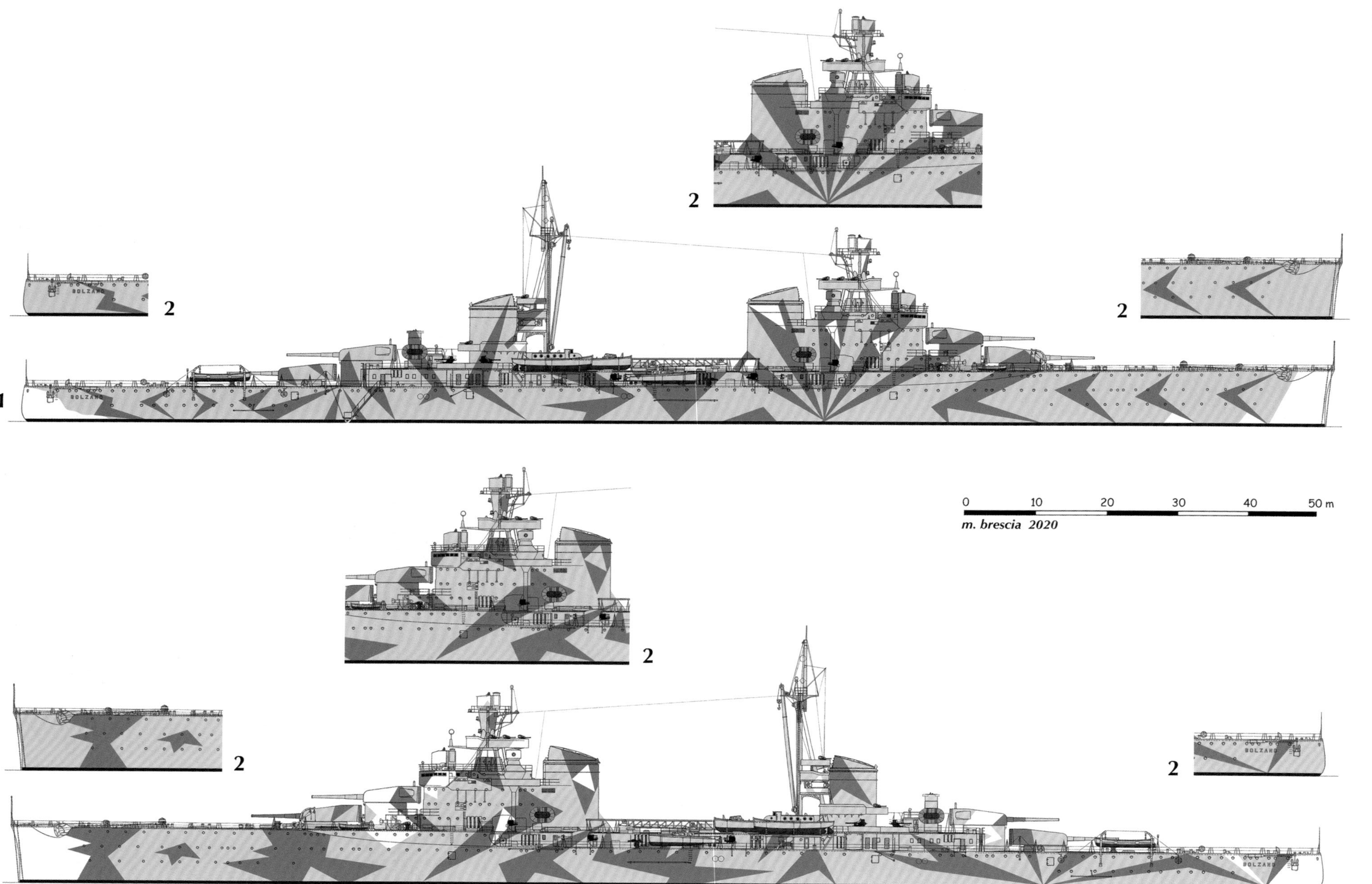

Heavy cruiser *Bolzano*
1: Spring 1942 (two-tone 'standard' scheme in light and dark grey with white areas fore, aft and on superstructures)
2: Summer 1942 (light grey replacing areas previously white)
(Illustrations by M. Brescia)

1. *Fiume* in standard prewar light grey.
2. Starboard elevation of *Gorizia* in March 1942 wearing a 'Claudus' style camouflage.
3. As above, port side.
(Illustrations by M. Brescia)

Three rare 'Agfachrome' colour slides taken by the German photographer Hugo Jaeger on 9 May 1938 during the 'H Review' in the Gulf of Naples. From the top: a detail of the cruiser *Fiume* (with *Zara* and *Pola* in the background) moored at the 'Stazione Marittima' in Naples; *Zara*, *Pola* and *Fiume* passing the battleship *Cavour*; aboard the *Cesare*, a NSDAP member observes *Zara*, *Pola* and *Fiume* with the Faraglioni (rock stacks) of Capri in the background.

March/April 1942: the *Trento* at Messina, with an experimental 'Claudus' type camouflage (E. Bagnaco collection).

These three ships were thus light grey on 10 June 1940 and between the end of the year and early 1941, funnel caps were overpainted in light grey to make the ships less conspicuous.

As built, the four *Zara* class cruisers were painted light grey overall, a colour used since 1929 that replaced the dark grey previously applied to these ships (as well as to all other Italian naval vessels) since the end of the First World War. Wood planking was left in its natural colour, and horizontal surfaces on superstructures – as a rule – were painted dark grey. After the battle off Calabria in July 1940 (when Italian aircraft mistakenly bombed Italian ships, luckily scoring no hits, when Admiral Campioni's ships were returning to their bases), a new means for identification of national ships from the air was introduced. On the forecastle deck, broad red and white diagonal stripes were painted to help air recognition; the stripes were 7ft to 15 ft wide and angled aft from port to starboard. The stripes began at the extreme bow and extended up to the breakwater (mostly in destroyers) or up to the barbette of No 1 turret (in some cruisers and battleships). These stripes were retained until the armistice of September 1943: sometimes they were painted on the aftermost part of the deck, but very few cases are well documented (the destroyer *Aviere* being one of these). *Pola* and *Zara* were lost at Matapan painted in this scheme.

After a trial period in January 1941, when the Regia Marina conducted trials of naval camouflage on small vessels, mostly in Pola Dockyard, technicians at La Spezia Dockyard drafted an experimental camouflage scheme for *Fiume*, issuing orders to make available paints and other items and to instruct Dockyard

Two rare colour photographs of the heavy cruiser *Zara* on 5 May 1938 during the review in the Gulf of Naples occasioned by the visit of the German Chancellor Adolf Hitler.

personnel. Colours to be used for *Fiume* would have been the standard light grey and a dark blue-grey for irregular patches to be overpainted on the light grey. The *Fiume* arrived in Taranto on 2 March arousing much curiosity, but, unfortunately, photographs showing this scheme are very scarce, and only two black and white images are known: one of the starboard side, taken from a great distance and rather unclear, with the cruiser moored at a buoy in Taranto in the first days of March 1941 (with the

Above: Bolzano leaving La Spezia for sea trials in June 1942. (E. Bagnasco collection)

Below: Trieste at La Spezia in 15 July 1942. Atop the main mast, there is the platform for an EC 3 ter 'Gufo' radar, never fitted. (E. Bagnasco collection)

The *Bolzano* in Genoa in May 1942 at the end of the refit begun in October 1941 to repair the torpedo and bomb damage of August–September 1941 in Messina. On completion, the cruiser was painted in her first 'standard' colour scheme in light and dark grey. (E. Bagnasco collection)

water tanker *Metauro* alongside, partially covering the starboard side forward); and one while steaming in the Ionian Sea on the morning of March 27 (the day before the loss of the ship in the night clash off Cape Matapan), where *Fiume* is seen in the far distance, in an almost stern view. In this last image *Fiume*'s colours, because of their darker shade, are quite different from those of the other two cruisers in the photograph, *Pola* and *Zara*, painted in light grey.

From studying these two photographs – as no other images have been traced up to now – scholars and enthusiasts have somehow 'reconstructed' *Fiume*'s experimental scheme, which was probably the same on both sides; but the results are far from certain as consistent and real data available on the matter is really very scarce. *Fiume* was sunk just less than one month after this camouflage was applied, so there is no official report (and, as far as it is known, no archival documents at all) on this scheme's effectiveness.

In March 1942 *Gorizia* was painted in a 'Claudus' camouflage scheme (named after the marine painter Rudolf Claudus, who studied naval camouflage both from a technical and chromatic point of view). This was a pattern of light grey and dark grey in very similar shades to those used in 'standard' camouflage patterns applied from late spring that year; there were also white areas in the bow, stern and amidship, deleted later in September 1942. *Gorizia* was still painted in this scheme when she was found half-sunk in La Spezia at the end of the war; soon after she was broken up still wearing this scheme.

March 1941: the *Fiume* at Taranto in one of only two photographs known to date showing the cruiser with her experimental camouflage painting. (E. Bagnasco collection)

In late spring of 1942, as one of the first experiments carried out by the Regia Marina in the field of naval camouflage, *Trento* too – after taking part into the '2nd Sirte' encounter – was

Cruiser *Fiume* in the late 1930s steaming at high speed, painted in the light grey overall scheme she carried prior to the short-lived experimental pattern applied in early 1941. (E. Bagnasco collection)

painted with an experimental 'Claudus' camouflage including dark grey polygonal areas (either with straight or curved edges) on a light grey background. The bow and stern were painted white in order to simulate a shortening of the length (bow) and greater speed (stern); some small triangular areas in white were also painted on the hull sides and superstructures. Some sources state that, shortly before the 'Mezzo Giugno' operation in which *Trento* was lost, the whites were overpainted in light grey, but the very scarce photographic evidence available does not permit a definitive judgment on this.

In May 1942, when camouflage patterns in light and dark grey became commonplace, *Trieste*'s camouflage showed a pattern with triangles, polygons and lozenges in dark grey that extended both on the hull and on the superstructures on a light grey background. At the bow, stern and on the funnels there were areas in light green as on other Italian ships (cruiser *Regolo*, destroyer *Legionario*, destroyer escort *Tifone*). By June at the latest, the light green had been replaced by white and was definitively overpainted light grey in August; after that *Trieste* never altered her camouflage scheme.

In May 1942, during repairs to the damage inflicted by HM S/m *Triumph* on 26 August 1941, *Bolzano* was painted in a 'standard' camouflage with light and dark grey, as for *Trieste*, showing dark grey polygons and white areas on the bow, stern, superstructure and funnels Amidships on the starboard side there was a 'radial' element found also on a few other ships, like the battleship *Vittorio Veneto* and troopship *Oceania*. In early summer white areas were overpainted in light grey as applied to almost all Italian ships by late autumn 1943, as it had been found that white was often visible both in sunny daylight or in clear moon-lit nights, as is often found in the Mediterranean.

Bolzano was severely damaged in August 1942 wearing this 'standard' two-tone grey colour scheme that was roughly maintained when the ship was repaired in La Spezia Dockyard; a photograph taken in September 1943 (see page 177) shows that the funnels and superstructure were repainted with darker colours on some areas – probably shades of green and brown – in an attempt to blend the ship into the surrounding coastline.

Until the end of the war decks covered by teak planking (*ie Bolzano*'s upper deck and *Trento* and *Trieste*'s deck aft of No 2 turret to the stern) were usually maintained in a natural wood colour. At the bow, decks were painted dark grey (*grigio piombo*, *ie* 'lead grey'), and this was later also applied to surfaces covered by the wooden planking.

The *Gorizia* at Messina in March 1942, shortly after a 'Claudus' type camouflage had been applied. (E. Bagnasco collection)

Chapter 6

PRE-WAR ACTIVITY OF ITALIAN HEAVY CRUISERS (1929–1940)

This description of the pre-war service of heavy cruisers, subdivided by years and not by classes, covers only the main events from their commissioning until Italy's entry into the war. In this period, heavy cruiser activity was much greater than that of battleships (indeed, only the rebuilt battleships are relevant), both for intensity and for the length of service. For reasons of space, the coverage is limited to the main political and military events in which they were involved, as well as some significant aspects of their operational activity. To avoid repetition, we refer to the volume, *Italian Battleships: Conte di Cavour & Duilio Classes 1911-1956* (also published by Seaforth; see bibliography), where certain activities and operations (*eg* the 'Rivista H' and the occupation of Albania) have already been dealt with.

1927

On 4 September, at the launch of *Trento*, attended by the Sovereigns of Italy and the Minister of Communications Costanzo Ciano, the hull came to a halt on the slipway, after having moved 47.5 metres, slightly misaligned with respect to the longitudinal plane and with the stern partially in the water already. Attempts to move the ship failed and the ceremony was

Trento during early sea trials. (Cantiere Orlando, Leghorn, E. Bagnasco collection)

Trento at Messina in the 1930s with *Trieste*'s superstructure in the foreground. (E. Bagnasco collection)

suspended. Attempts made in the following days were also unsuccessful and the *Trento* remained sadly in that position for almost a month. On 4 October, in the presence of only technicians and workers, by increasing the means of pushing on the slipway and using the towing force of the liner *Principe di Udine*, the launch was successfully achieved. Investigations began immediately and gave rise to a hypothesis of sabotage by mixing sand with tallow (the animal fat used to lubricate the vessels on the slipway and allow the poppet, on which the hull rests, to slide). This version gained strength after the Second World War, but those responsible were never identified. A second hypothesis – technically difficult to reconcile with the first – remained a minority view, namely that it was an accident due to the poor quality of the tallow used.

1928

On 21 December, in Trieste, at the San Marco shipyard of the Stabilimento Tecnico Triestino, the *Trieste* was delivered to the Regia Marina, not yet fully fitted out.

1929

3 April. The *Trento* was delivered to the Regia Marina at the Orlando shipyard in Livorno.

11 May. The *Trento* and *Trieste*, still undergoing fitting-out and working up, became the 'Divisione Incrociatori' (Cruiser Division) with the *Trento* as flagship.

5 June. The Cruiser Division was disbanded in anticipation of the *Trento*'s cruise to South America, to show a modern, large

Trento moored in the Gulf of La Spezia in the late 1930s. (E. Bagnasco collection)

Late summer 1931: *Fiume* during sea trials off Trieste, still without the after 203mm turrets. (G. Alfano collection)

Italian warship to the authorities and people of Brazil, Uruguay and Argentina and the many large colonies of Italian emigrants. On 23 July the *Trento* sailed from La Spezia and during the outward voyage visited the islands of Cape Verde, Rio de Janeiro, Santos, Montevideo, Buenos Aires, Ilha Grande and, on the way back, Bahia, the Canary Islands and Tangier, reaching La Spezia on 10 October.

30 August. Before the *Trento* returned, the two cruisers formed 1st Division which became part of the I Squadra, after the 'Armata Navale' had been disbanded in 1928.

1931

On 20 October and 23 November respectively, the *Zara* and *Fiume* were handed over to the Regia Marina, pending completion of fitting out.

12-13 December. On 12 December, the *Trieste*, flying the flag of Admiral Ernesto Burzagli, Commander in Chief of the I Squadra, left La Spezia to rescue the naval tug *Teseo*, which had run into a strong gale with force 8 and 9 winds while sailing from La Maddalena to Civitavecchia. The light cruiser *Ancona*, the MS *Caralis* and the steamers *Piave* and German *Trapani* also took part in the rescue operations. The *Trieste* arrived on the scene during the night of the 13th, when the first attempts to rescue the crew had already been unsuccessful. Due to the bad weather conditions and with the *Teseo* in risk of sinking, it was impossible

The *Fiume* entering 'Mar Piccolo' at Taranto through the 'Canale Navigabile' in a 1935-vintage postcard. (Foto Priore, Taranto)

to give a tow, to get too close to *Teseo* or even to lower boats into the sea. At first light the people on the tug and the passengers had to jump into the water with the sole help of lifebuoys and were rescued by ropes and ladders. At 09:40 the *Teseo* sank about 16 miles to the east-northeast of the island of Tavolara. In all, 62 of the 81 men of the crew were rescued and 50 of the 67 sailors who were passengers were rescued; 47 men were rescued by *Trieste*, 44 by *Caralis*, 20 by *Piave* and one was rescued during the night by *Trapani*, which later departed. After the sinking, the *Trieste*, the

Spring 1931: the forecastle of the heavy cruiser *Fiume*, during sea trials – the ship is steaming full astern at the speed of 15.6 knots.

The *Fiume* seen from the quarterdeck of a battleship during an exercise before a review in the Gulf of Naples.

Caralis and the *Piave* headed for Golfo Aranci, where the survivors disembarked during the night of the 14th. In the morning, all survivors were transferred to the *Trieste*, which returned to La Spezia.

On 23 December, the *Gorizia* was handed over to the Regia Marina.

1932

Following the Japanese occupation of Manchuria in September 1931 and the subsequent Sino-Japanese incidents in Shanghai, in order to protect its national interests, the Italian government decided to reinforce the Far East Naval Division, then

Cruiser *Trieste* in Toulon harbour in the 1930s.

The *Trieste* in Taranto's Mar Grande in the early 1930s. The secondary armament is still composed of eight twin 100/47 guns which in 1937 would be reduced to six, the two after mountings being replaced with four twin 37/54 Breda AA machine guns. (Foto Priore, Taranto)

consisting of the protected cruiser *Libia* and the gunboats *Caboto* and *Carlotto*. To this end, on 4 February, the *Trento* – flying the flag of Adm. Div. Domenico Cavagnari and with a company of the San Marco battalion aboard – and destroyer *Espero* set sail from Gaeta heading for Shanghai. Navigation was organised in such a way as to minimise refuelling and, in the final stretch, in order to gain time, the *Trento* proceeded alone, arriving in Shanghai on 4 March, followed by the *Espero* on the 7th. In Shanghai and while the *Trento* remained in these waters, Adm. Cavagnari assumed command of the Division. The arrival of the two ships in China coincided with an easing of tension. Although no major events took place, the mission of *Trento* strengthened the Italian presence in the region and provided first-hand information on Chinese and Japanese military efficiency (the latter did not shine in the fighting in Shanghai). The *Trento* returned to Italy via Hong Kong on 19 May, arriving in La Spezia on 30 June after intermediate stops. The *Espero* did not return to Gaeta until 3 December.

On March 21st, the *Zara* became part of the 1st Division of the I Squadra, but became fully operational only in the following month of May.

In the second half of the year, with the commissioning of *Gorizia* and *Bolzano*, the naval forces were reorganised in such a way as to concentrate the two heavy cruiser divisions in the I Squadra: the 1st included the three *Trento*s, the 2nd the first three *Zara*s.

On 21 December 1932 the *Pola was* delivered to the Regia Marina.

1933

In June 1933 the *Pola* became part of the 2nd Division, with the *Gorizia* (flagship) and the *Fiume*, and the *Zara* became flagship of the II Squadra.

The *Fiume* entering 'Mar Piccolo' at Taranto through the 'Canale Navigabile' in 1934. (Foto Priore, Taranto)

The cruisers *Trento* and *Trieste* moored at 'Calata Zingari' in the port of Genoa; the liner *Conte Grande* is at left. (G. Parodi collection)

Pola and *Zara* moored off Venice's 'Bacino di San Marco' in summer 1933. (Foto Baschetti, Venice)

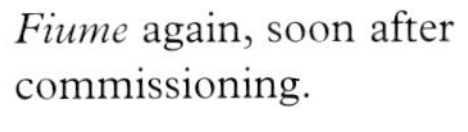

Fiume again, soon after commissioning.

August. During a cruise in the western Mediterranean, the *Trieste* and 2nd Division (*Gorizia*, *Zara* and *Fiume*) with the 7th and 8th Destroyer Squadriglia (*Freccia* and *Folgore* classes) made a stopover at Villefranche (Southern France). It was one of the rare occasions in which major Italian ships entered a French port between the two wars.

19 August. The *Bolzano* was delivered to the Regia Marina not yet completely fitted out and, together with the *Trento* (flagship) and the *Trieste* that became part of the 1st Division of the I Squadra; the *Gorizia* (flagship), the *Fiume* and the *Pola* made up the 2nd Division; the *Zara*, flagship of the I Squadra, was attached to the 1st Division.

2 December. The I Squadra was reorganised: the three *Trento*s went to form the 2nd Division and the *Zara*s the 1st, with the name-ships as flagship.

1934

23-30 June. On 8 June in Durazzo (Albania), by order of King Zog of Albania, nominally for budgetary reasons, almost all Italian instructors of the Army and Navy were removed from service in the Albanian National Defence forces and expelled from the fortifications; in addition, four Mas boats were seized. On 23 June, the I Squadra sailed from Taranto and without warning arrived at Durazzo. Although the visit was declared friendly, it generated extreme apprehension among Albanian authorities. After Tirana's assurances of willingness to negotiate to resolve any issue with Rome, in the afternoon of 25 June the I Squadra left Durazzo and proceeded on a cruise in the Adriatic, except for the *Fiume* and a Squadriglia of destroyers which remained there until the 30th, as a means of pressure, until the *status quo ante* was restored.

July. The 2nd Division with the three *Trento*s changed its ordinal number to 3rd and remained so until its end in April 1943.

Cruiser *Bolzano* in 1938. (USMM, courtesy F. Fontana)

1935

On 4 and 6 January in the Gulf of La Spezia, aboard the *Fiume* (on which a wooden flight deck had been fitted), an autogyro model 'La Cierva' C.30A, the ancestor of the helicopter, carried out take-off and landing tests, with the ship stationary and in motion. The results were promising and the Navy, keen to continue the experiments, ordered two more gyroplanes. These, however, were not followed up, also due to the intervention of the Regia Aeronautica, which claimed a monopoly on the possession and use of all types of aircraft.

From the summer there was escalating tension between London and Rome over the Ethiopian affair which took the form, for dissuasive purposes, of the strengthening of the Mediterranean Fleet and British positions in the Mediterranean, military collaboration agreements with coastal countries and the application of economic sanctions against Italy (November 1935) by the League of Nations. The Regia Marina General Staff studied and prepared plans for a possible conflict with the United Kingdom. These plans, among other things, provided for the reunification of the 1st and 2nd Squadron in the Forze Navali Riunite (FNR) under a unified Headquarters aboard *Pola*, which, pending formal appointment, already began to operate by standardising the engagement rules of the FNR. In the absence of battleships – the two *Cavour*s were undergoing reconstruction and the fighting value of the two *Duilio*s was almost zero – the seven heavy cruisers constituted the backbone of the fleet, composed of modern surface ships and a large underwater force.

22 November. In spite of the renewed tension with Athens because of its adhesion to the Geneva sanctions against Italy, the *Trento* was designated to serve as an honorary escort from Brindisi to the Ionian Sea, for the Greek vessel returning King George II of Greece from exile in London after the restoration of the monarchy.

1936

January. In the event of a conflict with the United Kingdom, the General Staff of the Regia Marina planned to open hostilities on the morning of the first day with a 'surprise' bombardment of the British ships at Alexandria. The heavy cruisers of the I Squadra and, first and foremost, the three *Trento*s would be assigned to

The swing-bridge at Taranto opens to allow *Gorizia* to enter the 'Mar Piccolo' in 1935. (Foto Priore, Taranto)

this operation due to their high speed. From an operational standpoint, the greatest problem was represented by the approach, to be carried out in peacetime without alerting the enemy. Three possibilities were considered: the first, sailing south of Crete, to make it seem as if it were proceeding towards Cyprus or Haifa; the second, skirting the coast of Marmarica (Libya) to make it seem as if it were transferring to Tobruk, in view to further operations; the third, passing through the Aegean and the Scarpanto (Karpathos) channel, to aim for Alexandria. The last was preferred, as it was more suitable for concealing the real objectives of the mission. The favourable and rapid progress of the war in Ethiopia and the intention of London and Rome not to extend the African conflict, extinguished the threat of conflict and in July 1936 led to the lifting of sanctions, the withdrawal of the Home Fleet's ships from the Mediterranean and the end of the anti-Italian Mediterranean agreements. The reorganisation of the FNR, which remained divided into two Squadre, was also implemented: the 1st squadron was stationed in Taranto and the 2nd squadron in La Spezia.

July. From the beginning of the Spanish Civil War the Italian Navy was employed – as it was until the end of the conflict in March 1939 – to support the Nationalists indirectly and directly and, until 18 November 1936, to rescue Italian citizens and other nationalities along the coasts in Republican hands. On 22 July, Adm. Div. Iledebrando Goiran on the *Fiume* left Taranto for Barcelona, where from the 24th he assumed command of Italian naval ships in Spanish waters. The *Fiume* remained there until 15 August along with other Italian and foreign warships; on the same date Goiran transferred to the light cruiser *Alberto di Giussano*. From Barcelona the *Fiume* moved to Alicante, remaining there until 19 August to protect the re-embarkation of Italian diplomatic personnel. Finally, *Fiume* moved to Palma de Majorca, where the Regia Marina, especially in the person of Carlo Margottini, commanding officer of the scout *Lanzerotto Malocello*, contributed to the reorganisation of the Nationalist forces that would lead to the failure of the Republican landing in Majorca and the conquest of all the Balearic Islands except Menorca. The *Fiume* returned in Italy at the end of August.

July-August. On 25 July, the *Gorizia* with Admiral Riccardo Paladini, Commander of the 1st Division, sailed from Taranto to

The *Bolzano* moored in Venice in June 1934. The seaplane on the catapult is a Piaggio P.6; later the CANT.25 AR was used, but the Ro.43 became the 'standard' aircraft on Italian ships during the war, and was in fact embarked from 1937 onwards. Some twin 100/47s and secondary fire directors still have to be fitted. (Courtesy Museo Storico Navale, Venezia)

The *Bolzano* at La Spezia on 10 May 1938. (A. Fraccaroli collection)

Kiel to attend the regattas of the Berlin Olympics (8–20 August 1936). On 31st July, *Gorizia* stopped off in Gijon to protect Italian residents while clashes were underway between Nationalists, supported by the light cruiser *Almirante Cervera*, and anarcho-communist ships. This was the *Gorizia*'s only participation in the events of the Spanish civil war. After a visit from 1 to 4 August to Le Verdon (mouth of the Gironde), which was well received by the French authorities and population, the *Gorizia* reached Kiel on 8 August through the canal of the same name, where she remained until 19 August. Here Paladini received a visit from Admiral Erich Raeder, Commander in Chief of the Kriegsmarine, and was received by the Führer and Reich Chancellor Adolf Hitler aboard the sloop *Grille*. During the return voyage to Italy, *Gorizia* suffered an unfortunate accident on the evening of 24 August at Tangier. An explosion of petrol vapours from the seaplane fuel stowage blew two symmetrical gashes, each 25 square meters long, on both sides of the bow. There were no casualties, nor was buoyancy compromised, but the opening of the exterior plating prevented normal navigation, due to the risk of extending the hull tears. Since it was not possible to carry out even brief repairs in Tangier, agreements were made with the British authorities, who authorised the *Gorizia* to go to Gibraltar to be drydocked and undergo a temporary repair. She arrived there on 25 August, down by the stern, towed by a British tug and escorted by the scout *Luca Tarigo*.

The drydocking from 26 August to 9 September allowed the British to measure the volume of the hull and ascertain that the actual standard displacement of these cruisers was more than 1000 tons above the limits set by the Washington Treaty. There were no consequences because of the British desire not to exacerbate the tension with Rome after the Mediterranean crisis and to encourage Italy's accession to the Second London Naval Treaty of 1936. The *Gorizia* returned to La Spezia on 1 September – in the meantime, Paladini had already returned home – for the final repairs, which were completed the following November. The investigation, carried out on 3 October, found that the causes were an exceptional leakage of vapours that affected some adjacent areas, an explosion caused by an electrical fault when shutting down a log reel, and some carelessness on the part of the personnel in charge.

On 3 September, the *Pola* left Gaeta for Barcelona, where the situation was still confused. Arriving there on the 5th, she stayed until the 11th, when she went to Palma de Majorca, where she remained until 3 October and returned to Italy on the 4th.

27 November. The 1st and 3rd Divisions (flagships *Trento* and *Bolzano*) took part in the naval review in the Gulf of Naples in honour of the Regent of Hungary, Nicholas Horthy, a guest on *Zara*, in the presence of the King, the Crown Prince, Mussolini and some of the highest political and military personalities of the two countries. A total of 105 ships and submarines took part.

December. Due to Moscow's massive aid to Republican Spain and the influx of large combatant forces of overseas volunteers (the International Brigades), Mussolini decided, unilaterally, to provide Franco with a large expeditionary force in an attempt to force a rapid conclusion to the conflict. The sea transportation to Spain of the Volunteer Troops Corps (63 ship sorties for 46,200 men and 35,000 tons of materials) was organised between 17 December to 22 February 1937 (the day before the Non-Intervention Pact came into force). Its distant protection was entrusted to revolving patrols by ships of the II Squadra, while the I Squadra with the '10,000s' was held in readiness in the ports of Sicily and the Tyrrhenian and Ligurian seas.

1937

7 June. The II Squadra took part in the naval review in honour of the Reich Minister of War, Field Marshal Werner von Blomberg, who was visiting Italy, with Mussolini attending, aboard the light cruiser *Duca d'Aosta* between Gaeta and Naples. There were 131 ships in all, including 74 submarines. At the end of the visit, von Blomberg expressed rather negative judgements on the Army's readiness, armament and training, and more flattering opinions on the Air Force and Navy.

8-12 June. In the afternoon of the 8th, the *Bolzano* with the VII Destroyer Squadriglia left Naples for Palma de Mallorca, to transfer the bodies of six men from the auxiliary cruiser *Barletta*, victim of a Soviet air attack. The *Bolzano* arrived in Palma on the morning of the 10th and, after embarking the coffins, left at noon for Naples with the VII Destroyer Squadriglia where it arrived at 06.00 on the 12th. The bodies disembarked at 08.00 and were followed by a solemn funeral ceremony with great public participation. It was the only mission of the *Bolzano* in Spanish waters during the civil war.

16 August. The 3rd Division (*Trento* and *Bolzano*) participated in the combined exercises of opposing parties in western Sicily, with Mussolini present, aboard the *Pola*. These were the first landing exercises with direct collaboration between the three service arms. The outcome was not considered satisfactory. In particular, the Army criticised the Navy for lack of operational preparation, means and men.

1938

2 May 1938. The 3rd Division became part of the II Squadra.

5 May 1938. The 1st and 3rd Divisions took part, with almost the entire surface and underwater naval forces, in the naval review in the Gulf of Naples in honour of Adolf Hitler, from which its name 'H' was derived. The H review was characterised by the execution of exercises depicting brief tactical and firing actions,

Zara steaming at slow speed around 1935–1936.

in addition to the traditional parades of formations with crews manning the rails of most ships, and by the participation of a large mass of submarines in motion, either on the surface or underwater. The phases were planned in such a way as to follow each other in a varied and uninterrupted manner, featuring elaborate and showy manoeuvres, such as the spectacular diving and surfacing of a formation of 81 submarines at the same time. Numerous passenger ships were provided to ensure the maximum participation of Italian and German political, military and civil representatives, media and the general public (12,000 guests, including tourists, in addition to the representatives). On this occasion the *Fiume* and the *Zara*, separated from the 1st Division, carried out firing against the radio-controlled target ship *San Marco* at a distance of 15,000m, with aerial observation by two catapulted Imam Ro.43s, and against a simulated aerial target; the section then rejoined the rest of the division. (For details of the review, see *Italian Battleships: Conte di Cavour & Duilio Classes*, pages 109-112).

13-31 May. The I and II Squadrons and the I and II Submarine Groups took part in exercises in the Tyrrhenian and Ligurian seas in the presence of Mussolini, who was aboard the *Cavour* (13–14 May), and in the subsequent visit to Genoa. In addition to the usual numerous ceremonies, exchanges of visits and courtesies with local authorities and personalities, the number of visitors to the fleet was estimated at 650,000, 220,000 of whom came from the rest of Liguria, Piedmont and Lombardy by 110 special trains, in addition to ordinary trains and road transport. The ships were visited by the general public in the afternoon of each day and in the morning also on some days. Each visitor was guaranteed a visit to a ship, a submarine and a tour of the port on board a tugboat. The warships left Genoa between the afternoon of the 30th and the morning of the 31st. (For details see *Italian Battleships: Conte di Cavour & Duilio Classes*, pages 112–114).

13-20 November. On 2 October, Mussolini, in agreement with Franco, ordered the repatriation from Spain of those legionnaires who had taken part in the civil war for 18 consecutive months, in accordance with the agreement of 5 July 1938 reached in the Non-Intervention Committee and in order to implement the Easter agreements with London. A total of 382 officers and 9769 non-commissioned officers and military personnel were concentrated in Cadiz, to board the steamers *Sardegna*, *Liguria*, *Calabria* and *Piemonte*, which would take them to Naples. The *Trieste*, flying the flag of Admiral Wladimiro Pini, Commander in Chief of the II Squadra, the X Destroyer Squadriglia (*Maestrale*, *Camicia Nera*, *Grecale*, *Scirocco*) and the XIV Destroyer Squadriglia (*Ugolino Vivaldi*, *Antonio da Noli* from Cagliari and *Antoniotto Usodimare* and *Luca Tarigo* from Palma di Maiorca) were assigned to the escort. The *Trento* and destroyer *Lanzerotto Malocello* were also supposed to take part in the mission, but both had to transfer some of their personnel to the remaining ships, to make up for those who were on leave or furlough. The *Trieste* and the X Squadriglia set sail from Messina on the evening of the 13th, following the routes less frequented by merchant traffic. On the 15th, the *Trieste* and the XIV Squadriglia arrived separately at

Stern view of *Zara* during an exercise in the mid-1930s.

Cadiz, where personnel embarkation on the four steamers had already begun on the 14th, while the X Squadriglia was sent to refuel at Ceuta. The convoy and escort left Cadiz on the evening of the 15th. During the night of the 16th the 10th Squadriglia joined them from Ceuta. The convoy and escort proceeded at an average speed of 10 knots, with weapons at the ready. On the afternoons of the 17th, over the meridian of Menorca, and the 19th, to the east of Sardinia, the Elmas Air Force Wing carried out two aerial reconnaissance missions over the sea areas that the convoy would cross. To the south of Sardinia, the XIV Squadriglia was detached to Cagliari and in the Tyrrhenian Sea the convoy met, as agreed, the nationalist cruiser *Navarra*. Since there was no risk of surprise attacks, in the afternoons of the 18th and 19th, evolutions, simulated torpedo attacks and aircraft launches were carried out for propaganda purposes, in which a seaplane from the *Trento* also took part. On the morning of the 20th, the convoy reached Naples, where, after the landing of the legionnaires, the welcoming ceremonies took place with a review before the King and the Crown Prince, while the *Trieste* headed for Gaeta to rejoin the *Trento*. It was the first explicit recognition by the King of the Italian intervention in the Spanish war. The mission revealed difficulties in keeping the steamships in formation and in the operation of their communications service, so much so that the warships had to make up for the lack of equipment and personnel training.

22 November 1938. Upon returning from an exercise (ET3) in the Ionian Sea, the *Pola* collided with the destroyer *Lampo*. The cruiser was the second in line of a formation with *Fiume* (flagship of the division) at the head and battleship *Giulio Cesare* at the rear. On the port bow, at a distance of 2000m from the *Fiume*, was the 8th Destroyer Squadriglia (*Lampo*, *Fulmine*, *Baleno*) and, on the starboard side, the 9th Destroyer Squadriglia (*Vittorio Alfieri*, *Giosuè Carducci*, *Saetta*). The formation proceeded at 21 knots in a 6-7 knot wind and a rough sea, which required the destroyers to make frequent turns in order to cope with the conditions. Shortly before 14:30 on the *Lampo*, due to a sudden failure of the steering gear, the rudder jammed at a 15° angle to starboard. Her commander, Francesco Ruta, after an initial, unsuccessful attempt to steady the course with engines and after having reported the failure, ordered to proceed at maximum speed in order to pass the bow of the *Fiume*; however, after having avoided the lead ship, he was still unable to steer with engines and the destroyer continued to pull to starboard at a high speed, hitting the oncoming *Pola* on the bow. Although the *Pola* was reducing from full speed and started to turn to port, imitated by the *Cesare*, the impact, which occurred at a 70° angle, was extremely violent. The *Lampo*, pivoting on the bow of the cruiser, broke in two at the level of the forward 120/50 gun; the bow sank rapidly, while the rest of the hull scraped along the side of the cruiser, still afloat; 4 people were killed. The *Pola* had her bow damaged and twisted to the left, but the watertight bulkheads held up well with limited leakage. More than three minutes passed from the moment of the rudder failure to the impact. The *Lampo*'s remaining hull, from frame 46 (forward of boiler room No 1), was salvaged and towed to Taranto after more than a day of hard work, initially assisted by the *Cesare* and the *Fiume*; the *Pola* reached the base under her own power the same day without difficulty. The enquiry, which was soon opened, relieved Ruta of all blame and attributed the greatest responsibility to the command of the 1st Division on the *Fiume*, since the latter had kept the course unchanged, instead of turning to port and signalling the manoeuvre to the other ships. Post-war studies raise, instead, doubts about the conduct of the *Lampo*'s commander, at least because he should have tried to stop the ship before or after passing the *Fiume* – having sufficient time and space – instead of trying to maintain course, manoeuvring with the engines. The *Pola* was again in service at the end of January 1939, and the *Lampo*, whose bow was rebuilt, at the end of the following May.

1939

Early March. At the end of the Spanish Civil War, the 1st and 5th Divisions (flagships *Conte di Cavour* and *Giulio Cesare*) of the I Squadron formed the 'Interception Force' which, together with the 'Scouting Force', were designated to interdict any attempt by the Republican fleet, which had left Cartagena on 5 March with 500 civilians on board, to reach the Soviet Union, from where it would be difficult for the new Spanish government to bring them back. The I Squadron was to intercept it and force it to divert to Augusta, without the use of force, except in the case of refusal or resistance. On the morning of the 7th the two divisions set sail from Taranto, the 5th with the sole purpose of moving to Messina. In the meantime, for most of the morning of the 6th, there were no sightings of the 'red fleet' until it was discovered by aircraft from the Balearics off Algiers and followed for the rest of the 6th until Bizerte, where it took refuge and was interned. No contact was, however, established at sea, but Rome was aware of its movements through the Italian Naval Mission in Spain. On 7 March, having learned of the internment in Bizerte, it was ordered to end of the emergency. (For a more detailed description of the events see *Italian Battleships: Conte di Cavour & Duilio Classes*, pages 117–118). It has only to be added that France restored the interned ships to the new Spanish government on 6 April, the day they returned to Cadiz.

5–7 April. During the landings and occupation of Albania (Oltre Mare Tirana Operation, OMT), the *Pola* and the *Zara* with the VIII Torpedo Boat Squadriglia were engaged in covering duties, in Durazzo and Vlora respectively, of the evacuation of diplomatic personnel and their dependents. In Durazzo, the evacuation was carried out by tanker *Tirso* and by torpedo boat *Lupo*, in Vlora by the tanker *Garigliano*. Once these had been disembarked in their homeland between the 6th and the 7th, these ships went back to Italy, except for the *Lupo* and the *Libra* which returned off Durazzo. (For general background and details of the OMT operations, see *Italian Battleships: Conte di Cavour & Duilio Classes*).

7-9 April. (Oltre Mare Tirana Operation, OMT). The expeditionary corps was structured in three groups for a total of 22,000 men: the first constituted the landing force, while the others were to fan out and garrison the penetration zones and continue towards the interior. The Regia Marina contributed with an impressive deployment of forces (I Squadra, Command School Division and smaller ships) to protect the transportation of the expeditionary force, as well as occupying the landing places, using the San Marco battalion and its own detachments, and initially covering the advance of the Army columns towards the interior. The Regia Aeronautica intervened with an air force (Albania Squadron) of 384 transport, bombing and fighter aircraft.

On 4 April, the steamers began to arrive in the designated ports (Bari, Brindisi and Taranto) and men and material embarked as they arrived. On the 6th, after some uncertainty, the order to execute OMT was made at 12:46. For the 2nd Group – the most important, since the Army units (column 'Messe'), having taken Durazzo, had to march to Tirana – the convoy left Brindisi in the late afternoon, while the 1st Division did so only during the night, due to its higher speed. The Division was preceded by the *Lupo* and *Libra*. At first light on the 7th, the landing companies of the cruisers and destroyers and the Army divisions embarked on them came ashore, entrusted with the task of occupying the important points of the city. They encountered some resistance with losses even among the *Fiume*'s personnel. The defence was soon overcome, also thanks to destroyers and torpedo boat gunfire, and at 09:30 Durazzo was fully occupied. The subsequent advance on Tirana, which saw the bulk of the 'Messe' column engaged, proceeded slowly due to some organisational and logistical errors in the planning. After brief reconnaissance cruises, the 1st Division returned to Taranto in the early afternoon of the 9th along with the 5th from Vlora. The OMT ended on 10 April with the occupation of all of Albania.

11 May. The 3rd Division took part, along with the II Squadra, the torpedo boat ships of the Command School, the 4th, 8th, 9th and 10th Mas Squadriglie, the 2nd Submarine Group, other ships and smaller vessels from Naples in the review, named 'J' in honour of the Prince Regent of Yugoslavia Paolo Karagjorgjevic, who was aboard the *Trieste*, flagship of the II Squadra. The review took place in the Gulf of Naples and, although on a smaller scale, with 106 ships taking part, it followed the pattern of the 'H' review, with exercises depicting short tactical and manoeuvring

Calisthenics for *Fiume*'s crew at Naples in 1939.

actions, in addition to the traditional sail-pasts in single and double columns. *Trento* and *Bolzano* fired against the *San Marco* radio-controlled target ship and anti-aircraft fire was directed against a simulated aerial target.

June 1939. At the beginning of the month, with the civil war in Spain having just ended, the General Staff of the Navy planned a training cruise of the I Squadra in the western Mediterranean and eastern Atlantic with port calls in Spain and Portugal as well as Tangier, a territory subject to a special international regime. The *Conte di Cavour*, the 1st and 8th Divisions and four submarines took part. On 19 June, the *Cavour*, flagship of Admiral Arturo Riccardi, Commander in Chief of the I Squadra, sailed from Naples with the 10th Destroyer Squadriglia (*Maestrale*, *Grecale*, *Libeccio*, *Scirocco*), the 1st Division (*Fiume*, *Zara*, *Pola*, *Gorizia*) with the 9th Destroyer Squadriglia (*Vittorio Alfieri*, *Giosuè Carducci*, *Vincenzo Gioberti* and *Alfredo Oriani*) and the 8th Division (light cruisers *Duca degli Abruzzi* and *Giuseppe Garibaldi*) with the 7th Destroyer Squadriglia (*Freccia*, *Saetta* and *Strale*). Separately, two sections of submarines also sailed from Naples and La Spezia: *Atropo* and *Guglielmotti*, *Mocenigo* and *Giuseppe Finzi*. The squadron called at Palma de Mallorca (21–24 June), Lisbon (27 June–1 July) and Tangier (2–7 July 1939), and returned to Taranto on 9 July, except for the 8th Division which proceeded independently, stopping in Valencia (25–28 June), Barcelona (29 June–3 July) and Mahon on the island of Menorca (4–6 July). (For details of this cruise, which was the only one to see the participation of a 'modern' battleship across the Straits, see *Italian Battleships: Conte di Cavour' & 'Duilio Classes*, pp. 120-121.

13 December. In the late afternoon, during a mooring manoeuvre in the Mar Grande at Taranto, the *Pola* struck the chain of a small buoy of an underwater obstruction while the engines were stopped, causing some abrasions to the starboard propeller which did not affect its efficiency. The few repairs were carried out at the end of January 1940 when she was already scheduled for docking.

Chapter 7

WARTIME CAREERS
(June 1940 – May 1945)

Details of the activities of the Regia Marina's most important warships during the Second World War have already been comprehensively and thoroughly covered in two previous Seaforth volumes:

- E Bagnasco, A de Toro, *The Littorio Class – Italy's Last and Largest Battleships*, 2011 (hereinafter abbreviated to *Littorio Class*);
- E Bagnasco, A de Toro, *Italian Battleships: Conte di Cavour and Duilio Classes 1911–1956*, 2021 (hereinafter abbreviated to *Italian Battleships*).

These two books also cover the fleet activity of Italian heavy cruisers from 1940 to 1943 when operating with the battleships. Consequently, this chapter only discusses specific events or naval battles where the Regia Marina's heavy cruisers were the main protagonists, as well as the circumstances of their loss. For all other events, readers are referred to the above books for further details.

At Italy's entry into the war (10 June 1940), all heavy cruisers were united in the 1st and 3rd Divisions of the II Squadra, with the *Pola* flagship of the Commander in Chief, as reported in Appendix I. All ships were operational, except the *Trieste*, which was at La Spezia for a refit, which prevented her from participating in the first operations of the war, including the battle of Punta Stilo.

The Battle of Punta Stilo (6–15 July 1940) – see *Italian Battleships*

The first clash between the Regia Marina and the British Mediterranean Fleet involved six of the Italian heavy cruisers (*Trieste* was refitting). In a very long range exchange of fire, *Warspite* hit *Cesare* with a 15in (381mm) shell and the Italian fleet withdrew. During the shooting, *Bolzano* was hit by three 6in (152mm) AP shells from *Neptune* or *Orion* (for details of damage see Appendix A).

By 9pm on the 9th, the *Cesare* and 3rd Division had entered Messina, while the 7th Division continued across the Straits to Palermo and the bulk of the force went on to Augusta. As early as the 7th, thanks to a partial decryption of a cipher, Supermarina had indications of a planned air raid on the base. Later, on the 10th, Navy cryptographers in Rome decrypted a 9:24am Cunningham transmission about upcoming movements that clearly suggested an evening attack against the Ionian bases. Acting on the decryption of the 7th, by the evening of the 9th, Supermarina had alerted the naval bases and ordered Paladini to leave Augusta, where he had just arrived, and move to Naples with the *Pola*, *Cavour*, and the 1st Division, which he did during the night of the 10th after a quick refuelling. On the morning of the 10th, it was the turn of the 9th and 11th Destroyer Squadriglia while the 8th and 4th Divisions continued late in the afternoon towards Taranto. The 7th Division, which had already entered the Tyrrhenian Sea, was also diverted to Naples due to fears arising from the presence of Force H in the western Mediterranean. The *Cesare*, on the other hand, like the 3rd

Punta Stilo, 9 July 1940: two well known images of *Zara* class cruisers in action during the battle. *Top*: *Zara*, *Gorizia* and *Fiume* during the deployment phase of the combat; *bottom*: the *Fiume* firing astern.

Amidship view of *Pola* in 1939; the two after 100/47 gun mounts have been removed pending their replacement with four twin Breda 37/54 machine guns.

Punta Stilo, 9 July 1940: *Pola* under bombardment by aircraft of the Regia Aeronautica that attacked the Italian units at the end of the battle – mistaking them for British – but, fortunately, without hitting them.

Division, remained in Messina to disembark the wounded and fallen and to tidy up the ship.

The air raid on Taranto

Regarding the British operation MB.8 (6–14 November 1940) and the air raid on Taranto (Operation 'Judgment', 11–12 November 1940), see *Littorio Class*, pp170–173 and *Italian Battleships*, pp157–162. Here we simply note that all seven heavy cruisers were present at the base: the 1st Division (*Zara*, *Gorizia* and *Fiume*) in the Mar Grande along with six battleships; the *Pola* and the 3rd Division (*Trieste*, *Trento* and *Bolzano*) in the Mar Piccolo: the *Trieste* and the *Bolzano* moored at the buoys, the *Pola* and the *Trento* at the Torpediniere dock. During the second wave of 7 plus 2 Swordfish (the latter took off late from the aircraft carrier *Illustrious*), that reached the target shortly before midnight

9 July 1940: a well-known image of the *Zara* during the Punta Stilo battle, with the 203/53 guns at maximum elevation.

Punta Stilo, 9 July 1940. The *Bolzano* along with *Pola* (in background) and the heavy cruisers of the 1st Division; on the *Bolzano* the torpedo tubes are ready for use. Note that the height of the after mast has been reduced. (E. Bagnasco collection)

Punta Stilo, 9 July 1940: from left, *Fiume*, *Gorizia*, *Zara* and *Pola* (emitting smoke) are about to turn to port astern of the *Trento* (from where the photo was taken).

on the 11th, the delayed bomber attacked the ships in the Mar Piccolo at 00:30 on the 12th, succeeding in hitting *Trento* with a 250lb (113.5kg) SAP (semi-armour-piercing) bomb, which was slightly damaged (for details see Appendix A). The *Gorizia*, on the other hand, was probably responsible for the shooting down of one of the two Swordfish lost during the first wave, which arrived over Taranto around 23:00.

An immediate consequence of the Taranto air attack was the cancellation of the naval bombardments of Suda and Zakynthos, planned on 10 November by Supermarina, in which the heavy cruisers would have played an important part.

Transfer from Taranto to Naples and bombing of Naples, December 1940 – see *Littorio Class* and *Italian Battleships*

Counters to Operation 'White' (16–18 November 1940) – see *Littorio Class* and *Italian Battleships*

One of the balloons, towed by small units for local use, which should have contributed to the anti-aircraft defence of the Taranto naval base in the autumn of 1940, shortly before the attack carried out by the aircraft of the Mediterranean Fleet on the night of 11 November. In the background, the cruiser *Fiume* may be seen.

Counters to Operation 'Collar' and the Battle of Cape Teulada (26–28 November 1940)

The necessity to supply Greece and Malta induced the British to dispatch a fast convoy from Great Britain (MT) through the Mediterranean with two merchant ships for Malta and one for Alexandria and, at the same time, a convoy of four merchantmen from Alexandria to Malta (MW.4) and a convoy of five from Malta to Alexandria (ME.4).

The first news of the two operations reached Rome on the morning of 25 November: to the west, from observers around Gibraltar; to the east, from a civilian airliner that sighted heavy enemy forces, including an aircraft carrier and a battleship, 150 miles southeast of Malta. In the absence of more precise information, and given the presence of aircraft carriers, Supermarina assumed that there were to be enemy attacks on Italian bases. Therefore, he put the coastal defences on alert and ordered the departure of the 10th Squadriglia from Trapani to watch the waters off Cape Bon, an ambush of 9 Mas boats in the Sicilian channel, a deployment of 4 submarines south of Sardinia and one of 3 near Malta, as well as the preparation of I and II Squadra in Naples and Messina. Since it was not possible, given the dispersion of the Italian fleet and the presumed superiority of the British Mediterranean Fleet to the east, it was decided to concentrate on Force H to the west. In the mid-morning of the 26th, Supermarina issued operational orders to the two squadrons, establishing that they would be located south of Sardinia in the morning of the 27th, but that they would commit themselves to battle only if the situation was favourable. The I Squadra and the 1st Division left Naples around 12 noon on the 26th and at 17:40 reunited in the southeastern Tyrrhenian Sea with the 3rd Division which left Messina at the same time. The Italian naval forces were composed as follows:

- I Squadra: *Vittorio Veneto* (flagship of the Commander in Chief of the I Squadra and senior commander at sea, Adm. Campioni), *Cesare*; XIII Destroyer Squadriglia (*Granatiere*, *Fuciliere*, *Bersagliere*, *Alpino*); VII Destroyer Squadriglia (*Freccia*, *Saetta* and *Dardo*).
- II Squadra: *Pola* (Flagship of the Commander in Chief of the II Squadra, Adm. Iachino); 1st Division (*Fiume* and *Gorizia*), IX Destroyer Squadriglia (*Oriani*, *Carducci*, *Gioberti*); 3rd Division (*Trento*, Sansonetti's flagship, *Bolzano*, *Trieste*); XII Destroyer Squadriglia (*Lanciere*, *Carabiniere*, *Corazziere*, *Ascari*).

The first contact occurred during the night of the 27th. At 00:33, the torpedo boat *Sirio*, on patrol in the Sicilian channel, sighted near Cape Bon the ships of Force D (including the battleship *Ramillies*) proceeding northwest. At 00:55am, after a fruitless and unnoticed torpedo attack, *Sirio* sent the discovery signal, immediately received by Supermarina and *Vittorio Veneto*. At first light on the 27th, Campioni ordered a reconnaissance with the shipboard aircraft. The *Sirio*'s message was also intercepted by the British who thus knew they had been discovered. By mid-morning, the first reports from their respective scouts, uncertain as to the composition and routes of the enemy, reached both commands at sea. Campioni, who had reached the 8th meridian southwest of Sardinia, received the report from *Bolzano*'s aircraft; he learned that the enemy force included only one battleship and therefore considered engaging it. However, at 11:00, he ordered his ships to turn 70°, thus on a course away from the probable origin of the enemy; only at 11:28 did he turn 135°, orienting the normal deployment to the probable direction of the enemy's origin.

The Italian naval forces had just taken up the deployment ordered by Campioni on course 135°, when more precise information was received from an Air Force scout. He thus learned

This photograph documents the difficult weather conditions encountered by the *Gorizia* and other ships of the Regia Marina engaged in the unsuccessful attempt to counter the British Operation 'Hats' between late August and early September 1940. (E. Leproni archive)

Gorizia in the Ionian Sea on 1 September 1940 facing heavy weather.

Cape Teulada (Spartivento to the British), 27 November 1940. The *Bolzano* at high speed and making smoke to evade the large-calibre 15in (381mm) guns of the British battlecruiser *Renown*, two shells of which exploded near her stern. (USMM, Foto LUCE)

that he was facing two battleships and an aircraft carrier and that there was a convoy; he judged, therefore, that he found himself in an unfavourable situation, especially due to the presence of the aircraft carrier, and, in strict adherence to Supermarina's instructions, not to engage. At 12:07, he ordered the subordinate commands to fall back to the east and the II Squadron not to engage, to increase speed to 30 knots and to rejoin the battleships, some 24,000m away.

At the moment Campioni ordered the retreat, the British cruisers, followed by the *Renown*, which, due to engine trouble, could not reach 28 knots, sighted the Italians and Somerville learned from aerial reconnaissance their exact composition. The five British cruisers closed the distance by advancing on a line of bearing in the direction of the Italian ships and, at 12:20, opened fire at the limit of range of their 6in (152mm) guns. At 12:24 the *Renown* joined in at 23,800 yards; at 12:26 the *Ramillies*, unable to reach her nominal 21 knots, fired her only two salvoes to verify distance, which turned out to be remarkably short, after which she remained on the fringes of the fight. The Italian cruisers responded, between 12:21 and 12:22, at an average distance of 21,500 yards for the 3rd Division and 22,000 yards for the 1st Division, while, following Campioni's orders, they headed east and increased their speed. At this stage, British fire, including that of the *Renown*, was mostly directed at the nearest 3rd Division (first on the *Trento* and then the *Bolzano*), while initially the *Pola*, *Fiume* and *Bolzano* concentrated their fire on the *Berwick* and the *Gorizia* on one of the light cruisers. The situation worried Iachino, who ordered Sansonetti's 3rd Division to move at

The forward turrets of the *Bolzano* scarred by the impact of shrapnel from a 152mm projectile that exploded against the muzzle of one of the 203mm guns. (E. Bagnasco collection)

maximum speed northward with his stern to the enemy, while he and the 1st Division proceeded northeast to rejoin the battleships. The gradual withdrawal of the 3rd Division was covered by smoke screens and firing only with its after turrets until it ceased firing at 12:50 when the enemy was out of range at 28,000m. This induced the British to concentrate their fire on the 1st Division, which was unable to gain ground due to boiler problems in the *Fiume* which made it difficult to exceed 28 knots. The 1st Division thus ended up bearing the brunt of the fighting, engaged at this point by the *Renown*, which, however, could not get any closer, and by the five British cruisers.

The action between the cruisers continued, at varying intensity, in a north-east direction until 13:15 at distances between 22,500m and 17,000m, with the Italian ships firing in retreat and the British in pursuit. At 12:50 the 3rd Division ceased fire as the enemy was now out of range. The British fire was judged to be neither orderly nor effective (no salvoes reached the targets), but with well grouped salvoes; the Italian fire was successful, but with more dispersed salvoes. At about 13:00 Somerville sighted the two Italian battleships and prepared to engage them in formation with the *Ramillies*. However, the slow speed of *Ramillies*, the fact that the two Italian battleships were moving away to the north-east, while the 1st Division was already within its firing range, made it preferable to engage the latter with the *Renown* alone. *Renown*'s fire against the 1st Division was also ineffective, but worried Iachino, who was disappointed to see himself without the support of his own battleships. At 13:00 the *Vittorio Veneto* had come within firing range due to a difference in speed, and although retiring opened fire; in the space of 10 minutes, she fired seven salvoes with her 381mm (15in) after turret alone for a total of 19 rounds against the *Manchester*, at distances between 28,500m and 32,500m. The 5th and 7th salvoes were on target, but the cruiser was only hit by shrapnel. The *Cesare* did not even get within range (28,600m). At 13:12, Somerville broke off the action, disengaging towards the south-east, and 3 minutes later, the 1st Division also stopped firing, when the distance had increased to 26,000m. Somerville gave up the pursuit for a number of reasons: the worsening visibility due to smoke and fog; the difficulty of pursuing the faster Italian ships, not so far slowed by torpedo bombers, and his lack of confidence in the prospects for repeat air attacks due to the poor training of the pilots; the risks of attacks by the Italian Air Force and of ambushes by submarines as they approached the Sardinian coast; and above all, the need to give priority to the safety of the convoy continuing towards the Strait of Sicily. For Iachino, too, there would have been a chance to usefully continue the fight, assuming that he would face the *Renown* alone without the slower *Ramillies*.

The cruiser *Trento* in 1941 from the *Bolzano*. (E. Bagnasco collection)

Gunnery contact between major ships was concluded. In the initial phase, the *Berwick* was hit by two 203mm (8in) shells from the *Pola* or *Fiume*: the first (12:22) pierced the barbette of 'Y' turret, putting it out of action, killing 7 men and wounding 9; the second (12:35) penetrated and exploded in the officers' quarters without serious consequences, but destroying the electrical distribution board at the stern, which momentarily deprived the aft quarters, including 'X' turret, of power; the *Berwick* held her place in formation. It has recently been learned that the *Southampton* was also hit on the armour belt (76-127mm), obviously by a 203mm projectile, which did not explode, perhaps due to the small angle of impact.

The British operation went on and ended as planned and without losses despite the ambush force set up by Supermarina in the Strait of Sicily on the afternoon of the 27th (10th torpedo boat Squadriglia, 12 Mas, 2 of which had to return because of damage, and 2 submarines).

The Italian squadrons returned divided into three groups on

AMMUNITION EXPENDITURE AT CAPE TEULADA (SPARTIVENTO)

Ship / calibres (mm)	381	320	203	Grand total
Vittorio Veneto	19			
Cesare		/		
Pola			110	
Gorizia			123	
Fiume			210	
Trieste			96	
Bolzano			27*	
Trento			92	
Totals	19	/	658	677

Ship / calibres (mm)	381	203	152	Grand total
Ramillies	?**			
Renown	86			
Berwick		380		
Sheffield			718	
Newcastle			503	
Manchester			912	
Southampton			750	
Totals	86**	380	2883	3271

* The *Bolzano* fired only a few salvoes, as the aiming was disturbed by smoke from the *Trento*.

** The *Ramillies* fired two 381mm [15in] salvoes with an unknown number of rounds to ascertain the target range, which has not been taken into account here.

The *Trieste* at high speed in March 1941. (A. Fraccaroli collection)

independent routes: the I Squadra was in Naples shortly after 13:00 on the 28th; the 3rd Division, after escorting the *Lanciere* to Cagliari, rejoined the 1st Division on the morning of the 28th near Ponza and together they reached Naples in the early afternoon.

The gunnery phase took place in excellent visibility conditions, except for the disturbances caused by smoke and fog curtains, with calm seas and an ENE wind force 2. The number of rounds fired by the two sides is summarised in the table above.

Considering that only three 203mm shells reached the target, the percentage of hits scored by the Italian ships was 0.44% or 0.60% if the superficial damage caused by the 381mm exploded near the *Manchester* is also taken into account. The percentage of hits scored by the British was much lower (0.09%), but it must be said that the light cruisers almost always fired at distances close to their maximum range. For the rest, the performance of the main armament of the Italian cruisers was judged to be excellent; few failures were reported, which were immediately resolved, and only one shot was lost (on the *Bolzano*); on the other hand, there were problems due to the quality of some optical equipment and targeting systems. However, in contrast, the AA armament proved to be unsatisfactory due to the inadequacy of the 100/47 mountings and the aiming systems, especially for the machine guns, as well as personnel training. The machinery gave a good performance: the 3rd Division reached and maintained a speed of 34 knots while disengaging; the *Bolzano* complained of some damage to the centre engines due to the concussion of the shot and defects in the lubrication circuits. The *Fiume*, on the other hand, took part in the operation with its machinery in poor shape, as did the *Berwick* and the *Newcastle* on the opposing side. Major damage was done to the superstructures and some fire control and electronic equipment located on the bridge tower, due to blast damage from the forward turrets when firing abaft the beam during the retreat. The *Pola* was most affected. No damage was done to the main structures and the damage was quickly repaired after returning to base.

This action is known as the Battle of Cape Spartivento in British sources.

The naval bombardment of Genoa and the failure to counter Operation 'Grog' (8–11 February 1941) – see *Littorio Class* and *Italian Battleships*

Operation 'Gaudo' and the drama of Matapan (26–29 March 1941) – 1. The Gaudo clash

The genesis of this operation has been summarised in *Littorio Class*, pp170–171 and was the result of increasing pressure from the Kriegsmarine, beginning with the conference of 13–14 February in Merano between the leaders of the two navies, to intervene against the intensified British convoy traffic between North Africa and Greece in support of the Greek Army (Operation 'Lustre'). The idea, however, was also put forward independently by Iachino and, finally, shared by Supermarina. The idea was strengthened by the erroneous news of the torpedoing on 16 March of two of the three battleships of the Mediterranean Fleet by the X Fliegerkorps (news corrected on the 26th), inducing Supermarina to plan a double offensive sortie south of Crete and in the Aegean Sea, in which the *Vittorio Veneto*, the two heavy cruiser divisions and one light cruiser division would take part. The squadron would be divided into two groups:

- Group 1 (or *Vittorio Veneto* group), formed by the battleship and the 3rd Division, from the Strait of Messina would steam southeast towards the lower Ionian Sea and from here, at 20:00 on 27 March, it was to turn east under cover of darkness, to

The *Trento* in August 1941. It should be noted that the funnel caps (added the previous year) are now painted in light grey like the other vertical surfaces in order to make the ship's silhouette less conspicuous. A Ro.43 seaplane rests on the forecastle catapult, obstructing the firing arcs of the forward 203mm battery. (A. Fraccaroli collection)

reach a point 20 miles south of Gaudo at 07:00 on the 28th. From here it would turn back, so as to be 100 miles west of Cape Chios (southwestern extremity of Crete) at 12:00 on the 28th, from where it would then return to base.

- Group 2 (or *Zara* group), formed by the 1st and 8th Divisions, would rejoin Group 1 in the western Ionian Sea and from there would continue south-east towards the lower Ionian Sea. Under cover of darkness, at 20:00 on the 27th it would head ENE towards the Aegean Sea, passing between Cerigotto and Cape Spada until reaching a point close to that sea at 08:00 hrs on the 28th. From here it would return to the Ionian Sea, passing again between Cape Spada and Cerigotto, to reach at 13:00 on the 28th the point 90 miles west of Cerigotto, from where, not far from Group 1, it would return to base.

In daytime, the two groups would head south-east to confuse enemy observation and, in the dark, would head for their respective targets and attack shipping and any enemy forces, provided the odds were in their favour. Special importance was placed on the cryptographic service with the embarkation of dedicated personnel on the *Vittorio Veneto*, on aerial support (reconnaissance, escort and offensive) and inter-service cooperation through agreements with the X Fliegerkorps, Superaereo and the Higher Command of the Aegean Armed Forces (Egeomil). Plans were also made to send the submarines *Nereide*, *Dagabur*, *Ascianghi* and *Ambra* to the eastern Mediterranean and the *Galatea* to the Caso Strait, all already at sea. Unfortunately, these submarines, although well positioned along the approach routes, would not prove to be of any help, also due to the vagueness of the operational orders received, which did not specify the purpose of the exploration. The operation, which would later take the name 'Gaudo', was based on secrecy, effective air cooperation, given the distance from the bases, and on the assumption that the bulk of the Mediterranean Fleet, even if not crippled, was in port at Alexandria.

On 22 March, the *Vittorio Veneto* had left La Spezia for Naples, where it arrived on the morning of the 23rd, awaiting the start of the operation. This began in the evening of the 26th with the participation of the following naval forces:

from Naples
– *Vittorio Veneto* (flagship of C in C of SN, Adm. Iachino);
– X Destroyer Squadriglia (*Maestrale*, *Libeccio*, *Scirocco*, *Grecale*)
from Messina
– 3rd Division: *Trieste* (Adm. Sansonetti), *Trento*, *Bolzano*;
– XII Destroyer Squadriglia (*Corazziere*, *Carabiniere*, *Ascari*);
– XIII Destroyer Squadriglia (*Granatiere*, *Fuciliere*, *Bersagliere*, *Alpino*).
from Taranto
– 1st Division: *Zara* (Adm. Carlo Cattaneo), *Pola*, *Fiume*;
– IX Destroyer Squadriglia (*Alfieri*, *Oriani*, *Carducci*, *Gioberti*).
from Brindisi
– 8th Division: *Abruzzi* (Adm. Legnani), *Garibaldi*;
– XVI Destroyer Squadriglia (*da Recco*, *Pessagno*).

Vittorio Veneto sailed from Naples for the Strait of Messina at about 21:00 escorted by X Destroyer Squadriglia; having passed the Strait, she joined the 3rd Division, which left Messina at 05:30 on the 27th, keeping 15,000m astern. As escort to the battleship, XIII Destroyer Squadriglia replaced the X Squadriglia, which put in to Messina to refuel; although ordered to remain ready for sea, in fact it would take no further part in the operation. Finally, on the evening of the 26th, the 1st and 8th Divisions left their respective bases.

The preparations for Operation 'Gaudo' did not pass unnoticed by the British. On 25 and 26 March, the British cryptographic organisation at Bletchley Park – intelligence from this source was known as 'Ultra' – had decoded some messages transmitted from Rome to Egeomil using the Enigma cipher machine, in which Supermarina announced an operation in the Aegean for the 28th and gave instructions for air operations in the sector. From this information, which was not entirely comprehensive and, moreover, contradicted by other decryptions of the 25th, Cunningham came to the precise conclusion that the Italian Navy was preparing a sortie against Operation 'Lustre' convoys. On the afternoon of the 26th, even before the Italian ships had set sail, he issued a series of operational commands, ordering: the suspension of convoys in the Aegean Sea, an air alert over the entire eastern Mediterranean and reconnaissance over Taranto, Messina, Brindisi, and Naples, submarine patrols, the reinforcement of the Suda base with the AA cruiser *Carlisle*, the alerting of Greek naval forces and the exit from Piraeus of Force B, the 7th and 3rd Divisions (*Orion*, *Ajax*, *Perth*, *Gloucester* under Vice-Adm. Pridham-Wippell); 'Ultra' provided two more decrypted messages from Supermarina at Egeomil and a four-engined Short Sunderland sighted the 3rd Division at 12:25, but not the *Vittorio Veneto*. On the evening of the 27th, Force A (battleships *Warspite*, flagship, *Barham*, *Valiant* and four destroyers of the 14th Flotilla) left Alexandria in the utmost secrecy in order to rendezvous with Force B the next day 20 miles south of Gaudo; five destroyers of the 10th Flotilla (Force C) were sent ahead, again to rendezvous with Force B; three destroyers (Force D) were kept ready to move from Piraeus. Force A's departure had been preceded at 15.30 on the 27th by that of the aircraft carrier *Formidable* – which had arrived in Alexandria via Suez a few days before, replacing the damaged *Illustrious* – to receive some aircraft on board. Force A's progress was temporarily slowed to 20 knots by trouble with *Warspite*'s condensers, delaying the rendezvous with Force B. Finally, the RAF also made the necessary preparations to attack any Italian forces that came within range of its aircraft stationed in Greece. Thus, both the British and Italian fleets converged, almost without each other's knowledge, on the same point, on the same day and at the same time.

The navigation of the two Italian groups, reunited in the late morning of the 27th, proceeded without surprise until after noon, when the Sunderland sighted the 3rd Division, which was 12,000m ahead of the *Vittorio Veneto*. This fact alone was enough to destroy any element of surprise, but Supermarina did not interrupt the operation, assuming from W/T interceptions that the battleship had remained undetected, that there was a good chance of intercepting light forces south of Crete and that at 14:30 the bulk of the Mediterranean Fleet was still in Alexandria. However, at 21:00, instead it cancelled the risky thrust of Group 2 into the Aegean, both because in the meantime information had arrived on the absence of shipping in that sea, and because the Aegean Air Force could not provide cover to both groups, as well as to achieve a strong preponderance of forces south of Gaudo. If at that point in the evening of the 27th the Mediterranean Fleet had put to the sea – as effectively happened – the prevailing speed of the Italian ships would have always allowed them to disengage. In the early afternoon, in order to mislead enemy reconnaissance, which had not been interrupted by Axis fighters, Iachino had briefly headed toward the Libyan coast and anticipated the separation of Group 2 at 19:00, which from that moment set course for the Cerigotto channel. Half an hour later, at dusk, Iachino headed east with Group 1 toward the point 20 miles south of Gaudo. However, around 22:30, Group 2 received an order from Supermarina, intercepted by Iachino, to cancel the Aegean run and rejoin Group 1 at dawn on the 28th. In any case, Group 2

The *Trieste*, 3rd Division flagship, south of Gaudo in March 1941. (A. Fraccaroli collection)

ended up being significantly outnumbered and unable to take part in the following morning's battle.

In the late evening of the 27th, Supermarina detected the presence at sea of a battleship and an aircraft carrier from Alexandria and cruisers from Piraeus from radiotelegraphic (W/T) traffic and from sightings by X Fliegerkorps. At the same time Iachino, who after the war complained that he had not been informed by X Fliegerkorps about the torpedoing of two British battleships, was fully informed of the full efficiency of all three battleships of the Mediterranean Fleet. In fact, their efficiency had already been ascertained on 24 March – a fact which did not worry Supermarina as long as they remained in Alexandria – and Iachino must have been aware of this before leaving Naples. He was not, however, informed of the clear signs of the presence of battleships at sea. Unfortunately, in the afternoon of the 27th and, above all, in the morning of the 28th, there was no aerial reconnaissance that could have shed light on the situation in Alexandria.

At dawn on the 28th, the Italian squadron was south of Cape Crio heading southeast with the 3rd Division about 10,000m ahead of the *Vittorio Veneto* and Group 2 still 30,000m astern of the battleship. On the opposite side, Force B, coming from Piraeus, was south of Gaudo heading south-east, while Force A, joined during the night of the 28th by *Formidable*, was steaming 150 miles away to the north-west. In the early dawn of the 28th, both carried out aerial reconnaissance, thanks to which the Italians gained a clearer picture of the situation than the British: at 05:35, *Vittorio Veneto*'s Ro.43 sighted and recognised Force B's cruisers, while *Formidable*'s scouts sighted cruiser groups twice, at 07:20 and 07:39, in two different positions, leaving Cunningham and Pridham-Wippell in doubt as to whether or not they were friendly. None of the opposing battleships were discovered.

After the aerial sighting, Iachino ordered Sansonetti to head towards the enemy and increase speed to 30 knots. At 07:52 Force B, having sighted and recognised the Italian cruisers coming from the north but mistaken for the *Zara* class, turned away towards the southeast, increasing speed to 28 knots. In turn, Sansonetti, as soon as he sighted the enemy cruisers to the south (08:00), turned together in that direction, increasing his speed to 32 knots to shorten the distance, but soon resumed his course to the southeast, roughly parallel to that of the enemy, to keep them within the optimum arcs for his guns. On this course, at 08:12, the *Trieste* opened fire at a range of 22,000m, when she had the first fire control solution, immediately followed by the *Trento* and the *Bolzano*, but resulting in a range of 24,000–26,000m, outside the range of the British 152mm (6in) guns, but also at the limit of the Italian 203mm (8in). Due to the long distance and the gloomy atmosphere, the firing was conducted at a slow pace, with each salvo being observed to fall; initially, fire was concentrated on the *Gloucester*, at the tail of the British line, which, due to engine trouble, should not have exceeded 24 knots, but which actually managed to reach 30. The battle was initially conducted in a south-easterly direction. At 08:20, Force B turned decisively to the south, followed by the Italian cruisers, and at 08:29, when she was down to 23,500 yards, the *Gloucester* returned fire, but all salvoes fell short. At 08:31, Iachino, suspicious that the British were refusing to fight, ordered Sansonetti to fall back if he could not reduce the distance. With this in mind, at 08:36, the 3rd Division also turned south together, increasing its speed to 33 knots. The battle continued until 08:49, when the Italian cruisers ceased firing, with no hits and only one salvo on target, and turned back to the west. So did the *Vittorio Veneto* and the distant Group 2, as did Pridham-Wippell, whose force followed the 3rd Division at a distance.

By 09:00 the entire Italian squadron was on its way home, always tailed by Force B. It was at this point that Iachino thought he could take advantage of the fact that the enemy was unaware of the battleship's presence by preparing an ambush. It was a matter of reversing the *Vittorio Veneto*'s course to bypass it from the north; a little later, further south, the 3rd Division would do the same, so as to catch the enemy between two fires. At 10:35 the *Vittorio Veneto* turned to the east, increasing her speed to 28 knots; at 10:50 she sighted the enemy cruisers and at 10:56 headed south-southeast, in order to close the distance, imitated at 10:59 by the 3rd Division. Almost at the same time, the British also spotted the battleship, but Pridham-Wippell remained uncertain as to its identity, thinking it might be Force A that had overtaken him, and had the *Orion* make a visual recognition signal. In response, at 10:57 the *Vittorio Veneto* opened fire with all 381mm turrets on *Orion*, the leading ship, at an estimated range of 22,800m. With the battleship's identity revealed, Force B sped off to the south, increasing its speed to 30 knots, zigzagging and covering itself with smokescreens spread even by the destroyers of the 2nd Flotilla. The 3rd Division, on the other hand, was unable to get close enough to intervene. The *Vittorio Veneto*'s fire was quite accurate, even if the salvoes were rather scattered: the *Orion* was near-missed several times, but was only hit by shrapnel which caused negligible damage. After a short pause, due to the concealment of the targets, the firing switched to the *Gloucester*, the easternmost ship and the only one partially visible. She, too, was bracketed, but only hit by shrapnel with minor damage. At 11:22, when the estimated distance had increased to 26,000m, the *Vittorio Veneto* suspended firing due to the difficulty of observation because of the artificial smokescreens and smoke from the enemy cruisers and reversed course, heading west-northwest, at a time when a serious threat was looming from the sky. The 3rd Division performed a similar manoeuvre.

Thus ended the Gaudo battle. Iachino's manoeuvre was only partially successful: Force B found itself further north than Iachino had estimated and this brought forward the sighting; then

The cruiser HMS *Gloucester* steaming off Plymouth in spring 1939.

The *Leander* class light cruiser *Orion* in 1940.

opening fire at the recognition signal meant it had to take up the pursuit immediately, and therefore the 3rd Division's manoeuvre became pointless. Apart from the effect of smoke screens, both shooting phases were carried out in good visibility conditions, calm seas and an ENE wind force 2. The results of the firing can be summarised as follows:

Ship/calibre (mm)	Rounds fired	Rounds failing	Hits on target	Near misses (with little damage)
Vittorio Veneto, 381	94	11	/	2 (allegedly, *Orion* and *Gloucester*)
Trieste, 203/50	132	/	/	/
Trento, 203/50	214	/	/	/
Bolzano, 203/53	189	/	/	/
Total 203	535	/	/	
Grand total	629	11	/	/

The results were therefore disappointing. As for the 3rd Division, Iachino attributed this to the difficulties in targeting due to the uncertain light conditions at long distances, the age and type of the *Trieste* and *Trento*'s coincidence rangefinders, and the poor optical characteristics of the APGs, so that the silhouettes of the enemy ships appeared as shapeless blobs and the firing was initiated with data from the firing directors; on the other hand, there was no noteworthy damage to the artillery equipment. The *Vittorio Veneto*'s firing was accurate despite the considerable interference of the smoke screens and several of the 29 shots fired bracketed the targets (*Orion* and *Gloucester*), but their dispersion reduced the chances of direct hits. Iachino judged the performance of the equipment to be good, as there were no noteworthy failures: as on the cruisers, at the end of the battle all of *Vittorio Veneto*'s weapons were able to fire regularly. In truth, the number of failed rounds, 12% of the total, was excessive and above the average of those occurring during exercises, and one was fired off on the 29th during the return leg of the mission. It must be said, however, that, especially in the first phase of the battle, combat distances were always greater than those considered optimum for good shooting (19,000–21,000m for the 381s, 17,000–19,000m for the 203s), beyond which there was a greater longitudinal spread of the salvoes – at 'Gaudo', for the 381s, this was around 350-400m.

Operation 'Gaudo'. 2. The night of Matapan and the end of the 1st Division

While the 'Gaudo' engagement was underway, Cunningham had learned from Pridham Wippell of the sighting of three Italian cruisers (08:27) and, at 09:05 from one of *Formidable*'s aircraft, of the presence of a group of ships further north with three battleships: they were the *Zara*s and the battleships were the two *Abruzzi*, mistaken for the *Cesare* class. At the first of these reports he was 90 miles away heading west-northwest. He increased his speed from 20 to 22 knots, the maximum speed that the *Barham*, and at that time the *Warspite*, could achieve, and had the *Formidable* ready a squadron of Albacores with two Fairey Fulmar escorts for a torpedo attack. They took off at 09:38, still uncertain about the presence of an Italian battleship, but at 11:00, after being vainly attacked by two Junker Ju 88s of the X Fliegerkorps, they found the *Vittorio Veneto*, while Cunningham learned from Pridham-Wippell that he was engaged by a battleship (11:07). The Albacores attacked shortly before 11:30. Launches, executed in several waves from the forward sectors, from distances of approximately 2000m were easily avoided by the *Vittorio Veneto*, but assisted the disengagement of Force B. At 11:30, after manoeuvring to escape the torpedo attack, Iachino took a west-northwest course at a speed of 28 and then 25 knots.

This was the first air raid the Italian squadron was subjected to that day. In the afternoon, it was repeatedly attacked by RAF, Greek and Fleet Air Arm (FAA) aircraft from *Formidable* and Maleme (Crete).

The events at 'Gaudo' had a paradoxical effect. Iachino's manoeuvre, which endangered Force B, ended up bringing him closer to Cunningham, so much so that the latter hoped to make contact around 12:30 and had already taken the relevant tactical measures, while the torpedo attack had induced Iachino to reverse course and, therefore, to distance himself from the main British force. Cunningham had no choice but to rely on the torpedo bombers to slow down the Italian battleship and reach it before nightfall. Now, even the Italian admiral knew of the presence of an enemy carrier; around noon, Supermarina belatedly informed him of the presence of an enemy carrier, and shortly before, the cryptographers on the *Vittorio Veneto* also ascertained the presence of the British flagship at sea. However, in the absence of confirmation from aerial reconnaissance, Iachino formed the idea that the enemy ships were far away and posed no immediate threat. Even the 12:15 sighting of a battleship and an aircraft carrier 80 miles east of the *Vittorio Veneto* by a squadron of torpedo bombers, which arrived at 14:25, did not worry him too much, also because the important detail that the torpedo bombers had then attacked the aircraft carrier was omitted, a circumstance which would have given the message a very different implication. Another message from the X Fliegerkorps arrived around 12:30 reporting the sighting of only four cruisers, which reinforced Iachino's belief that the British battleships were still in Alexandria's waters. Nor did he worry about the radio direction-findings, communicated by Supermarina around 15:00, which placed a battleship and an aircraft carrier 170 miles southeast of the *Vittorio Veneto* at 13:15.

By early afternoon, the Italian squadron was south of Cape Crio proceeding west-northwest at 25 knots with the ships widely spaced: the *Vittorio Veneto* was in the centre, the 3rd Division 25 miles ahead on the port side and the 1st and 8th 30 miles ahead on the starboard side. Force A's effective distance from the Italian battleship was 65 miles. In the early afternoon the Italian squadron was subjected to further air raids, conducted without much determination by the RAF and FAA stationed on Crete and which remained unsuccessful, while *Formidable* was preparing to launch a second torpedo attack against *Vittorio Veneto*. This was conducted around 15:20 in conjunction with an attack by four Blenheim twin-engined bombers. It was during this action, executed with excellent coordination between bombers and torpedo bombers, that the *Vittorio Veneto* was hit by a torpedo on the port side of the stern, suffering serious damage to the propulsion system on that side and, to a lesser extent, to the rudders and taking on 3800 tons of water. Despite the extent of the damage, within an hour the starboard engines and the main rudder were working fairly smoothly again and the speed was increased first to 12, then 16, until it reached a steady 19 knots in the evening (for details see *Littorio Class* p199 and pp333-335).

Nevertheless, the situation had become difficult. The *Vittorio Veneto* was still 420 miles from Taranto and more torpedo attacks were to be expected; if she was hit a second time, she would have had little chance of survival. Iachino was not so much concerned about being met by enemy battleships – at 16:00 he received a message from Rome that a Ju 88 had sighted a battleship, four cruisers and twelve destroyers 170 miles south of the *Vittorio Veneto* (actually 70 miles), heading west-northwest – as he was worried about new torpedo attacks. He then decided to protect the battleship, gathering all ships in a close formation in five columns with the destroyers on the outside, the heavy cruisers in the second line – the 3rd Division on the port side and the 1st on the starboard side – and the *Vittorio Veneto* in the centre, preceded and followed in line by two sections of the XIII Squadriglia. The intention was to create a barrier of fire, smoke screens and beams

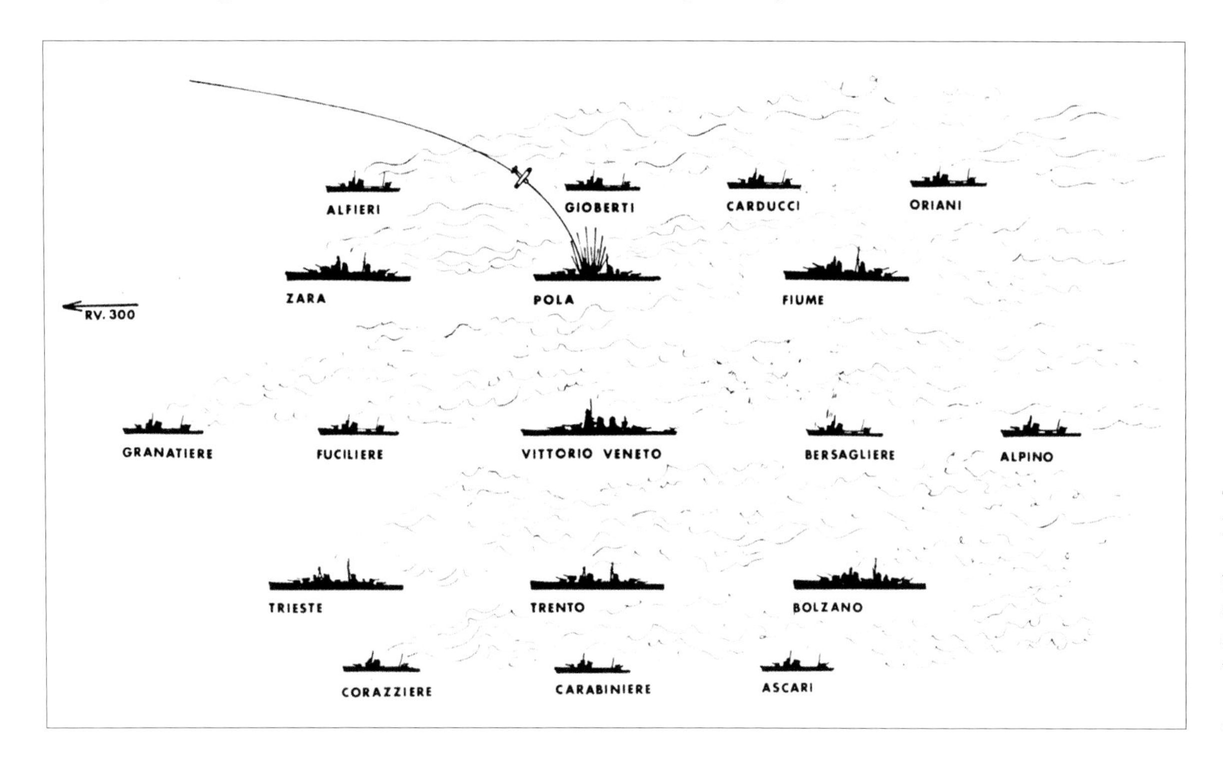

The formation ordered by Admiral Iachino on the evening of 28 March 1941 to protect the damaged battleship *Vittorio Veneto*. The very tight formation was concealed in a curtain of artificial fog when *Pola* was torpedoed and immobilised. (Drawing by V. Gay in E. Andò, *Zara class heavy cruisers*; see Bibliography).

of light around the battleship, but the formation was also rather rigid with the risk of collisions in the event of evasive manoeuvres by individual ships. The deployment was completed at 18:40, after the 1st Division, coming from the northwest, had joined the main body and the 8th had been sent back to Brindisi. In the same hours, interceptions by cryptographers aboard the *Vittorio Veneto* confirmed the feared attack at sunset. It should be remembered that throughout the afternoon of the 28th, the squadron did not enjoy any of the expected German air cover, except for the unnoticed appearance of a few heavy fighters of the X Fliegerkorps, that no Italian air activity in the sector was planned for that afternoon, which would have been problematic in any case due to the limited autonomy of the Italian fighters stationed in Sicily and Rhodes.

In the afternoon, having learned of the torpedoing of the Italian battleship, Cunningham took measures to bring about its destruction: he ordered *Formidable* to launch a new torpedo attack at sunset, Pridham-Wippell to re-establish contact with the cruisers and the 2nd and 24th Destroyer Flotillas to attack during the night. If that did not lead to her sinking, he would intervene with Force

At the naval battle of Matapan, besides the three heavy cruisers, the destroyers *Alfieri* and *Carducci* were also lost. These two images show both ships at Taranto 1939. (Foto Priore, Taranto)

A, and if during the night she was not tracked down, Force A would proceed northwest to re-establish contact the next morning.

The British torpedo bombers, eight from *Formidable* and two from Maleme, made contact at about 18:30 and for almost an hour kept their distance, studying the Italian deployment. Shortly after sunset (18:51) Iachino, with the disposition described above, turned 270°, in order to make the ships less illuminated, ordered all ships to turn on their searchlights and, finally, had the destroyers gradually extend smoke screens. The attack began at 19:28, in the last remains of twilight, with the attackers out of the dark. The attackers found it difficult to overcome such a barrage and the torpedo launches took place in an uncoordinated manner, so much so that, when at 19:50 the action ended, the searchlights were turned off and the firing was suspended. Aboard the *Vittorio Veneto*, as on almost all other ships, it was thought that all had gone well. At 20:05 Iachino changed deploy-

HMS *Barham* in the mid-1930s painted in the overall Home Fleet Dark Grey.

HMS *Warspite* in Malta's Grand Harbour in 1937. (Wright & Logan)

The aircraft carrier *Formidable* in late 1941.

ment for night navigation, ordering the 1st Division to move 5000m forward, the 3rd 5000m aft of the battleship and the XIII Squadriglia to take up close escort on both sides of the battleship. But, at 20:15, he received the news that the *Pola* had been torpedoed – at the end of the attack the cruiser had been hit amidships and immobilised. It was the *Fiume*, which had been next in line, who noticed this as it passed to starboard. At 19:54, he informed Cattaneo and the latter, in turn, Iachino, requesting authorisation to detach two destroyers to assist the *Pola*.

At the same time, information arrived on the *Vittorio Veneto* that might otherwise have guided Iachino's decisions. At 20:05 he was informed by Supermarina that radio direction-finding placed an enemy command complex 75 miles (actually 55 miles) east-southeast of the *Vittorio Veneto* at 17:45. He assumed that it was the usual group of cruisers following him or destroyers. Between 19:45 and 20:48, messages were intercepted regarding a 17:35 torpedo bomber attack on a convoy south of Crete, where it was well known that there could be no convoys. Even this news did not arouse Iachino's suspicions or move him from the conviction that British ships were not in the vicinity or had even returned and that the smaller ships did not constitute a serious danger, neither during the night nor the following morning, not even for the 1st Division that he was about to send to help *Pola*. He even declared himself convinced that the British were neither prepared nor willing to sustain night combat with larger ships. He was even more convinced of this when, at 19:45, messages were decoded in which Pridham-Wippell ordered his cruisers to reduce speed;

The battleship HMS *Valiant* in 1943, on completion of repairs carried out in the United States following the damage sustained in Alexandria by the men of the Decima Mas on the night of 18 December 1941. (IWM)

evidence, in his view, that they had no intention of engaging in darkness either. At 20:18, estimating that the two destroyers requested could do no more than scuttle the *Pola* and not even save the entire crew, and that only the division commander could properly appreciate the situation and take the most appropriate measures, including towing, he ordered Cattaneo to reverse course with the rest of the division and IX Squadriglia. Cattaneo, instead, understood the riskiness of the mission – as confirmed after the war by surviving officers present with him on the bridge – and hesitated to carry it out, trusting that Iachino would change his mind. This did not happen; at 20:45 and 21:00 the order was confirmed, but then he was authorised (20:14) to abandon the *Pola* in case of an encounter with superior enemy forces.

At 21:06 the 1st Division reversed course with the *Zara* in the lead, followed by the *Fiume* and the IX Squadriglia, a little astern, at a speed of 16 knots (briefly at 22); this rather slow speed was due in part to the fact that the destroyers had just enough fuel remaining to return to base. Perhaps this was also one of the reasons why Cattaneo decided not to deploy the destroyer squadron in front of the cruisers as a screen, as the manoeuvre would have required a significant increase in speed.

After the turn, at 21:24, the *Zara* informed the *Pola* of its imminent arrival, and finally, at 21:57, the *Zara* signalled the *Fiume* to be ready to take the crippled cruiser in tow. This was his last radio message. What happened on board the *Pola* after the torpedoing is explained in Appendix A. Here it is only necessary to remember that at 22:25, the captain, Manlio De Pisa, having sighted, at a distance of about 1.5 miles, some dark shapes coming from the southeast, the opposite direction to the one from which the 1st Division should have arrived, launched a red Very flare (seen by everyone, including the distant *Vittorio Veneto*) to signal his position, under the mistaken assumption that these shapes were the pair of cruisers that had overtaken him without sighting him.

On the opposite side, on the basis of the radar warnings of the *Orion* at 19:15, sent with Force B in search of the Italian squadron, Cunningham thought he had formed a clear idea of the position (33 miles ahead) and of the elements of the Italian squadron's motion (course 295°, speed 13 knots) and at 20:37 he decided to launch a torpedo attack entrusted to the 2nd and 14th Flotilla (eight destroyers in all) under the command of Capt. Philip Mack on the *Jervis*. However, his assessments were wrong: the distance amounted to 57 miles, the course had been changed by Iachino from 300° to 323° (*ie* in the direction of Capo Colonne, the easternmost promontory of Calabria), and the speed was 19 knots. This was the only major error made by

1938: the destroyer HMS *Nubian* leaving Portsmouth with Spanish Civil War 'neutrality bands' painted on the shield of the 'B' twin mounting. (Wright & Logan)

Cunningham during the entire operation, but it was such that it compromised Mack's mission. The latter, intending to overtake the Italian squadron from the west and attack it from ahead, ended up, instead, slipping astern of Iachino, who was already far away. A second mistake, which Cunningham came to regret, was made by Pridham Wippell; he failed to establish visual contact with the Italian squadron before nightfall and, therefore, to guide the destroyers toward the objective; furthermore, around 22:00, he sighted the incoming 1st Division, mistaking it for Mack's forces; in an effort not to interfere, he diverted northward, driving Force B further away from the Italian squadron. Finally, when Cunningham gave the general order to retreat to the north-east in order to reorganise his forces, except for those engaged in the search for the Italian fleet, Pridham-Wippell executed it to the letter, leaving the search area permanently, to Cunningham's disappointment.

By 20:15, therefore, the *Orion* had discovered the hulk of the *Pola* on radar, but without sighting it visually, and then continued on its way west. At 20:40 it communicated the results of its reconnaissance to Cunningham, some twenty miles away. Cunningham was confident that it was the *Vittorio Veneto* and prepared to destroy it. At 21:11 he changed course from west-northwest to west with the heavy ships in line (*Warspite*, *Valiant*, *Formidable* and *Barham*) preceded by the destroyers of the 10th Flotilla in two columns (*Stuart* and *Havock* on the starboard side, *Greyhound* and *Griffin* on the port side), until, at 22:03, the radar of the *Valiant* (the only battleship so equipped) detected the *Pola* dead in the water at a distance of 8 or 9 miles to the left. Force A turned to port together (22.10), then rebuilt the line and passed alongside the *Pola* on that side, with almost all their 15in guns ready to fire as soon as the target was sighted visually. *Greyhound* and *Griffin* were moved to starboard to clear the field of fire. While executing the manoeuvre, at 22:23, the *Stuart* suddenly sighted two large dark silhouettes off the port bow a couple of miles away, preceded by a smaller one (this was a mistake; no Italian ship was ahead of the *Zara*) and followed by three more, also small. Soon after, the sighting was also made by the other British ships. Force A turned together onto a course of 280°, recomposing the line so as to pass parallel to the sighted ships, with their guns now pointing at the new target. At the same time, the *Formidable* was moved out to distance it from the engagement area.

During the same minutes, the 1st Division spotted the *Pola*'s red Very light on the port bow. It then reduced speed and turned slightly to the left. Up to that moment, no one aboard the Italian ships had any inkling of the presence of the enemy and their attention was focused on spotting the *Pola*, towards which signals were directed, first with the Donath flasher and then with the VHF short range radio. Perhaps a moment before the British opened fire, the 1st Firing Director of the *Zara* recognised dark silhouettes which could not have been Italian ships. At that instant, a searchlight from the *Greyhound*, the closest to the Italian ships, illuminated the *Fiume* (where it was mistaken for a searchlight from the *Pola*), in order to aid the battleships' gunfire. At 22:28, at a distance of about 3000m, with the searchlights switched on, the *Warspite* opened fire, followed by the other battleships. The action lasted about three minutes and the course of fire is summarised in the table below.

The Italian cruisers were devastated, unable to react. Only the

BRITISH FIRING AT MATAPAN: OPENING PHASE

Ship	Calibre (in)	Salvoes	Total AP shells	Target in time sequence	Calibre (in)	Salvoes	Target in time sequence
Warspite	15	2+4+1	40	*Fiume, Zara, Alfieri*	6	?*	*Fiume, Zara, Carducci, Havock*
Valiant	15	1+5	39	*Fiume, Zara*	4.5	7+5**	*Fiume, Zara, Oriani* (?)
Barham	15	1+5	21	*Alfieri* (?), *Zara*	6	7	*Zara*
Total		19	100			?	

*44 HE shells in total; **120 shells in total

The destroyer HMS *Jervis*, name-ship of the 'J' class, moored at Portsmouth in 1939. (Wright & Logan)

The British destroyer *Greyhound* off Norway in April–May 1940. (IWM)

Zara fired a few rounds of 37/54 machine guns at *Barham*. Cattaneo was unable to give orders and the two ships to starboard after a while came to a stop under fire. The *Fiume* began to sink, heeling over to starboard – the disengaged side – due to a 15in shell that had passed right through the hull; she sank at 23:15. The *Zara*, which was half-destroyed in its topside and superstructure, remained afloat and an engine was still operating; it was stopped to allow the ship to be abandoned without waiting for dawn, and it sank after 02:00 on the 29th (for details see Appendix A).

In the meantime, in the light of the searchlights, explosions and fires, the destroyers of IX Squadriglia appeared clearly visible, following the cruisers in line and briefly targeted by the main and secondary armament of *Warspite* and *Barham*.

At this point (22:32), once the destruction had been completed, the British battleships turned off their searchlights and turned away 90° (towards the North) to avoid possible torpedo attacks by Italian destroyers. The 10th Flotilla was left to finish off the still floating wrecks.

Brief mention should be made of the fate of the IX Squadriglia's destroyers:

Alfieri, squadron leader. Badly hit by the *Barham*, turned away, ordering the other destroyers to lay down a smoke screen; severely damaged in the engine and steering system, she turned a complete circle before stopping. Shortly after 23:00 she was attacked and hit by the *Stuart* and finally finished off with a torpedo from the *Havock*. She responded – the only Italian ship to do so – by launching three torpedoes and firing machine guns and the 120mm (4.7in) forward gun at the *Stuart*. She sank in flames around 23:30.

Carducci. The third ship in the line, she initially hauled out of the line, only to turn to port shortly afterwards in an attempt to lay down a smoke screen to cover the other destroyers. She was severely hit by two medium calibre shells from the *Warspite*, but as she passed astern of the *Gioberti*, which was ahead of her, her smoke screen was able to cover her sister ship, and perhaps even the *Oriani*, making it easier for them to disengage. *Carducci*'s manoeuvre and its effectiveness were the subject of a long and controversial debate after the war, but no definitive conclusion was reached. Immobilised, without power and with fires on board, the ship was scuttled at 23:45, all hope of saving it having been lost.

Gioberti. The second ship in the line, also left the line and was slightly damaged. She managed to disengage, perhaps also thanks to the smoke screen of the *Carducci*, and reached Augusta under her own power in the late morning of the 29th. She underwent repair work at Taranto from 2 to 13 April 1941.

Oriani. The last ship in the line performed the same evasive manoeuvre as the other destroyers. she was hit by a 4.5in shell and suffered serious machinery damage; around 23:20 the ship was reported to have been engaged and again hit by the *Stuart*. However, she managed to get away and reached Augusta with difficulty on the morning of the 30th, towed in the final phase by the torpedo boat *Simone Schiaffino* and assisted by the destroyers *Libeccio* and *Maestrale*, the torpedo boat *Giuseppe Dezza* and the auxiliary cruiser *Lago Zuai*. She underwent repairs from 10 April to 2 July 1941 in Livorno.

The heavy cruiser *Pola* in December 1940. (Courtesy Gruppo ANMI Torino, A Lovera collection)

This photograph, taken from the *Garibaldi* at about 11:00 on 27 March 1941, is perhaps the best known of the few related to Operation 'Gaudo' and the last known image of the three *Zara* class cruisers lost during the night of 28–29 March 1941. The *Fiume*, camouflaged in an experimental pattern, is the third from the left and appears darker than the other ships (from left to right *Zara*, *Pola* and *Duca degli Abruzzi*). (E. Bagnasco collection)

The *Pola*, which until then had watched helplessly as the tragedy engulfed its division, was sighted by the *Havock* at 23:45, which mistook her for the *Vittorio Veneto*, informing Cunningham and Mack at 00:20. The latter abandoned the search and immediately reversed course (from west-northwest to east-southeast), continuing in this direction even after having received, at 01:34, a correction from the *Havock* regarding the exact nature of the immobilised ship. Finally, the *Pola*, once again spotted by British destroyers, was sunk with two torpedoes by the *Jervis* and the *Nubian*, after the latter had rescued those remaining on board (for details, see Appendix A).

The two squadrons returned to their bases – on the afternoon of the 29th for the Italians, and on the afternoon of the 30th for the British – without any events worthy of note other than those described in *Littorio Class*, p201. It is sufficient to add that during the return voyage to Alexandria the Mediterranean Fleet was attacked at 15:30 on the 29th without success by a squadron of Ju 88s; one was shot down and a Fulmar was also lost in an accident. Finally, on the morning of the 30th, an S.79 was shot down during a reconnaissance sortie.

Operation 'Gaudo' had thus reached its epilogue. The loss of three British aircraft and three airmen and negligible damage to two cruisers cost the Italian Navy three of its largest and best cruisers, two modern destroyers and serious damage to the *Vittorio Veneto* and a destroyer, as well as the loss of two aircraft, one of which was German. The loss of life was equally severe, as reported below.

CASUALTIES ON ITALIAN SHIPS DURING OPERATION 'GAUDO'

Ship	Officers	Petty officers	Sailors	Airmen	Military and civilians	Grand total
Vittorio Veneto			1			1
Zara	35	123	619		23	800
Fiume	37	85	681	6	5	814
Pola	9	52	265		2	328
Alfieri	7	17	184		2	210
Carducci	4	22	145			171
Oriani			3			3
Total	92	299	1898	6	32	2327

To these must be added 1162 prisoners, among the survivors, as listed below. Their rescue, except for those immediately rescued by the British, was slow and laborious and cost much sufferings to those who perished or survived at sea on makeshift lifeboats up to five days after the events. For further details see *Littorio* Class.

Pola personnel recovered by *Jervis*	257
Survivors picked up by British destroyers	766
Survivors picked up by Greek destroyers *	139
Survivors picked up by hospital ship *Gradisca* (31 March– 2 April)	161
Total	1323

* Except for those who died in captivity and those transferred to British hands, they returned home after the capitulation of Greece.

The destruction of the 'Duisburg' convoy (7–9 November 1941)

From April to July 1941, the 3rd Division was deployed on six convoy escort missions to Libya unopposed by British surface forces. However, on 21 October 1941, Force K was formed in Malta under the command of Capt. W G Agnew, consisting of the two small light cruisers *Aurora* and *Penelope*, from Scapa Flow, and the two modern destroyers *Lance* and *Lively*, and expressly intended to attack Italian convoys to Libya. They had already been subjected to effective air and underwater attacks – in September, among others, the large and splendid liners *Oceania* and *Neptunia* were sunk – but London considered this effort insufficient to compromise supplies to the Italian-German Armoured Army (ACIT) in view of the offensive in Cyrenaica in the autumn.

The presence of the two cruisers on the island did not escape Rome's notice. However, after a brief suspension of traffic, it was decided to resume the system of remote escort with cruisers since supplies to ACIT could not be interrupted. For the first ten days of November, a large convoy of seven merchant ships with a total load of 15,400 tons of fuel, 1600 tons of ammunition, 14,000 tons of various materials, 389 vehicles and 244 Italian and German soldiers and civilians was sent to Tripoli. It took the name of 'Beta' but became better known as 'Duisburg' after the German steamship that provided the convoy leader's flagship. Initially, it was thought that it would be routed to the west, via Trapani, suggested by Superaereo, where it would enjoy easier air cover; in this case it would be entrusted with the escort of the 8th Division (*Abruzzi* and *Giuseppe Garibaldi*). But, in the end, even though it was a slow convoy, the decision was made to take the eastern route (via Messina), with the 3rd Division providing a remote escort, deployed there very much with Force K in mind. This was the final composition of the convoy and of the escort forces, naval and air.

'Beta' or 'Duisburg' Convoy
From Naples (7 November 1941, at 06:30)
– German steamers *Duisburg*, *San Marco*;
– Italian steamers *Sagitta*, *Maria*, motor tanker *Minatitlan*.
Direct escort:
– X Destroyer Squadriglia.: *Maestrale* (Capt. Ugo Bisciani), *Euro* (added), *Fulmine*;
– XIII Destroyer Squadriglia (*Granatiere*, *Fuciliere*, *Alpino*, *Bersagliere*) up to Messina

Sardinian Sea, August 1941. The cruisers of the 3rd Division in a photo probably taken from aboard the *Trieste* - showing, from the closest, *Trento*, *Gorizia* and *Bolzano*. (E. Bagnasco collection)

From Messina (coming from Palermo, 8 November 1941, at 03:30)
– Italian steamers *Rina Corrado*, tanker *Conte di Misurata*.
Direct escort:
– X Destroyer Squadriglia: *Grecale*, *Libeccio*, *Oriani*

Long distance escort (from Messina 8 November 1941, at 12:00)
– 3rd Division (*Trieste* flagship of Adm. Bruno Brivonesi and *Trento*);
– XIII Destroyer Squadriglia (*Granatiere*, *Fuciliere*, *Alpino*, *Bersagliere*).
At Messina, ready to steam at 2 hours notice: *Gorizia* and XII Destroyer Squadriglia (*Corazziere* and *Carabiniere*).
A/s patrol south of the Messina Strait: torpedo boat *Giuseppe Dezza*.
Daytime air escort (of the convoy and of 3rd Division): 64 aircraft in multiple shifts (6 employed for asw warfare).

The deployment of air power was remarkable. The Sicilian Air Force and the 5th Air Squadron in Libya would provide direct and indirect escort and carry out constant reconnaissance on possible movements from Malta; the air forces of the High Command of the Aegean would do the same on those from Alexandria and Tobruk. Night air strikes on Malta were repeated with the maximum of available forces and proved to be very ineffective. Anti-submarine protection in the Ionian Sea would be provided by Marina Messina's Maritime Reconnaissance and in Libyan waters by Marina Tripoli's Maritime Reconnaissance. Three submarine ambushes were arranged, for scouting and attack purposes (which did not produce results), two to the east of Malta and one to the west; perhaps, given the importance of the operation, it would have been preferable to direct them all to the east. According to Supermarina's dispositions, once the convoy was out of the Strait, it was to reunite with the 3rd Division, would have headed east until 22:00 on the 8th, attempting to suggest – a bit naively, given the size and the bases of departure – that it was headed for Greece or Benghazi, and then head south and proceed toward Tripoli, keeping outside the range of British torpedo boats by making course changes away from danger where necessary. The 3rd Division would accompany the convoy until 19:00 on the 10th at Misurata and then return to Messina; the convoy's arrival in Tripoli with only a direct escort was scheduled for 24:00 on the 10th.

Initially, the mission went almost as planned. The bulk of the convoy left Naples in the early hours of 7 November with some delay due to the smoke caused by an air raid on the port. Navigation towards Messina proceeded without any surprises until early afternoon. During daylight navigation, the 3rd Division kept 5 miles astern of the convoy, zigzagging at 16 knots alternately to port and starboard of the convoy's 9-knot course. In the darkness, after experimenting with more pronounced zigzags, in order to maintain visual contact with the convoy and sufficient speed to allow acceptable manoeuvrability for the cruisers, Brivonesi decided to move out to the starboard side of the convoy, the most exposed to attack from Malta, at a speed of 12 knots and 1500m from the escorts. Until 19:30, the fleet continued steaming east, then, at 19:30, it turned to the southeast and, at 19:55, to the south-southeast. In the meantime, in the afternoon, a Martin Maryland reconnaissance aircraft of 69 Squadron spotted it from a high altitude about 40 miles east of Cape Spartivento Calabro. The Maryland had been seen and news reached Rome immediately, but Supermarina did not divert the convoy, as Superaereo had suggested; only aerial countermeasures were taken, which did not produce tangible results. The Maryland reported the sighting on its return to Malta – it had avoided radio communication – and gave a fairly approximate indication of its position, course (to the east), speed and composition; however, the presence of the 3rd Division was missed and, in any case, these elements were insufficient to allow for a precise interception of the Italian convoy, lacking any information on subsequent changes of course. The decisive information on its composition – although the 3rd Division was still missing – and its route were provided by 'Ultra' intelligence thanks to the timely decryption of messages transmitted with the Enigma cipher machine.

At 00:39 on the 9th, about 180 miles east of Malta, the convoy was sighted visually by the *Aurora* (radar played no part) on a polar bearing of 30° and at a distance of about 7 miles. At that moment there was a light breeze, the sea was barely rough, the sky was cloudy and visibility was excellent with the Italian ships silhouetted in the moonlight. The convoy was proceeding south-southeast, while the 3rd Division, 4000 yards astern on the starboard side, had just reversed its course to the south and was beginning to steam upwind; a situation theoretically favourable for engaging Force K, which was proceeding on the opposite course. In fact, with coolness and confidence in his own ability and means, Agnew did not immediately attack the convoy, but, even though he risked being discovered in turn, he turned north, reducing his speed from 28 to 20 knots, to place the convoy up-moon, and giving the signal for enemy in sight. During the manoeuvre he spotted, again visually, the 3rd Division on the opposite course, mistaking it, however, for another, smaller convoy; he preferred to ignore it in order to concentrate on the main objective. Once he had crossed the convoy's course, he turned decisively to attack from the starboard quarter and at 00:57 the *Aurora* and *Penelope* opened fire from a distance of about 5200m, using radar Type 284, without the use of illuminating projectiles, so as not to be spotted, soon imitated by the *Lance* and *Lively*. At 00:59, Force K turned south, then enveloped the head of the convoy and continued on the opposite side in an anti-clockwise direction. The Italian ships were taken completely by surprise. They were immediately hit: the *Grecale*, at the rear of the convoy, badly; the *Maestrale* at the head, slightly, but having had the radio aerials shot away with a momentary inability to transmit; on the starboard side, the *Fulmine*, which responded with the forward 120mm (4.7in) gun, but sank shortly after a boiler explosion, and the *Euro*, which suffered minor damage. The *Euro* was the only destroyer to attempt a torpedo attack, but aborted it, fearing that it was facing the 3rd Division. The *Maestrale*, initially assuming an air attack, like many of the ships in the convoy, failed to get a clear idea of the situation and began to lay down a curtain of smoke, refusing to counterattack; at 01:06, when many transports were in flames, she turned away at high speed, first to the south and then to the east – the direction in which the transports had also headed – thinking that she could do nothing now to save them and to gather the escorts for a later action. She was followed by the *Oriani* and *Libeccio*, and finally by the *Euro*, which also tried to conceal the convoy with smoke screens, but in this way, after being engaged again by Force K, they ended up moving away from the convoy, failing in every function, defensive and offensive. Most of the merchantmen were destroyed or burnt by 01:07, a couple between 01:15 and 01:29. Force K continued undisturbed in its enveloping manoeuvre, passing to the south of the convoy between 01:25 and 01:45 on the 9th, and continuing to fire at the burning transports and the retreating Italian destroyers; finally, having rounded the wrecks from the north, at 02:06, the force moved west-southwest towards Malta.

As for the 3rd Division, from 00:30, the *Trieste* began intercepting the *Aurora*'s signals which increased in intensity and proximity, without, however, identifying the source (they were initially attributed to a submarine). Just before the *Aurora* opened fire, she was spotted by the *Bersagliere* at 7000m ahead, but the sighting report did not reach the *Trieste* until the action was in progress and did not influence the events. Upon sighting the gun flashes, the two cruisers increased speed to 16 knots and turned together to starboard, in order to bring all guns to bear on the enemy; it would also clear the firing arcs from the two leading destroyers and from the transports themselves and avoid blast damage to the seaplanes on the forecastle catapults, which might have generated fires which would make them easy targets. This manoeuvre was criticised after the war because it took the 3rd Division away from Force K and delayed the opening of fire – it was argued that it would have been preferable to engage as soon as possible, even with only the forward turrets, and to try to get between the enemy and the convoy. However, it corresponded to tactical doctrine then in force, being prescribed even in the case of night combat, so much so that Brivonesi received no censure of his tactics in the enquiries that followed the battle. At 01:03 on the 9th, at a distance initially estimated at 8000m and then corrected to 9800m, the *Trieste* opened fire, followed two minutes later by the *Trento*, against the *Penelope* and the *Lively*, attempting to take advantage of illuminating fire from the 100/47 guns. However, due to insufficient range, this actually worsened, rather than improved, the light conditions. The first 203mm salvoes were short, but the following rounds appeared to be on target. Due to a series of circumstances the XIII Squadriglia remained on the fringes of the battle, without attempting to counterattack with torpedoes; only the *Bersagliere* opened fire. In this firing phase the British, who mistook the Italian cruisers for destroyers, intermittently directed their fire at the *Trieste* and the *Bersagliere*, without hitting them.

At 01.08, as Force K, proceeding at 20 knots to the south, increased its distance and fell into the aft firing sectors of the Italian cruisers, Brivonesi returned 180°, but bringing the speed down to only 18/20 knots, with the result that the firing continued at increasing ranges. It was directed at the *Penelope*, *Lively* and *Lance* and continued unsuccessfully until 01:25, when at a distance of 17,000m it was suspended as it became impossible to observe the fall of shot. It was only then that the 3rd Division increased its speed to 24 knots, while Force K began to execute an outflanking manoeuvre and disappeared from sight behind the smoke of the artificially generated screens and the burning merchant ships. Brivonesi sensed exactly that the enemy would outflank the convoy from the east and north and then return to Malta, and he reversed course, heading 360° at a speed of 24 knots with the intention of intercepting them on their return. But he soon changed his decision. At 01:13 on the 9th Supermarina had warned him of probable torpedo bomber attacks, which Brivonesi thought were coming from aircraft carriers, since the Maltese Swordfish did not have sufficient range – incidentally, the Mediterranean Fleet had not had any aircraft carriers since the end of May 1941 – and, at 01:43, he received a radio message from the *Maestrale* indicating that it was crossing to the south of the convoy, leading him to think that the enemy might be moving away from here as well. At 01:45, without having made any contact, Brivonesi headed northwest (toward the Calabrian coast), informing Supermarina. His reasons for this were: because he had no information on the enemy's position and movement; in order not to expose the cruisers to air and underwater attacks in an area illuminated by fire; in order not to approach Malta, the probable origin of these attacks; in order to approach the Italian coast and facilitate the meeting with the air escort; and to resume the search for the enemy in the light of day. This decision did not affect the possible interception of Force K because at 01:45 Brivonesi had passed the theoretical intersection point with Force K's re-entry route, which at that time was still 7 miles to the southwest and which the 3rd Division could have sighted only if it had stayed in the area, which it had no intention of doing. While Brivonesi was mulling over these decisions, Force K completed its outflanking manoeuvre, continuing to fire undisturbed at the flaming wrecks and searching, to no avail, for further targets. At 02:06, rounding them from the north, they continued on to Malta at 25 knots, where they arrived at 13:05 on the 9th, vainly attacked during the morning by four waves of Sicilian Air Force torpedo bombers.

During the night on the Italian side, the surviving escort ship guided by the *Maestrale*, after having gone 17 miles eastward, turned back at 18–20 knots, reaching the sea area strewn with flaming hulks, shipwrecks and debris at 03:06 on the 9th. Brivonesi did the same at dawn, after informing Supermarina of the destruction of the convoy and ordering the *Maestrale* to rescue the survivors. Rescue operations took up most of the morning and involved the XIII and the still efficient destroyers of the X Squadriglia, while the *Trieste* and *Trento* provided cover. The rescue operation was saddened at 06:46 by the torpedoing of the *Libeccio* by the submarine *Upholder*, which blew off its stern. The *Upholder*, along with the *P 34* and the *Urge*, was part of an ambush line 120 miles east of Malta and, after witnessing the destruction of the convoy from afar, was able to reach those waters in time (11:08), to target the *Trento*, which avoided the closest of the three torpedoes launched. Shortly thereafter, the *Libeccio* sank, despite the *Euro*'s attempt to tow it to safety, and at the same time the 3rd Division began its return to Messina, where it arrived the evening of the 9th. The hospital ships *Virgilio* (from Augusta) and *Arno* contributed to the rescue effort and remained in the waters of the disaster until dawn on the 10th. A total of 704 survivors were rescued by the warships, 55 by the hospital ships plus 5 from a seaplane damaged by ditching. Finally, 13 were rescued on a launch. The *Grecale* was also saved, which was towed for part of the way by the *Oriani* and returned to Crotone on the evening of the 9th.

'Alfa' and 'C' Convoys and torpedoing of the *Trieste* (21–23 November 1941)

The disaster of the 'Duisburg' convoy was followed by intense discussions between Italian and German military leaders on solutions to the convoy crisis, such as increasing traffic to Benghazi, which was less exposed to enemy attacks, using military vessels (light and auxiliary cruisers, destroyers, submarines) to transport personnel, fuel and ammunition, as well as small steamers and motor sailers, or convoys of fast motor ships, escorted by strong naval forces.

The last of these solutions took shape with the dispatch of two fast convoys, decided in mid-November, that is, before the beginning of the British offensive in Cyrenaica: 'Alfa' (German MV *Ankara* and MV *Sebastiano Venerio*) with the escort of the X Squadriglia (*Maestrale*, *Oriani*, *Gioberti*) and 'C', departing from Naples, respectively on 19 and 20/21 November, and bound for Tripoli with the distant escort of the 3rd Division (*Gorizia*, flagship of Adm. Parona, *Trieste* and *Trento*). Joining the convoy, the 3rd Division placed itself at the rear with the 8th Division in the lead. Until 21:45, the formation sailed parallel to the Sicilian coast, when it assumed the night sailing formation with the 3rd Division on the port side and the 8th on the starboard side; it headed east in order to get out of range of Malta's torpedo bombers as quickly as possible and to disorientate the reconnaissance aircraft tracking it.

In this case, too, 'Ultra' intelligence played an important role, identifying the composition and route of convoy 'C' as of 15 November. Thus, as far as the Tyrrhenian Sea, the convoy was kept in sight by an RAF Short Sunderland from Malta and followed by enemy scouts even south of the Strait. Here the submarine *Utmost*, patrolling in the area, was alerted and torpedo bomber attacks by Albacore and Swordfish of 828 and 830 Naval Air Squadrons whose aircraft were equipped with flares.

At 23:10 the *Utmost* launched four torpedoes against the last cruiser of the 3rd Division (actually the second, the *Trieste*), 13 miles south of Cape dell'Armi, while proceeding at a speed of 13 knots, damaging her severely with a single hit (see Appendix A for details). At 00:38 on the 22nd, south-southwest of Cape Spartivento Calabro, the *Abruzzi* was hit by a torpedo from a torpedo bomber, with less serious damage. Both cruisers succeeded in reaching Messina the following morning: the *Abruzzi* was assisted by the *Garibaldi* and XIII Squadriglia, which immediately enveloped it in screens of smoke, joined by the destroyer *Turbine* and tugs which had left the base; the *Trieste* was assisted by the *Corazziere* and *Carabiniere* as well as the torpedo boat *Perseo*. Due to the continuing air threat and doubts about the reported presence of an enemy force at sea, the convoy, after having dispersed, was diverted to Taranto escorted by the remaining ships. Here they arrived unharmed in the late morning of the 23rd.

The double mission ended in failure, putting two cruisers out of action, although no merchantmen were lost or damaged.

After minor repairs in Messina, on 3 December the *Trieste* left under its own power, escorted by four torpedo boats, for La Spezia, where she arrived without incident on the 4th. The *Abruzzi* was also destined for restoration work in La Spezia, where she completed her work on July 4th, 1942.

Operation 'M 42' and the First Battle of Sirte (16–19 December 1941)

After the cancellation of Operation 'M 41', in which the 3rd Division (*Gorizia* and *Trento*) was supposed to take part as an escort group for one of the three planned convoys (see *Littorio Class*, pp209ff), Supermarina was strongly urged by Mussolini and of the Chief of the General Staff, General of the Army Ugo Cavallero, to prepare a new supply operation for Libya, this time with only two convoys, which would leave Taranto together at 14:00 on 16 December and would separate at 18:00 on 17 December north of the Gulf of Sirte, the first heading to Tripoli and the second to Benghazi, where they should arrive at first light on 18 December. Convoy No 1 consisted of three merchant ships with the direct escort of six 'Navigatori'-type destroyers; Convoy No 2 consisted of one motor vessel escorted by one destroyer and one torpedo boat.

A group comprising the *Duilio* and the 7th Division (*Aosta*, *Attendolo* and *Montecuccoli*) with the XI Destroyer Squadriglia. (*Aviere*, *Ascari*, *Camicia Nera*) was assigned to the close escort, which would depart from Taranto at 15:00 on the 16th. A support group formed by the *Littorio* (Iachino's flagship), the *Doria* and the *Cesare*, the 3rd Division (*Gorizia*, Parona's flagship) and *Trento*), the XIII Squadriglia (*Granatiere*, *Fuciliere*, *Bersagliere*, *Alpino*), from XII Squadriglia (*Corazziere*, *Carabiniere* plus the *Usodimare*) and from X Squadriglia (*Maestrale*, *Oriani*, *Gioberti*) with departure from Taranto at 20:00 on the 16th. The 'Littorio' group would assume cover in the east, manoeuvring independently from the convoy. The 'Duilio' group would maintain visual contact with it, the battleship to the east and the 7th Division to the west in case Force K were to intervene. On the night of the 18th, the 'Duilio' group would rejoin the convoy and return to Taranto, as would the 'Littorio' group. Supermarina also prepared a deployment of submarines, while the reconnaissance and air escort would be carried out by divisions of Naval Aviation and the Air Force.

At the same time, the British had arranged for the naval supply ship *Breconshire* (converted to carry fuel oil) to be sent from Alexandria to Malta, escorted by the 15th Cruiser Squadron (*Naiad*, flying the flag of RAdm. Philip Vian, and *Euryalus*), the *Carlisle* and the 14th Destroyer Flotilla [hereafter DF], while Force K (light cruisers *Aurora*, *Penelope* and 4th DF) would leave Malta to join Vian and, in the afternoon of the 17th, Force B (light cruiser *Neptune* and destroyer *Kandahar*) to search for the

Italian convoy. Cunningham chose not to employ his two remaining battleships due to a shortage of destroyers. Vian left Alexandria late in the evening of the 15th (the *Carlisle* and two destroyers soon returned to Alexandria due to breakdowns) and at 08:30 on the 17th joined Force K north of Cyrenaica, continuing towards Malta. 'Ultra' intelligence on 'M 42' was also precise and timely, especially in the initial phase, but aerial reconnaissance from Malta on the 17th was not as effective as on previous occasions in following the movements of the Italian forces. This did not help Vian's search for the convoy to Benghazi, but in any case, his priority was to protect *Breconshire* until the evening of the 17th and only afterwards to search out and attack the convoy.

But the Italian decryption service also worked well and by midnight on the 16th, Iachino knew he had been discovered. From the morning of the 17th, Vian's formation was spotted several times by German and Italian aircraft, including the two from the *Littorio*, which, however, consistently mistook the *Breconshire* for a battleship. This heavily influenced Iachino's decision to adjust his approach and engage the enemy with all three battleships, rather than with the faster *Littorio* and the 3rd Division alone; in this case he could always fall back on the two slower battleships if he found himself in the presence of superior forces. However, with an hour to go before sunset, Iachino felt that he could not intercept the enemy before dark and had the convoy and the 'Duilio' group reverse course to avoid possible night-time attacks, while the support group, with the 3rd Division at 10,000m ahead, would continue south. At the same time, shortly before 17:30, while Iachino was thinking about measures for the night, there were unexpected sightings of British forces on the port side of the *Littorio*, divided into two groups and subjected to one of the many air attacks of the day. Iachino, still convinced that he had at least one battleship in front of him, immediately moved in that direction until he was within firing range and, having reached 32,000m, he turned his force together southwards to bring all his artillery into play, but gave up on further reducing the distance.

Vian, who had also sighted the Italian forces, all of which were out of range, had *Breconshire* proceed south with two destroyers at her maximum speed (16 knots) and executed a diversionary manoeuvre to the north with the remaining forces, spreading smoke screens. The battle began at 17:53, in the feeble twilight, which favoured the British ships who had darkness behind them. The *Littorio* opened fire on the cruisers at the initial distance of 32,000m, followed by the *Doria*, and by the 3rd Division, which was more advanced to the south and closer to the enemy cruisers, but a few minutes later, as the latter were now concealed by the smoke screens, the Italian major ships directed their fire on the nearest destroyers of the 14th Flotilla. Shortly thereafter, the XIII and X Squadriglia countered a suspected attack by British destroyers. Despite the enormous distance and the impending darkness to the east, the *Littorio*'s fire seemed accurate to the British, but no hits were made. At the same time, the British ships were subjected to German air attacks. In the end, only the destroyer *Kipling* was superficially damaged by bombs and a 203mm shell from the *Gorizia* exploded in close proximity, resulting in one casualty and the destruction of the radio aerials. This very short burst of fire by the Italian ships can be summed up as follows.

Ship	Fire beginning at	Estimated range	Fire ceasing at	Nº of rounds
Littorio	17:53	32,000m	18:02	27
Andrea Doria	17:53	32,000m*	17:59	13
Giulio Cesare	/	30,000m**	/	/
Gorizia	17:55	22,400m	18:04	58
Trento	17:57	22,400m	18:02	34

* The maximum range of the 320/44 guns of the *Duilio* class battleships was 29,400m.

** The maximum range of the *Cesare*'s 320/44 guns was 28,600m; the distance shown here is that registered by its rangefinders.

As darkness fell, Iachino broke off the action, altering course and ordering the destroyers to rejoin the main force. At 18:26 he headed north, the direction in which the convoy and the 'Duilio' group had been proceeding for half an hour. Until late in the evening, the convoy and its escort continued on this course, which temporarily took them into less dangerous waters, but also took them away from their destination and brought them closer to Malta. On the other hand, the manoeuvre eluded enemy reconnaissance and compromised Vian's search for the convoy, who only during the night learned of the course change through 'Ultra'. At 22:00, Iachino had the convoy and the 'Duilio' group head southwest, while the support group again provided cover to the east, proceeding in the same direction. During this phase, in the early hours of the 18th, while reorganising the battleship escort, Iachino ordered the XII Destroyer Squadriglia to move to the starboard side of the battleships, *ie* to the side where torpedo attacks might occur, favoured by the darkness to the west. During the manoeuvre, the *Granatiere* and the *Corazziere* collided and both suffered the loss of their bows. The *Granatiere* under tow by the *Oriani* and the *Corazziere* by the *Gioberti* reached, respectively, the bases of Navarino and Argostoli (Cephalonia), while the 3rd Division, escorted by the *Maestrale*, joined by the *Geniere* and the *Scirocco*, brought in from Taranto, returned to the Apulian base around noon on the 19th.

In the meantime, at 12:30 a.m. on the 18th, at the entrance to the Gulf of Sirte, the two convoys split up with their respective escorts: No 1 for Tripoli, No 2 for Benghazi, arriving at their destinations on the morning of the 19th. In the early afternoon of the 18th, the *Duilio* joined the 'Littorio' group. Around 15:00 the combined group set course for Taranto, where it arrived at 17:00 on the 19th without incident. Only the 7th Division continued to escort convoy No 1 until the evening of the 18th for fear of Force K and returned on the 19th, after having avoided torpedo attacks from the submarines *Unbeaten* and *P 31* that same morning.

Vian's main concern, too, was to bring the *Breconshire*, which had sailed south of the Italian forces, to its destination. He

Right: Central Mediterranean, 22 March 1942: *Trento* rolls heavily during the Second Battle of Sirte. Note the Battle Ensign partly torn away by the fierce sirocco wind of that day. The box on the left is a schematic indication of the area of the battle. (E. Bagnasco collection)

SICILIA
LIBIA

assigned Force K to its escort, reinforced on the morning of the 18th by Force B, which had been searching in vain for the Italian convoy in the previous hours. The *Breconshire* arrived in Malta at 15.00 on the 18th. Vian, however, was already steaming back to Alexandria, after a mistimed attempt to intercept convoy No 2 off Benghazi. Force K, having just resupplied in Malta, went back to sea that same evening in search of the Italian convoy in the waters off Tripoli, but during the night of the 19th ran into the 'T' mine barricade, laid in June 1941 by the 4th and 7th Divisions. The *Neptune* and *Kandahar* were sunk, the *Aurora* was badly damaged and the *Penelope* was slightly damaged. For a few months the surviving ships continued to operate from Malta, but without the original offensive vigour.

Operation 'M 43' (3-6 January 1942) – see *Littorio Class* and *Italian Battleships*
Countering the British Operation 'MF5' (14–16 February 1942) – see *Italian Battleships*
Operation 'K 7' (21–24 February 1942) – see *Italian Battleships*

Countering the British Operation 'MG1' and the Second Battle of Sirte (20–23 March 1942) – see also Littorio Class

Second Sirte was one of the events – the most spectacular, but also the least important – in the course of the British 'MG1' operation and the Axis counter-attack, the consequences of which were highly charged and should be mentioned in order to form a complete picture.

During the night of the 23rd, a gale reached its peak with winds up to Force 9 or 10 and all Italian ships came out with varying degrees of wear and tear (for the *Gorizia* and *Trento*, see Appendix A). On the morning of the 23rd, the destroyers *Lanciere* and *Scirocco*, the latter having failed to reach the squadron, sank due to machinery failures, which made them unable to cope the sea and the flooding; of the former there were 16 survivors, of the latter only two. The Italian ships returned to their bases separately. Of the larger ships, the *Littorio* narrowly escaped an unnoticed launch of four torpedoes from the

22 March 1942: a 203mm salvo from the heavy cruiser *Gorizia* during the 'Second Sirte' naval battle. The cruisers *Gorizia*, *Trento* and *Bande Nere* fired from a great distance at the British cruisers *Cleopatra*, *Euryalus*, *Dido* and *Penelope* but no shots hit the target. (A. Fraccaroli collection)

The *Gorizia* moored at Messina in March 1942. (G. Vaccaro collectiom, courtesy *STORIA militare*).

submarine *Upholder* around 16:00 on the 23rd, and reached Taranto a few hours later, escorted only by the destroyers *Ascari* and *Bersagliere*, and the *Antonio Pigafetta*, which had been sent from Taranto for this purpose; the *Gorizia* reached Messina in the early afternoon of the 23rd; the *Trento* – sent at 10:30 of the 23rd by Iachino to rescue the sunken *Lanciere* – reached Messina on the morning of the 24th. The *Bande* Nere also reached Messina at 13:00 at the end of a lucky voyage. All Italian ships were damaged by the force of the sea and required more or less long periods of repair.

On the British side, though for different reasons, the outcome was even worse. Iachino's tactic of interposing himself between the convoy and Malta, although unsuccessful, delayed their arrival but the air attacks of the 22nd, although also fruitless, had led to a high consumption of AA ammunition. Thus, on the morning of the 23rd, the merchantmen were still far from Malta and the II Fliegerkorps resumed its attacks: the motor vessels *Talabot* and *Pampas* managed to reach the island without serious consequences, but the *Clan Campbell* was sunk and the *Breconshire* severely damaged; the *Legion* also suffered further damage from near-misses. But the air attacks continued with extreme violence in the following days. On 24 March, the 'Hunt' class escort destroyer *Southwold* sank on a mine, while assisting the *Breconshire*; on the 26th, the *Talabot* and the *Pampas* were sunk in port, and on the 27th, the *Breconshire*, which was laboriously towed to an anchorage on the island. Ultimately, all the merchantmen of Operation 'MG1' were lost and of the 25,900 tons of material, only 5000 could be landed with a further 2500 tons salvaged later from the sunken hulls. Vian's ships also suffered during the return voyage from the air attacks and from the sea, although to a much lesser extent than the Italians: the most damaged were the *Zulu* and the *Lively*; the latter had to make for Tobruk, unable to make more than 14 knots. The *Carlisle* and four of the five 'Hunts' sailed from Malta on 25 March; the *Avon Vale*, damaged in a collision, on the 29th headed for Gibraltar instead.

The Battle of 'Mezzo Giugno' and the sinking of the *Trento* (11-16 June 1942) – see also *Littorio* Class

This was the name given to the Italian Fleet action against

Operation 'Vigorous', a British attempt to resupply Malta with a convoy from Alexandria. At the same time Operation 'Harpoon' sought to fight through a separate convoy from the west. The Italian surface forces, led by the battleships *Littorio* and *Vittorio Veneto*, concentrated on 'Vigorous', for which the distant protection was largely provided by a submarine patrol line and, predominantly, shore-based aircraft.

The Italian surface forces were subject to numerous attacks as they sailed south towards the convoy. The first British attack was carried out between 02:33 and 03:56 on the 15th against two cruisers of the 9th Division by a section of torpedo bombers; coordination between the two ships was not good: the illuminating star-shells were launched at too great a distance from the Italian formation, which effectively defended itself by spreading dense smoke screens covering the surface of the sea.

The second attack was conducted in the morning twilight of the 15th, shortly after 05:00: nine Bristol Beaufort twin-engined torpedo bombers of 217 Squadron attacked in three waves simultaneously. Their target was the cruiser group proceeding in line (*Garibaldi*, *Aosta*, *Gorizia*, *Trento*), flanked by a section of destroyers of XI Squadriglia on each side: the first wave against the 8th Division, the second against the *Gorizia* and the third against the *Gorizia* and *Trento*. The Beauforts approached low over the water at high speed and on intersecting courses; those targeting the leading ships got no closer than 1000m, hampered by the destroyers' defensive fire, but those targeting the rear of the line, protected by fewer destroyers, were able to get closer. At 05:16, a Beaufort launched a torpedo from just 200m off the starboard quarter of *Trento*, and hit her in the forward boiler room, immobilising her (for details on damage see Appendix A); all other ships avoided the torpedoes by rapid manoeuvring.

AA fire proved to be fairly effective, especially from the 6in-armed light cruisers which hindered the torpedo aircraft's approach, but it was made difficult at short distances by the very rapid changes in range due to the high angular speed and evasive action of the aircraft and by the need to defend simultaneously against those coming from different and changing sectors; the destroyer screen proved useful for the leading ships. The *Gorizia* claimed to have shot down two aircraft, which were in fact only damaged.

Within minutes, a group of three more Beauforts also attacked the 9th Division, concentrating on the *Vittorio Veneto*. All torpedoes were avoided by manoeuvre (for details of this and subsequent air attacks against the 9th Division, see *Littorio Class*, p222ff). Ranged fire from the 152mm and 90mm guns of the battleships and the 120mm of the destroyers proved effective, hampering the approach and forcing the planes to drop torpedoes at considerable distances, thus making it easier to avoid the torpedoes. All of these attacks took place without any air cover over the Italian fleet.

The third air attack was carried out almost simultaneously by high-level bombers and torpedo aircraft. From 08:16 to 18:50, a formation of eight US Consolidated B-24 Liberators from Egypt (a ninth had to return due to damage) attacked the 9th Division in three successive groups from an estimated altitude of 4000m (13,000ft), on an opposite course and with the sun behind them. A 500lb (227kg) bomb hit the *Littorio* on the barbette of Turret 1, causing minor damage; others exploded nearby, without consequences, but putting the two Ro.43 floatplanes out of action due to shock damage. Simultaneously with the Liberator raid, between 08:40 and 08:46 the two battleships were attacked by five Beaufort torpedo bombers from Malta, part of an original formation of twelve, seven of which had been previously shot down or forced back by Messerschmidt Bf 109 fighters. Again, the launches, although well coordinated, were carried out at long ranges and the torpedoes were easily avoided. One Beaufort was so badly damaged by AA fire that it was destroyed on landing in Malta. For the duration of the attack, the 9th Division had been escorted by four Ju 88s, which had been overhead since 07:00, but which, to Iachino's disappointment, would not take action against enemy aircraft, either by interdiction or pursuit.

While the Italian fleet continued southeast and then east-southeast towards the enemy sightings, the drama of the *Trento* was unfolding. After the torpedoing, Iachino had detached the

The *Trento* moored at Messina in late spring 1942 painted in a 'Claudus' experimental dazzle scheme. (E. Bagnasco collection)

Camicia Nera, the *Pigafetta* and the *Saetta* to assist the cruiser, immobilised and with an oil fire on board, and Supermarina had ordered that the torpedo boat *Partenope* moved from Patras and tugs from Crotone. At 09:10, when the *Trento* was about to get underway with its own power, it was torpedoed again by the British submarine *P 35* in line with the forward magazine, which exploded causing the almost instantaneous sinking of the ship (for details, see Appendix A). The *P 35* belonged to the westernmost line of submarines crossed by the Italian fleet at the time of the torpedo bomber attacks in the morning twilight, and, at 05:46, it had already launched a salvo of four torpedoes against the *Vittorio Veneto* at a distance of 5000m without success and which went unnoticed.

Operation 'Vigorous' ended in failure when the British convoy MW11 was ordered back to Alexandria, the main cause of which was the Italian surface fleet, as was unanimously acknowledged by the British enemy and the German ally. While it is true that all British losses were caused by Axis air and submarine forces, it was the presence of the Italian fleet at sea that forced the convoy to turn back, demonstrating that their contribution was decisive in preventing a large convoy from reaching its destination. Indeed, it can be said that this was the only clear and decisive success achieved by the Italian fleet during the entire conflict. The painful sinking of the *Trento* and the minor damage to the *Littorio* constituted a material price more than compensated for by the sinking and damage to warships and merchantmen incurred by the British. In these circumstances, Supermarina and the higher command at sea gave proof of determination and a clear vision of the situation, having recognised which convoy was the most important, understanding that it was necessary to engage it as far east as possible and that some risk had to be taken, even in the absence of air cover.

Operation 'Harpoon', which took place in the same days, had a more controversial outcome. It culminated on the morning of the 15th in a battle off Pantelleria, in which the 7th Division played a leading role, but failed to prevent the arrival of the convoy's surviving merchantmen in Malta. Two of them reached the island with 15,000 tons of material, enough to revitalise the island, although not enough to solve its problems long term. The price paid by the British was very high: as a result of Italian-German and 7th Division air and underwater attacks, convoy WS19/Z lost four of its six merchantmen, two destroyers and a minesweeper; it also suffered damage to a merchant ship, two light cruisers, of which the *Liverpool* remained out of service for 13 months, four destroyers and a minesweeper, while on the Italian side the *Vivaldi* was seriously damaged and the *Eugenio* and *Montecuccoli* suffered slight damage. Only the air losses in the two operations as a whole were greater for the Axis: 42 aircraft against 30 Allied aircraft; an acceptable result, if one considers that a good part of the Italian-German offensive effort was focused on air power.

On the other hand, the British air strikes, even if they did not have the desired effect on the two Italian fleet operations, left a strong impression on the Italian naval commanders and had no small influence on subsequent operations. They were carried in a well-coordinated manner by torpedo bombers and aircraft, mostly from Malta, which were much faster and with much greater range, although less manoeuvrable than the Fleet Air Arm Swordfish and Albacores, demonstrating that the island had recovered much of its offensive capability and extended its range, and that Italian surface ships now had to deal with much more dangerous aircraft. Conversely, cover by Axis air forces seemed to be lacking – in fact, almost non-existent – and the defence of the ships remained entrusted to manoeuvre and AA fire. This was still effective, as was the ranged barrage which disrupted the attacking formations, but at close range, the 37mm and 20mm machine gun fire was inadequate – new gunnery direction equipment was not yet ready, the ammunition was inadequate against large aircraft, even when repeatedly hit, and the training conducted up to that point did not reflect reality. Even in night attacks, the rules of engagement, which consisted of placing smoke screens between ships and the star-shell illumination, could no longer be considered effective, since every single major ship had to be completely concealed for the tactic to work. Improved AA defence required more effective smoke generators, which were in the process of being adopted, a greater number of escort ships and better tactical coordination between escorts and major ships.

A rare image – unfortunately of mediocre quality – of *Trento* during her last wartime mission in June 1942. This picture, taken from the light cruiser *Duca d'Aosta*, is probably the last surviving image of the *Trento* before she was sunk on the morning of 15 June in the central Ionian Sea. (N. Siracusano collection)

The *Gorizia*, the only serviceable cruiser in the 3rd Division, remained in Taranto until 5 July, when she returned to Messina along with the XI Destroyer Squadriglia.

The Battle of 'Mezzo-Agosto' and the second torpedoing of the *Bolzano* (10–15 August 1942)

The only major Italian surface units to be committed against Operation 'Pedestal' – a massive attempt to resupply Malta from the west – were the Cruisers of the 3rd and 7th Divisions, but they had no opportunity to intervene.

The submarine *Unbroken*, commanded by Lt. A C G Mars, was part of a group of eight boats deployed north and south of Sicily to defend the British convoy from ambushes by the Italian fleet. The boat had been entrusted with a patrol area in the waters

La Spezia Dockyard, spring 1942: the *Bolzano* moored at the 'Veleria' quay with the cable-layer *Città di Milano* alongside; in the left foreground is a German Type VII U-boat. (Courtesy L. Braeuer)

off Palermo and Milazzo, where it had also been the target of fighter aircraft and anti-submarine ships. Having moved 30 miles further north, between the islands of Stromboli and Salina, and informed himself of the movements of the Italian cruisers, Mars assumed that they would pass through the Aeolian Islands. He sighted them at 07:25 on the 13th, southwest of Stromboli at a distance of 12,000m. He then manoeuvred to launch against the nearest cruiser, the *Bolzano*, waiting for the corresponding cruiser of the outer column, the *Attendolo*, to partially overlap it, so as to have a larger target, and for the destroyers forming the port screen to pass by. A few minutes after 08:00, the *Unbroken* fired a salvo of four torpedoes from a distance of 1800m.

On the Italian side, at 08:13, while the *Gorizia* had begun to turn to port to launch the seaplane, the *Fuciliere* sighted the submarine's periscope 400m to the left and immediately gave the alarm with flags and machine gun fire in the direction of the periscope. Of the four torpedoes, only three were sighted: the middle torpedo passed astern of the *Gorizia*, which increased the turn in progress, and was avoided by the *Bolzano*, which turned to starboard, but hit the the bow of *Attendolo* which had changed course too late, not having seen the signals from the *Fuciliere*; the leftmost torpedo hit the *Bolzano* amidships while she was manoeuvring to avoid the previous one; the rightmost torpedo passed a few metres ahead of the *Gorizia*; nothing threatened the *Trieste*, but as a precautionary measure she turned to starboard, putting on maximum power; the fourth torpedo was not seen by anyone. Neither the two Cant Z.506 aircraft of the escort nor the sonars of the *Fuciliere* and *Grecale* had detected the presence of the submarine.

The *Bolzano*, hit on the port side just aft of the bridge tower, almost came to a halt, down by the bow and with a very violent fire that immediately enveloped the superstructure and the hull forward. The *Attendolo*, hit about 10m from the stem, had its bow almost removed or crumpled for 25m and stopped immediately, slightly bow-down and heeling to port by 3°-4°. Immediately after the double torpedoing, the *Fuciliere* and the *Camicia Nera* searched for the *Unbroken* and dropped depth charges at the location of the last sighting, while the *Gorizia* and the *Trieste* zigzagged away at a speed of 25 knots, escorted by the *Corsaro* and the *Camicia Nera*, once they had abandoned the hunt for the submarine. Assisting the two damaged cruisers were the *Aviere*, *Ascari*, *Geniere*, *Legionario* and *Grecale*. Only the *Fuciliere* continued to hunt for the *Unbroken* with depth charges.

Both cruisers survived, the *Bolzano* being initially beached off Panarea, but despite a number of schemes for reconstruction, the ship was never returned to service.

The heavy cruiser *Trieste* in the southern Tyrrhenian Sea on the morning of 13 August 1942. The ship was part of the 3rd Division (Adm. Angelo Parona) along with the *Gorizia*, the *Bolzano*, the light cruiser *Attendolo* and eight destroyers. The formation was heading for Messina when, just northwest of Panarea (Aeolian Islands), the *Bolzano* and the *Attendolo* were hit and severely damaged by a torpedo salvo from the British submarine *Unbroken* lurking in those waters. (E. Bagnasco collection)

The end of the 3rd Division at La Maddalena and its disbandment (April 1943)

In early April 1943, the US Air Force's North African Air Force (NAAF) planned a daytime high-altitude air attack on La Maddalena, the major Italian naval base on Sardinia. Since the Allied landings in Algeria and the progressive occupation of Libya, bombing raids had been systematically carried out against the rear echelons of the Tunisian front and, in particular, on the source and destination ports of supply convoys. But the main naval forces were also among the top-priority targets, with the intention of destroying them or driving them away from the central Mediterranean; this was the case with the bombing of Naples on 4 December 1942 and of Messina at the end of January 1943, which led to the abandonment of those bases by the 9th and 8th Divisions, respectively. The planned bombing of La Maddalena seems to have been influenced by an additional consideration, namely an erroneous appreciation of the meeting in Rome between the Commanders in Chief of the Regia Marina, Adm. Arturo Riccardi, and the Kriegsmarine, Grand Admiral

The *Bolzano* in a photo taken from the light cruiser *Muzio Attendolo* shortly before both ships were almost simultaneously hit by two torpedoes from a salvo launched by HM/SM *Unbroken* on the morning of 13 August 1942 in the waters off the Aeolian Islands. (Photo Rev. Tarcisio Beltrame, A. Rastelli collection)

Karl Doenitz, in mid-March 1943 regarding the organisation and defence of convoy traffic with Tunisia. The Americans reached the conclusion, in line with the widespread prejudice against the Italian Navy, that a German admiral would take command of the fleet (in truth, the Germans had actually been pursuing this objective for some time). Fearing that this would mean a more aggressive naval policy, the Americans wanted to eliminate the ships stationed at La Maddalena as soon as possible, inasmuch as they constituted the closest threat to Anglo-American shipping along the Algerian coast.

After an accurate photographic reconnaissance located and recognised the exact mooring places of the two cruisers, the attack was finally carried out in broad daylight, at 14:50 on 10 April 1943, by 84 Boeing B-17 Flying Fortress four-engined bombers of the NAAF's 12th Air Force at an altitude of 19,000 feet, adopting the 'area saturation' bombing technique. Thirty-six B-17s of the 97th Group and 2nd Group flew over *Gorizia*, 24 of the 99th Group over *Trieste* and the remaining 34 of the 301st Group over the naval base. Only the two destroyers *Camicia Nera* and *Gioberti*, moored to the buoys at Santo Stefano, were left out. As evidence of the perfect knowledge of the location and characteristics of the targets and of the meticulousness with which the attack was planned, the B-17s destined for the two cruisers were armed with 1000lb (454kg) armour-piercing bombs with fuses set to pierce armoured decks 2in and 3in (51mm and 76mm) thick, respectively, the thickness of the decks of *Trieste* and *Gorizia*, while the aircraft attacking the base were armed with 250lb (113.5kg) bombs.

Formations of B-17s suddenly arrived over the targets in several groups, initially coming from the direction of the sun (south-southwest). The weather conditions were very good with clear skies and fair winds. The alarm from the base was sounded at 14:35, a few minutes before the bombers appeared over the base and the AA defences on the ships and ashore swiftly went into action with heavy fire and apparently well directed. However, their effectiveness was practically nil due to the high altitude of the attacking aircraft and the speed with which the raid took place, estimated at only 6 minutes. None of the enemy aircraft were shot down or damaged and their action was not even appreciably disrupted. On the other side, the *Trieste*, the *Gorizia*, the naval base and some of the ships located there were hit in rapid succession. The two destroyers suffered no damage, because they were not attacked.

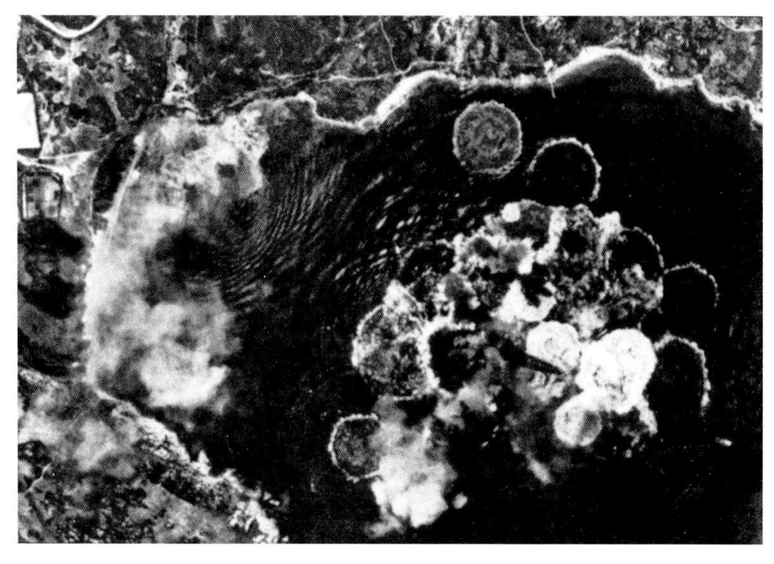

An image of the 10 April 1943 bombing raid that sank the *Trieste* in the Mezzo Schifo harbour in Palau (north-eastern Sardinia) (USAAF).

Shortly after 14:35 the *Trieste* was bracketed by at least four or five salvoes of extremely heavy bombs. Of these, three 1000lb armour-piercing bombs certainly hit the *Trieste* directly; others exploded in the immediate vicinity. As a result of the damage received, almost all power was lost and it became impossible to contain the extensive flooding; attempts to tow the cruiser into shallower waters to prevent its complete sinking also failed. The *Trieste* sank, capsizing, at 16:13 at her mooring place (for details see Appendix A).

The *Gorizia* was also simultaneously framed by numerous bombs (estimated at 60), although here the B-17 drops did not appear to be as accurate. She was, nevertheless, hit by three 1000lb armour-piercing bombs, while others exploded in the immediate vicinity. The cruiser was badly shaken and damaged. However, the skill and the efficiency of the damage control parties prevented the sinking and kept the vital parts of the ship in a reasonable working state (for details on the damage and how the *Gorizia* stood up to it, see Appendix A). It should be noted that the overall efficiency of the cruiser on 1 April 1943 was estimated at 80% of its maximum, to which deficiencies in electrical equipment contributed.

Heavy damage was also sustained by the base, which had many of its structures destroyed, including the power plant, and large sections of the docks in the port area. The three Ro.43s of the two cruisers on shore were also destroyed. The losses of the ships present were more limited: the five submarines (*Mocenigo*, *Sirena*, *Topazio*, *Aradam*, *Dandolo*) were almost unharmed; *MAS 501* and *MAS 503*, three motor sailboats, later recovered, and some floats were lost. No damage was caused to La Maddalena itself and the surrounding villages.

As a result, the 3rd Division ceased to exist and on 30 April was formally disbanded, although the *Gorizia* proved to be salvageable.

The 10 April bombardment of La Maddalena proved easy to execute and impressively effective, both for the precision of the bombing and for the fact that the action took place suddenly and undisturbed. As on previous occasions, such as the bombing of the port of Naples on 4 December 1942, the enemy action highlighted, more than had already been perceived, the inadequacies of the warning system (the bombing began only a few minutes after the alarm) and of the AA defence of Italian naval bases, which was also ineffective in disrupting the enemy, as would be confirmed shortly thereafter by the bombing of La Spezia, a base that was certainly better protected and defended than La Maddalena. Last but not least, the affair highlighted once again the weakness of Supermarina's thinking, centred on the preservation of the fleet's major units, with the declared goal of exploiting their ability to deter possible enemy initiatives in Italian home waters. The daytime bombing raids conducted by the American Air Force at high altitudes were demonstrating that the Italian fleet was even more insecure in port than at sea. In the days

The wreck of *Gorizia* at la Spezia in 1946. (Photo A. Fraccaroli)

immediately following the air raid on La Spezia, when systematic bombing of the Italian fleet began, concern arose that the fleet would succumb without a fight, as Bergamini wrote to Supermarina the day after the 5 June 1943 bombardment, which put the battleships *Roma* and *Vittorio Veneto* out of action for some time (see *Littorio Class*, pp263–264).

In the end, as a result of the destruction suffered and the difficulties in defending it, the base ended up being downgraded, as the Stato Maggiore della Marina (Naval General Staff) deemed it unsuitable to host major ships and submarines, but only a few Mas boats and possibly, at a later date, a couple of destroyers and a few submarines.

Italian '10,000-ton' cruisers: the epilogue (1943–1951)

Once in La Spezia, the *Bolzano* changed berth several times: first at the Scali dock (Duca degli Abruzzi outer dock); then, in the first months of 1943, at the Mancina dock of one of the inner docks of the Arsenal; in the spring of the same year at the Varicella pier (Duca degli Abruzzi dock) and, finally, again at the Scali dock.

At the armistice of 8 September 1943, the vessel was abandoned at her mooring without scuttling, as she was completely unusable and practically unrecoverable. The Germans took possession of the ship in the days that followed, when they occupied La Spezia and the Arsenal, and when, it seems, the ship had already been largely robbed of its fittings and equipment by the civilian population. In the following months, the German naval authorities ordered the final stripping of the ship, depriving it of all weapons and any material that could be used again. The *Bolzano*, by then reduced to a derelict wreck, was finally moored to the buoys in an enclosure of anti-torpedo nets located almost in the middle of the La Spezia harbour in front of Punta Pezzino.

In that position, during the night of 22 June 1944, the hulk was attacked by British raiders from an underwater assault craft of the 'Chariot' type, which was approached together with a second 'Chariot' by Italian craft of the Assault Craft Command of the Southern Navy (destroyer *Grecale* and motor torpedo boat *MS 74*), in order to prevent the wreck – along with the *Gorizia*, which, however, was not attacked – from being used to obstruct the entrances to the roadstead; an accurate assumption, at least as far as the *Gorizia* was concerned. After a few hours, the explosion of the charge placed on the hull by the 'Chariot' caused it to sink (see Appendix A, p178). Also participating in the assault were Italian 'Gamma' frogmen transported by modified torpedo

Left: Another view of the wreck of *Gorizia* at la Spezia in 1946.

Below: A detail of the port side of the wreck of *Gorizia* in 1946. (Photo A. Fraccaroli)

motorboats (MTSM), taken aboard the *Grecale*, targeting other vessels in the La Spezia base; there is no precise information on the results of their action. The sinking of the *Bolzano* on 22 June preceded by a few days a German plan to carry out experiments with underwater explosive charges on the hull, which were then instead carried out on the incomplete *Impero* at Capodistria (Trieste) in the summer of 1944.

At the end of the war the wreck of the *Bolzano* was found upside down with part of the hull submerged. After the war it was raised and broken up.

The fate of the *Gorizia* was similar. The badly damaged ship arrived in La Spezia from La Maddalena on 14 April 1943, and in the following days she was prepared to be drydocked (4 May 1943). The work proceeded rather slowly due to the bombings which damaged the shipyard in the following months and to the greater priority accorded to the three *Littorio*s, which absorbed some of the ship's resources, especially personnel; but the work was never suspended. On the contrary, the numbers of workers assigned were increased, including the few carrying out maintenance of what was still serviceable on the *Bolzano*. On 1 September 1943, the *Gorizia* was nominally added to the 9th Division and work was expected to be completed by 30 November 1943. Even if this deadline had been met, considering the time required for trials, it would have been difficult to have the ship ready before the beginning of 1944. From photographic evidence of the wreck dating from the very first months after the war, however, it can be deduced that the repairs to the superstructure had been completed.

On 8 September 1943, the *Gorizia* was still drydocked and the commander, Carlo Dessì, after having dismissed the remaining crew, decided to sabotage the cruiser, by letting water into the dock and opening the sea water intakes to scuttle the ship. The operation was immediately suspended, however, given that the ship could not be serviceable for a long time and that the Italians

Aerial view of one of the drydocks in the La Spezia Dockyard with the capsized hull of *Trieste* in June 1950. (E. Bagnasco collection)

The capsized wreck of the *Trieste*, salvaged at La Maddalena, in a drydock at La Spezia Dockyard on 20 June 1950. (E. Bagnasco collection)

The wreck of the *Trieste*, towed by the Dutch tug *Thames*, outside Cartagena on 3 September 1951. The salvaged hull of the cruiser, still found to be in acceptable condition, had been purchased by the Spanish Navy, which intended to rebuild her as an aircraft carrier but, in spite of these ambitious plans, it was instead scrapped at El Ferrol between 1956 and 1959. (E. Bagnasco collection)

hoped for a rapid Allied advance. With the German occupation of the Arsenal, the ship was stripped of its materials and equipment. Later, as the German Navy needed to use the basin and the Arsenal for its own needs, which were increased by the capture of Italian ships, the *Gorizia* was taken out of the basin and moored in the roadstead. The *Gorizia* also escaped the German intention of experimenting with underwater charges, as it was already intended as a block-ship. At the end of the conflict, it was found half-submerged near the merchant port and, since it had no reuse value, once it was refloated it was sent for breaking up.

The fate of the wreck of the *Trieste* was different and curious. The hull was raised from the sea-bottom of La Maddalena in 1950 by the salvage company Micoperi. Still upside down, it was towed to La Spezia and put into the basin to prepare for righting. The hull was then put up for sale at the end of the same year.

At that time the Spanish Navy was considering a low-cost naval unit and was looking for hulls of the right size to enable it to build a light aircraft carrier. Attention was drawn to the hull of the *Trieste*, which, despite having spent seven years underwater, was still in good condition. After a positive inspection by a commission of the Spanish Navy, the hull was purchased in May 1951 and towed to Cartagena the following June. But a change in the leadership of the Spanish Navy led to a reconsideration of the whole project and the conclusion that it would not be worth completing. The following September, however, the hull of the *Trieste* was towed to the Ferrol arsenal, the site of the planned reconstruction. Having discarded proposals for other conversions and for reusing the engines, none of which made economic sense, it was decided to dismantle the ship, which was carried out on site between 1956 and 1959. Only small elements were ever reused.

Chapter 8

CONCLUSIONS AND COMPARISONS

A comparison between the *Trento*s and the *Zara* class.

In outlining the origins of the Italian '10,000' type, the authors have highlighted the different concepts that inspired their design and have pointed out that the *Zara*s were not a development of the *Trento*s – if anything, the *Bolzano* was – nor were the two classes homogeneous, even in their criteria of employment, although the exigences of war eventually blurred and cancelled the differences. It is necessary to remember that until the eve of the conflict, the General Staff of the Regia Marina conceptually divided the main naval forces into 'light' (and fast) groups, and a 'battle force'. The former had just been completed by the 12 large 'scouts' of the *Attilio Regolo* class of the 1938 supplementary programme and included the 3 *Trento*s and the 6 light cruisers of the *Bande Nere* and *Diaz* classes. The 'battle force' comprised the 8 battleships (4 *Littorio* and the 4 rebuilt *Cavour* and *Duilio* classes), the 4 *Zara*s, the 6 light cruisers of the *Montecuccoli*, *Aosta* and *Abruzzi* classes, together with the more modern destroyers (the 'Soldati', 'Poeti'

TECHNICAL CHARACTERISTICS OF THE ITALIAN '10,000-ton' CRUISERS

Main characteristics at commissioning	*Trento*, 1929 (*Trieste*, 1929)	*Bolzano*, 1933	*Zara* class, 1931–1932
Standard displacement (t)	10,511 (10,505)	11,065	11,502 / 11,870
Full Load displacement (t)	13,358 (13,540)	13,885	14,168 / 14,560
Dimensions (m)			
- overall length	196.6	196.9	182.8
- maximum breadth	20.6	20.6	20.6
- depth at full load	6.8	6.8	7.2
Machinery	12 boilers, 4 geared turbines, 4 shafts	10 boilers, 4 geared turbines, 4 shafts	8 boilers, 2 geared turbines, 2 shafts
- maximum power (shp)	150,000	150,000	95,000
- maximum speed (knots)	35	35	32
- range at 16 knots (miles)	4160 (4208)	4432	4480/5400
Weapons (mm)			
- main calibre (in twin turrets)	8 – 203/50	8 – 203/53	8 –203/53
- medium calibres	16 – 100/47	16 – 100/47	16 – 100/47
- automatic weapons	4 – 40/39; 4 – 12.7; 8 – 13.2	2 – 40/39; 4 – 12.7; 8 – 13.2	4/6 –40/39, 8 – 13.2
- torpedoes (mm)	8 – 533	8 – 533	/
- aircraft	1 catapult, 3 aircraft	1 catapult, 2 aircraft	1 catapult, 2 aircraft
Protection (mm, max)			
- vertical	70	70	150
- horizontal	50	50	20+70
- transverse bulkheads	50	50	120
- turrets (front)	100	100	150
- barbettes	70	60	150
- conning tower	100	100	150
Electrical power (Kw)	2 –150 Kw turbogenerators, 1 –160 Kw turbogenerator, 2 –150 Kw diesel generators. Total 760 Kw	Similar to *Zara* class	3 –180 Kw turbogenerators, 2 –150 Kw diesel generators. Total 840 Kw
Crew (officers / POs & sailors)	25 / 756	28 / 760	31 / 810
Initial cost (lire)	95,100,000 (95,100,000)	101,600,000	from 106,000,000 to 114,700,000

HULL WEIGHTS

	Trento	%	*Trieste*	%	*Bolzano*	%	*Zara*	%
Hull, machinery and fittings (t)	5447	53.6	5432	53.0	5398	53.1	4693	42.6
Protection (t)	888	8.7	888	8.7	856	8.5	2688	24.4
Weapons (t)	1017	10.0	1014	9.9	1102	10.9	1372	12.5
Machinery	2292	22.6	2281	22.2	2205	21.7	1407	12.8
Other weights (t)	522	5.1	636	6.2	590	5.8	850	7.7
Total (t)	10,166	100.0	10,251	100.0	10,160	100.0	11,010	100.0

and *Maestrale* classes): The former would have the task of acting in the western Mediterranean against French shipping, while the latter force would be more of a traditional battle fleet. The doctrinal basis of both was the concept of the fleet in being – or, more accurately, the conservation of forces – already enunciated in previous years and which would influence the conduct of Italian naval warfare throughout the conflict. The 'battle force' would have the task of imposing on any adversary an enormous deployment of forces for any offensive operation it wished to undertake in the Mediterranean, especially in the central-eastern basin; the 'light groups' would create a threat in the western Mediterranean such as to force an adversary either to abandon this basin or to continuously deploy large forces there, subjecting them to the wear and tear of insurgent warfare. These ideas had already been outlined in the mid-1930s, when, under the Cavagnari undersecretariat, there was a shift in favour of battleships, and it is worth bearing this in mind when comparing the Italian heavy cruisers.

The data shown in the accompanying tables should be considered representative, as they are not exactly uniform in origin and are subject to calculations and simplifications to make them comparable. In addition, from the outset the figures for the Italian ships were adjusted to make them agree with the limits set by the Washington Treaty; thus, for example, from other sources, it appears that the armour of the two *Trento*s amounted to 900 tons and not to the reported 888 tons here.

The *Trento*s and other first generation heavy cruisers

More useful is a comparison between the *Trento*s and the other 10,000-ton cruisers of their generation – that is, ships which came from the same technical, political and doctrinal uncertain-

The heavy cruiser *Trento* shortly after commissioning; two further 'legs' were added to the tripod above the tower. The secondary armament was originally composed of eight twin 100/47 guns. (Fotocelere, Torino)

ties of the 1920s and which more or less all arrived at the concept of a 'large light cruiser', highly armed and fast, but with little or no protection and sometimes not very robust.

By these criteria, the *Trento* was not one of the worst designs. None had the protection to withstand the onslaught of 8in (203mm) guns at the foreseeable combat distances. Structurally, they were less robust and seaworthy than the *Kent* class, which, like their successors, were designed to operate on the open oceans, but this did not reflect their strength and capacity to withstand damage. For example, the 21in torpedo which hit the aft quarters of the *Bolzano* on 26 August 1941 had less serious consequences than those suffered by the *Kent*, which was struck on 17 September 1940 by a 450mm (17.7in) torpedo from a torpedo bomber, or by the more highly rated German heavy cruisers *Lützow* and *Prinz Eugen*, which were hit in the same areas by 21in torpedoes on 11 April 1940 and 23 February 1942, respectively. The loss of the *Bolzano* at Panarea was due, not so much to structural failure as to the extremely violent fuel oil fire, less efficient damage control than the ship had previously achieved, and uncertain command. In similar circumstances *Trieste* and *Trento* put in a good performance, including on the occasion of their sinking. Paradoxically, the newer *Pola* performed more poorly, both during the bombardment of Naples on 14 December 1940, when she was at risk of sinking because of a single 250lb bomb, and during the torpedoing of 28 March 1941 at Matapan, when her entire propulsion system was rendered useless by an 18in torpedo, even though she did not suffer serious damage or extensive flooding. In both circumstances a major part was played by the poor efficiency of damage control, which was very common in the first months of the war on Italian ships. From this point of view, both bitter experiences proved providential, because they highlighted the shortcomings of the ship's equipment, insufficient subdivision of the machinery and hull and allowed for their almost complete elimination in the following months.

More significant was the structural lightness – at least of the first two *Trento*s – which was the source of vibration in the hull and superstructure at high speeds, which compromised the efficiency of the fire control equipment, as well as the steering

TECHNICAL CHARACTERISTICS OF THE *TRENTO, TOURVILLE,* (*SUFFREN*) AND *KENT* CLASSES

Main features on commissioning	*Trento*, 1929 (*Trieste*, 1929)	*Tourville* class, 1929 (*Suffren**, 2 ships, 1930–1931)	*Kent* class**, 7 ships, 1928
Standard displacement (t)	10,511 (10,505)	10,160 (10,160)	9596 – 9709
Full load displacement (t)	13,358 (13,540)	12,634 (13,345)	13,614 – 13,736
Dimensions (m)			
- overall length	196.6	191.0 (194.0)	192.1
- maximum breadth	20.6	19.0 (19.3)	20.9
- draught at full load	6.8	6.45 (6.51)	6.2
Machinery	12 boilers, 4 geared turbines, 4 shafts	8 boilers (6+2), 3 geared turbines, 4 (3) shafts	8 boilers, 4 geared turbines, 4 shafts
- maximum power (shp)	150,000	120,000 (90,000)	81,110
- maximum speed (knots)	35	34 (32)	31.5
- range at 16 knots (miles)	4160 (4208)	5000 at 15 knots (4600 at 15 knots)	8000 at 10 knots
Weapons (mm)			
- main (in twin turrets)	8 – 203/50	8 – 203/50 (8 – 203/50)	8 – 203/50 [8in]
- secondary	16 – 100/47	8 – 75/50 (8 – 76/50 - 90/50)	4 – 102/45 [4in]
- MGs	4 – 40/39; 4 – 12.7; 8 – 13.2	8 – 37/50 (8–6 – 37/50)	16 – 40/39 [2pdr]
- torpedoes	8 – 533	6 – 500	8 – 533 mm
- aircraft	1 catapult, 3 aircraft	1 catapult, 3 aircraft	1 catapult, 1 aircraft
Protection (mm, max)			
- vertical	70	/	30 (30)
- horizontal	50	20–30 (50)	25.4–102
- transverse bulkheads	50	24+18 (20)	25.4–76
- turrets (front)	100	/ (20)	/
- barbettes	70	30 (30)	25.4
- conning tower	100	/ (/)	25.4
		/	External torpedo bulges
Electrical power (Kw)	2 150 Kw turbogenerators, 1 160 Kw turbogenerator, 2 150 Kw diesel generators; total 760 Kw	2 turbogenerators, 2 diesel generators (*ditto*)	4 300 Kw turbogenerators; total 1200 Kw
Crew (officers / PO & ratings)	25/756	total 637 (731)	total 585–710

* *Foch* similar (2 units). ** *London* (4 ships) and *Dorsetshire* (2 ships) similar

The cruisers *Trieste* (foreground) and *Trento* moored at 'Calata Zingari' in the port of Genoa in late May 1938. (E. Bagnasco collection)

The heavy cruiser *Trento* steaming at high speed towards the end of 1938.

HULL WEIGHTS: *TRENTO, TOURVILLE, SUFFREN* and *KENT* CLASSES

	Trento	%	*Tourville* class	%	*Colbert*	%	*Kent* class	%
Hull, machinery and fittings (t)	5447	53.6	5404	53.2	5569	54.8	5659	56.0
Protection (t)	888	8.7	459	4.5	762	7.5	1008	10.0
Weapons (t)	1017	10.0	1335	13.1	1346	13.3	1002	9.9
Machinery	2292	22.6	2271	22.4	1810	17.8	1855	18.4
Other weights (t)	522	5.1	691	6.8	673	6.6	577	5.7
Total (t)	10,166	10.0	10,160	100.0	10,160	100.0	10.101	100.0

system. The strengthening of the original tripod with two extra legs, adopted immediately after completion, did not remedy the problem, nor did the improvements made to the motion-dampening of this equipment in the summer of 1942 work at speeds of over 26 knots. But the same phenomena was not uncommon in the first 10,000-tonners, including the *Kent* class; the problem was reduced in later designs, but not completely eliminated. On the other hand, the armament of the first two *Trento*s revealed other limitations. These were in addition to those of a more general nature concerning the weapons of Italian ships and were due to the technical solutions adopted to limit the weight of the 203mm guns and to the adoption of inaccurate coincidence rangefinders; all of these problems were highlighted both before and during the war, when the additional inconvenience of barrel wear emerged (the rifling of the bores could not be replaced cold). At the time of commissioning, the anti-aircraft (AA) armament was superior to that of contemporary cruisers, but the 100/47 mountings, despite their good ballistic performance, were compromised by the technical solutions described earlier, which greatly reduced their effectiveness. Despite the gradual transition to automatic AA power mountings and from barrage firing at predetermined distances to pursuit firing, it was not possible to produce calculation accuracy and speed of reaction to the angular changes to target individual aircraft of the time; this was evident on the eve of the conflict and was confirmed by wartime experience. In short, the AA weapon system proved to be ineffective even before the war and was mainly suited to barrage firing.

Another note concerns their machinery, usually judged to be of poor performance and unsatisfactory operation, so much so that during the war period it was unable to propel the three cruisers at speeds above 31 knots at full load displacement. This is a judgement that must be qualified. With displacements of around 14,000 tons and without any boiler or engine failures, the entire 3rd Division reached a speed of 34 knots during the battle of Cape Teulada (Spartivento) and 33 knots during the first phase of the 'Gaudo' battle. During the latter it was unable to gain ground on the retreating British cruisers, but this was due to the fact that they had to alter course to widen the firing arcs and to free the *Bolzano* from the *Trento*'s funnel smoke. On 15 May 1942, during speed trials following the repair of the torpedo damage, the *Bolzano* easily maintained a speed of 34 knots for an hour with a displacement of approximately 14,000 tons. Finally, the efficiency reports of the *Trieste* of 1 October 1941, 1 January 1942, 1 October 1942, and 1 January 1943, for displacements between 13,500 and 14,460 tons, gave maximum speeds between 33.5 and 34 knots; for the *Trento*, the reports of 1 October 1941 and 1 January 1942 gave a maximum speed of 34.5 knots with a displacement of 13,000 tons.

Finally, the common judgement on these – and indeed most Italian naval vessels, including the most modern and largest battleships – must repeated: if, in terms of design, materials and construction, they could be considered, more or less, equivalent and sometimes even better examples of naval architecture than contemporary foreign ships, in the more advanced technologies, such as electronics, communications and fire control systems, especially AA, they lagged behind, nor did they make significant progress between the beginning and end of the conflict.

The *Zara*s and other second-generation heavy cruisers

There is no need to add to what has already been said about the comparison between the *Zara*s and the three *Trento*s. More useful is a comparison between the *Zara*s and the second generation of heavy cruisers (the third generation was produced once the treaty restrictions were abandoned and which only applied to the US Navy). There was no British second-generation design (although the *Kent* class was modified for later classes), so for the sake of simplicity, the comparison has been restricted to the French *Algérie*, expressly conceived as an answer to the *Zara*s – with the

HULL WEIGHTS: *ZARA* CLASS, *ALGÉRIE* and *ADMIRAL HIPPER* CLASS

	*Zara**	%	*Algérie*	%	*Admiral Hipper*	%
Hull, machinery and fittings (t)	4693	42.6	3837	37.8	7492***	51.9
Protection (t)	2688	24.4	2035	20.0	2436	16.9
Weapons (t)	1372	12.5	1526	15.0	1216	8.4
Machinery	1407	12.8	1335	13.1	2357	16.3
Other weights (t)	850	7.7	1427**	14.1	939	6.5
Total (t)	11,010	100.0	10,160	100.0	14,440	100.0

* Please note the cautions in the comparison between the *Trento*s and the *Zara*s.

** Auxiliary machinery and fittings included.

*** Including protection incorporated into the hull structure.

TECHNICAL CHARACTERISTICS OF *ZARA* CLASS, *ALGÉRIE* and *ADMIRAL HIPPER* CLASS

Main features on commissioning	*Zara* class, 1931–1932	*Algérie*, 1934	*Admiral Hipper* class*, 1939
Standard displacement (t)	11,502 – 11,870	10,271	14,247 – 14,475
Full load displacement (t)	14,168 – 14,560	13,677	18,600 – 18,694
Dimensions (m)			
- overall length	182.8	186.2	202.8
- maximum breadth	20.6	20.0	21.3
- draught at full load	7.2	6.3	7.7
Machinery	8 boilers, 2 geared turbines, 2 shafts	5+1 boilers, 4 geared turbines, 4 shafts	12 boilers, 3 geared turbines, 3 shafts
- maximum power (c.v.)	95,000	84,000	132,000
- maximum speed (knots)	32	31	32.5
- range (miles)	4480/5400 (at 16 knots)	8000 (at 15 knots)	6500 (at 17 knots)
Weapons (mm)			
- main (in twin turrets)	8 – 203/53	8 – 203/50	8 – 203/60
- secondary	16 – 100/47	12 – 100/45	12 – 105/65
- MGs	4/6 – 40/39, 8 – 13.2	4 – 37/50, 16 – 13.2	12 – 37/83, 8 – 20/65
- torpedoes	/	6 – 500	12 – 533
- aircraft	1 catapult, 2 aircraft	1 catapult, 2 aircraft	1 catapult, 3 aircraft
Protection (mm, max)			
- vertical	150	110	80 (70 + 20-40)
- horizontal	20+70	22+80/30 (sides)	30+30/50 (sides)
- transversal bulkheads	120	70	70
- turrets (front)	150	100	160
- barbettes	150	100	80
- conning tower	150	100	105
	40mm amidship (internal)	20 internal longitudinal bulkhead	
Electrical power (Kw)	3 180 Kw turbogenerators, 2 150 Kw diesel generators; total 840 Kw	4 300 Kw turbogenerators, 2 100 Kw diesel generators; total 1400 Kw	4 400 Kw, turbogenerators, 2 230 Kw diesel generators, 3 150 Kw diesel generators; total 2510 Kw
Crew (officers / PO & ratings)	31/810	746	42/1340

* *Prinz Eugen* similar.

actual protection (and displacement) characteristics from French sources – and to the German *Admiral Hipper* class.

With the exception of the *Gorizia*, the war gave no opportunity to demonstrate the fighting qualities of the *Zara* class, which was nevertheless held in high regard even by the enemy. The loss of the *Zara* and the *Fiume* at Matapan cannot be taken as a criticism of their protection, because the damage received would have been fatal for any type of warship. A similar consideration can be made for the *Blücher*, lost in the Oslo fjord on 9 April 1940. However, the events surrounding the loss of the *Pola* are still astonishing today, especially when compared to the notable resilience demonstrated by the *Gorizia* during the bombardment of La Maddalena (see Appendix A).

The main armament of the *Zara*s corresponded in number and calibre to that of all European heavy cruisers. From the reports of training activities in the pre-war period, the 203/53 revealed drawbacks and tuning problems, common to similar cruisers of other navies, such as the *Kent* class, and similar to those of the 203/50 of the first two *Trento*s. The main problem remained the dispersion of the salvoes, especially at long distances. The perception of this problem and its causes by the Italian naval leadership is outlined in Chapter 3. In the years of training before the war, the efficiency of the 203/53 did not prove to be much greater than that of the 203/50, although in the exercises of 1939–1941 things went better (see Chapter 3), but not entirely satisfactorily, as was confirmed by the course of the battles of Punta Stilo, Cape Teulada and the First Sirte. The equipment and arrangements for daytime firing proved to be acceptable: even at long distances targets were quickly straddled and only the excessive dispersion of the salvoes prevented any appreciable results from being achieved.

During the war, the machinery performed somewhat below expectations: the maximum operational speed was between 30 and 31 knots and was subject to a certain amount of wear and tear, which in the case of the *Gorizia* from mid-1942, limited its efficiency due to the postponement of major work on the ship and the poor quality of some replacement parts.

Like the *Zara*s, the *Algérie* represented a break with the classes which had preceded her and, even if the actual standard displacement was a bit higher than declared due to the expedients adopted in calculating the equipment, the final result was equivalent to her Italian opponents, with a slight advantage in terms of protection. However, it should be noted that the *Algérie* was the only '10,000' to be expressly equipped with underwater protection, even if it was limited to the midships part of the hull along the machinery spaces. On paper, it should have been able to absorb the bursting energy of 300kg of high explosives – equivalent to that expected of a modern battleship. It should be added that the *Algérie*'s lower displacement was made possible by the extensive use of electric welding, which was absent from Italian cruisers. On the whole, the two types of ships can be considered equivalent.

The *Admiral Hipper*, designed after the conclusion of the Anglo-German naval agreement of June 1935 and more advanced technically than the *Zara* design, were conceived for a higher speed than the *Dunkerque* and overall characteristics not inferior to the *Algérie* as well as being able to wage war on the open oceans. They are, to this day, considered among the best in their class. The main armament showed excellent performance, on a par with all large German ships. But their propulsion, characterised by very high-pressure boilers, like the *Gneisenau* class battleships and the destroyers, revealed significant and recurrent operating problems due to the advanced, but insufficiently tested, design; this condemned these ships to prolonged periods of inactivity and even to compromise the progress of ongoing operations. Even their autonomy proved insufficient for oceanic warfare, despite increases in fuel supplies. The so-called 'pocket battleships' equipped with diesel engines proved to be more suitable for these tasks, although they were not as fast. In line with the other major German ships, protection was developed more in coverage than in thickness. Apart from the bombing raids of the last weeks of the war, for which there are no adequate records, it was tested only once, in the Battle of the Barents Sea on 31 December 1942. On that occasion, a single 6in (152mm) shell from *Sheffield* hit the 80mm armour belt at a distance of about 10,000m, piercing it with relative ease and eventually going through the entire hull. It should be noted that this was not the shot that knocked out two-thirds of the evaporator apparatus, which had passed under the armour belt. This experience, although isolated, leads to the conclusion that the vertical protection of these ships was not sufficient to withstand 203mm (8in) guns.

More than even the '35,000-ton' battleship, which, all things considered, represented a natural end point of battle fleet development, the '10,000-ton' cruisers were the most 'political' of the ships that emerged in the age of treaties, and one with the most uncertain role. At the beginning of the 1930s they were also candidates to replace battleships as capital ships, when the prospect of their abolition was being canvassed. It is also difficult to compare and judge them in terms not only of their mere technical characteristics, but also of the criteria for which they were built and the operations they actually performed. From the first point of view, the *Zara* class, even with the limitations highlighted several times, can ideally be considered the most balanced and successful of the European 10,000-tonners; but from the second point of view, it was probably the *Kent* class that proved to be the most flexible and provided the most convincing results during the conflict.

Algérie, the last French '10,000-ton' cruiser, visiting Venice in June 1935. She was probably the nearest foreign equivalent to the *Zara* class. (Augusto de Toro collection)

Appendix A

DAMAGE AND LOSSES DURING THE SECOND WORLD WAR

TRENTO

Trento, air raid on Taranto, night of 11/12 November 1940

During the second-wave torpedo bomber attack on Taranto, at 00:30 on the 12th, the *Trento*, moored at the Torpediniere dock, was hit by a 250lb armour-piercing bomb, dropped from low altitude. The bomb hit the forward 100/47 gun on the port side. The shelter deck was not penetrated; only two plates of the smoke duct grating were deformed. The only consequence was the temporary breakdown of the portside boiler No 1 due to a ruptured smoke duct. The deck was repaired with on-board equipment. The rest of the repairs were carried out between 13 and 14 November in Messina after the transfer from Taranto. There were no casualties among the personnel.

Trento, 2nd Battle of Sirte, 22–23 March 1942

During the 2nd Battle of Sirte, the *Trento* was not damaged by enemy fire. Instead, she sustained damage due to the combined effect of the blast damage of her own guns and the sea conditions. Unfortunately, no detailed documentation has been found, except in regard of the gunnery branch, where the effective work of its personnel overcame the problems, which did not affect firing, with only the partial exception of the port twin 100/47 gun. The worsening weather conditions during the night and morning of 23 March caused significant flooding, resulting in damage to the electrical and weapons systems and difficulties in keeping the sea, which forced the ship to change course. There is also no documentation on the repair or remedial work, except that the 'tidying up' took place in Messina after her return from the operation.

Trento, operation 'Mezzo Giugno', 15 June 1942

In the initial phase of operation 'Mezzo Giugno', shortly after 05:00 on 15 June, in the morning twilight the *Trento* was attacked, while proceeding at 24 knots, by twin-engine Bristol Beaufort torpedo bombers and hit on the starboard side in the forward boiler room by an 18in (450mm) Mark XII type torpedo with a burst charge of 176kg of TNT, released at a distance of only 200m and therefore not avoidable, despite the prompt evasive manoeuvre.

The explosion caused the immediate flooding of the room with the loss of all personnel and broke through the bulkhead separating the central boiler room, where there was considerable water ingress and a worrying fire of vapourised fuel oil which produced a huge plume of smoke from the forward funnel. The four forward boilers were immediately put out of action and the four midships boilers also went out due to breakages in the fuel pipes and the flooding of the space; here, however, the personnel managed to escape. The four aft boilers also stopped due to the shutdown of the oil burners because of water infiltration in the fuel manifold. The forward engines stopped first due to lack of steam and the after ones slowed and then stopped. At 05:16 the *Trento*, with about 2500 tons of water on board, was immobilised, listing 2° to starboard and slightly down by the head. Other damage included the hydraulic transmission of the rudder and the APG of the 1st Director and there were slight leaks in the firing station and magazine of Turret 2; the battery deck (protected) and its doors remained intact. In general, the ship's situation was serious, but not hopeless: with the after boilers and the four engines in operation, she was able to undertake the return voyage at 10 knots, although she would not be safe from air and underwater attacks due to difficulties in manoeuvring.

The destroyers *Camicia Nera*, *Antonio Pigafetta* and *Saetta* were detached to assist the cruiser and provide smoke screens. On board, the forward bulkheads of the forward and aft engine rooms and the aft bulkheads of the order room and firing station were shored up and strengthened, as they were showing signs of collapse, the former due to the high temperatures generated by the fire in the central boiler room, the latter due to the pressure of the water on board. The high-volume pumps were brought into action in order to reduce the water level in No 2 magazine and the forward engine room; the 100mm ammunition and the 13.2mm machine guns were transferred to the extreme stern under wet hoods and mats in order to keep them away from the heat of the fire, the backup manual rudder system was brought into operation, the after boilers were connected to water and unpolluted oil and the towing hawser was prepared. Shortly after 08:00, as the difficulties in starting the aft boilers persisted due to water contamination in the fuel oil pipes leading to the sprayers, the captain, Stanislao Esposito, took the decision to start the engines. Esposito decided to have the *Pigafetta* tow from the bow. At 09:00 all seemed to be going well: the flooding was contained, the fire in the central boiler room was out, the after boilers were back on stream and the after engines were ready to start, while the *Pigafetta* was laying out the tow-rope.

A few minutes later, however, the cruiser was hit by a second torpedo launched from the submarine *P 35*, which at first light had spotted the tall column of smoke rising from the recently torpedoed cruiser. The 21in Mark VIII torpedo with a 340kg

TNT burst charge hit the ship at 09:10 on the port side at Turret 2 and was followed by the massive explosion of the forward magazine. The ship was devastated: all the deck was lifted on the portside ahead of the forward turrets, the pentapod structure was demolished with all its decks and platforms, including the bridge – it remained for two minutes supported by a single leg and then plunged into the sea to port; the forward funnel was ripped open, the forward 100/47 mounting and the port illuminating howitzer were thrown into the sea, the after mast was knocked down, while a large mass of wreckage and metal plating was blown into the air. At 09:13 the *Trento*, heeling heavily to port, sank by the bow, lifting her stern vertically and breaking in two. The captain, the commander and all the personnel on the bridge or on the forecastle handling the towing equipment perished almost instantaneously and the order to abandon ship was given by Lt-Cdr. Umberto Paolicchi. The abandonment took place with discipline and to cries of 'Viva il Re, viva il Duce, viva il *Trento*'. Many men, however, hesitated to throw themselves into the sea and went down with the ship. In all, 406 men were killed, including 28 officers, 69 non-commissioned officers, 306 other ranks and 4 military and civilians; 580 survivors were picked up by the *Pigafetta*, which had promptly cast off the tow, and by the *Saetta*. The behaviour and demeanour of the officers and crew, from the first torpedoing until the sinking, was judged excellent, as was that of the destroyers that assisted them.

TRIESTE

Trieste, 'C' convoy escort, 21/22 November 1941

While escorting convoy 'C' from Naples to Tripoli, at 23:10 on 21 November 1941, the *Trieste*, proceeding at less than 13 knots, was hit by one torpedo out of a salvo of four launched from the British submarine *Utmost*, 13 miles south of Capo dell'Armi. The 21in (533mm) Mark VIII torpedo, with a burst charge of 340kg of TNT, hit the cruiser on the port side at boiler No 3 (forward boiler room).

The detonation of the warhead was compounded by the explosion of boiler No 3. The ship was jolted several metres and violently whipped so much that it was feared that the pentapod or the topmasts might come down. There was a large leak and the water flooded the forward and middle boiler rooms, the firing station, part of the orderly room and two alcoves; but the bulkheads of the flooded rooms held well; they were, however, shored up. The fire caused by the combustion of vapourised naphtha in both boiler rooms was extinguished without human intervention by the escaping steam. On fire and without lighting, the *Trieste* came to a standstill, as the four after boilers also had to be extinguished as their water supply had been cut off. However, the diesel dynamos of the two groups of turrets and the one in the bow were quickly put into operation and, finally, one of the turbogenerators, which brought light back to the ship.

Shortly after midnight, the destroyers *Corazziere* and *Carabiniere* and the torpedo boat *Perseo* arrived on the scene, keeping watch in the surrounding waters, without, however, preparing for towing. At 00:45 on 22 April, the after boilers were lit and the *Trieste* was once again ready to move with steering from the bridge. Moving slowly, she returned to Messina at 06:45 without the aid of tugs (all of which had been sent to assist the *Duca degli Abruzzi*, torpedoed at the same time), mooring at the Customs House dock. During the return voyage, no major problems were reported, other than minor failures to the electrical circuits and the high-volume pumps, which were soon removed. Losses among personnel amounted to 22 killed and 6 wounded, all non-commissioned officers and ratings. The officers and crew behaved in a highly commendable manner and the ship demonstrated high efficiency in all departments.

The hit suffered by the *Trieste* was almost identical to that suffered by the *Trento* at 'Mezzo Giugno', with the only difference being the higher torpedo burst charge and the effects on the hull and services were similar, as was the amount of water that flooded part of the hull, no less than 2500 tons.

Trieste, bombardment of La Maddalena, 10 April 1943

During the raid on La Maddalena, the *Trieste* was moored within an enclosure of anti-torpedo netting in the bay of Mezzoschifo. Shortly after 14:35 on 10 April 1943 the ship was bracketed by at least four sticks of carefully calibrated bombs, released from an altitude of 5000–6000m. These were all 1000lb (454kg) armour-piercing bombs with fuses set to pierce 2in and 3in (51mm and 76mm) armour decks – the thickness of those of the *Trieste* and *Gorizia*, respectively, while the bombs intended for the base were

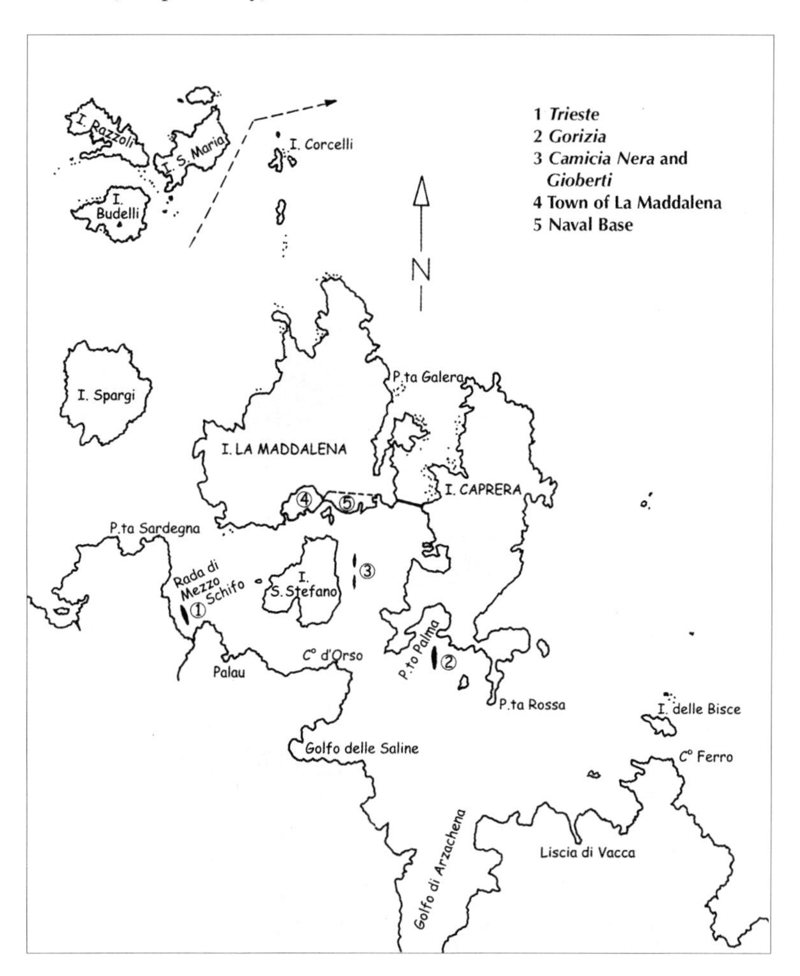

The anchorage and naval base at La Maddalena showing the positions of the ships when attacked on 10 April 1943.

500lb (227kg) high explosive. Of the AP bombs, three certainly hit the cruiser and others exploded in the vicinity:

- one hit the deck at the extreme aft end, on the starboard side, at the rudder port, piercing it and causing a large hole in the area, with rapid flooding of the ice and rudder rooms;
- two hit the pentapod at the same time, demolishing the bridge, its bulwarks and the fire control panels; one went on through the deckhouse, pierced the port side of the deck and probably exploded on the battery deck (deck protected with 50mm armour) in line with the smokebox of boiler No 1, devastating the whole area. The other pierced the battery deck on the same side and exploded in the forward boiler room, wrecking it and causing a leak in the joint between the protected deck and the armoured belt on the starboard side.

The other bombs, which exploded in the water in the immediate vicinity, caused:

- a large breach and rupture of the outer and inner plating strakes on the starboard side in line with the after boiler and engine rooms, with rapid flooding of the same and pouring of fuel oil from the side tanks;
- puncture of the outer plating on the port side between the forward engine and the after boilers;
- deformation of the aft watertight bulkhead of the forward engine room and leakage through the inner plating at the same bulkhead;
- breakage of the inner and outer plating courses on the starboard side in line with the forward and middle boiler rooms with opening of waterways and oil spillages;
- a rupture in the plating under the forward diesel dynamo room with consequent water and oil spillage and putting the forward power plant out of action;
- a minor fire in the forge room (workshop), which was soon extinguished with the use of fire extinguishers.

As a result of the attack, the entire propulsion system was put out of action, with the exception of the auxiliary boilers, which were turned on despite the lack of power to the electric compressors. The same was true for all the electric power generators and the mobile pumps, except for the stern diesel dynamo, which continued to supply power to the stern lighting circuits; with this they struggled to power the large electric pumps 3 and 2, before the compartment was in turn flooded. The same fate befell the radio aerials and wireless telegraph equipment, so that communications with the Navy Command ashore were reduced to a semaphore signal through the Guardiavecchia traffic light.

After the first bombs, the AA response was reduced; gun mountings were decimated and many men ended up in the sea due to the columns of water and the shock-waves to which the ship was subjected. However, within a few minutes, AA fire was reorganised for the guns remaining in working order.

As a result of extensive and uncontrollable flooding, the cruiser went down by the stern with an increasing list to starboard, enhanced by the pull exerted by the dead bow section on the starboard side, from which she was moored. At 15:13 a request to send in pumping equipment was transmitted ashore. Once he realised that there was no possibility of saving the ship, the CO, Capt. Rosario Viola, tried to prevent the ship from sinking completely by having her towed out of the net enclosure to beach her in the shallows; at 15:20 he asked for the assistance of tugs. He also ordered the starboard bow and stern moorings to be released, but waited to release the port one, as the traction exerted slowed down the increasing list.

Two small tugs and a motor sailer were ready to intervene, but, due to their small size, they were unable to open or cut the obstructions closing the net enclosure on the south side in time. Serious difficulties were also encountered on board when it came to releasing the shackles of the mooring cables from the buoys or

1950, La Spezia Dockyard: bow-on view of the refloated (but still capsized) hull of the *Trieste*. The cruiser had been sunk on 10 April 1943 in the Bay of Mezzo Schifo (Palau, north-western Sardinia) during an attack by USAAF heavy bombers. (E. Bagnasco collection)

dealing with dead bodies due to breakdowns in the chain of command on deck. In the meantime, with the help of three Mas boats, motor sailers and motorboats, the injured personnel and those not strictly necessary for operations on deck were evacuated, as well as the bodies of the fallen, all in an extremely orderly manner. Shortly after 16:00, when the ship's heel had reached 40 degrees and any other efforts would have been futile, Viola gave the order to abandon the ship to the few remaining personnel, not before giving the order to salute the King, the Duce, and the *Trieste*. At 16:10, he was the last to abandon the cruiser, which at 16:13, having completed its capsize to starboard, sank.

Sixty-seven people died, including two officers, and 69 were wounded, including two officers. The conduct of the personnel on board was exemplary and Damage Control did all it could in the conditions prevailing on the ship. In the captain's opinion, 'with the obstructions [net defence] open, moorings released, and suitable tugs ready, it might have been possible to bring the ship ashore, if starting the manoeuvre immediately after the attack,' since, after all, 98 minutes passed from the beginning of the attack to the final sinking.

Comparing the *Trieste* to the *Gorizia*, which was badly damaged at the same time but in fairly good condition in her vital parts, one could easily conclude that the inferior horizontal protection of the *Trieste* made the difference. Both of the bombs that hit the *Trieste* amidships – even if, perhaps, one of them did not completely penetrate – were able to overcome the thinner armoured deck (50mm compared to 70mm for the *Gorizia*) and contributed significantly to depriving the ship of any source of power, without which it was impossible to cope with the widespread and substantial flooding. The injuries received by the *Trieste*, including those produced by the near-misses, were significant, and in themselves do not indicate a particular structural fragility of the ship and would have been fatal for many ships of this type and generation.

BOLZANO

Bolzano, Battle of Punta Stilo, 9 July 1940

At 16:05 during the Italian fleet's disengagement, the *Bolzano* was hit in rapid succession by three 6in [152mm] armour-piercing shells fired from the light cruiser *Neptune* (according to some sources from *Orion*) and the effects of other rounds of the same calibre landing nearby.

The first shell hit the ship on the starboard side between frames 67 and 68 AD (on the *Bolzano* the frames were numbered from the main section towards the bow and stern) with an impact angle of 53°, penetrated the hull and, after having pierced the platform deck with the 20mm splinter shield armour protecting the steering gear, exploded in the starboard alcove adjacent to the local manual rudder. The explosion and splintering caused flooding of these compartments, severed various power lines, including those supplying the rudder electric pump No 2, which stopped, while No 1 continued to operate. At the time of the explosion, the rudder was in the process of being put over 15° or 20° to port, but suddenly the cruiser turned sharply in that direction, immediately suggesting an emergency. It turned out that, in addition to the direct hit, a second 6in projectile had exploded simultaneously in the water, again on the starboard side in the vicinity of the rudder, and that the explosion had violently accelerated the movement of the rudder, causing disruption of the steering gear hydraulic mechanisms and jamming the rudder hard over to the left. The combination of the two explosions caused two different failures that made the ship unmanageable and confused the search for the nature of the damage for a few minutes. The first attempts to move the rudder, using electric pump No 1, had to continue the operation manually because the compartment was flooding; this failed. Only after inspecting the steering gear was it possible to take effective action and, thanks also to the stabilising effect of the ship's high speed, bring the rudder back under control. Some small punctures and minor deformations affected the port centre propeller and the rudder blade. The time between the loss and the restoration of the ship's steering was 6 (or 9) minutes, after which control returned first to the order room and then to the armoured command tower. At this juncture, the cruiser had performed a complete heart-stopping 360° turn to port, before resuming her place in formation. Minor failures involved pumps and pipework for fire, washing and sanitation services and, momentarily, the No 4 high-capacity pump. The ship took on 316 tons of water which did not significantly affect her trim, stability or speed; minor leaking affected the port central shaft tunnel and some of the recesses of the magazine for Turret 4.

The second 6in shell hit the starboard 203mm gun of Turret 2 one metre from the muzzle. The gun was badly damaged and the core tube laid bare. Incredibly, the gun continued to fire in this condition without any further incident. The left gun was also damaged by shrapnel, removing between 1 and 2 metres of metal from the muzzle, but it also continued to fire. Other shrapnel hit a sighting device on the same turret and slightly damaged the right-hand head of the 7.20m rangefinder base, piercing the bridge and the deckhouses below.

The third 6in projectile hit the port broadside between frames 31 and 32 AD at an impact angle of 57°, pierced the deck gunwale plate, penetrated the after torpedo room, where it was deflected by various structures and exploded after bouncing off the battery deck (50mm protected deck). The explosion and the resulting splinters caused: the breakage or deformation of some horizontal and longitudinal structures in the affected area, the severance of some pipes and cables of the lighting circuit, the destruction of all light parts of the rigging on the starboard side of the torpedo room, some plate breakage of the engine room skylight, without any effect on the machinery, and enough minor damage to the after port torpedo room to render it unusable.

In addition to the hit near the stern, other near-miss salvoes during the 360-degree turn and aerial machine-gun fire caused further damage, namely: the deformation of the stiffening plates of the starboard after torpedo tubes, the destruction of the starboard bow projector, minor injuries to the port projector and a 13.2mm machine gun, and holes in the superstructure. Minor damage was caused by the blast of the forward turrets, while they were firing in retreat – a problem common to most ships armed with guns – producing slight deformations to the rangefinder turret of the fire directors on the starboard side and more delicate failures in the three lookout stations on the starboard side of the bridge.

At the end of the battle, the efficiency of the ship was only reduced in its offensive power, with two 203mm guns and four of the eight torpedo tubes out of action; the damage to the secondary armament and some fire control equipment was unimportant. The ship's steering was restored and the flooding at the stern was under control. Ultimately, the *Bolzano*, having regained its place in formation, would have been able to resume combat if necessary. The battle did, however, highlight some deficiencies in construction and shipboard services, which were present on other Italian ships at the time and which, at least in part, were remedied in the following months.

The machinery had worked very well. The only drawback was the distillation system for the reserve water for the boilers, which was insufficient to supplement consumption during prolonged wartime steaming. Damage Control demonstrated good organisation and readiness, but also the absence or inadequacy of pump capacity and means of automatically extinguishing boiler and electricity fires, such as autonomous foam generators and mobile motor pumps (only one was on board). Internal communications proved inadequate, starting with the lack of a telephone switchboard allowing direct and immediate communication between machinery control and the engine and boiler rooms, and the lack of a communication line between the machinery and the Fire Safety Service. In the tactical phase, this resulted in difficulties in getting fire extinguishing equipment into or out of the affected areas and in the transmission of orders for the operation of the engines, for which it was necessary to resort to verbal communications from officers and non-commissioned officers.

The horizontal protection (50mm armoured battery deck) proved adequate to resist 6in armour-piercing shells with a high angle of impact and the resulting splinter showers. In fact, it suffered only a few dents and kept the effects of the explosion from the areas below, except for some ricocheting shrapnel which fell harmlessly into the after engine room through the skylight grating. The same cannot be said for the protection of the

Morning of 26 August 1941, about 10:00, the *Bolzano* enters the port of Messina assisted by tugs, with stern submerged by flooding through the hole caused by the torpedo from submarine HM S/M *Triumph*, which struck it just over three hours earlier at the northern entrance to the Strait. (E. Bagnasco collection)

steering gear, defended only by 20mm armour plating (platform deck) which was easily penetrated by a similar shell. Here the consequences could have been very serious, since, if the rudder failure had not been corrected within a few minutes, the ship would have found herself without steering and isolated with superior enemy forces approaching.

Bolzano, opposition to Operation 'Mincemeat', 26 August 1941

At 06:41 on 26 August, as the 3rd Division was returning to Messina, the *Bolzano* was proceeding at a speed of 16 knots when she was hit by a torpedo launched from the British submarine *Triumph* in the vicinity of Cape Peloro. The 21in (533mm) Mark VIII type torpedo, with a 340kg TNT burst charge, struck the hull just aft of Turret 4 at an impact angle of about 145°.

The explosion caused very strong shocks and vibrations along the entire hull and opened a hole about 15m long and 10m high, extending from the keel almost to the deck; on the opposite side it broke the sheer of the deck, causing extensive damage for long stretches aft of Turret 4 with crumpling of the plating as well as lifting, gashes and lacerations on the platform decks (20mm of armour), on the battery and on the main decks. The flooding affected, totally or partially, almost all the compartments aft of the bulkhead of the after engine room, including the ammunition magazines of Turrets 4 and 3, up to and above the battery deck, with the ship down by the stern and a slight list to starboard. In spite of the deformations, it was possible to close the watertight doors of the bulkhead corresponding to AD 62, thus preventing the flooding towards the bow above the battery deck and the complete flooding of the magazine of Turret 3, which, besides making the ship heavier, would have increased pressure on the entire surface of the bulkhead of the after engine room. An initial assessment estimated that she had taken on 2000 tons of water.

As for the machinery, the starboard after engine was immediately unusable due to serious deformation of the shafts and the inner propeller; the same was true for the port aft shaft, although to a lesser extent. Extensive water infiltration affected the lubrication circuits, resulting in leaks and oil pollution, so that the engine continued to operate slowly but at low oil pressure. Only the forward engines ran smoothly without water leaking into the lubrication circuits. The evaporator apparatus did not suffer any damage, but after four hours, during the return trip, a combination of the strong draught, the low speed and only some of the engines working produced abnormal variations in the levels in the

The *Bolzano* in drydock at Genoa in October 1941 to repair the damage sustained in the torpedoing of 26 August 1941 outside Messina. (A. Fraccaroli collection)

water feed tanks, so four boilers were shut down, reducing steam production to only six forward boilers.

In addition, the large high-capacity pump room No 4 was destroyed. Lacerations and deformations were found in the forward steering machinery room, concentrated on the left side of the gangway, the hand steering room, the winch room, some fuel tanks and the officers' quarters on the platform and battery decks.

After the explosion, the commander, Captain Francesco Ruta, immediately stopped engines, but soon had them restarted at slow speed to move away from the area of the attack. The outside propellers worked normally, but there were noticeable vibrations in the hull and a periodic oscillation in the longitudinal direction. The following operations began immediately: balancing, to contain the variations in trim, and shoring up the bulkheads adjacent to the flooded compartments; cutting all electrical circuits, to prevent dangerous short circuits of steam, water and fuel oil in the stern area; activation of the large high-capacity pump No 3 to drain the shaft tunnels of the after engines.

Since the state of the ship's buoyancy was still unclear, Capt. Ruta manoeuvred with engines only in the approach to the Calabrian coast, at the same time preparing for a tow from forward; the destroyer *Corazziere* remained nearby, in case she was needed for the tow. Between 07:45 and 10:55, with the assistance of four tugs and after the rest of the division had returned to Messina, the *Bolzano* completed the difficult navigation through the Strait and entered port, mooring at the Etiopia pier. Three officers and four sailors were killed or missing; two more officers and 19 non-commissioned officers and ratings were wounded.

Once moored, the draught at the stern was measured at 9.10m (8.80m immediately after the torpedoing) and 5.60m at the bow compared to the normal 6.80m average draught. Here, the pumping, plugging and shoring operations begun at sea continued with the help of external equipment which had been rushed in, and port service was resumed with only one main boiler in operation. It was also possible to ascertain that the area between AD 81 and the stern to starboard was almost torn away from the rest of the ship, being joined to it by part of the plating on the port side, by some plates of the main deck and the battery deck, and by other brackets and plates below the waterline, all very deformed. On the other hand, from a rough calculation of residual stability, the *Bolzano* still had a metacentric height of at least 60cm. The conditions of buoyancy and stability therefore appeared quite reassuring.

Considering the extent of the damage, the ship was fairly secure. Damage control had operated promptly and efficiently, so that the flooding was quickly controlled and contained, and two engines continued to operate. However, her salvation was also due to the fact that she was only a short distance from Messina – a circumstance that was almost taken for granted, given the fact that British submarines preferred to ambush in narrow passages – and to the fact that she was promptly rescued by tugs, which were decisive for manoeuvring, made difficult by rudder failures and the currents in the Strait. Had the torpedoing occurred at a greater distance, as in the case of the torpedoing during the Battle of 'Mezzo Agosto' at Panarea (see below) or the similar damage to *Trento* during the Battle of 'Mezzo Giugno', the salvage operation would have been more complicated due to the ship's prolonged exposure to additional underwater and aerial attacks.

Bolzano, air raid on Messina, night of 10 September 1941

During the air raid on the night of 10 September on Messina, the *Bolzano* was hit at 00:08 on the 10th by a bomb dropped from a low altitude. The bomb, probably a 250lb (113.5kg) semi-armour-piercing bomb, arrived at the target at a drop angle of about 64°, grazed the catapult on the starboard side, pierced the deckhouse ceiling and the deck at the air service room and exploded on the protected battery deck (50mm) in the forward torpedo room between the two torpedo tube mountings, whose weapons had fortunately been landed the day before. The protected deck was not pierced, but only suffered a small 20cm tear. However, the explosive shock-wave, unable to vent because the space was effectively airtight, caused considerable damage locally; on the other hand, this prevented the fires from feeding due to lack of oxygen. The explosion generated an intense cloud of shrapnel and a violent blaze that devastated the torpedo room; furthermore, the flames escaped through the tear in the deck, the access hatch and the ventilation ducts, into the space underneath housing the AV (forward) engine, whose geared turbines were immediately shut down. As a result, the lighting and power lines on the starboard side failed and, after 5 minutes, the entire ship's electricity supply was cut off. The back-up lighting was immediately activated, which worked very well, and the stern diesel generators were started up (the after geared turbines were kept at a standstill so as not to damage the surrounding bulkheads, which were being repaired to eliminate the leaks caused by the previous month's torpedoing), but it was only possible to initially supply electricity to the aft area due to the severance of connections between the two distribution panels and the numerous power lines passing through the damaged spaces. In a short time, it was possible to supply the lighting circuits in all the forward compartments by means of temporary connections.

The fight against the fires in the torpedo room and the AV power plant, where they had spread rapidly along the electrical cables, took longer. They were extinguished with fire extinguishers, foam appliances and from a tanker alongside the ship from which a fire hose had been rolled out, using minimal water so as not to damage the electrical equipment further, but also thanks to the fact that the fires were extinguished by suffocation. In the deckhouse, the least worrying outbreak was extinguished with fire extinguishers, blankets and quilts. At 05:00 on the 10th, the fire was almost out, except for a few small outbreaks, for which the dispatch of a fire-fighting tug was requested.

Casualties were 12 dead and 34 wounded, many of them seriously burned. Damage control functioned well, as it did on the occasion of the torpedoing, and in the opinion of the commander, Capt. Francesco Ruta, the conduct of the personnel was praiseworthy with episodes of heroism and sacrifice. The damage sustained did not delay the ship's preparation for transfer to La Spezia (4–6 October) and then to Genoa for a thorough repair.

Bolzano, Operation 'Mezzo Agosto', 13 August 1942

At 08:13 on 13 August, while returning with the 3rd and 7th Divisions to Messina, while proceeding at a speed of 18 knots, the *Bolzano*, was hit by one torpedo of a salvo of four launched from the British submarine *Unbroken* near the island of Panarea (Egadi Islands). The 21in (533mm) torpedo, with a burst charge of 340kg of TNT, struck amidships on the port side, abreast boiler rooms 1-2 (just abaft of the bridge tower). The explosion shook the ship violently, opened a 16m x 8m hole between frames 35 and 54 AV (forward, counting from the frame on the main section), caused the keel to buckle, but not to break, and caused extensive destruction and a violent fire in the affected area. Boiler rooms 1-2 and 3-4 were flooded immediately with seawater, and the corresponding fuel tanks were breached, spilling a large quantity of fuel, initially estimated at 380 tons, which spread the flames through all openings (forward funnel and smokebox, ventilation ducts) to the deck; another 200 tons caught fire later. Towards the bow, the order room was flooded and the machinery control station was put out of action. With six boilers out of action, the steam pressure in the forward engines fell, and they were stopped, while the boilers and the after engines, after a short interruption, were brought back on line, allowing the ship to move slowly for a while. Due to the flooding, the *Bolzano* lurched to the left and immersion increased, but without, for the time being, serious problems of buoyancy and stability.

The fire, fed by the copious spillage of fuel oil, spread upward and towards the bow until it caused explosions around the forward 100/47 guns and the 20/65 MGs, which produced gashes and breaks in the surrounding structures, which in turn aided flooding towards the bow. In a matter of minutes, the fire reached alarming proportions, scorching and deforming decks, bulkheads, hatches and other structures directly affected; it enveloped the superstructure and the forward funnel in flames and smoke, destroying them, significantly raising the temperatures of adjacent compartments not directly affected by the fire, and dividing the ship into two zones. The bridge, soon isolated from the rest of the ship due to the complete interruption of the telephone networks, was immediately evacuated by the personnel, who descended to Turret 2, as all other routes were impassable. The captain, Mario Mezzadra, struggled hard to get to the stern, where he continued to carry out his duties from a makeshift position, operating the rudder by hand and transmitting orders by voice chain.

Mezzadra, who had already taken measures to deal with the flooding and fires, ordered the ship to continue on to the island of Panarea, a few miles away, where he hoped to run the ship aground. Soon, however, boiler rooms 5 and 6 had to be abandoned, as they were flooded with water and fuel oil due to the collapse of the forward partition bulkhead and the failure of Pump No 2 due to a short circuit; nor was it possible to verify the closure of the collision bulkhead at the bow and fight the fire amidship due to serious damage to the fire-fighting service piping on both sides.

Half an hour after the torpedoing, a new emergency arose, namely the heating of the magazines under Turrets 2 and 1, whose temperature, verified by telethermometers, had risen from 28° to 51° and 48°, respectively. Mezzadra ordered them to be flooded as a precaution, aware that this would increase the ship's immersion. This operation also proved problematic due to the smoke, flames and high temperatures in the compartments, which prevented personnel from approaching the magazines.

Panarea, 14:25 on 13 August 1942: the *Bolzano* shortly after being skilfully run aground with the assistance of the destroyer *Geniere* – visible on the right – to avoid sinking after being torpedoed by submarine HM S/M *Unbroken*. (E. Bagnasco collection)

Turret 2's could not be reached, but it was verified that it was flooding on its own; the one in Turret 1 was reached with great difficulty, from forward, but the attempt to open the seawater intakes did not succeed perfectly due to the deformation of the mechanical transmissions and the valves or the expansion of the metals. At the same time, they tried to correct the ship's attitude, which had heeled about 6° to the port side, by transferring fuel oil and to stem the flames by extending all available hoses from the bow and stern onto the battery and main decks, connecting to any fire mains which were still intact. But this too was in vain, as was the use of fire extinguishers, fire-retardants and other devices, including those used by the destroyer *Geniere*, which remained along with *Aviere* in the vicinity for rescue. With these means exhausted, the fires could only be contained by closing the watertight doors and the hatches on the battery and main decks.

After 09:00, when the ship was heading towards Panarea, Mezzadra decided to approach the island stern-on, but due to a turbine failure on the starboard engine, he ordered the *Geniere* and the *Aviere* to take the bow and stern of the cruiser in tow and head for the Lisca Bianca shoal, east of Panarea. The hawsers were taken at 09:46, but they soon parted and the manoeuvre was attempted again with more caution by the *Geniere* alone, while the *Aviere* came alongside the cruiser to transfer the wounded. A little later, due to the rocky nature of the seabed at Lisca Bianca, Angelo Parona, commander of the division, ordered Mezzadra to head for the sandy bottom of Punta Peppemaria, also east of Panarea.

In the meantime, the flooding had greatly extended towards the bow, both because of the existing water passageways and because of the failure or impossibility of closing any more hatches. The after engines also ceased to function for unknown reasons. At 10:35, after the *Geniere* had resumed towing from the stern and the *Aviere* had left the ship due to a submarine alarm, with the sea at deck level forward and about 2m from the stern, listing to port about 15° and with the fire expanding, the captain became convinced that the ship was about to capsize and ordered abandon ship. The majority of the crew, who had gathered some time previously and not without confusion, at the extreme bow and stern, carried out the order by means of boats, rafts or throwing themselves overboard, while a final group of 200 people, including Mezzadra, transferred to the *Geniere*, which,

The *Bolzano* shortly after she was run aground at Panarea on 13 August 1942 after being torpedoed by the British submarine *Unbroken*; note that the ship is listing to port and the smoke caused by the fires still burning in the tower and funnel area. (F. Petronio collection)

after having broken the towing hawser again, brilliantly manoeuvred alongside the cruiser's starboard side.

Some time later, seeing that the ship's attitude had not altered, Mezzadra ordered the towing to be resumed from astern and, to this end, he sent a motor launch aboard the *Bolzano*, manned by personnel from the cruiser and the *Geniere*, to prepare the towing cables, ensure the closure of the bulkheads aft of the fire and cut the electrical cables which had proved to be deadly spreaders of the flames. The operation was successful and was decisive for the partial salvage of the ship.

At 13:30 the *Geniere*, replaced at the last moment by *Tug 92* from Messina, brought the *Bolzano*, with its stern towards the land, to beach on the sandy bank of Punta Peppemaria at an average depth of 12m, perpendicular to the coast 130m away. By means of other rescue vessels from Messina, the ship was hauled a few metres closer to the shore. At that moment the ship, still on fire, was heeling 20° to port, with the bow almost completely submerged and the stern lifted out of the water with the outer starboard propeller protruding. It was estimated that she had 4500 tons of water on board; at 14:00 she rested her bow on a 13.5m seabed with the forecastle deck mostly submerged. In the following hours she was assisted by numerous rescue craft from Messina, including the *Camicia Nera* with Parona aboard, and the torpedo boats *Giuseppe Cesare Abba* and *Giuseppe Sirtori*, but she continued slowly to sink with an increasing list to port, until laying completely on the bottom, inclined 35°–40°, in danger of capsizing. The situation stabilised at 19:00 after the ship had settled on the bottom with the heel decreasing to 16°.

The fire was completely extinguished only on the morning of 15 August. At this point the *Bolzano* was sunk, but salvageable. Losses amounted to 4 dead and 70 wounded, mostly burned, a few of them serious. The low casualties were attributed to the fact that at the time of the explosion, boilers 1 and 2 had been closed down and the boiler room was unmanned, while in the remaining forward boiler rooms the watches were being changed.

The partial loss of the *Bolzano* was primarily due to the exceptional nature of the fire, against which little could have been done and without whose effects the destruction and flooding caused by

Panarea, late August 1942. A detail of the damaged *Bolzano*'s forward funnel while work is underway to bring the ship on to an even keel. (N. Siracusano collection)

Panarea, early September 1942: a detail of the aft superstructure of the *Bolzano* while salvage operations continue. (N. Siracusano collection)

Left: The *Bolzano* undergoing salvage work at Panarea in the first half of September 1942; at top left is the crane jib of the pontoon *GA 232*, transferred to the island to help lighten the cruiser. (N. Siracusano collection)

Right: The cruiser *Bolzano* moored in La Spezia in a rare image dated September 1943. The serious damage received in August 1942 has only been partially repaired and the ship, without a crew, was still awaiting a final decision on her fate. In this condition, she was abandoned at the proclamation of the armistice and fell into German hands. The Kriegsmarine carried out the progressive dismantling that was still in progress at the time of her sinking. (N. Siracusano collection)

the torpedo explosion alone could have been controlled, since the ship had proved capable of floating with three adjacent compartments flooded, as had been planned. In this respect, the cruiser proved to be sufficiently well built; otherwise, the complete abandonment proved to be untimely and would have resulted in her total loss without the return of volunteers aboard, which allowed the towing to be resumed by the *Geniere* and the cruiser to be beached. However, the matter had a certain aftermath with very harsh remarks from Parona and, to a lesser extent, from the Commander in Chief of the Naval Forces, Admiral Angelo Iachino, towards Mezzadra and some of the officers and crew, who were not seen as up to the task.

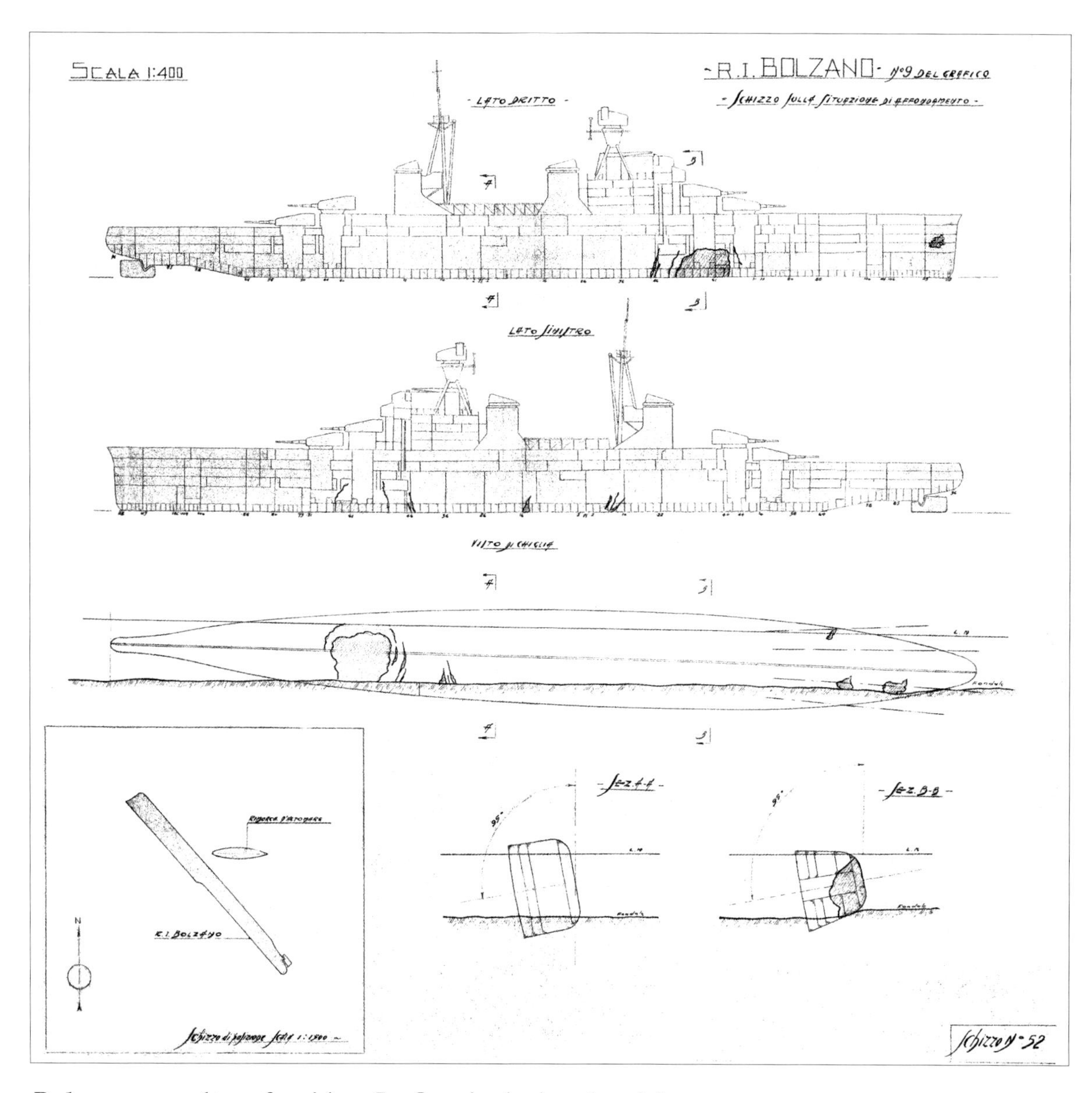

A 1945 drawing by La Spezia Dockyard technical officers showing the state of *Bolzano*'s wreck. (AUSMM, fondo 'Naviglio militare'. B.G4, F.R.I. Gorizia [*sic*])

Bolzano, assault craft raid on La Spezia during the night of 22 June 1944

During the night of 22 June 1944, the wreck of the *Bolzano*, completely abandoned and moored to the buoys near anti-torpedo nets in the middle of La Spezia harbour, was attacked by British underwater raiders manning the LVII underwater self-propelled craft of the 'Chariot' type, who applied a 245kg high explosive charge to the hull. The charge exploded after a few hours and produced a large hull breach which caused extensive flooding, not counteracted by open or ineffective internal bulkheads, and the rapid sinking of the ship.

The wreck of the *Bolzano* partially emerging from the waters of La Spezia harbour on 17 June 1946. (Photo A. Fraccaroli)

ZARA

Zara, Battle of Cape Matapan, 28 March 1941

During the night events at Cape Matapan on 28 March 1941, the *Zara*, followed by the *Fiume*, was surprised by the bulk of the Mediterranean Fleet coming in the opposite direction. From 22:29 to 22:32 the *Zara* was hit on the port side by four 15in [381mm] salvoes and as many 6in [152mm] salvoes from the *Warspite*, five 15in salvoes (35 rounds) from the *Valiant* and one from the *Barham*, fired from a range of about 3000m. A high proportion of the rounds hit the target (20 out of 62 fired according to British estimates).

The *Zara* was hit in the bow and amidships: Turret 1 was destroyed and the muzzles of the guns of Turret 2 were deformed; the structures of the bridge were damaged and the night firing posts became untenable, as well as the secondary armament and the howitzer on the port side, with considerable losses among the personnel. Fires broke out in the middle of the ship and around Turret 1; as a precaution, the flooding of No 1 magazine was ordered, but it is not clear if it was carried out. As for the machinery, boilers Nos 4 and 5 were destroyed with the total loss of personnel; Nos 7 and 8, apparently undamaged, were unusable due to lack of personnel, perhaps evacuated; there is no clear information about No 6; Nos 1 and 2 and, perhaps for a while, also No 3 were still operational and managed to power the starboard engine. There was almost no electricity. The loss of personnel was very high, but the ship remained afloat and could still manoeuvre, albeit with difficulty. There was almost no reply: the after main turrets, which remained undamaged, began to traverse but were stalled due to lack of power, and it was not even possible to operate the diesel dynamo for that turret group; the secondary armament was put out of action due to the high losses among the crews; only a twin 37/54 machine gun managed to fire. Under enemy fire the commander, Capt. Luigi Corsi, ordered the helm hard to starboard and the engines full ahead, a manoeuvre which was only partially successful, as the starboard engine could barely be powered and the rudder responded to commands only with difficulty. For a while the *Zara* continued to move slowly, turning to starboard. The machinery was finally stopped by order of Cattaneo, who, having ascertained the impossibility of saving the ship and in order to avoid any risk of an enemy boarding, decided to abandon her without waiting for dawn and, therefore, to sink the ship by exploding charges. The evacuation took place gradually and in reasonable order, despite some premature abandonment. Around 02:00 hours on the 29th, the explosion of the charges in the forward ammunition magazine was carried out. The ship sank around 02:30, capsizing to starboard. There is no record of it being hit by torpedoes from British destroyers, sent to finish off the still floating wrecks of Italian ships. Lost with the *Zara* were 35 officers, including Cattaneo and Corsi, who were awarded the Medaglia d'Oro al Valor Militare, 123 non-commissioned officers, 619 sailors and 23 civilians.

FIUME

Fiume, Battle of Cape Matapan, 28 March 1941

During the night events at Cape Matapan on 28 March 1941, the *Fiume*, following the *Zara*, was equally surprised by the bulk of the Mediterranean Fleet coming in the opposite direction. The cruiser had ceased battle stations and had ordered normal sea stations with only two main armament turrets, one per group, on stand-by. At that moment she was illuminated by a searchlight from the destroyer *Greyhound* and soon after, between 22:27 and 22:28, was hit on the port side, at an average distance of 3000m, by two 15in salvoes from *Warspite* (6 + 8 shells) and four 6in salvoes and one 15in salvo from *Valiant* (4 rounds). At least six 15in rounds hit the target. *Barham*, after initially directing her fire at the *Zara*, also moved on to the *Fiume*, against which she fired six salvoes of 15in (21 shells) and seven of 6in (34). At 22:32 the British battleships ceased firing and disengaged by all turning away together.

The *Fiume* was hit by at least six 15in [381mm] shells and a few 6in [152mm]. Initially, the following were hit: Turret 4; Boiler No 8 (starboard aft) by a projectile which passed through the hull and exploded in a cofferdam on the opposite side of the ship, producing a large hole; the forecastle; the forward superstructure; Boilers Nos 3 and 4. In a second onslaught, the bridge, the auxiliary fire director, Turret 2, and a gun from Turret 3 were hit.

As a result of the hits, night firing direction, helm orders from the bridge and the armoured command tower, the 100/47 guns, Boilers 3, 4 and 8, and Turret 4 were destroyed; the aft deck was heavily bowed upwards and a huge gash was opened in the centre of the ship. Electrical power was almost completely cut off, the port engine stopped and the cruiser sank, lurching noticeably to the opposite side (starboard) from the damage, a circumstance which, at first, led to the erroneous assumption of a torpedoing. The starboard engine was unharmed, as were boilers 1 and 2. Violent fires, which they vainly tried to fight, broke out in Turret 4, amidships and forward of Turret 2. At first the order was given for the highest possible speed (10 knots), but soon after, realizing that it was impossible to save the ship, the captain ordered the engines to be stopped so that the ship could be abandoned. The *Fiume* maintained steerageway for about ten minutes, slowly turning to port. Finally, judging it unnecessary to set the scuttling charges, the commanding officer, Capt. Giorgis, ordered abandon ship. The *Fiume* sank at 23:15, capsizing on her starboard side. Due to the extent of the damage, the lack of electrical power, the interruption of communications and the jettisoning of the 100/47 ammunition, any attempt at a response fell through. Seventeen officers, including the commander who was awarded the Medaglia d'Oro al valor Militare, 85 non-commissioned officers, 681 ratings, five civilians, one officer, one non-commissioned officer and four airmen all disappeared.

The primary cause of the *Fiume*'s sinking was the single 15in hit in the vicinity of boiler No 8 and the destruction of the bulkheads as a result of the other hits that encouraged the rapid spread of the flooding, as well as the lack of any means of pumping due to the loss of all sources of power. Otherwise, the ship would have floated motionless and in flames, as happened to the *Zara*.

GORIZIA

Gorizia, 2nd Battle of Sirte, 22–23 March 1942

During the course of the 2nd Battle of Sirte, the *Gorizia* was bracketed several times by enemy cruiser fire; numerous pieces of shrapnel fell on board, but without effect. Damage and inconveniences occurred, however, due to the combined effect of blast from the firing of the main calibre guns, the sea conditions, which worsened considerably after sunset, and the worn state and design shortcomings of some of the fittings. During and after the battle there were complaints of water entering or seeping in, even to some extent:

- in the main and on the battery decks through the deck hatches and the valves closing the ventilation ducts on the weather decks, the deck openings of the ammunition hoists for the 100/47 guns, as well as the scuppers and discharge pipes, unhinged or deformed by their own weight;

- in boiler rooms 1-2 and 4-5 and in the forward engine room through the intake openings of the turbo fans, causing them to malfunction;
- in the forward magazines (charges and shells), with inconveniences and failures of the electric fans, due to infiltration through the closing systems without doors in the ventilation ducts on the forecastle and constantly submerged by the water that broke and accumulated on that deck;
- in the 203mm turrets through the gunports and the sighting apertures, with blurring of the optics by salt and combustion residues;
- in the stators of the electric motors for the traverse and elevation of the 100/47 guns due to the bad seal of the already worn-out gaskets producing frequent short circuits;
- in the hangar due to the failure of the aircraft loading hatch to seal due to air displacement caused by the distorting weight of the forward turrets;
- in the chain locker, partially flooded, due to insufficient closure of the hawse pipes on deck;
- in some accommodation and in the cofferdam between port side frames 75-83 through corroded tubing in the scuppers.

The only structural damage, because of the considerable stresses caused by the force of the sea, consisted in the deformation of some brackets and stanchions under the beams of the battery and 1st decks and of the area in the bow between frames 148 and 157. In the past, the problem had occurred further forward in the area between frames 157 and 165 and had been remedied by reinforcing the structure. The gale during 2nd Sirte showed that the problem, instead of being solved, had moved immediately aft of the aforesaid ordinates; if, therefore, the strength members had been also reinforced in this area, there would have been the risk of moving the phenomenon aft of ordinate 148, to the area which, due to the presence of the hangar and the elevator shaft, was structurally the least resistant of the ship.

Thanks to the timely and constant intervention of the crew, the damage described above did not affect the fighting efficiency of the ship during the battle and the return to base. In the end, no major damage was reported, but only inconveniences, especially to the electrical equipment of the fire direction stations and the 203mm and 100mm guns. The *Gorizia* withstood the bad weather conditions better than the other ships, demonstrating good seakeeping qualities. Returning to Messina without too much difficulty, the ship was always ready to move at 6 hours' notice.

To remedy these failures in future, the ship's commander, Paolo Melodia, proposed a series of modifications and improvements, some of which could be carried out any time the ship was in a dockyard, while other work could be done whenever the ship was not ready for sea, but some would have to be part of a major refit. The modifications mainly concerned the doors and hatches of the weather decks, the methods of making them watertight and drainage into the sea (scuppers), the ventilation ducts and the electrical system. The most significant modification involved the aviation facilities, which were no longer used – the removal of the hangar, the elevator shaft and its platform and the aircraft loading hatches, which would allow the reinforcement of the longitudinal and transverse structures and the restoration of the continuity of the deck. This would make it possible to reinforce the area between frames 148 and 157, where the deformations in question had occurred.

It is not known what work was actually carried out. From 29 May to 14 June 1942 the *Gorizia* was transferred to Taranto, where she was docked and underwent major repairs. But the adaptation of the hangar was only authorised in January 1943 and never carried out.

Gorizia, bombardment of La Maddalena, 10 April 1943

During the raid on La Maddalena in the early afternoon of 10 April 1943, the *Gorizia* was moored at Porto Palma protected by torpedo nets. Shortly after 14:35 she suffered three direct hits by 1000lb (45kg) armour-piercing bombs, dropped from an altitude of 5000m to 6000m, of the estimated 60 which fell within the enclosure, causing considerable, but not lethal, damage.

Two hit simultaneously amidships, on the port side: one near No 4 twin 100/47 gun, the other between frames 83 and 85; both pierced the upper deck (20mm of armour) and exploded on the battery deck (main armoured deck 70mm thick), which withstood the impact, being only damaged and distorted. The violence of the explosions caused the total destruction of the area, which was reduced to a pile of wreckage; the broadside plating was opened on the port side above the armour belt and the deck was ripped apart and lifted fore and aft. Two 100/47 guns were destroyed: No 4 (centre) was blown overboard, No 6 (aft) was left hanging on the deck plate twisted towards the stern; a portion of the same deck was thrown up, to fall back amidships, on the opposite side, where it temporarily immobilised No 3 and No 5 100/47 mountings. The ship remained almost completely open on the port side above the battery deck between ordinates 65 and 95 and the structure was detached from the upper edge of the armoured belt in the interval between two ordinates (82 and 83).

The third bomb hit Turret 3, pierced the roof armour (100mm) and exploded in the rear of the turret, blowing the shield down onto the deckhouse, and detaching all other vertical and horizontal armour elements; the explosion and the shrapnel also damaged two of the twin 37/54 machine guns, wreaking havoc among the crews, piercing the deckhouse, the tripod mainmast, the signal bridge and demolishing the searchlights.

The three explosions on board and the many near-misses shook the cruiser violently and caused the chain of the starboard mooring to break and the anchors with the cables to fall into the sea. Fires in No 4 boiler room – the only one lit at the time of the attack – in the crew's galley and in the engineering petty officers' quarters were extinguished with relative ease, despite failures in the fire-fighting network. Bombs exploding in the vicinity broke up and detached some of the hull plating, opening up various parts of the hull to leaks and flooding.

The areas towards the bow between frames 165 and 175 (chain lockers, log room and boatswain's sea cabin) were open to the sea and rapidly flooded, as well as the port cofferdam between frames 42 and 52. More worrying was water, from both external and internal sources, entering the ice room above the rudder, the compartments housing the two steering engines, and the magazine for No 4 turret at both levels (shells below and charges above). Internal leaks of fresh water or fuel oil affected the after engine room, the lower ammunition (shell) room of No 3 turret, the forward engine room (starboard) and boiler rooms Nos 4 and 5. As a result of the flooding, the *Gorizia*, which at the time of the attack had a displacement of 14,150 tons, took on 400–500 tons of water, bur without any appreciable change in trim. All of the flooded areas, except those directly open to the sea, were drained or contained using only the ship's own resources.

The efficiency of the ship was greatly reduced, but not compromised, especially in terms of buoyancy and the supply of power. The boilers below the affected area, Nos 4 (the only one in operation, but closed down after half an hour due to leaks of fuel oil and water), 5, 6 and 7 were unusable due to ruptures in the water and smoke pipes and the dismounting of the air intake fans, as were the two auxiliary boilers; but boilers No 1 (turned on after half an hour), No 2, No 3 and No 8 were usable with only slight steam leaks. The engines remained in good condition and ready for operation. More serious were the failures of the steering gear, with only one rudder engine in working order.

Turret 3 was heavily damaged, but the rest of the main armament was also out of action due to failures in the ventilation and electrical circuits and transmissions. Of the six 100/47 mountings, Nos 3 (centre starboard), 5 (aft starboard) and 2 (aft port) remained operational. Of the six twin 37/54 machine guns, only the two forward ones were out of action; the others remained unserviceable. The eight 20/70 machine guns and four 13.2mm guns all remained operational. Shock damage of varying degrees affected the power supply, the firing directors and transmissions for Turrets 3 and 4 and all 100/47 mountings.

Both turbogenerators and diesel generators remained serviceable. The power, light and telephone lines on the port side were destroyed, but those on the starboard side continued to work. The explosions caused all radio aerials and several telephone networks to break down. All aerials were soon restored to service and 40 out of 70 telephones were reactivated.

Crew losses amounted to 63 killed and missing, including 4 officers, 6 non-commissioned officers, and 95 wounded, including 4 officers and 6 non-commissioned officers.

The *Gorizia* therefore took very heavy blows and suffered considerable damage, but was not at risk of sinking, thanks to the effectiveness of the horizontal protection, which limited the damage to vital organs, and to the efficiency of the Damage Control department, which within 30 minutes managed to activate one boiler (No 8 after closing down No 4), to locate and deal with the main sources of flooding, infiltrations and internal leaks, and, albeit with makeshift connections, continuously ensure the supply of steam and electricity, with lighting in at least some of the compartments, and the operation of the drainage pumps (high-capacity and bilge pumps, as well as mobile pumps).

POLA

Pola, bombing of Naples on 14 December 1940

During the air raid on Naples during the night of 15 December 1940, a few minutes after 21:00, the *Pola* was moored at the Italo Balbo pier (formerly Ponte di Massa) when she was hit by two 250lb (113.5kg) semi-armour-piercing (SAP) bombs, causing some damage.

The first hit the deck on the port side amidship between frames 97 and 98 at 2.80m from the hull side; it went through the deck (20mm of armour) and exploded on the main armoured deck (70mm thick), without penetrating it completely, but causing a tear of about 1m^2. However, numerous pieces of shrapnel penetrated into the boiler room No 3 below, which was lit for port services, and damaged the steam pipes and auxiliary machinery. The compartments on the battery deck were also extensively damaged with a fire, which was soon extinguished.

The second went through the shield of No 2 100/47 mounting (port centre) and pierced the deck at frame 92, near the gunwale, a short distance from the impact point of the other bomb. It penetrated in succession the battery deck (main armoured deck, tapered near the hull side and the junction with the upper edge of the armoured belt and characterised by an irregular profile due to the presence of a scupper), detaching its plates, the platform deck and the upper orlop; finally, it exploded in a cofferdam used as an oil tank in boiler room No 3, near the junction of the watertight bulkhead separating it from boiler rooms Nos 4 and 5. The explosion detached the bulkhead and blew a 3m x 2.5m hole in the hull in line with frame 91, about 4m below the waterline. This went undiagnosed for many hours and caused the flooding of boiler room No 3, which also housed the three turbogenerators of the forward power plant, Nos 4 and 5, and the forward (starboard) engine room as well as abundant oil spills inside and outside the hull. Water and fuel oil leaked through the transverse balancing system and increasingly into boiler rooms 1, 2, 6 and 7. There were 22 dead and 33 injured, all caused by the first bomb.

As a result of the flooding, the *Pola* soon assumed a list of 7 degrees to port and went down by the bow by 1degree; but, more seriously, she was left without power and lighting due to the breakdown of the only boiler in operation, No 3. In order to take a direct view of the situation, Adm. Angelo Iachino, Commander in Chief of the 1st Squadron, Adm. Carlo Cattaneo, Commander of the 1st Division, Adm. Vladimiro Pini, Commander in Chief of the Maritime Military Department of the Lower Tyrrhenian Sea, and technical officers from their respective General Staffs made attempts to improve the transverse and longitudinal trim, to contain infiltration into the boiler rooms adjacent to the flooded ones, to reignite at least one boiler, and to lighten the ship by discharging fuel, water, ammunition, and other weights onto lighters; but little was achieved. Attempts to start the boilers and the auxiliary machinery, which had remained unharmed, failed, either because the fuel pumps were sucking up fuel oil mixed with water due to pollution of the fuel stores or due to the progress of the flooding, with the result that the turbogenerators could not be activated. After a couple of hours, the small amount of electricity generated was just enough to power the lighting circuits, but not the large drainage pumps.

At first, not even the help of the port salvage vessels proved decisive. From 22:30 the *Pola* was assisted by local tugs, but there was still no knowledge of the position and extent of the leak, so for some time their pumps merely sucked water from compartments open to the sea. It was only from 02:30 on the 15th, having verified the exact position and extent of the damage, that they could be profitably put to work containing the flooding in the compartments adjacent to those open to the sea. Due to the size of the damage, with the jagged edges blown outwards, and the presence of many other splinter holes, the attempt to stop up the openings had to be abandoned. The offloading of excess weights onto the barges, which had been alongside the ship during the night, also proceeded slowly and with much difficulty.

At 05:00 on the 15th, however, the port heel was reduced to 5 degrees and the longitudinal trim to ¾ of a degree, but it was not until 08:30 that the submarine *Luciano Manara* could be postioned on the port side of the *Pola*, where her diesel-electric machinery made it possible to supply power to the large-capacity drainage pumps. At 09:00 Iachino ordered the cruiser to be towed into the basin, despite the fact that the lightening work was far from complete. The manoeuvre failed, when at 11:46 the *Pola*'s bow grounded in front of the dock and was not until 13:00 on the 16th that the ship was able to enter the dock, where the lightening and remedial work was completed.

In itself, the damage to the *Pola* was not very serious. What is surprising, however, was the ease with which two 250lb SAP bombs, dropped from low altitude, had been able to pierce both protected decks and the disproportion between the damage received and its consequences, with the entire condenser system out of action and the ship almost completely deprived of power. Without external help, which was not very effective at first, the situation would have quickly become critical, to the point of compromising the buoyancy of the cruiser. As was soon discovered, these effects were due to imperfect fitting-out (permeability of the watertight bulkheads), the unsatisfactory performance of the auxiliary machinery and the poor efficiency of the electrical system, which compromised the efforts of the damage control service itself, as had already emerged on the battleships torpedoed at Taranto a month earlier. Iachino concluded in one of his reports to Supermarina that 'if the ship had been hit in open sea, with no possibility of receiving power and aid from outside, and far from a dry dock, it would most likely not have been saved.' Some time later, Supermarina was less pessimistic, merely observing that if the ship, left without power sources, was not in port, it would encounter serious difficulties.

After the experiences of Taranto and Naples, on the larger ships improvement work was carried out on the internal arrangements and on the shipboard systems, which improved their resilience, although there would still be some nasty surprises.

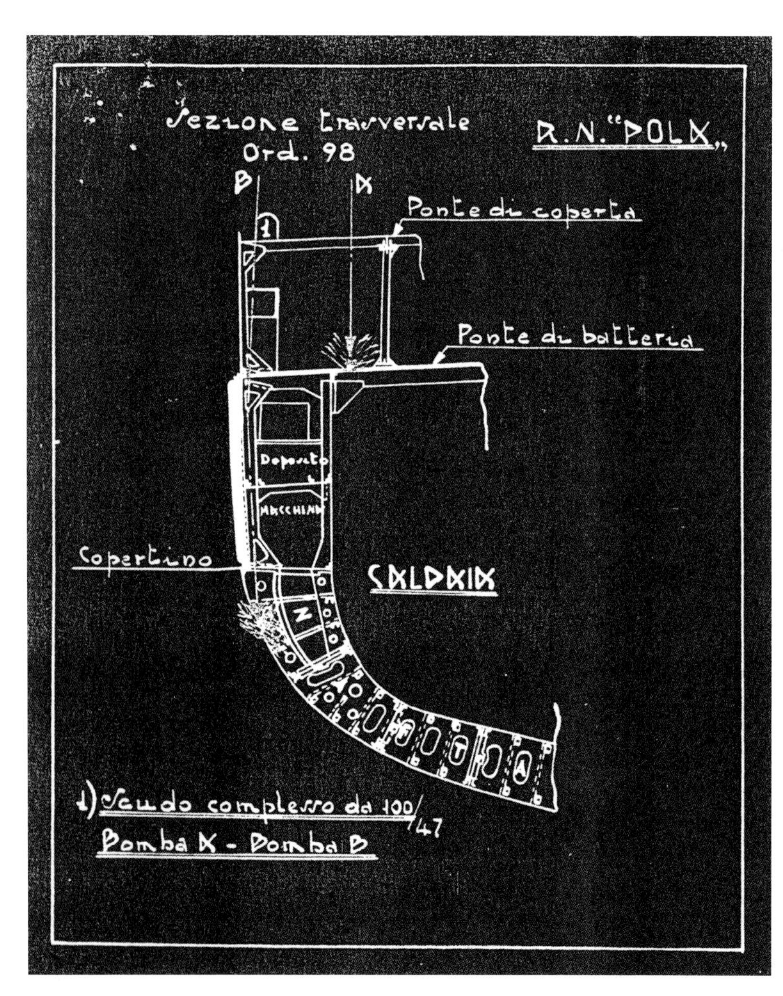

Pola: bomb impacts, 14 December 1940.

Pola, Operation 'Gaudo', torpedoing off Cape Matapan, 28 March 1941

At 19:50, during the air attack at dusk on 28 March, an 18in Mark XII torpedo, with a burst charge of 176kg of TNT, struck the *Pola* on the starboard side, in line with boiler room Nos 4 and 5, without any visible water column. The space was immediately flooded and due to the collapse of the bulkheads, the forward engine room (starboard) and boiler room No 3 were inundated as well, while the after engine room (port) and boiler rooms Nos 6 and 7 were also flooded, but here it was considered containable as soon as the large-capacity drainage pump could be brought into action. Boilers Nos 1, 2 and 8 remained almost untouched, but in order not to trigger the safety valves, the ship's commanding officer, Capt. Manlio De Pisa, ordered them to be closed down. The ship came to a halt. The aft diesel generator failed, although the forward one continued to operate normally. Despite the extensive flooding, the buoyancy was still sufficient, without any noticeable change in trim. The first measures involved shoring up the bulkheads that bordered the flooded compartments towards the bow and stern, and relighting boilers 8, 1 and 2, to power the turbogenerators and the after engines. Boiler No 8 and, it seems, a turbogenerator and large-capacity pump No 3 were successfully started, but not the after engines. Attempts to relight boilers No 1 and 2 failed, and the ignition of No 8 itself was suspended due to the production of smoke, on the grounds that it might betray the presence of the cruiser to the enemy, despite the brightly illuminated night, the belief that there were no enemy ships in the area and the order for the crew to stand down. In addition, having mistaken a steam leak from the forward engines for a fire, De Pisa ordered the ammunition in the magazines to be thrown overboard, with the consequence that the remaining guns could only be restocked by hand. Around 20:20, as soon as she was notified of the intended rescue by the 1st Division, the *Pola* began preparations for towing. At 22:00, shadows were sighted 1.5 miles to starboard (the *Pola* was still facing west), which matched the estimated time of the 1st Division's arrival, but from the opposite direction than expected. At about 22:25, thinking that he had not been sighted by his own ships, De Pisa fired a red Very light to attract their attention. A few moments later, the battleships of the Mediterranean Fleet, which were preparing to open fire on the *Pola*, targeted and destroyed the incoming 1st Division.

Pola watched helplessly. Battle stations were ordered once again, but the chance of a response seemed minimal: orders could not be transmitted due to the lack of power; the four 203mm turrets could only be handled manually (the forward turrets could also fire electrically) and under local control, except for makeshift connections with the night firing direction station; only a few rounds were reaching the 100/47 mountings, two of which were damaged. Some purely symbolic gunfire would have been possible, but this, according to De Pisa, would not only have been in vain, but would also have attracted an enemy reaction with serious losses among the personnel. At 23:15 he gave the order to abandon ship and to open the sea cocks. During these operations, at 23:45, the *Pola* was again discovered by the British destroyer *Havock* that illuminated her and opened fire, hitting twice and causing as many fires on the battery deck aft and on the deck-house amidships. There was no reaction, as the ship was sinking. The scuttling and abandonment proceeded slowly: the former due to communication failures and a temporary halt to the procedure; the latter due to some confusion among the crew – several men who had jumped overboard during the *Havock*'s attack, returned aboard due to the biting cold and were fortified with alcohol and had their wet clothes changed; others proved reluctant to go overboard at all. Between 01:00 and 02:30 on 29 March 29, the British destroyers *Greyhound*, *Griffin* and *Havock* approached within voice range; at 03:25 the destroyer *Jervis* came alongside the stern of the *Pola*, when the deck was about 1m from the surface of the sea, and transferred via a gangway the remaining men (257), the last of whom was De Pisa. It does not appear that any Englishmen had boarded the ship and some colourful and sarcastic descriptions of the disorder on board and the sorry state of the personnel are doubtless wartime exaggerations. At the end of the rescue operation, the *Jervis* and the *Nubian* finished off the *Pola* with a torpedo each, which sank at 04:03 on the 29th. Of the crew 328 were killed, almost all after jumping into the water.

Compared to the events in Naples, the *Pola* gave a better performance, managing to float in good buoyancy with three contiguous compartments flooded, also thanks to the work of the Damage Control service which stemmed the leaks from the adjacent compartments, even with a shortage of pumping resources; the ship was slow to sink even after the scuttling measures were implemented and having received the second torpedo hit. Had the attempts been successful in restarting boilers Nos 1 and 2, which were still in good condition, and had No 8 not been shut down, she might have been able to escape her fate that night. However, the electrical system and many details of the machinery set-up, especially the boiler feeds, still proved to be vulnerable: one torpedo was enough to almost completely extinguish the power sources on the ship.

The wreck of the *Trieste* in La Spezia drydock in 1950 after its salvage at La Maddalena. Note the large hole in the hull forward of the propeller shaft produced by one of the bombs that exploded close to the hull. These near-misses were just as decisive as actual hits in causing the sinking of the cruiser. (Augusto de Toro collection)

Appendix B

PLANS FOR MODIFICATIONS AND RECONSTRUCTION OF *BOLZANO*

After the ship's recovery off Panarea and the transfer of the *Bolzano* to Naples in September 1942 for an initial repair, it became clear that the severity and extent of the damage to the ship would require far more than merely restoring it to its original condition.

As early as the beginning of October, in order to save labour and materials, the Shipbuilding, Outfitting and Testing Inspectorate (Marinalles) had proposed to the Naval General Staff (Maristat) not to repair boilers 1 and 2 but instead to remove all equipment in the boiler room and to replace them with one double boiler, in order to increase the ship's range, and with a diesel-electric generator unit for port service, so as to ensure greater operating safety, lower fuel consumption and less wear than using a boiler. According to Marinalles' calculations, the range would have increased from 3680 to 4040 miles at 14 knots and from 3690 to 4060 miles at 16 knots, while speed would have suffered by 0.5 knots, as two independent homogeneous engines would have been obtained, each powered by 4 boilers, with a maximum speed of 33 knots at full load displacement, still higher than the 32 knots of the *Trieste* and the 30 of the *Gorizia*. Even the changes in stability appeared acceptable with a reduction in metacentric height of 3cm when unloaded and an increase of 4cm when fully loaded. In mid-November 1942 the proposal was agreed in all detail by Maristat. This was the only modification to the *Bolzano* that was accepted by the Navy, but it was not followed up.

A second proposal, regarding the replacement of the forward superstructure destroyed in the fire with a bridge tower of the 'Pugliese' type, as on the light cruisers of the *Duca degli Abruzzi* or *Duca d'Aosta* classes, was made by the then commander of the *Bolzano* to Maristat. Maristat submitted the proposal to the Committee for the Design of Ships (Maricominav), which, at the beginning of December, merely passed on a report by the commander of the *Eugenio di Savoia* regarding the poor suitability of this type of tower for the requirements of war, but which, above all, rejected the idea of refitting the *Bolzano* in its original form due to the excessive amount of time needed (about ten months) to procure materials (fire control and electrical systems), which were difficult to obtain, and because it would have been a refit of an outdated type of ship, which was already controversial at the time of its construction.

Instead, Maricominav submitted to Maristat an outline project for her transformation into an anti-aircraft ship, also suitable for the fast transport of 3500 tons of materials in five holds, and capable of embarking and launching by catapult 12 fighter or torpedo aircraft of the Reggiane RE.2000 type. The work would have taken about 5 months, provided that the outfitting was kept simple, and would have concerned:

- eliminations of boilers 1 and 2, as already decided in the case of restoration to the original design;
- splitting the forward funnel, which, in any case, would have to be rebuilt, into two smaller side-by-side funnels;
- removal of the forward superstructure;
- adaptation of the aft superstructure to a merchant-type bridge;
- removing both the main armament and the torpedo launchers;
- alteration of the ammunition magazines into cargo holds;
- fitting of new AA armament (5 single 90/53 guns per side for a total of 10 AA guns, but the final outfit was still to be defined)
- installation of a 'Heinkel'-type catapult, using one already available at La Spezia and adopting the launching techniques already employed by the Allies on merchant ships converted for the aerial protection of convoys. *(see drawing on page 92)*

Underwater protection would remain entrusted, as before, to internal subdivision, improved and extended to the upper decks.

Maristat made its decision as early as 24 February 1943. It judged Maricominav's proposal to be technically valid, but rejected it for operational reasons, since the launching of the planes by catapult would inevitably be slow and would not allow for the formation of an appreciable group of fighters in the air for simultaneous action; furthermore, once the aircraft were launched, there would be no role for the ship. But, more importantly, with the same note also addressed to Marinalles and to the General Directorate of Naval Armaments and Weapons (Marinarmi), Maristat definitively suspended any decision on the fate of the *Bolzano* and, in the meantime, there was to be no activity on board, except for the maintenance of machinery that might still have a use.

Appendix C

MOVEMENTS AND DEPLOYMENTS OF ITALIAN HEAVY CRUISERS IN THE SECOND WORLD WAR

The following schedules of movements and dislocations are based on the 'Statini dell'attività bellica delle navi' kept in the AUSMM (Arcgivio Ufficio Storico della Marina Militare) fund of the same name. This is a second-hand source, having been compiled after the war for administrative purposes on the basis of other documentation, but together they constitute an organic and complete collection of the movements of every single ship in the conflict and, above all, the most easily usable. Although they are not free of inaccuracies and gaps, for reasons of homogeneity it was decided to reproduce their layout and data, making corrections and additions on the basis of other archival documentation (war diaries, navigation, exercise and mission reports) only in the event of significant differences. For a better understanding it should be borne in mind that, in principle:

- the time protocols of arrival and departure, rounded to the nearest 5 minutes, refer to the end and beginning of the mooring and unmooring manoeuvres;
- for the hours underway, the criterion of indicating hours and minutes (sixtieths of an hour) separated by a comma has been adopted
- the indications of attacks on naval bases and ports are reported only if the ship has had a confirmed part in them due to damage received or anti-aircraft activities
- the hours of air raids refer to the beginning and end of the raid or the beginning and end of anti-aircraft fire and not to the first alarm or the end of the alarm, as reported in the 'statini', in order to better circumscribe the war episode.

TRENTO

Date	Hour	Location (from/to)	Hours underway	Nautical miles	Notes
10.06.1940 11.06.1940	19:05 12:30	Messina Messina	17,25	246	Exit of II Squadra to cover 2nd Division and minelayers for laying the 'L.K.' mine barrage in the Sicilian Channel.
12.06.1940 12.06.1940	00:10 18:20	Messina Messina	18,10	390	Exit of II Squadra, 1st and 8th Divisions (from Taranto) to search for enemy naval forces in the Ionian Sea. No contact.
22.06.1940 24.06.1940	17:45 07:15	Messina Messina	37,30	846	Exit of II Squadra (2nd Division from Palermo) and 1st Division (from Augusta) in support of a 7th Division raid in the Sardinian Sea against French traffic. No contact.
07.07.1940 10.07.1940	15:30 00:20	Messina Messina	56,45	1198	Exit of the naval forces (henceforth FN) in the Ionian Sea to cover and escort two convoys directed to Libya (Operation TCM). In the late afternoon of the 8th the II Squadra is attacked by bombers without result. Battle of Punta Stilo (09.07.1940); from 13:10 and to 16:12 the II Squadra is attacked by torpedo bombers in vain; from 15:55 to 16:12 the II Squadron engages the battleship *Warspite* and enemy light cruisers. From 16:10 to 16:45, in the disengagement phase, torpedo attacks against the *Trento* and the *Bolzano* were carried out without success. Until the evening, there is a succession of accidental attacks by Italian bombers on the FN without consequences.
30.07.1940 01.08.1940	18:25 12:20	Messina Messina	41,55	822	Exit of II Squadra and 1st Division for long-distance escort of 3 convoys to Libya (Operation TVL).
16.08.1940 16.08.1940	03:15 17:50	Messina Naples	14,25	281	Transfer and exercises of the 3rd Division.
29.08.1940 30.08.1940	12:35 17:15	Naples Messina	28,40	327	Transfer and exercises of the 3rd Division.

Continued overleaf

Date	Hour	Location (from/to)	Hours underway	Nautical miles	Notes
31.08.1940 02.09.1940	06:00 00:30	Messina Taranto	42,30	687	FN exit in the eastern Ionian Sea to counter the British Operation 'Hats'. No contact with enemy naval forces.
07.09.1940 09.09.1940	14:45 11:05	Taranto Messina	44,20	880	FN exit south of Sardinia to counter an alleged Force H sortie from Gibraltar.
27.09.1940 28.09.1940	10:25 04:30	Messina Messina	18,05	293	Exit of the 3rd Division for exercises.
29.09.1940 01.10.1940	19:55 08:30	Messina Messina	36,35	644	FN exit in the central Ionian Sea to counter the British Operation MB5. No contact with the enemy. At 15:05 AA fire at enemy aircraft.
06.10.1940 06.10.1940	08:35 23:00	Messina Messina	14,25	240	Exit of the II Squadra to cover a convoy for the Aegean (Operation CV). The operation is suspended due to erroneous sighting of enemy
12.10.1940 12.10.1940	07:55 18:30	Messina Messina	10,35	234	Assistance to XII Squadriglia destroyers after an encounter with British cruisers. At 11:49 and 12:55 AA fire at enemy aircraft.
21.10.1940 22.10.1940	20:05 10:00	Messina Taranto	13,55	255	Transfer of the 3rd Division.
04.11.1940 04.11.1940	11:35 19:00	Taranto Taranto	07,25	...	Exercises.
12.11.1940 12.11.1940	23:10 00:30	Taranto			Fleet Air Arm raid on the Taranto base (Operation 'Judgment', part of Operation MB.8). At 00:30 the *Trento* is hit by an inert bomb, suffering minor damage.
12.11.1940 13.11.1940	12:40 03:10	Taranto Messina	14,30	...	Transfer of the 3rd Division. At 13:01, during manoeuvres out of the Mar Piccolo AA fire at enemy aircraft.
16.11.1940 19.11.1940	08:55 01:35	Messina Messina	64.40		FN exit to counter the British Operation 'White' in the western Mediterranean. No contact with enemy naval forces, but FN presence at sea contributes to failure of enemy operation.
26.11.1940 28.11.1940	12:25 14:40	Messina Naples	50,15	...	Exit of the FN to counter the British Operation 'Collar'. Battle of Cape Teulada or Spartivento (27.11.1940); from 12:20 to 13:01 the 3rd Division is engaged by the battlecruiser *Renown* and enemy cruisers; at 15:35 enemy bomber attack on 3rd Division is unsuccessful.
28.11.1940 29.11.1940	20:00 08:10	Naples Messina	12,10	...	Transfer of the 3rd Division.
02.12.1940 03.12.1940	19:20 10:40	Messina Naples	15,20	...	Transfer.
04.12.1940 06.12.1940		Naples			In drydock.
06.12.1940 07.12.1940	19:05 15:15	Naples Messina	20,10	...	Transfer of the 3rd Division.
15.12.1940 16.12.1940	18:25 11:15	Messina Cagliari	16,50	...	Transfer of the 3rd Division.
19.12.1940 20.12.1940	20:10 13:05	Cagliari Messina	16,55	...	Transfer.
07.01.1941 07.01.1941	11:55 23:35	Messina Messina	11,40	193	Exit of the 3rd Division for exercises.
10.01.1941 11.01.1941	18:35 12:05	Messina Messina	17,30	260	Moving from one berth to another.

Date	Hour	Location (from/to)	Hours underway	Nautical miles	Notes
13.01.1941 14.01.1941	23:35 12:35	Messina Messina	13,00	240	Sortie of the Squadra Navale (henceforth SN) to search for the damaged aircraft carrier *Illustrious* in the Sicilian channel. Operation suspended.
31.01.1941 31.01.1941	11:15 19:00	Messina Messina	07,45	95	Exercises of the 3rd Division.
08.02.1941 11.02.1941	07:10 12:05	Messina Messina	76,55	1413	SN exit to counter British Operation 'Grog' (naval bombardment of Genoa by Force H). No contact with the enemy.
01.03.1941 01.03.1941	13:00 22:55	Messina Messina	9,55	190	Exit of the 3rd Division for exercises.
07.03.1941 08.03.1941	12:25 00:50	Messina Messina	12,25	207	Exit of the 3rd Division for exercises.
12.03.1941 13.03.1941	14:30 13:55	Messina Messina	23,25	437	Exit of the 3rd Division for long range escort of a convoy to Libya.
15.03.1941 15.03.1941	13:30 23:00	Messina Messina	9,30	153	Exit of the 3rd Division for exercises.
27.03.1941 29.03.1941	05:00 17:00	Messina Taranto	60,00	1225	SN exit for offensive mission in the Eastern Mediterranean (Operation 'Gaudo'). From 08:12 to 08:54 on the 28th the 3rd Division engaged enemy light cruisers without success. At 12:08 torpedo bomber attack and at 15:15 enemy bombers attack the 3rd Division without success. At 19:21 new torpedo attack and AA barrage fire.
23.04.1941 24.04.1941	17:15 09:55	Taranto Messina	16,40	295	Transfer.
05.05.1941 06.05.1941	18:45 23:40	Messina La Spezia	28,55	490	Relocation for refit.
07.05.1941 21.07.1941		La Spezia			Refit. On 6 June, the *Trento* administratively placed in reserve, until 18 July.
22.07.1941 22.07.1941	07:40 18:50	La Spezia La Spezia	11,10	163	Machinery tests and exercises.
04.08.1941 05.08.1941	05:20 11:00	La Spezia Messina	22,40	505	Transfer.
18.08.1941 18.08.1941	06:35 11:15	Messina Messina	4,40	98	Exit of the 3rd Division for exercises.
20.08.1941 21.08.1941	15:35 05:00	Messina Messina	13,25	206	Exit of the 3rd Division for exercises.
23.08.1941 26.08.1941	10:10 07:55	Messina Messina	69,45	1320	SN sortie as far south as Sardinia to counter the British Operation 'Mincemeat'. No contact with enemy naval forces.
10.09.1941 10.09.1941	07:55 14:05	Messina Messina	6,10	117	Exercises
26.09.1941 29.09.1941	13:50 00:55	Messina La Maddalena	64,00	1130	SN sortie as far south as Sardinia to counter the British Operation 'Halberd'. No contact with enemy naval forces.
10.10.1941 10.10.1941	03:05 22:30	La Maddalena Messina	19,25	375	Transfer of the 3rd Division.
08.11.1941 09.11.1941	12:15 20:35	Messina Messina	32,20	633	3rd Division long range escort of convoy 'Duisburg' to Libya. From 01:05 to 01:25 on the 9th unsuccessful fire against enemy light cruisers that attacked and destroyed the convoy.

Date	Hour	Location (from/to)	Hours underway	Nautical miles	Notes
21.11.1941 22.11.1941	19:05 18:05	Messina Taranto			Exit of 3rd and 8th Divisions for long range escort of a convoy to Libya. At 23:34 AA fire at enemy aircraft.
16.12.1941 19.12.1941	17:25 12:50	Taranto Taranto	27,65	1338	Exit of the SN for Operation M42 (convoy escort to Libya). First battle of Sirte (17.12.1941). From 17:57 to 18:02 on the 17th, the *Trento* opened fire on enemy ships without success
03.01.1942 05.01.1942	17:55 16:30	Taranto Messina	46,35	869	SN participation in Operation M4 (convoy escort to Libya).
14.02.1942 16.02.1942	23:00 16:00	Messina Messina	41,00	840	Exit of battleship *Duilio*, 3rd and 7th Divisions to counter British Operation MF5 (convoy for Malta). Operation aborted; no contact with enemy naval forces.
21.02.1942 24.04.1942	18:00 12:05	Messina Messina	66,05	1136	Participation of battleship *Duilio* and 3rd Division in Operation K7 (long range escort of convoys to Libya). At 14:18 on the 22nd *Trento* fires at enemy aircraft.
22.03.1942 24.03.1942	00:15 10:10	Messina Messina	57,55	1070	FN exit in central Mediterranean to intercept British convoy MW10 from Alexandria to Malta. Second Battle of Sirte (22.03.1942). From 14:36 to 19:00 on the 22nd the 3rd Division intermittently engaged enemy forces, causing light damage to light cruiser *Cleopatra* (hit by the light cruiser *Giovanni delle Bande Nere*) and to destroyer *Sikh*. *Trento* suffered damage due to heavy seas during the return to base.
25.03.1942 27.05.1942		Messina			Refit to repair damage sustained during the return voyage after the Second Battle of Sirte.
26.05.1942		Messina			British air raid.
27.05.1942		Messina			British air raid.
28.05.1942 29.05.1942	18:00 09:20	Messina Taranto	15,20	296	British air raid on Messina and transfer of the 3rd Division
14.06.1942 15.06.1942	13:30	Taranto			Exit of the FN in the central-eastern Mediterranean to counter the British Operation 'Vigorous'. Battle of 'Mezzo Giugno' (11–16.06.1942). No contact with enemy naval forces, but FN interposition between them and Malta causes the operation to fail. At 05:00 on the 15th the *Trento* was hit and immobilised by enemy torpedo bombers. At 09:10, while the towing cables were being passed to destroyer *Antonio Pigafetta* and *Trento* was preparing to steam under her own power, *Trento* was torpedoed by the British submarine *P 35* with the explosion of the forward ammunition magazine. The ship sank in a few minutes with a high toll of human lives.

TRIESTE

Date	Hour	Location (from/to)	Hours underway	Nautical miles	Notes
10.06.1940 22.07.1940		La Spezia			Refit.
23.07.1940 23.07.1940	09:10 16:20	La Spezia La Spezia	7,10	151	Sea trials and exercises.
26.07.1940 27.07.1940	05:20 07:30	La Spezia Messina	26,10	548	Transfer.
16.08.1940 16.08.1940	03:20 18:00	Messina Naples	14,40	292	Transfer and exercises of the 3rd Division.
29.08.1940 30.08.1940	12:35 07:00	Naples Messina	18,25	317	Transfer and exercises of the 3rd Division.

Date	Hour	Location (from/to)	Hours underway	Nautical miles	Notes
31.08.1940 02.09.1940	06:00 00:30	Messina Taranto	42,30	665	FN deployment in the eastern Ionian Sea to counter the British Operation 'Hats'. No contact with enemy naval forces.
07.09.1940 09.09.1940	14:55 08:40	Taranto Messina	41,45	857	FN exit as far south as Sardinia to counter an alleged Force H sortie from Gibraltar.
27.09.1940 28.09.1940	10:35 01:40	Messina Messina	15,05	283	Exit of the 3rd Division for exercises.
29.09.1940 01.10.1940	20:05 07:10	Messina Messina	35,05	644	FN exit in central Ionian Sea to counter British Operation MB5. No contact with enemy naval forces. At 15:05 fire at enemy aircraft.
06.10.1940 06.10.1940	08:55 21:00	Messina Messina	12,05	234	Exit of II Squadra to cover a convoy to the Aegean (Operation CV). The operation is suspended due to erroneous sighting of enemy naval forces.
12.10.1940 12.10.1940	08:00 17:30	Messina Messina	9,30	225	Assistance of 3rd Division to XII Squadriglia destroyers after a clash with British cruisers. At 11:47 AA fire at enemy aircraft. At 13:00 AA fire against enemy bombers.
21.10.1940 22.10.1940	20:15 09:55	Messina Taranto	13,40	252	Transfer of the 3rd Division.
04.11.1940 04.11.1940	11:35 18:35	Taranto Taranto	7,00	126	Exit of the 3rd Division for exercises.
12.11.1940 13.11.1940	12:00 02:50	Taranto Messina	14,50	261	Transfer of the 3rd Division after an enemy air raid on Taranto. At 12:45, coming out of the Mar Piccolo, the air alarm is given and the batteries of the base open fire. Shrapnel falls on the *Trieste* wounding some of the crewmen.
16.11.1940 18.11.1940	09:00 12:10	Messina Messina	51,10	930	FN exit to counter the British Operation 'White' in the western Mediterranean. No contact with enemy naval forces, but FN presence at sea contributes to failure of enemy operation.
26.11.1940 28.11.1940	12:00 15:05	Messina Naples	51,05	983	Exit of the FN to counter the British Operation 'Collar'. Battle of Cape Teulada, or Spartivento (27.11.1940); from 12:20 to 13:01 the 3rd Division is engaged by battlecruiser *Renown* and enemy cruisers; at 15:35 unsuccessful enemy bomber attack on 3rd Division.
28.11.1940 29.11.1940	20:35 07:50	Naples Messina	11,15	182	Transfer of the 3rd Division.
15.12.1940 16.12.1940	18:25 10:35	Messina Cagliari	16,10	349	Transfer of the 3rd Division.
19.12.1940 20.12.1940	20:55 12:30	Cagliari Messina	15,35	348	Transfer of the 3rd Division.
07.01.1940 07.01.1941	11:50 22:10	Messina Messina	10,20	190	Exit of the 3rd Division for exercises.
10.01.1941 11.01.1941	18:30 09:55	Messina Messina	14,25	257	Movements in port.
14.01.1941 14.01.1941	00:05 11:30	Messina Messina	11,25	229	SN moves to search for the damaged aircraft carrier *Illustrious* in the Sicilian channel. Operation suspended.
31.01.1941 31.01.1941	11:35 17:00	Messina Messina	5,25	93	Exit of the 3rd Division for exercises.
08.02.1941 11.02.1941	07:10 10:50	Messina Messina	75,40	1420	SN exit to counter British Operation 'Grog' (bombardment of Genoa by Force H). No contact with the enemy.

Continued overleaf

Date	Hour	Location (from/to)	Hours underway	Nautical miles	Notes
01.03.1941 01.03.1941	13:40 23:10	Messina Messina	9,10	184	Exit of the 3rd Division for exercises.
07.03.1941 07.03.1941	12:45 21:25	Messina Messina	8,40	136	Exit of the 3rd Division for exercises.
12.03.1941 13.03.1941	14:50 13:05	Messina Messina	22,15	423	Exit of the 3rd Division for long range escort of a convoy to Libya.
15.03.1941 15.03.1941	13:40 23:10	Messina Messina	9,30	161	Exit of the 3rd Division for exercises.
27.03.1941 29.03.1941	05:20 16:20	Messina Taranto	59,00	1221	SN exit for offensive mission in the Eastern Mediterranean (Operation 'Gaudo'). From 08:12 to 08:54 on the 28th the 3rd Division engaged enemy light cruisers without success. At 12:08 torpedo bomber attack and at 15:15 enemy bombers attack the 3rd Division without success. At 19:21 new torpedo attack and AA barrage fire.
23.03.1941 24.03.1941	17:35 08:40	Taranto Messina	15,05	284	Transfer.
27.04.1941 27.04.1941	11:00 16:20	Messina Messina	05,20	95	Exit of 3rd Division for long range escort of a convoy to Libya. Mission suspended due to sighting of enemy naval forces.
30.04.1940 02.05.1940	13:25 23:55	Messina Messina	58,30	1924	Exit of 3rd Division for direct and indirect escort of convoys to and from Libya.
24.05.1941 25.05.1941	16:20 19:35	Messina Messina	27,15	570	Exit of the 3rd Division for long range escort of a convoy to Libya.
26.05.1941 28.05.1941	15:55 13:55	Messina Messina	45,40	777	Long range escort of a convoy from Libya.
05.06.1941 05.06.1941	14:10 22:20	Messina Messina	8,10	162	Exit of the 3rd Division for exercises.
08.06,1941 09.06.1941	14:45 05:35	Messina Messina	14,50	301	Exit of 3rd Division for long range escort of convoy 'Esperia' to Libya.
19.06.1941 20.06.1941	17:05 03:05	Messina Messina	10,00	170	Exit of 3rd Division for exercises with destroyers of XII Squadriglia.
25.06.1941 26.06.1941	18:30 16:30	Messina Taranto	22,00	433	Exit of 3rd Division for long range escort of convoy 'Esperia' to Libya. Operation suspended due to intense air attacks.
27.06.1941 29.06.1941	16:50 11:10	Taranto Messina	42,20	845	Exit of 3rd Division for long range escort of convoy 'Esperia' to Libya. Operation suspended due to intense air attacks.
16.07.1941 18.07.1941	20:35 10:10	Messina Messina	37,35	826	Exit of 3rd Division for long range escort of a convoy to Libya.
18.08.1941 18.08.1941	06:30 12:40	Messina Messina	06,10	128	Exit of the 3rd Division for exercises.
20.08.1940 21.08.1940	15:30 03:00	Messina Messina	11,30	146	Exit of the 3rd Division for exercises.
23.08.1940 26.08.1940	10:10 07:30	Messina Messina	69,20	1312	SN sortie as far south as Sardinia to counter the British Operation 'Mincemeat'. No contact with enemy naval forces.
10.09.1941 10.09.1941	07:30 13:20	Messina Messina	5,50	107	Exit of the 3rd Division for exercises.

Date	Hour	Location (from/to)	Hours underway	Nautical miles	Notes
10.09.1941 11.09.1941	20:00 11:45	Messina Taranto	15,45	287	Transfer.
12.09.1941 24.09.1941		Taranto			Refit.
25.09.1941 29.09.1941	22:30 01:30	Taranto La Maddalena	75,00	1379	SN sortie as far south as Sardinia to counter the British Operation 'Halberd'. No contact with enemy naval forces.
10.10.1941 10.10.1941	03:05 22:00	La Maddalena Messina	18,55	365	Transfer of the 3rd Division.
08.11.1941 09.11.1941	12:15 20:25	Messina Messina	32,10	609	3rd Division long range escort of convoy 'Duisburg' to Libya. From 01:05 to 01:25 on the 9th unsuccessful fire against enemy light cruisers that attacked and destroyed the convoy.
21.11.1941 22.11.1941	18:30 13:15	Messina Messina	13,15	85	Exit of the 3rd and 8th Divisions for long range escort of a convoy to Libya. At 23:10 *Trieste* was torpedoed and seriously damaged by the submarine *Utmost*. At 00:38 *Trieste* managed to restart engines and returned to Messina under her own power.
03.12.1941 04.12.1941	07:00 20:00	Messina La Spezia	37,00	533	Transfer for repairs.
05.12.1941 14.07.1942		La Spezia			Refit.
15.07.1942 16.07.1942	12:50 03:50	La Spezia La Spezia	14,10	204	Sea trials and exercises.
09.08.1942 09.08.1942	08:25 19:45	La Spezia La Spezia	11,20	160	Sea trials and exercises.
12.08.1942 13.08.1942	00:50 12:30	La Spezia Messina	35.40	707	Exit of the 3rd and 7th Divisions to counter the British Operation 'Pedestal' (Battle of 'Mezzo Agosto'). The mission is suspended. During the voyage to Messina, at 08:20 *Trieste* manoeuvred to avoid a torpedo from the British submarine *Unbroken*.
10.10.1942 10.10.1942	07:00 12:00	Messina Messina	3,55	41	Exercises.
24.10.1942 24.10.1942	07:00 12:00	Messina Messina	5,00	73	Exercises.
09.12.1942 10.12.1942	19:25 14:40	Messina La Maddalena	19,15	435	Transfer of the 3rd Division.
22.03.1943 22.03.1943	07:15 09:25	La Maddalena La Maddalena	2,10	30	Exercises.
10.04.1943	14:35 16:13	La Maddalena			During an American air raid, the *Trieste* was hit at 14:40 by three bombs and damaged by others exploded nearby. She sank, capsizing on her starboard side at 16:13.

BOLZANO

Date	Hour	Location (from/to)	Hours underway	Nautical miles	Notes
10.06.1940 11.06.1940	19:00 13:05	Messina Messina	18,05	360	Exit of II Squadra to cover 2nd Division and minelayers for laying 'L.K.' mine barrage in the Sicilian Channel.
11.06.1940 12.06.1940	23:50 18:05	Messina Messina	18,15	365	Exit of II Squadra, 1st and 8th Divisions (from Taranto) to search for enemy naval forces in the Ionian Sea. No contact.

Continued overleaf

Date	Hour	Location (from/to)	Hours underway	Nautical miles	Notes
22.06.1940 24.06.1940	17:40 06:50	Messina Messina	37,00	740	Exit of II Squadra and 1st Division (from Augusta) in support of a 7th Division raid in the Sardinian Sea against French shipping. No contact with the enemy.
07.07.1940 10.07.1940	15:20 00:30	Messina Messina	33,10	1172	FN exit in the central Ionian Sea to cover and escort two convoys to Libya (Operation TCM). In the late afternoon of the 8th the II Squadra is attacked without success by bombers. At 18:27 AA fire against them. Battle of Punta Stilo (09.07.1940); at 13:10 and 16:12 the II Squadra is subjected to unsuccessful torpedo attacks; from 15:55 to 16:12 the II Squadra engages battleship *Warspite* and enemy light cruisers. The *Bolzano* was hit three times by 152mm [6in] shells from the light cruiser *Neptune* (or *Orion*), with some damage. From 16:10 to 16:45, during the disengagement phase, torpedo bomber attacks against the *Trento* and the *Bolzano* were carried out without success. Until the evening, there was a succession of mistaken attacks by Italian bombers on the FN without consequences.
12.07.1940 13.07.1940	00:30 20:03	Messina La Spezia	25,55	536	Transfer.
14.07.1940 03.08.1940		La Spezia			Refit.
04.08.1940 05.08.1940	10:00 11:30	La Spezia Messina	25,30	508	Transfer and exercises
16.08.1940 16.08.1940	00:50 18:25	Messina Naples	15,35	281	Transfer and exercises of the 3rd Division.
29.08.1940 30.08.1940	12:30 06:55	Naples Messina	18,25	322	Transfer and exercises of the 3rd Division.
31.08.1940 02.09.1940	05:35 00:20	Messina Taranto	42,45	685	FN exit in the eastern Ionian Sea to counter the British Operation 'Hats'. No contact with enemy naval forces.
07.09.1940 09.09.1940	15:25 19:35	Taranto Messina	41,40	866	FN sortie as far south as Sardinia to counter an alleged Force H sortie from Gibraltar.
10.09.1940 26.09.1940		Messina			Refit & small repairs.
27.09.1940 28.09.1940	20:20 07:15	Messina Messina	10,55	283	Exit of the 3rd Division for exercises.
29.09.1940 01.10.1940	20:20 07:15	Messina Messina	34,55	629	FN exit in central Ionian Sea to counter British Operation MB5. No contact with the enemy.
06.10.1940 06.10.1940	09:00 20:50	Messina Messina	11,50	234	Exit of II Squadra to cover a convoy to the Aegean (Operation CV). The operation is suspended due to erroneous sighting of enemy naval forces.
12.10.2940 12.10.1940	08:05 17:25	Messina Messina	09,20	228	Assistance of 3rd Division to XII destroyer Squadriglia after a clash with British cruisers.
21.10.1940 22.10.1940	20:25 09:45	Messina Taranto	13,20	262	Transfer.
04.11.1940 04.11.1940	11:15 18:40	Taranto Taranto	7,25	145	Exit of the 3rd Division for exercises.
12.11.1940 13.11.1940	12:40 03:15	Taranto Messina	14,35	261	3rd Division transfer.
16.11.1940 18.11.1940	09:00 12:15	Messina Messina	51,15	926	FN exit to counter the British Operation 'White' in the western Mediterranean. No contact with enemy naval forces, but FN presence at sea contributes to failure of enemy operation.

Date	Hour	Location (from/to)	Hours underway	Nautical miles	Notes
26.11.1940 28.11.1940	11:50 15:40	Messina Naples	51,50	1161	Sortie of the FN to counter the British Operation 'Collar'. Battle of Cape Teulada or Spartivento (27.11.1940); from 12:20 to 13:01 the 3rd Division is engaged by the battlecruiser *Renown* and enemy cruisers; at 15:35 enemy bomber attack on 3rd Division unsuccessful.
28.11.1940 29.11.1940	20:00 08:00	Naples Messina	12,00		Transfer.
30.11.1940 18.12.1940		Messina			Engine room repair.
19.12.1940 19.12.1940	10:40 15:25	Messina Messina	4,45	105	Trials sortie. Alleged enemy submarine attack.
07.01.1941 07.01.1941	11:45 20:05	Messina Messina	8,20	191	Exit of the 3rd Division for exercises.
09.01.1941		Messina			AA fire against aircraft flying over the city.
10.01.1941 11.01.1941	18:35 11:05	Messina Messina	16,30	262	Movements in port.
14.01.1941 14.01.1941	00:40 11:40	Messina Messina	11,00	230	Exit of the Squadra Navale (SN) to search for the damaged aircraft carrier *Illustrious* in the Sicilian channel. Operation suspended.
31.01.1941 31.01.1941	12:05 17:20	Messina Messina	05,15	91	Exit of the 3rd Division for exercises.
08.02.1941 11.02.1941	07:40 10:45	Messina Messina	75,05	1428	SN exit to counter British Operation 'Grog' (bombardment of Genoa by Force H). No contact with the enemy.
01.03.1941 01.03.1941	13:30 22:35	Messina Messina	9,05	175	Exit of the 3rd Division for exercises.
07.03.1941 07.03.1941	12:55 22:45	Messina Messina	9,50	193	Exit of the 3rd Division for exercises.
12.03.1941 13.03.1941	15:25 13:15	Messina Messina	21,50	433	Exit of the 3rd Division for long range escort of a convoy to Libya.
15.03.1941 15.03.1941	13:40 22:50	Messina Messina	9,10	169	Exit of the 3rd Division for exercises.
27.03.1941 29.03.1941	05:40 18:20	Messina Taranto	60,40	1236	SN exit for offensive mission in the Eastern Mediterranean (Operation 'Gaudo'). From 08:12 to 08:54 on the 28th the 3rd Division engaged enemy light cruisers without success. At 12:08 torpedo bomber attack and at 15:15 enemy bombers attack the 3rd Division without success. At 19:21 new torpedo attack and AA barrage fire.
30.03.1941 13.04.1941		Taranto			Refit.
14.04.1941 14.04.1941	14:05 14:45	Taranto Taranto	0,40	4	Change of mooring.
23.04.1941 23.04.1941	17:40 18:45	Taranto Messina	25,05	282	Transfer.
27.04.1941 27.04.1941	10:55 16:10	Messina Messina	5,15	92	Exit of 3rd Division for remote escort of a convoy to Libya. Mission suspended due to sighting of enemy naval forces.

Continued overleaf

Date	Hour	Location (from/to)	Hours underway	Nautical miles	Notes
30.04.1941 02.05.1941	13:10 00:20	Messina Messina	35,10	1091	Exit of 3rd Division for direct and long range escort of convoys to and from Libya.
24.05.1941 25.05.1941	15:35 20:00	Messina Messina	28,25	559	Exit of the 3rd Division for long range escort of a convoy to Libya.
05.06.1941 05.06.1941	13:40 22:55	Messina Messina	9,15	169	Exit of the 3rd Division for exercises.
08.06.1941 09.06.1941	14:25 06:00	Messina Messina	15,35	300	Exit of 3rd Division for long range escort of convoy 'Esperia' to Libya.
19.06.1941 20.06.1941	16:45 04:00	Messina Messina	11,15	186	Exit of the 3rd Division for exercises with XII destroyer Squadriglia.
11.07.1941 11.07.1941	14:10 23:45	Messina Messina	9,35	176	Exercises
16.07.1941 18.07.1941	20:45 10:00	Messina Messina	37,15	814	Exit of the 3rd Division for long range escort of a convoy to Libya.
19.07.1941 19.08.1941		Messina			Participation in the AA defence of the city of Messina.
20.08.1941 21.08.1941	16:10 00:30	Messina Messina	8,20	158	Exit of the 3rd Division for exercises.
23.08.1941 26.08.1941	10:05 10:10	Messina Messina	72,05	1306	SN sortie as far south as Sardinia to counter the British Operation 'Mincemeat'. No contact with enemy naval forces. At 06:43 the *Bolzano* was torpedoed and seriously damaged by the British submarine *Triumph*. She returned to Messina with the help of two tugs.
10.09.1941		Messina			During an enemy air raid, *Bolzano* is hit by a bomb at 00:08, which causes significant damage and casualties among personnel.
04.10.1941 06.10.1941	20:00 13:00	Messina La Spezia	41,00	485	Transfer for repairs.
09.10.1941 09.10.1941	10:00 14:30	La Spezia Genoa	4,30	65	Transfer for repairs.
10.10.1941 14.05.1942		Genoa			Refit.
15.05.1942 15.05.1942	05:20 13:30	Genoa La Spezia	8,10	146	Transfer and sea trials.
21.05.1942 21.05.1942	05:45 17:05	La Spezia La Spezia	11,20	142	Exercises.
25.05.1942 26.05.1942	13:25 01:45	La Spezia La Spezia	12,20	213	Exercises.
03.06.1942 03.06.1942	05:00 15:35	La Spezia La Spezia			Exercises.
11.06.1942 11.06.1942	13:50 15:30	La Spezia	1,50	136	Change of mooring.
19.06.1942 19.06.1942	17:30 24:00	La Spezia La Spezia	6,30		

Date	Hour	Location (from/to)	Hours underway	Nautical miles	Notes
05.07.1941 06.07.1941	00:00 03:35	La Spezia Messina	27,35	523	Transfer
12.08.1942 13.08.1942	09:00 12:00	Messina Panarea	27.00	700	Exit of the 3rd and 7th Divisions to counter the British Operation 'Pedestal' (Battle of 'Mezzo Agosto'). The operation was suspended. During the return voyage, at 08:13, the *Bolzano* was torpedoed and severely damaged by the British submarine *Unbroken*. Run aground off the island of Panarea.
14.08.1942 14.09.1942		Panarea			Ship rescue operations.
15.09.1942 16.09.1942	15:30 19:45	Panarea Naples	28,15	145	Transfer under tow.
17.09.1942 10.12.1942		Naples			Refit for partial repairs.
11.12.1942 11.12.1942	09:30 17:30	Naples Naples	8,00	15	Exit for sea trials and swinging for compass deviation.
21.12.1942 22.12.1942	15:30 15:00	Naples La Spezia	23,30	332	Transfer under her own power.
23.12.1942 08.09.1943		La Spezia			Ship awaiting decisions, subject only to minor maintenance.
08.09.1943		La Spezia			When the armistice was declared, the ship was simply abandoned, as it was completely unseaworthy.
22.06.1944		La Spezia			The wreck of the *Bolzano* is sunk by explosive charges applied by British underwater raiders.

ZARA

Date	Hour	Location (from/to)	Hours underway	Nautical miles	Notes
11.06.1940 12.06.1940	23:45 20:00	Taranto Taranto	20,15	489	Exit of 1st and 8th Divisions and II Squadra (from Messina) to search for enemy naval forces in the Ionian Sea. No contact. At 11:07, at 14:33 and at 16:39 alleged enemy submarine attacks.
21.06.1941 22.06.1941	17:45 07:20	Taranto Augusta	13,35	280	Transfer of 1st Division for offensive mission in the Western Mediterranean.
22.06.1941 24.06.1941	14:30 10:00	Augusta Augusta	43,30	1002	Exit of II Squadra (from Messina and Palermo) and 1st Division in support of a 7th Division raid in the Sardinian Sea against French shipping. No contact with the enemy.
07.07.1940 09.07.1940	18:05 23:50	Augusta Augusta	53,45	1120	FN sailed into the central Ionian Sea to cover and escort two convoys directed to Libya (Operation TCM). Battle of Punta Stilo (09.07.1940) At 13:17 on the 9th *Zara* was subjected to torpedo attacks without result. From 15:55 to 16:17 the 1st Division engaged battleship *Warspite* and enemy light cruisers. Into the evening, there is a succession of luckily unsuccessful attacks by Italian bombers on the FN without consequences.
10.07.1940 10.07.1940	01:45 15:55	Augusta Naples	14,10	285	Transfer to evade enemy torpedo attacks.
30.07.1940 01.08.1940	09:50 19:10	Naples Naples	57,20	1307	Exit of II Squadra and 1st Division for remote escort of three convoys to Libya (operation TVL).
16.08.1940 16.08.1940	06:35 16:00	Naples Naples	9,25	183	Exit of 1st Division for exercises.

Continued overleaf

Date	Hour	Location (from/to)	Hours underway	Nautical miles	Notes
29.08.1940 30.08.1940	09:40 18:15	Naples Taranto	32,35	620	Transfer of 1st Division.
31.08.1940 02.09.1940	04:35 01:50	Taranto Taranto	45,15	702	FN exit in the eastern Ionian Sea to counter the British Operation 'Hats'. No contact with enemy naval forces.
07.09.1940 09.09.1940	15:00 08:30	Taranto Palermo	41,30	819	FN sailed as far west as Sardinia to counter an alleged Force H sortie from Gibraltar.
11.09.1940 12.09.1940	16:05 10:25	Palermo Taranto	18,20	375	Transfer if 1st Division.
23.09.1940 23.09.1940	12:25 23:50	Taranto Taranto	11,25	178	Exit of the 1st Division for exercises.
24.09.1940 24.09.1940	15:20 18:55	Taranto Taranto	3.35	60	Exit of the 1st Division for exercises.
29.09.1940 01.10.1940	17:30 05:10	Taranto Taranto	35,40	621	FN exit in central Ionian Sea to counter British Operation MB5. No contact with enemy naval forces.
06.10.1940 06.10.1940	09:50 24:00	Taranto Taranto	14,10	279	Exit of II Squadra to cover a convoy to the Aegean (Operation CV). The operation is suspended due to erroneous sighting of enemy naval forces.
06.11.1940 06.11.1940	11:15 18:50	Taranto Taranto	7,35	123	Exit of the 1st Division for exercises. On return the *Zara* moored in Mar Grande.
11.11.1940 12.11.1940	23:10 00:20	Taranto			Enemy air raid on Taranto base (Operation 'Judgment', part of Operation MB8). *Zara* participates in the AA defence.
12.11.1940 14.11.1940	11:50 08:45	Taranto La Spezia	44.55	827	Transfer for refit.
15.11.1940 08.12.1940		La Spezia			In drydock.
09.12.1940 10.12.1940	10:00 09:10	La Spezia Naples	23,10	396	Transfer, sea trials and exercises.
15.12.1940 16.12.1940	16:30 09:55	Naples La Maddalena	17,25	255	Transfer of the 1st Division after enemy air raid on Naples.
19.12.1940 20.12.1940	21:05 12:50	La Maddalena Naples	15,45	237	Transfer of 1st Division.
22.12.1940 23.12.1940	16:30 14:50	Naples Taranto	22,20	439	Transfer of 1st Division.
29.01.1941 30.01.1941	10:20 02:45	Taranto Taranto	16,25	184	Exit of 1st Division for exercises.
13.02.1941 13.02.1941	09:50 19:50	Taranto Taranto	10,00	115	Exit of 1st Division for exercises.
11.03.1941 11.03.1941	10:15 13:50	Taranto Taranto	3,25	...	Exit of 1st Division for exercises.
17.03.1941 17.03.1941	09:20 12:30	Taranto Taranto	3,10	...	Exit of 1st Division for exercises.

Date	Hour	Location (from/to)	Hours underway	Nautical miles	Notes
26.03.1941 29.01.1941	21:00 02:40	Taranto Cape Matapan			SN exit for offensive mission in the Eastern Mediterranean (Operation 'Gaudo'). Following the torpedoing and immobilisation of the *Pola* at 19:12 on the 28th, the *Zara*, the *Fiume* and the IX destroyer Squadriglia are sent to her rescue. At 22:30, the Italian ships were surprised by the Mediterranean Fleet; the *Zara*, *Fiume* and destroyers *Vittorio Alfieri* and *Giosuè Carducci* were destroyed by the battleships *Warspite*, *Valiant* and *Barham* and by the 10th Destroyer Flotilla. The *Zara*, now a wreck in flames, was scuttled at 02:30 on the 29th south of Cape Matapan.

FIUME

Date	Hour	Location (from/to)	Hours underway	Nautical miles	Notes
11.06.1940 12.06.1940	23:40 20:10	Taranto Taranto	20,30	490	Exit of 1st and 8th Divisions and II Squadra (from Messina) to search for enemy naval forces in the Ionian Sea. No contact. At 14:35 alleged enemy submarine attack.
21,06.1940 22.06.1940	17:45 07:15	Taranto Augusta	13,30	287	Transfer of 1st Division for offensive mission in the Western Mediterranean.
22.06.1940 24.06.1940	14:30 09:55	Augusta Augusta	43,25	1024	Exit of II Squadra (from Messina and Palermo) and 1st Division in support of a 7th Division raid in the Sardinian Sea against French traffic. No contact.
07.07.1940 10.07.1940	18:10 17:10	Augusta Naples	71,00	1452	Exit of the Naval Forces (FN) in the central Ionian Sea to cover and escort two convoys heading to Libya (Operation TCM). Battle of Punta Stilo (09.07.1940). At 13:23 on the 9th enemy torpedo bomber attack and AA fire without result. From 15:55 to 16:17 the 1st Division engaged battleship *Warspite* and enemy light cruisers. From 16:20 to 19:30, during the disengagement phase, there were other air attacks, including Italian ones by mistake, luckily without success.
30.07.1940 01.08.1940	10:00 20:00	Naples Naples	58,00	1213	Exit of II Squadra and 1st Division for long range escort of three convoys to Libya (Operation TVL).
16.08.1940 16.08.1940	06:30 18:20	Naples Naples	11,50	185	Exit of 1st Division for exercises.
29.08.1940 30.08.1940	12:30 18:25	Naples Taranto	29,55	440	Transfer of 1st Division.
23.09.1940 23.09.1940	12:40 23:55	Taranto Taranto	11,15	183	Exit of 1st Division for exercises.
24.09.1940 24.09.1940	15:30 18:55	Taranto Taranto	3,25	60	Exit of 1st Division for exercises.
29.09.1940 01.10.1940	17:40 03:40	Taranto Taranto	34,00	640	FN exit in central Ionian Sea to counter British Operation MB5. No contact with the enemy.
06.10.1940 06.10.1940	12:30 24:00	Taranto Taranto	11,30	265	Exit of II Squadra to escort a convoy to the Aegean (Operation CV). The operation is suspended due to erroneous sighting of enemy naval forces.
06.11.1940 06.11.1940	12:30 24:00	Taranto Taranto	5,50	116	Exit of the 1st Division for exercises. On return the *Fiume* is moored in Mar Grande.
11.11.1940 12.11.1940	23:10 00:20	Taranto			Enemy air raid on Taranto (Operation 'Judgment', part of Operation MB8). *Fiume* participates in AA defence.
12.11.1940 13.11.1940	13:05 13:35	Taranto Naples	24,30	481	Transfer of the 1st Division after the air raid on Taranto.
16.11.1940 18.11.1940	09:40 15:10	Naples Naples	53,30	954	FN exit to counter the British Operation 'White' in the western Mediterranean. No contact with enemy naval forces, but FN presence at sea contributes to failure of enemy operation.

Continued overleaf

Date	Hour	Location (from/to)	Hours underway	Nautical miles	Notes
26.11.1940 28.11.1940	11:45 14:35	Naples Naples	50,50	910	Exit of the FN to counter the British Operation 'Collar'. Battle of Cape Teulada or Spartivento (27.11.1940); from 12:20 to 13:01 the 1st Division is engaged by the battlecruiser *Renown* and enemy cruisers; at 12:22 and 12:35 the *Fiume* or *Pola* hits the British heavy cruiser *Berwick*; at 15:25 British torpedo bomber attack against the 1st Division without result.
10.12.1940 11.12.1940	11:55 10:25	Naples La Spezia	22,30	377	Transfer.
12.12.1940 26.02.1941		La Spezia			Refit.
27.02.1941 27.02.1941	11:30 19:30	La Spezia la Spezia	8,00	140	Sea trials.
28.02.1941 02.03.1941	12:15 10:00	La Spezia Taranto	47,45	730	Transfer.
11.03.1941 11.03.1941	13:35 16:45	Taranto Taranto	3,10	50	Exit of 1st Division for exercises.
17.03.1941 17.03.1941	13:15 17:15	Taranto Taranto	4,00	70	Exit of 1st Division for exercises.
26.03.1941 28.03.1941	21:00 23:15	Taranto Cape Matapan			SN exit for offensive mission in the Eastern Mediterranean (Operation 'Gaudo'). Following the torpedoing and immobilisation of *Pola* at 19:12 on the 28th, *Zara*, *Fiume* and IX Destroyer Squadriglia are sent to her rescue. At 22:30, the Italian ships were surprised by the Mediterranean Fleet: *Zara*, *Fiume* and destroyers *Vittorio Alfieri* and *Giosuè Carducci* were destroyed by battleships *Warspite*, *Valiant* and *Barham* and by the 10th Destroyer Flotilla. *Fiume*, sank at 23:15 on the 28th south of Cape Matapan.

GORIZIA

Date	Hour	Location (from/to)	Hours underway	Nautical miles	Notes
11.06.1940 12.06.1940	23:40 20:25	Taranto Taranto	20,25	483	Exit of 1st and 8th Divisions and II Squadra (from Messina) to search for enemy naval forces in the Ionian Sea. No contact. At 14:46 and 16:47 alleged attacks by enemy submarines.
21.06.1940 22.06.1940	17:45 06:45	Taranto Augusta	13,00	1305	Transfer of 1st Division for offensive mission in the Western Mediterranean.
22.06.1940 24.06.1940	14:45 09:55	Augusta Augusta	43,10		Exit of 2nd Squadra (from Messina and Palermo) and 1st Division in support of a 7th Division raid in the Sardinian Sea against French shipping. No contact.
07.07.1940 09.07.1940	18:10 23:55	Augusta Augusta	53,45	1114	FN deployment in the Ionian Sea to cover and escort two convoys to Libya (Operation TCM). Battle of Punta Stilo (09.07.1940). At 13:20 of the 9th enemy torpedo bomber attack and AA fire without result. From 15:55 to 16:17 the 1st Division engaged battleship *Warspite* and enemy light cruisers. Then, until the evening there are attacks by Italian bombers on the FN without consequences.
10.07.1940 10.07.1940	01:55 16:40	Augusta Naples	14,45	300	Transfer.
30.07.1940 01.08.1940	10:00 19:25	Naples Naples	57,25	1279	Exit of II Squadra and 1st Division for long range escort of three convoys to Libya (Operation TVL).
16.08.1940 16.08.1940	06:20 16:35	Naples Naples	10,15	200	Exit of 1st Division for exercises.
29.08.1940 30.08.1940	12:55 18:20	Naples Taranto	29,25	618	Transfer of 1st Division.

Date	Hour	Location (from/to)	Hours underway	Nautical miles	Notes
31.08.1940 02.09.1940	04:35 00:05	Taranto Taranto	43,30	706	FN exit in the eastern Ionian Sea to counter the British Operation 'Hats'. No contact with the enemy.
07.09.1940 09.09.1940	15:30 09:35	Taranto Palermo	42,05	821	Transfer of 1st Division.
10.09.1940 11.09.1940	20:30 18:10	Palermo Taranto	21,40	398	Transfer of 1st Division.
23.09.1940 23.09.1940	12:40 18:10	Taranto Taranto	6,30	117	Exit of 1st Division for exercises.
24.09.1940 24.09.1940	15:30 24:00	Taranto Taranto	8,30	127	Exit of 1st Division for exercises.
29.09.1940 01.10.1940	17:40 03:50	Taranto Taranto	34,10	612	FN exit in central Ionian Sea to counter British Operation MB5. No contact with enemy.
06.10.1940 06.10.1940	10:25 24:00	Taranto Taranto	13,45	273	Exit of II Squadra to cover a convoy to the Aegean (Operation CV). The operation is suspended due to erroneous sighting of enemy naval forces.
06.11.1940 06.11.1940	12:00 18:55	Taranto Taranto	6,55	120	Exit of the 1st Division for exercises. On return, the *Gorizia* moored in the Mar Grande.
11.11.1940 12.11.1940	23:10 00:20	Taranto			British air raid on Taranto base (Operation 'Judgment', part of Operation MB8). *Gorizia* participates in the AA defence and probably shoots down one of the two British aircraft that were lost.
12.11.1940 13.11.1940	18:05 14:00	Taranto Naples	19,55	442	Transfer of the 1st Division after the air raid on Taranto.
16.11.1940 18.11.1940	09:20 13:50	Naples Naples	54,30	868	FN exit to counter the British Operation 'White' in the western Mediterranean. No contact with enemy naval forces, but FN presence at sea contributes to failure of enemy operation.
26.11.1940 28.11.1940	11:25 14:20	Naples Naples	50,55	837	Exit of the FN to counter the British Operation 'Collar'. Battle of Cape Teulada or Spartivento (27.11.1940); from 12:20 to 13:01 the 1st Division is engaged by the battlecruiser *Renown* and enemy cruisers; at 15:20 attacks by enemy torpedo bombers without success.
15.12.1940 16.12.1940	16:45 09:50	Naples La Maddalena	17,15	252	Transfer of the 1st Division after the enemy air raid on Naples.
19.12.1940 20.12.1940	21:20 13:05	La Maddalena Naples	15,45	238	Transfer of 1st Division.
22.12.1940 23.12.1940	06:30 15:10	Naples Taranto	22,40	427	Transfer of 1st Division.
26.12.1940 26.12.1940	09:00 16:15	Taranto Taranto	7,15	10	Change of mooring.
29.01.1941 30.01.1941	10:20 02:50	Taranto Taranto	16,30	175	Exit of 1st Division for exercises.
13.02.1941 13.02.1941	10:05 19:50	Taranto Taranto	9,45	120	Exit of 1st Division for exercises.
22.02.1941 22.02.1941	09:25 10:50	Taranto Taranto	1,25	6	Change of mooring.

Continued overleaf

Date	Hour	Location (from/to)	Hours underway	Nautical miles	Notes
28.02.1941 02.03.1941	13:35 15:35	Taranto La Spezia	50,00	933	Transfer for refit.
03.03.1941 28.04.1941		La Spezia			Refit.
29.04.1941 29.04.1941	14:00 17:50	La Spezia La Spezia	3,50	65	Sea trials.
01.05.1941 01.05.1941	08:00 19:10	La Spezia La Spezia	11,10	196	Exercises.
07.05.1941 08.05.1941	15:05 18:05	La Spezia Messina	27,00	510	Transfer
26.05.1941 28.05.1941	17:05 14:15	Messina Messina	45,10	781	Long range escort of a convoy from Libya.
05.06.1941 06.06.1941	14:15 01:30	Messina Messina	11,15	174	Exit of 1st Division for exercises.
19.06.1941 20.06.1941	17:30 02:20	Messina Messina	8,50	136	Exit of 1st Division for long along with XIII destroyer Squadriglia.
25.06.1941 26.06.1941	18:40 17:00	Messina Taranto	22,20	435	Exit of 3rd Division for remote escort of convoy 'Esperia' to Libya. Operation suspended due to intense air attacks.
27.06.1941 29.06.1941	17:25 11:10	Taranto Messina	41,45	861	Exit of 3rd Division for remote escort of convoy 'Esperia' to Libya.
21.07.1941 22.07.1941	15:15 00:20	Messina Messina	9,50	159	Exercises.
20.08.1941 21.08.1941	15:55 03:55	Messina Messina	12,00	213	Exit of the 3rd Division for exercises.
23.08.1941 26.08.1941	10:00 08:15	Messina Messina	70,15	1355	SN sortie as far south as Sardinia to counter the British Operation 'Mincemeat'. No contact with enemy naval forces.
10.09.1941 10.09.1941	07:50 12:15	Messina Messina	4,25	72	Exit of 1st Division for exercises.
26.09.1941 29.09.1941	14:00 01:50	Messina La Maddalena	59,50	1146	SN exit as far south as Sardinia to counter the British Operation 'Halberd'. No contact with the enemy.
10.10.1941 10.10.1941	03:15 23:30	La Maddalena Messina	20,15	194	Transfer of 3rd Division.
20.11.1941 21.11.1941	23:00 02:00	Messina			Air raid on Messina. *Gorizia* participates in the AA defence. Some bombs exploded on the mooring dock causing light damage and minor losses among the personnel.
21.11.1941 22.11.1941	18:15 18:40	Messina Taranto	24,25	370	Exit of 3rd and 8th Divisions for remote escort of a convoy to Libya.
13.12.1941 14.12.1941	18:40 03:55	Taranto Taranto	09,15	111	Operation M41 (long range escort of a convoy to Libya), later suspended.
16.12.1941 19.12.1941	17:15 12:45	Taranto Taranto	67,30	1341	SN exit for Operation M42 (convoy escort to Libya). First Battle of Sirte (17.12.1941). From 17:55 to 18:14 on the 17th *Gorizia* opened fire against British forces, slightly damaging destroyer *Kipling* with a near miss.

Date	Hour	Location (from/to)	Hours underway	Nautical miles	Notes
03.01.1942 05.01.1942	18:10 15:45	Taranto Messina	45,35	861	SN exit for Operation M42 (convoy escort to Libya).
14.02.1942 16.02.1942	23:15 15:20	Messina Messina	40.05	824	Exit of II Squadra and 3rd Division to counter British Operation MF5. No contact with enemy.
21.02.1942 24.02.1942	18:30 12:00	Messina Messina	65,30	1120	Exit of II Squadra and 3rd Division for Operation K7 (convoy escort to Libya). At 14:08 on the 22nd AA fire at enemy bomber.
22.03.1942 23.03.1942	00:55 14:20	Messina Messina	37,25	773	SN exit to counter British Operation MG1. Second Battle of Sirte. From 14:35 to 19:00 on the 22nd, the 3rd Division intermittently engaged enemy forces, causing minor damage to the light cruiser *Cleopatra* (hit amidship by light cruiser *Giovanni delle Bande Nere*) and destroyer *Sikh* (near-missed by *Trento*). *Gorizia* damaged by heavy seas during the return voyage.
24.03.1942 18.05.1942		Messina			Refit.
19.05.1942 19.05.1942	01:45 07:10	Messina Augusta	05,25	78	Transfer and exercises.
25.05.1942 25.05.1942	03:15 09:00	Augusta Messina	05,45	83	Transfer.
26.05.1942	22:25	Messina			British air raids on Messina. The *Gorizia* participates in AA defence.
27.05.1942		Messina			British air raids on Messina. The *Gorizia* participates in AA defence.
28.05.1942 29.05.1942	17:50 10:25	Messina Taranto	16,35	317	British air raid on Messina and transfer of the 3rd Division.
14.06.1942 16.06.1942	12:45 17:20	Taranto Taranto	52,35	1092	Exit of the FN in the central-eastern Mediterranean to counter the British Operation 'Vigorous'. Battle of 'Mezzo Giugno' (11–16.06.1942). No contact with enemy naval forces, but the interposition of FN between them and Malta makes the operation fail. At 08:12 on the 15th the *Gorizia* carried out AA fire against enemy aircraft.
05.07.1942 05.07.1942	04:15 18:35	Taranto Messina	14,20	301	Transfer.
12.08.1942 13.08.1942	09:30 12:00				Exit of the 3rd and 7th Divisions to counter the British Operation 'Pedestal'. Battle of 'Mezzo Agosto' (11–15.08.1942). The mission of the two divisions is suspended without contact with the enemy. During the return, at 08:20 the *Gorizia* manoeuvred to avoid a torpedo from the British submarine *Unbroken*.
09.10.1942 09.10.1942	13:25 17:55	Messina Messina	4,30	51	Exercises.
19.10.1942 19.10.1942	07:00 11:40	Messina Messina	4,40	69	Exercises.
09.12.1942 10.12.1942	20:25 14:05	Messina La Maddalena	17,40	385	Transfer of 3rd Division.
18.03.1943 18.03.1943	07:05 10:00	La Maddalena La Maddalena	02,55	37	Exercises.
10.04.1943	14:35	La Maddalena			During a US air raid, the *Gorizia* at 14:35 was severely damaged by three bombs and others exploded in the vicinity with serious loss of life.
12.04.1943 12.04.1943	23:30 16:55	La Maddalena La Spezia	17,24	231	Transfer for refit under her own power.

Continued overleaf

Date	Hour	Location (from/to)	Hours underway	Nautical miles	Notes
14.04.1943		La Spezia			Refit.
04.05.1943 07.09.1943		La Spezia			Drydocking for repairs.
08.09.1943 02.05.1945					At the proclamation of the armistice the ship was still under repair in the drydock, where she was captured by the Germans. The Germans then moved her to the Duca degli Abruzzi dock and later to the merchant port, where she was found half-submerged after the war.

POLA

Date	Hour	Location (from/to)	Hours underway	Nautical miles	Notes
10.06.1940 11.06.1940	19:00 12:45	Messina Messina	17,45	383	Exit of II Squadra to cover 2nd Division and minelayers for laying 'L.K.' barrage in the Sicilian Channel.
12.06.1940 12.06.1940	00:00 17:55	Messina Messina	17,55	453	Exit of II Squadra, 1st and 8th Divisions (from Taranto) to search for enemy naval forces in the Ionian Sea. No contact.
22.06.1940 24.06.1940	17:45 06:40	Messina Messina	36,55	890	Exit of II Squadra (2nd Division from Palermo) and 1st Division (from Augusta) in support of a 7th Division raid in the Sardinian Sea against French shipping. No contact.
02.07.1940 02.07.1940	03:00 06:30	Messina Augusta	3,30	72	Transfer.
07.07.1940 10.07.1940	18:00 15:15	Augusta Naples	69,15	1324	FN deployment in the central Ionian Sea to cover and escort two convoys to Libya (Operation TCM). Battle of Punta Stilo (09.07.1940). At 13:20 on the 9th enemy torpedo bomber attack and AA firing without result. From 15:55 to 16:17 the 1st Division engaged battleship *Warspite* and enemy light cruisers. Until the evening there is a succession of attacks by Italian bombers on the FN without consequences.
30.07.1940 01.08.1940	10:00 18:30	Naples Naples	56,30	1220	Exit of II Squadra and 1st Division for remote escort of three convoys to Libya (Operation TVL).
16.08.1940 16.08.1940	06:30 16:00	Naples Naples	9,30	178	Exit for exercises with 1st Division.
29.08.1940 30.08.1940	12:45 18:15	Naples Taranto	29,30	718	Transfer with the 1st Division.
31.08.1940 01.09.1940	04:30 24:00	Taranto Taranto	43,30	797	FN exit in the eastern Ionian Sea to counter the British Operation 'Hats'. No contact with enemy naval forces.
07.09.1940 09.09.1940	15:15 07:30	Taranto Palermo	40,15	754	FN exit as far south as Sardinia to counter an alleged Force H sortie from Gibraltar.
10.09.1940 11.09.1940	21:00 16:45	Palermo Taranto	19,45	367	Transfer with the 1st Division.
23.09.1940 23.09.1940	12:40 19:05	Taranto Taranto	6,25	125	Exit with 1st Division for drills.
24.09.1940 24.09.1940	15:30 23:05	Taranto Taranto	7,35	107	Exit with 1st Division for drills.
29.09.1940 01.09.1940	17:40 04:00	Taranto Taranto	34,20	583	FN exit in central Ionian Sea to counter British Operation MB5. No contact with enemy naval forces.
06.10.1940 06.10.1940	10:15 24:00	Taranto Taranto	13,45	275	Exit of II Squadra to cover a convoy to the Aegean (Operation CV). The operation is suspended due to erroneous sighting of enemy naval forces.

Date	Hour	Location (from/to)	Hours underway	Nautical miles	Notes
06.11.1940 06.11.1940	10:15 24:00	Taranto Taranto	7,00	275	Exit with 1st Division for exercises. On return, the *Pola* is moored in the Mar Piccolo.
12.11.1940 13.11.1940	13:15 13:20	Taranto Naples	24,05	458	Transfer with the 1st Division after the air raid on Taranto.
16.11.1940 18.11.1940	10:10 13:20	Naples Naples	51,10	867	FN exit to counter the British Operation 'White' in the western Mediterranean. No contact with enemy naval forces, but FN presence at sea contributes to failure of enemy operation.
26.11.1940 28.11.1940	11:50 14:00	Naples Naples	50,10	842	Exit of the FN to counter the British Operation 'Collar'. Battle of Cape Teulada or Spartivento (27.11.1940); from 12:20 to 13:01 the 1st Division is engaged by the battlecruiser *Renown* and enemy cruisers; at 12:22 and at 12:35 the *Pola* or *Fiume* hits the British heavy cruiser *Berwick*; at 15:25 unsuccessful British torpedo bomber attack against the 1st Division.
14.12.1940 15.12.1940	20:55 01:50	Naples			Enemy air raid. Two bombs hit the *Pola* at 20:57 and 22:25 causing not a lot of damage, but enough to risk sinking her.
16.12.1940	13:00	Naples			*Pola* drydocked.
17.12.1940 06.02.1941		Naples			Refit.
07.02.1941 07.02.1941	09:40 14:00	Naples Naples	4,20	92	Sea trials.
10.02.1941 11.02.1941	20:45 19:40	Naples Taranto	23,35	408	Transfer.
13.02.1941 13.02.1941	13:00 20:00	Taranto Taranto	7,00	146	1st Division exit for drills.
11.03.1941 11.03.1941	15:50 19:10	Taranto Taranto	3,20	60	1st Division exit for drills.
17.03.1941 17.03.1941	10:55 14:25	Taranto Taranto	3,30	60	1st Division exit for drills.
23.03.1941 23.03.1941	11:35 14:45	Taranto Taranto	3,10	60	Exercises.
23.03.1941 23.03.1941	19:25 00:45	Taranto Taranto	5,20	100	Exercises.
26.03.1941 29.03.1941	21:00 04:00	Taranto Cape Matapan	54,00	840	SN leaves for an offensive mission in the Eastern Mediterranean (Operation 'Gaudo'). At 19:12 on the 28th, during the return voyage, the SN was attacked by enemy torpedo bombers and the *Pola* was hit and immobilised south of Cape Matapan. *Zara*, *Fiume* and the IX Destroyer Squadriglia were sent to rescue her but at 22:30 they were surprised by the Mediterranean Fleet. *Zara*, *Fiume* and destroyers *Vittorio Alfieri* and *Giosuè Carducci* are destroyed by the battleships *Warspite*, *Valiant* and *Barham*. At 24:00 the *Pola* was shelled by destroyer *Havock* and, at 04:00, sunk with two torpedoes by destroyer *Jervis*, after recovering the survivors.

Appendix D

ITALIAN HEAVY CRUISER BRIDGE TOWERS

Roberto Maggi will be familiar to readers for the excellent plans and line drawings that illustrated *Italian Battleships: Conte di Cavour and Duilio Classes 1911–1956* by Erminio Bagnasco and Augusto de Toro (published by Seaforth in 2021). He has made a particular study of the design, configuration and differences of the tower bridge structures of Italian cruisers that took part in the Second World War, this section relating to the seven heavy cruisers being expressly written for this book.

Roberto Maggi is an engineer, naval draughtsman and skilled model-maker, so these pages are enriched by specially made drawings highlighting the differences between the seven Italian heavy cruisers, as well as exquisitely detailed models of their bridge structures. Those of *Fiume*, *Zara*, *Gorizia* and *Pola*, published for the first time, join those for *Trento*, *Trieste* and *Bolzano* which taken with the comprehensively detailed drawings, will enable scholars, enthusiasts and model-makers to visualise the differences in these structures, which have never before been fully described.

TRIESTE and *TRENTO*

These two cruisers were almost identical, though with some very visible differences in details left to the initiative of the shipyards. Their towers were repeatedly modified, starting from commissioning, because of continuing dissatisfaction on the part of the Regia Marina, which was never able to obtain an adequate configuration from an original design that was too tall and bulky, and not very functional in practice.

The main central superstructure consisted of a long deckhouse on the main deck, from the second to the third turret of the main armament. Initially, the tower was built around a tripod with a central tube of 80cm external diameter and two 50cm legs raked aft and stepped on the forecastle deck, either side of the large forward funnel, with an elliptical section and enormous smoke boxes (over 100m² protruding above the deckhouse), necessary to concentrate and dispose of the smoke produced by the eight forward boilers.

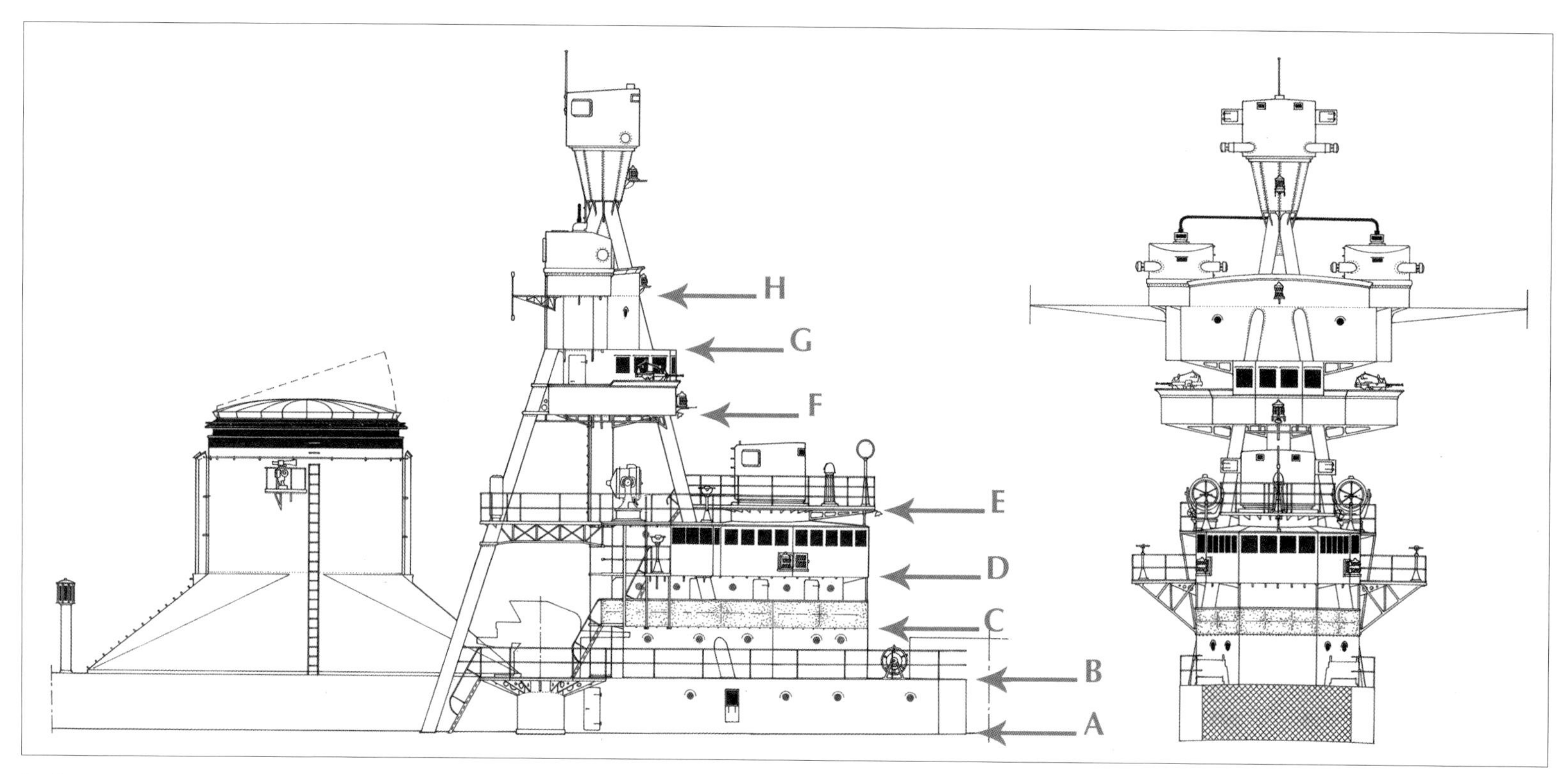

In the text, reference is made to the various levels of the towers of the cruisers *Trento*, *Trieste* and *Bolzano*, indicating them, from bottom to top, from 'B' to 'H' respectively. This is because it was decided to use the letter 'A' to indicate the main deck (for *Trento* and *Trieste*) or the forecastle deck (for *Bolzano*) where there was a deckhouse on which the tower of each ship was erected. The towers of the three ships were all distinguished by seven superimposed levels and the differences are identified by the elements indicated in the text.

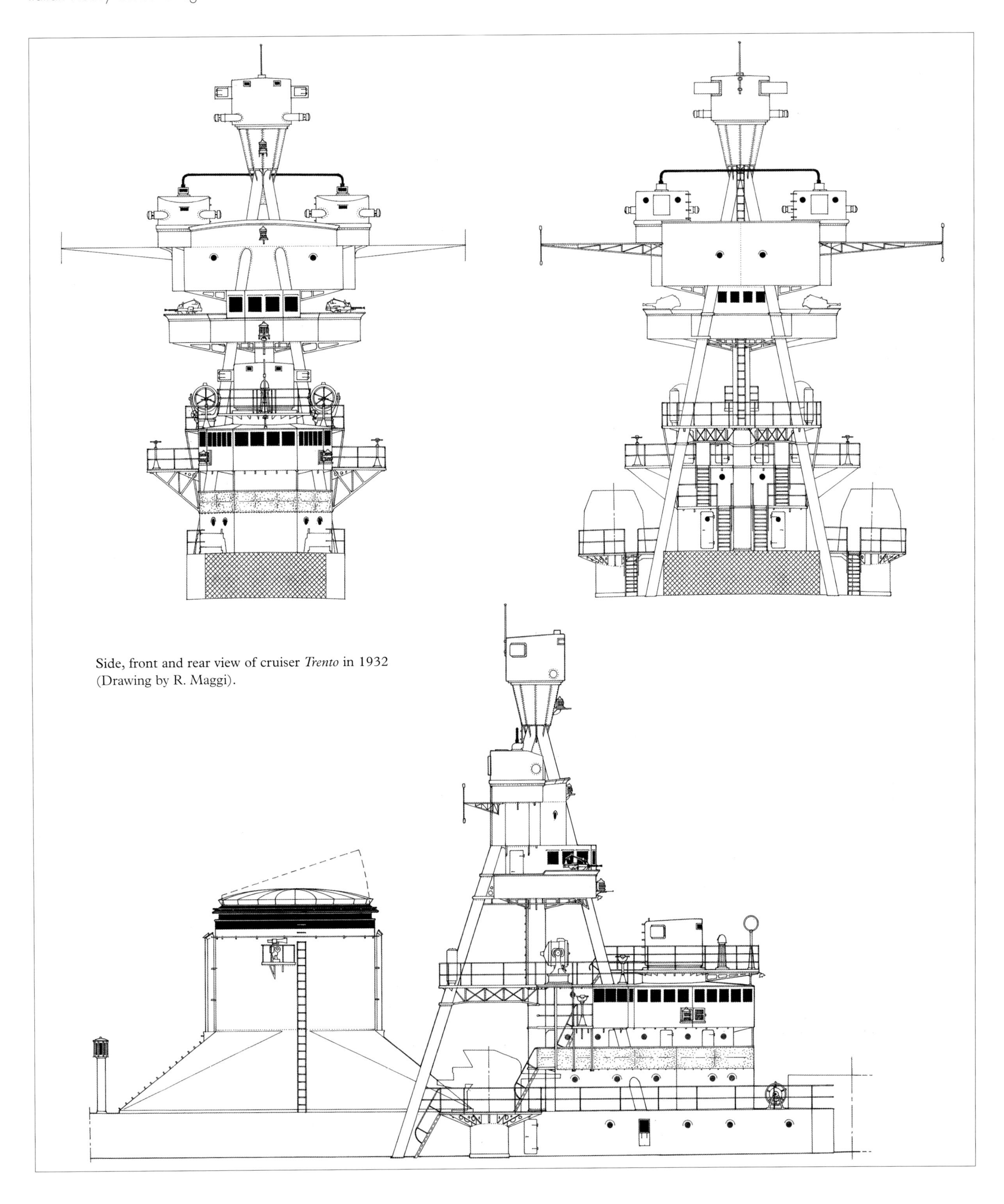

Side, front and rear view of cruiser *Trento* in 1932 (Drawing by R. Maggi).

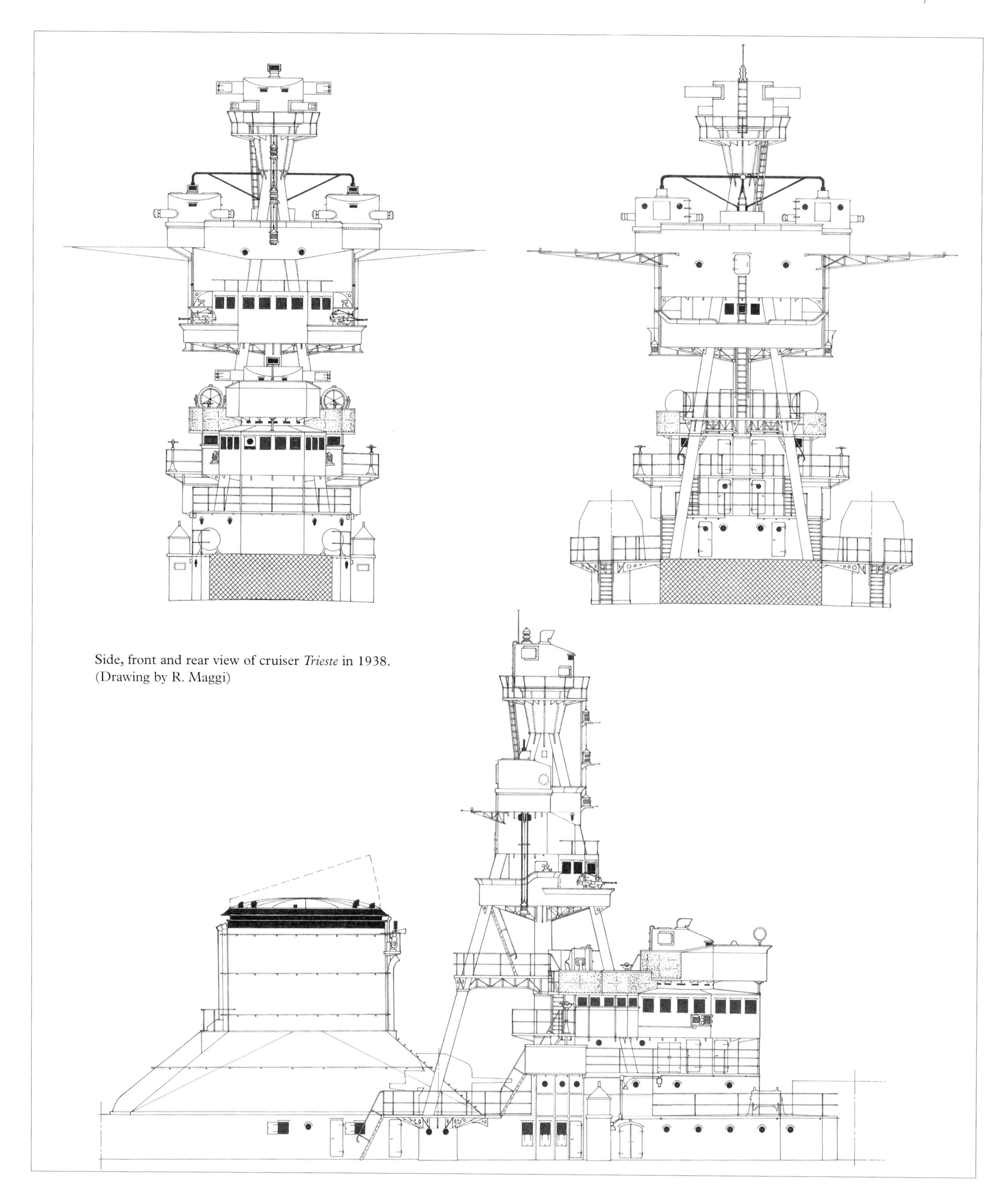

Side, front and rear view of cruiser *Trieste* in 1938.
(Drawing by R. Maggi)

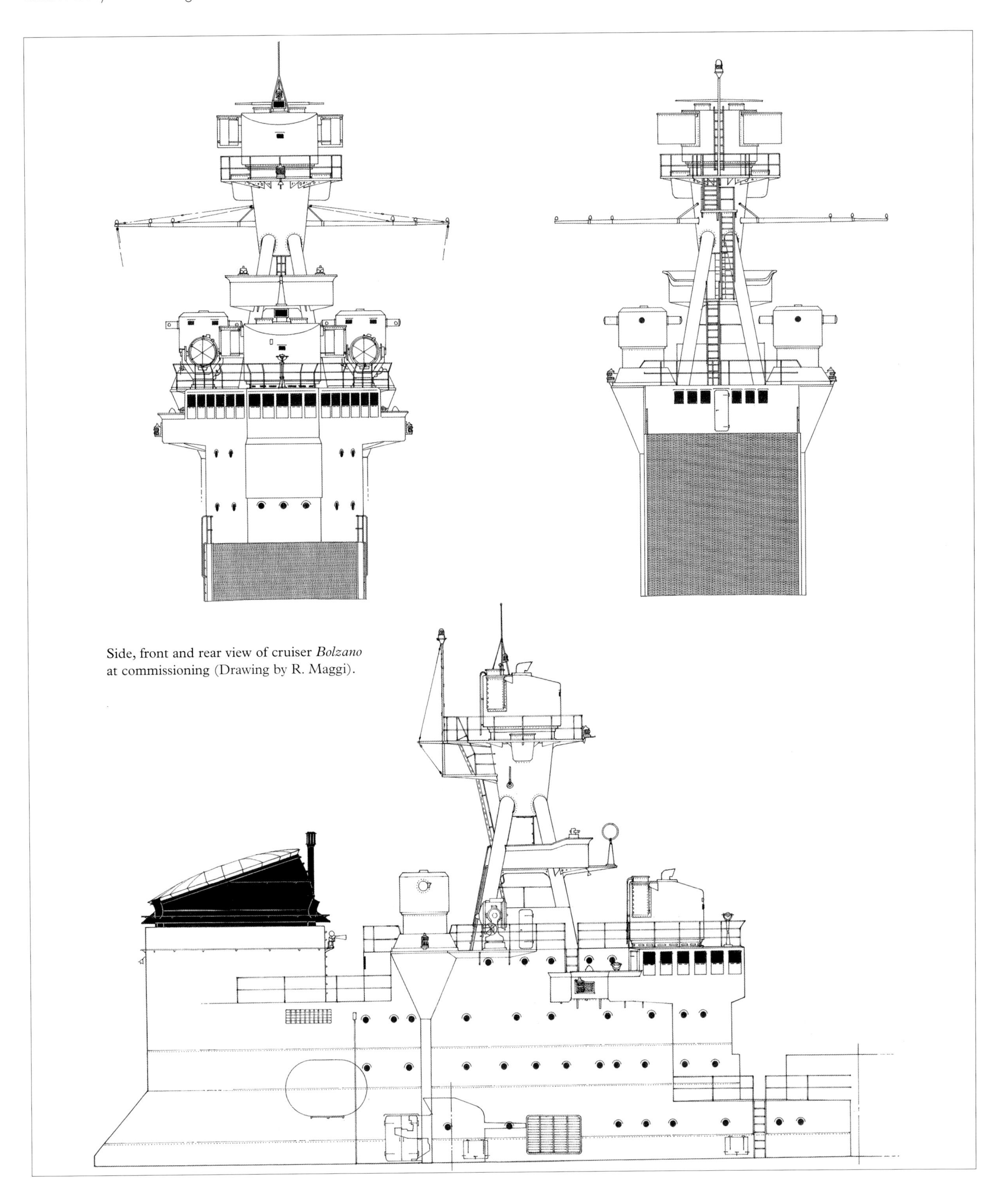

Side, front and rear view of cruiser *Bolzano* at commissioning (Drawing by R. Maggi).

To support the new platforms necessary to carry additional weapons and equipment, in 1930 the structure was stiffened by transforming the tripod into a pentapod, with the addition of two more prominent legs angled towards the bow, similar in size and inclination to the rear ones. This was in fact the configuration which these ships retained for the rest of their active lives.

The original tripod of the *Trieste* had a transverse opening of 7m on the main deck, with legs set back 6m with respect to the central pylon; the front legs, added in continuation of symmetry with an X plan, were only 5.5m forward, with a transverse opening limited to 6m. The *Trento* had a wider pyramid base, with the original rear legs more widely spaced (8.75m transversely and 6.75m longitudinally): this also led to a greater spacing of the additional front legs. In both cases, the pyramid converged in a geometric apex located 20.5m above the main deck.

The tower consisted of two distinct bodies, one at the bottom ahead of the central pylon and one at the top supported by the pyramidal scaffolding. The lower structure had four levels beyond the deckhouse (B deck, A being the basic deck, in this case the forecastle deck); while C deck was very small and left a wide external walkway all around the compartments, D deck was complex and contained the bridge and the various navigation and control equipment, with large windows and protruding wings. E deck was partly the bridge deck and partly a raised platform supporting the SDT2, magnetic compass, radio direction-finder antenna and the two 90cm searchlights. While the front legs of the pyramid passed through all the bridge decks, only deck E was connected to the rear legs by small platforms whose supports also served to stiffen the tripod.

The upper body, separated from the lower body by a clearly visible 'void' of about 4m in which only the tubes of the pyramid were visible, was composed of three levels: deck F was the admiral's bridge with sided platforms for the two twin 13.2mm machine guns; deck G was a massive structure supporting the bases of the sided directors of the anti-aircraft armament; deck H was an open bridge with the aforementioned directors on its sides.

The pentapod, at the height of a virtual level I, which did not exist, flowed into the inverted truncated cone supporting the main fire director, with double rangefinder around which – on the *Trieste* only – a circular platform was added after 1935, which could be reached with a ladder from the H deck. Initially, the two ships had four outrigger yards placed diagonally below the H deck; later, only the two rear ones were retained, with a total span of 19m.

On the whole, these towers were very massive and tall, therefore also very visible from great distance: the height of the main fire director rangefinder was 23m above the main deck and over 30m from the waterline. This excessive height was probably adopted to maximise the potential of the 203/50 guns, which had a theoretical range of 31,000m, but, obviously, no one could think of sustaining fire at such a distance, especially since the Ansaldo-Schneider mod 1924 guns with which these first major cruisers were equipped had an unacceptable dispersion of fire at long ranges. Therefore, the height was not only excessive, but also useless; in fact, in later cruisers, the tower was lowered by one or two decks.

Between the towers of the two cruisers there were many, though not great, differences, which increased with time, regarding the profiles of the various platforms, navigation lights, platforms, supports, ladders and the fire-control directors. To better document the differences, the accompanying drawings show the *Trento* around 1932 and the *Trieste* around 1938. The most obvious difference, however, was in the location of the 100/47 forward anti-aircraft guns, which on the *Trieste* were set further back compared to the *Trento*, with a different design of their gun supports. Note also the presence on *Trieste*'s funnel of iron rod handrails/footrests, and the different arrangement of the ladders reaching the various platforms.

The funnel caps added in 1941 are shown in hatched lines.

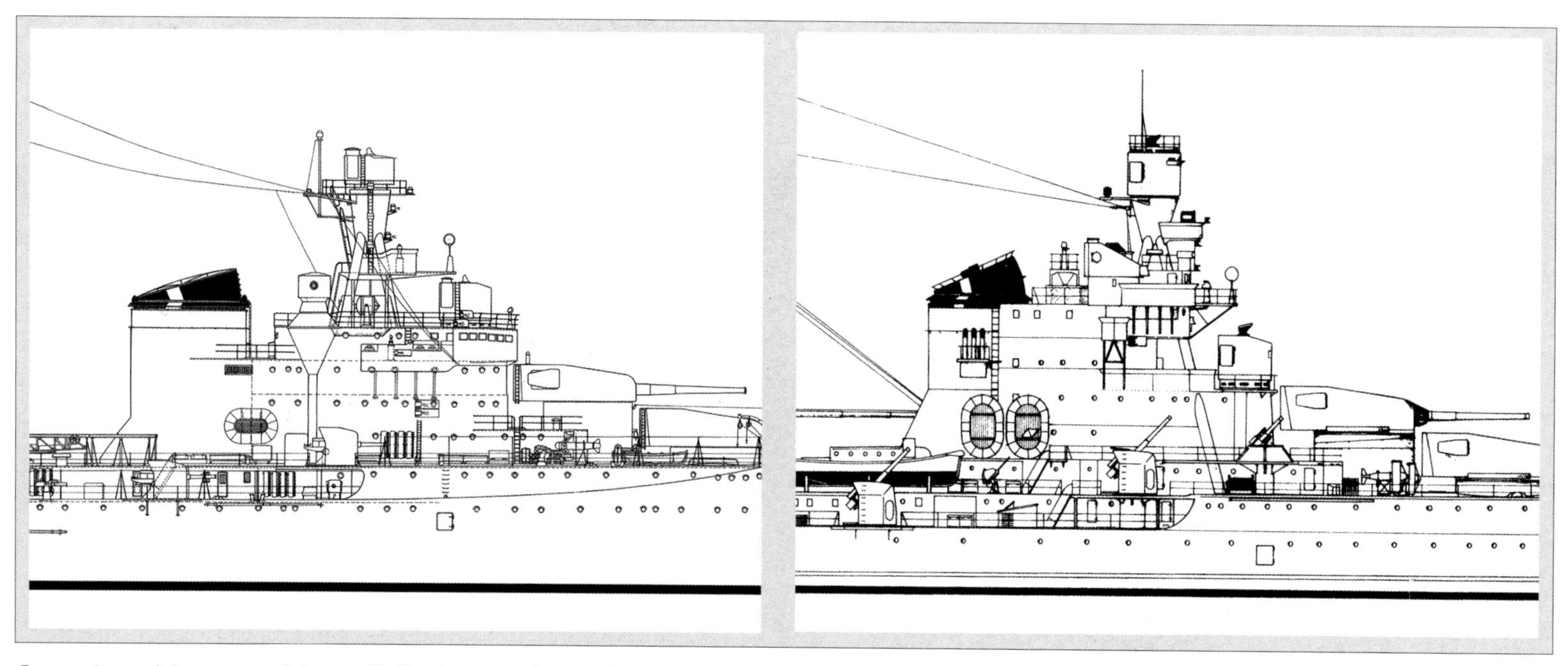

Comparison of the towers of the two Italian heavy cruisers with plating faired in to the forward funnel: *Bolzano* (left) and *Pola*.

BOLZANO

This cruiser was nominally the third of the class but was built to a different design, maintaining only the dimensions and technical characteristics of the *Trento*. In particular, the tower was redesigned along the lines of the modifications that were being studied for the heavy cruiser *Pola* of the *Zara* class; similar modifications were made to the tower-fore funnel arrangement of the *Trento*s in order to obtain that of the *Bolzano*. The tetrapod (obtained by eliminating the central support of the *Trento*s) was closed by continuous bulkheads, configuring the tower on the so-called 'casa popolare' model (see the *Pola*), which was faired into the funnel. The ensemble was lengthened, due to the larger overall dimensions of the ship (almost 15m longer), and the funnel had larger dimensions, as the *Bolzano* had machinery 50% more powerful than that of the *Zara*.

This produced the main differences, in particular:

- the secondary fire director placed one level higher
- the bridge placed one level lower
- the absence of the admiral's bridge
- the completely different rangefinders of the main fire directors (similar to those of the light cruisers of the *Di Giussano* and *Diaz* classes).

The *Bolzano*'s tower, while following the typology of 'tetrapod' towers, was of a different type and stood outside the continuity of development of the similar elements of the other ships.

FIUME

The tower of the cruisers of the *Zara* class (of which the *Fiume* was the first to be built) was clearly inspired by those of the *Di Giussano* class (tetrapod structure, same proportions, same number of levels, correspondence of the location of fittings and equipment). In addition, the towers were square rather than round at the rear.

The tower consisted of a central body built around the tetrapod, which in turn was made of steel tubes with an external diameter of 60cm, stepped on the deck and emerging from the forecastle deck; the front part of the deckhouse connected with the barbette of the 203mm forward superfiring turret. The funnel, elliptical in cross-section with a large 'cap' for better smoke evacuation, was separated from the deckhouse, and emerged directly from the forecastle deck level.

The height of the main rangefinder was 20.5m from the main deck, equal to 26m from the waterline: two metres less than the *Di Giussano*. This reduction was certainly not deliberate: in fact, the *Fiume*'s guns, with a longer range than those of the *Di Giussano*, would have benefited from a greater height; the lower height was due exclusively to the fact that the hull of the *Zara* class had two metres less freeboard, and it was not desired to burden the structure of the tower with an extra deck.

On the sides of the front legs of the tetrapod there were air intakes for the forward engine rooms, in separate structures from the tower; similar air intakes (for the central machinery spaces)

(continued on page 214)

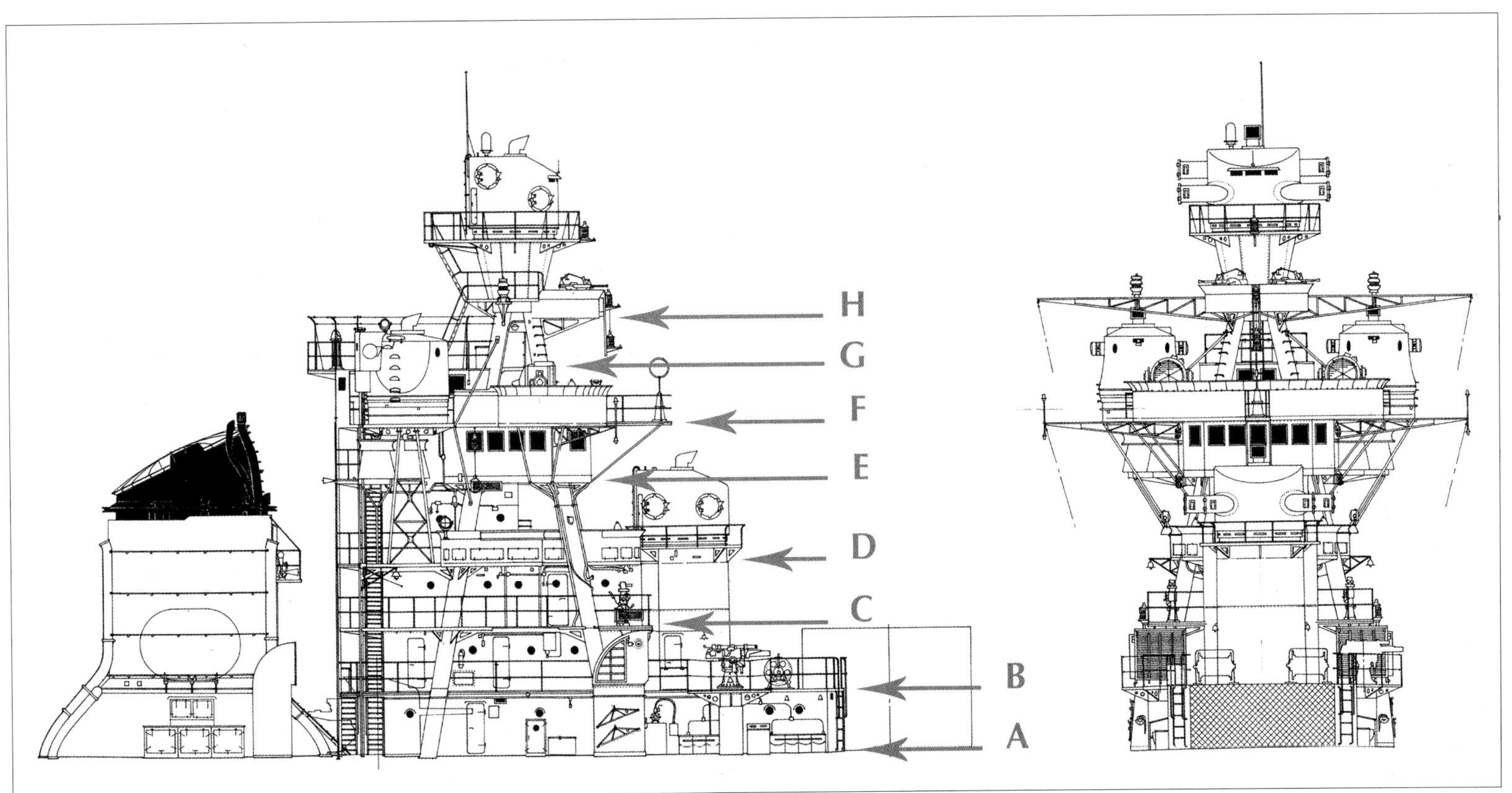

In the text, reference is made to the various levels of the towers of the cruisers *Fiume*, *Zara Gorizia* and *Pola*, indicating them, from bottom to top, from 'B' to 'H' respectively. 'A' indicates the forecastle deck where the deckhouse which formed the foundation of the tower of each ship was located. The towers of the four *Zara*s were all distinguished by seven superimposed levels and the differences are described in the text.

R.N. *Fiume*

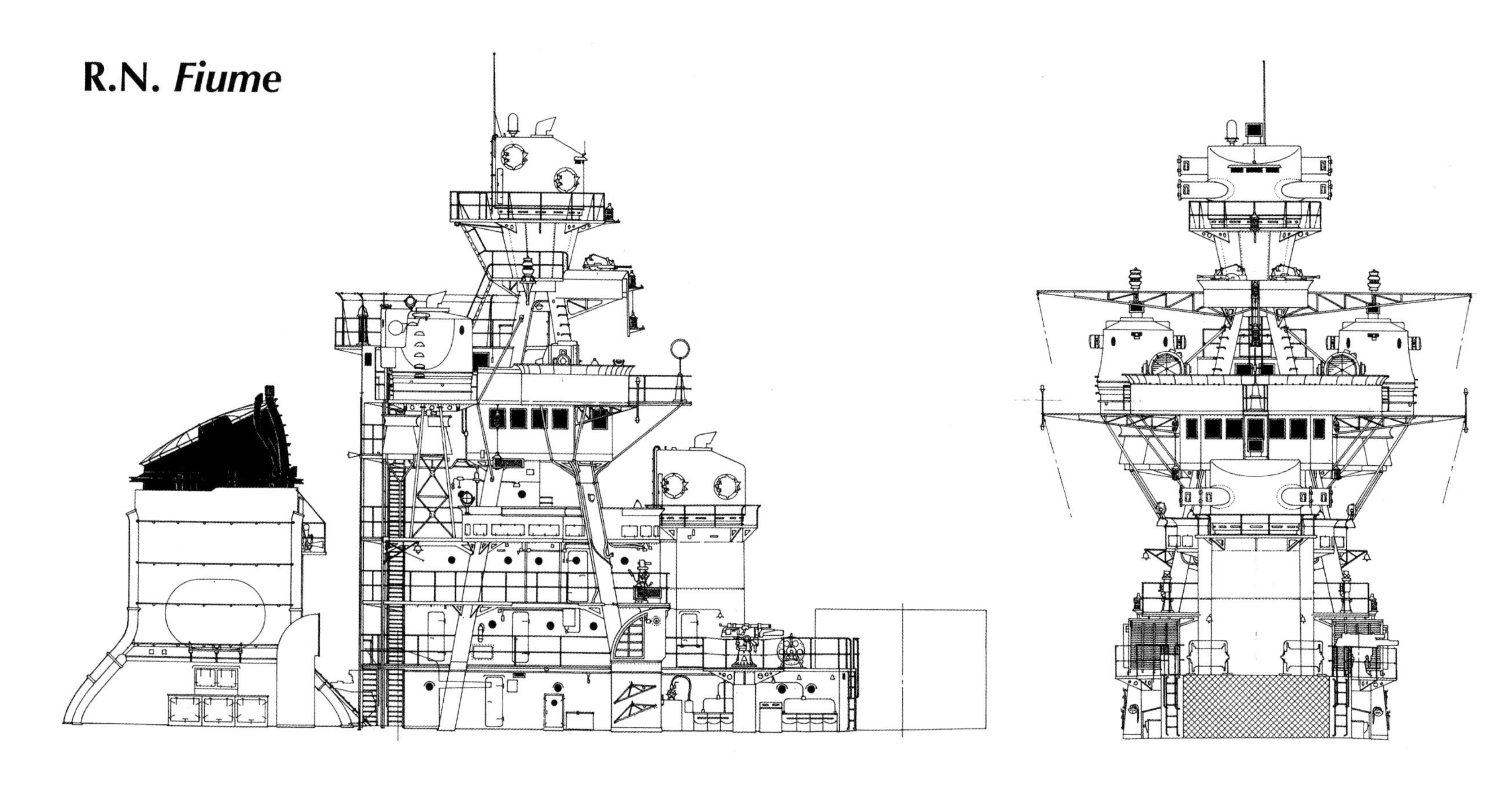

R.N. *Zara*

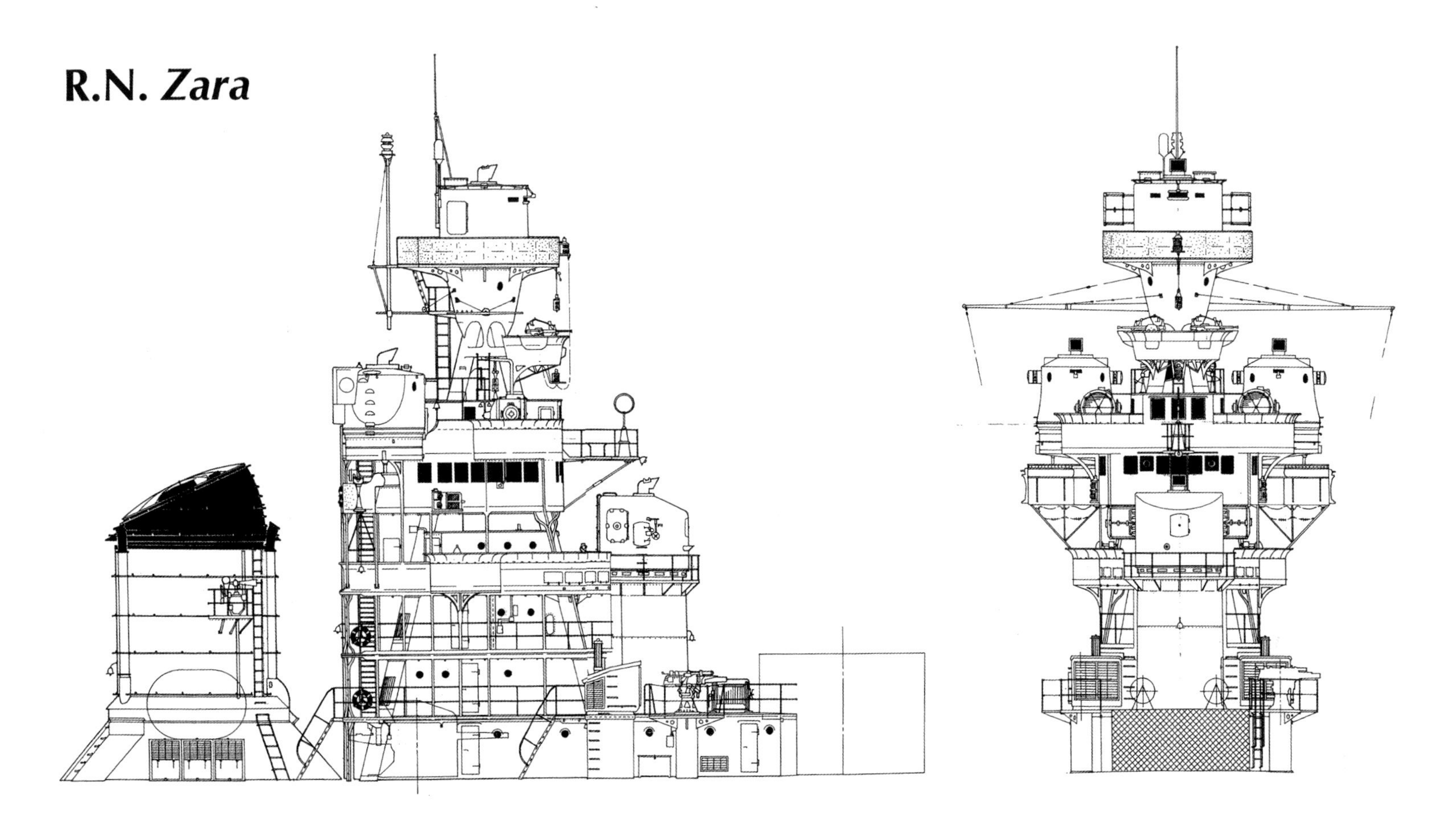

R.N. *Gorizia*

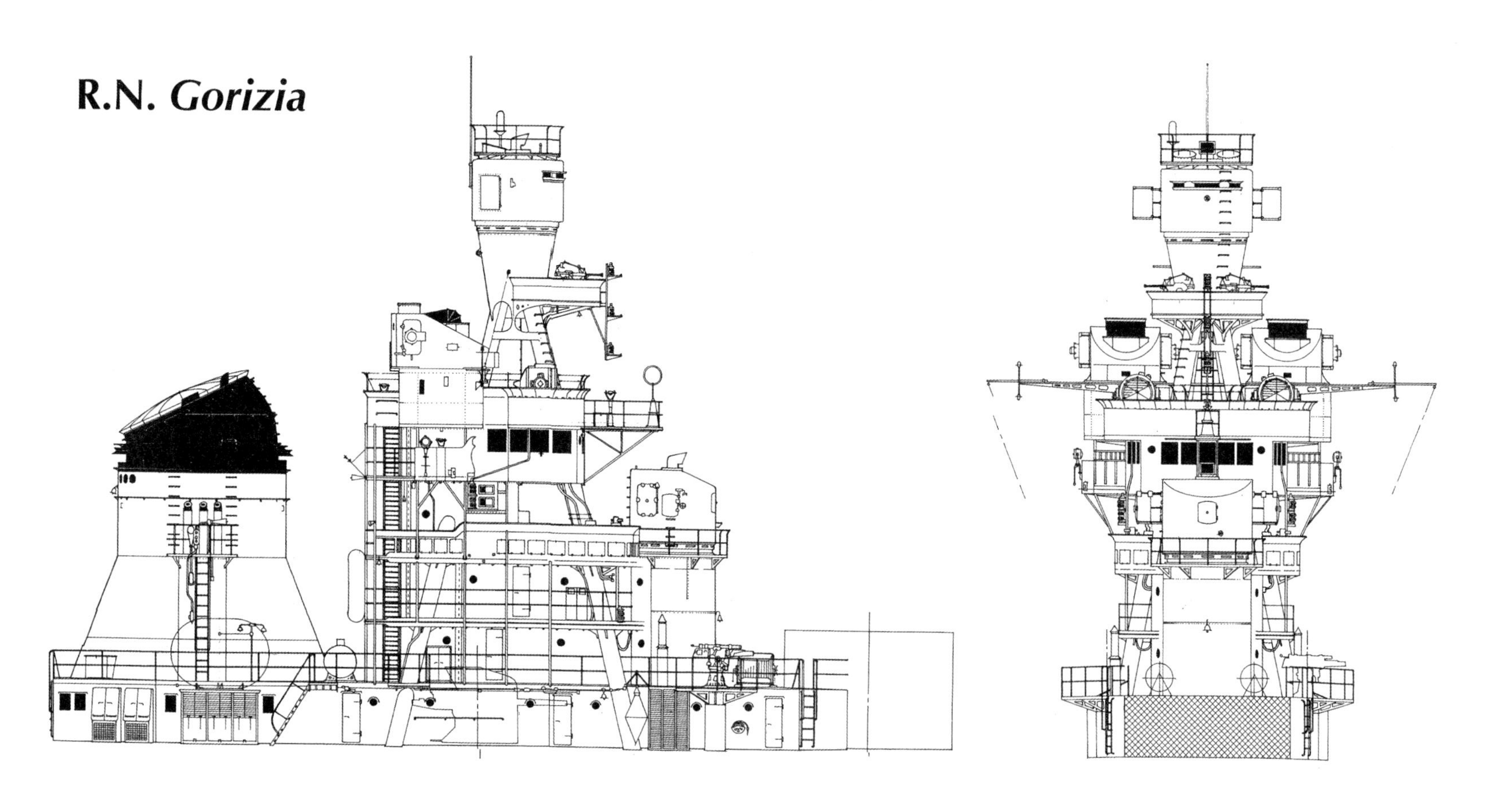

R.N. *Pola*

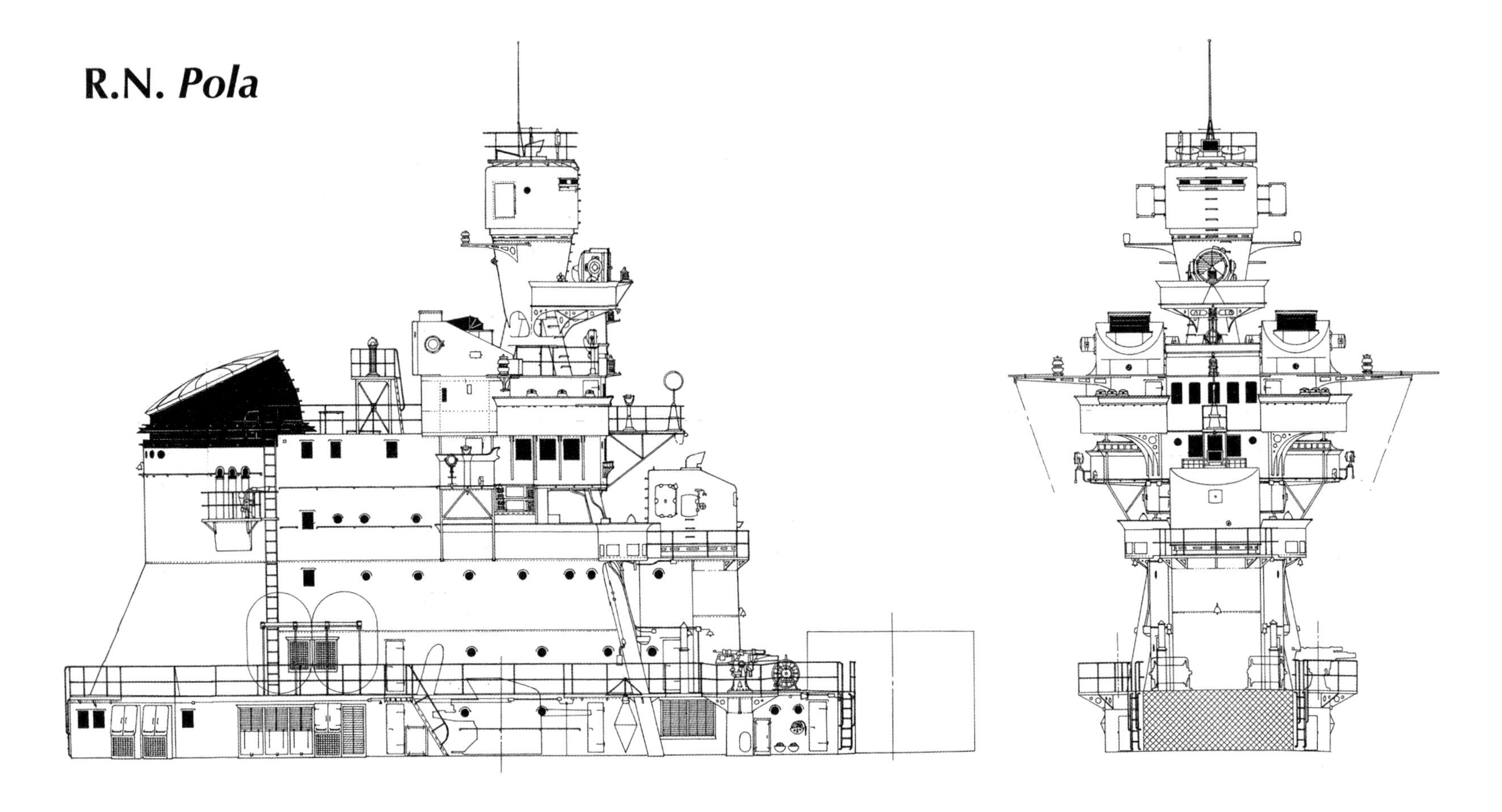

were positioned either side of the funnel. In front of the air intakes were the polygonal platforms for the 120mm howitzers. On either side and just aft of the rear legs of the tetrapod there were two 100mm anti-aircraft guns. Levels B and C left the legs of the tetrapod visible externally and were connected at the front to the cylindrical armoured conning tower. The fourth level of the tower (D), with a very small deckhouse, was entirely detached from the legs of the tetrapod. The secondary fire director was located forward, equipped with one 5m rangefinder one 3.5m rangefinder, surrounded by a circular walkway above the armoured wheelhouse.

The fifth level of the tower (E) completely enclosed the legs of the tetrapod and contained the polygonal navigating bridge, with four side windows, five front windows and one on each oblique angle. At the rear were the platforms with the gyrocompass repeaters, supported by lattice structures. The sixth level of the tower (deck F) consisted of an open navigating bridge, with the AA fire directors and their 3m rangefinders; these were cylindrical in shape, cantilevered out and supported by strong brackets. On the open bridge were the 105cm searchlights, a magnetic compass, the lookout stations, the radio direction-finding antenna and, abaft the legs of the tetrapod, the Signal Station. On G level were another magnetic compass, gyrocompass repeaters and signal lights. The tetrapod at the height of the H deck faired into the truncated cone supporting the main fire director, with a double 5m rangefinder, around which was circular platform accessible by two external ladders from level G. The H level consisted only of a platform with twin 13.2mm machine guns (both of the 'standard' type, with the operator on the right).

In the aft area of the tower, levels B to G were reached by ladders from the forecastle deck. The aft platform supports were reinforced with cross braces; the rear of level G had a windowed bulwark to protect the signal station. The *Fiume* had a double pair of lattice yardarms, supported by masts at levels F and H, for a maximum transverse span of 16m (12m and 16.5m from the main deck respectively).

Before the outbreak of war, the only modifications made to the *Fiume*'s tower were the adoption of a high continuous metal bulwark around the searchlights, with folding wind deflectors, including the forward gyro repeater, the forward extension of the lateral platforms projecting on level B and the adoption of canvas dodgers to protect the railings of the higher platforms.

Gorizia's forward guns and bridge tower; note the searchlights at the top of the tower and the 120/15 illuminating (starshell) howitzer just aft of the second 203mm turret.

ZARA

This cruiser showed some differences due to the latitude allowed to the building yards. However, the main difference between the two ships was the presence of an admiral's bridge on F level.

The main differences are as follows.

- Funnel of different design and with different piping, less slender and with a lower, squarer base.
- Different position of access ladders to B level.
- Smaller front air intakes connected directly to the bulkheads of level B, whose fore part was therefore inaccessible from the rear.
- Tetrapod more 'open' laterally (9m) and smaller and different transverse opening between front (7m) and rear (6.25m) legs.
- Larger platforms, encompassing the legs of the tetrapod and sustained by a framework of vertical structures supporting the navigating bridge.
- Fourth level of the tower (D) with an additional deckhouse that extended to the front legs of the tetrapod.
- Different shape (with rounded corners) and different windows of the bridge on level E, with seven side and seven front windows.
- Reduced size of the F level platform (in particular the areas with 105cm searchlights).
- Different rangefinders on main and secondary fire directors (only one 5m rangefinder with rectangular covers of the rangefinders' ends instead of circular covers).
- Different configuration of navigating lights and side and front lights.
- Presence of admiral's bridge on level F with three windows at the front.
- Lower and smaller 13.2mm machine gun platform (H level). The two starboard weapons were right-handed and left-handed on the port side, with the gunner's station projecting over an extension of the base. This made it possible to have smaller platform dimensions and to keep the gun barrels symmetrical on the centreline.
- Smaller rear window to protect the Signal Station on G deck.
- A platform around the main fire director of different shape and with different configuration of access ladders.
- Single transverse, needle-shaped yardarm protruding from the

Port side of *Pola*'s tower in early 1940. Note the 120/15 illuminating howitzer immediately abaft the second 203/53 turret.

truncated conical support of the fighting top, with a total width of 16m (17m above main deck).
- Presence of a large topmast abaft the fighting top.

Behind the tower, levels B to F were reached by ladders from the forecastle deck, while level G could only be reached by a vertical lateral ladder. The aft platform supports were reinforced by iron bracing and the aft edge of the various levels was straight. The 3m rangefinders for anti-aircraft fire control, cylindrical in shape, were identical to those on the *Fiume*.

Overall, the *Zara*'s tower had a more elaborate and less austere appearance than the *Fiume*'s; it also appeared to have more advanced engineering solutions in terms of supports and brackets. No obvious changes were made to the *Zara*'s tower before the war.

GORIZIA

The tower of *Gorizia* derived from that of the *Zara* through a process of simplification; the tetrapod was identical in position and openings and the most obvious differences were the absence of the admiral's bridge and the shape of the AA fire directors.

The main differences from the *Zara* were the following.

- The main deckhouse (level A) extended aft to support the funnel, which therefore emerged from the deckhouse and not from the forecastle deck.
- Fore funnel raised by one level and of a different design, with a much higher and more evident truncated cone base; side platforms on the funnels where sirens were located.
- Platforms for the illuminating howitzers were circular instead of polygonal, connected to the front air intakes, which only opened at the side instead of the front (demonstrating the evident use of more powerful pumps for forced air circulation).
- Smaller and generally less prominent platforms.
- Elimination of the additional deckhouse on the fourth level of the tower (D), so that the front legs of the tetrapod were 'free'.
- Different shape (angular) and different fenestration of the navigating bridge on level E (four side and five front elements, with two portholes).
- Even smaller size of the F level platform (in particular the wings with 105cm searchlights).
- Different AA fire directors, raised one level above the semicircular deckhouses of F level and more complex and square in shape; in contrast, the main and secondary fire directors with 5m rangefinders were identical to those of the *Zara*, with only minor marginal changes.
- Different configuration of navigating lights and side and front lights.
- Absence of the admiral's bridge on level F, where only the AA directors with their 3m rangefinders were located; a platform was placed all around (level G).
- H level for the 13.2mm machine guns was higher and wider, with 'standard' machine guns both with operators on the right.
- Absence of the fighting top platform and of the open signal station.

A crow's nest platform, small and rounded in shape, was located above the main rangefinder; the crow's nest and rangefinder were reached by external vertical ladders in addition to internal ladders. At the rear, levels C, D, E and F were reached by ladders from level B, while level G was only reached by a central internal ladder. The aft platform supports were not reinforced by crossed braces and the rear edge of the decks was straight as on the *Zara*. A single lattice yardarm was fitted just ahead of the supports for the AA directors, for a total width of 17m (14m above the main deck).

Overall, the tower of the *Gorizia* had a simpler and more compact appearance than that of the *Zara*, while retaining a considerable level of complexity. No obvious changes were made to the *Gorizia*'s tower before the war. Being the only survivor of the class, *Gorizia*'s tower was modified in 1942–43, with the addition of windows on the uncovered searchlight platform, the adoption of metal protections with wind deflectors instead and the addition of a small topmast abaft the crow's nest.

POLA

This last cruiser, which followed the *Gorizia*, was built in the same shipyard and was almost identical to this ship. Even the tower, which at first glance looked very different, was in reality structurally identical, even though all of the platforms were enclosed and the external bulkheads were connected to the sides of the forward funnel in such a way as to form a single block, with numerous portholes and windows, for which it was immediately given the nickname of '*casa popolare*' (which might be translated as 'apartment block'). This solution was similar to that adopted on the contemporary *Bolzano*, which had been built only a few months earlier.

The similarities and main changes made to the *Gorizia* are described below.

- Identical tetrapod, identical fighting top and main fire director (except for small differences in some details).
- Identical deckhouse on level A, with the same location for level B and fore funnel. Marginal differences: ladders, air intakes, polygonal instead of round illuminating howitzer platforms, the presence of two small gun tubs behind the funnel for two 40mm machine guns (later eliminated).
- Plating in of platforms connected to the funnel; internal access ladders; reduction in number and size of the top platforms; different positioning of the Carley-type life rafts. As a result of all this, the rear legs of the tetrapod were almost completely invisible, while the front legs were more prominent.
- The shape and fenestration of the E-level navigating bridge was different (three side and three front windows, plus two portholes). The structures supporting the gun tubs above were very evident.
- The shape and extension of the F-level bridge were different; the searchlights were removed from the wings of the bridge and replaced by protected lookout posts. A single 105cm search-

light was fitted on level H in place of the 13.2mm machine guns, which were relocated to the deckhouse.
- Presence of the admiral's bridge (with five front windows) connected with the semicircular bases of the AA fire directors.
- Magnetic compass on a small platform in front of the fore funnel.
- The AA fire directors were identical to those of the *Gorizia* as were the signal yards; the 5m rangefinders of the main and secondary fire directors also identical to those of the *Gorizia*.
- Different configuration of the navigating lights and the side and front lights.
- Addition of a pair of outrigger yardarms, just below the main director and angled aft.

Several modifications were made to *Pola*'s tower before the war: relocation of the searchlights and machine guns, extension of the admiral's bridge and its railings, adoption of metal bulwarks with wind deflectors.

The bridge and forward 203mm turrets of *Gorizia*, taken at Venice in 1938. The bridge most closely resembled *Zara*'s but the absence of an admiral's bridge on *Gorizia* was the most obvious difference. (Museo Storico Navale di Venezia)

Appendix E

FULL SPEED AND RANGE TRIALS WITH MAXIMUM FUEL ALLOCATION*

TRENTO CLASS

Ship	Date	Displacement (t)	Speed (knots)	Power (hp)	rpm	Fuel (t) Standard/Max	Reserve Feed Water (t)	Range (nautical miles) Maximum Speed	Economical Cruising Speed
Trento	11.03.1929	11,203	36.60	146,640	309.00	1702/2290	296	1150/34	4160/16
Trieste	14.03.1930	11,353	35.60	124,761	296.00	2150/2290	254	1221/33	4208/16
Bolzano	17.12.1932	11,022	36.81	173,772	333.14	2166/2200	279	1153/34.8	2240/16

Source: Direzione generale delle costruzioni navali e meccaniche (AUSMM).

* The data tables refer to full speed and range trials considered valid according to the contractual regulations set out in the special specifications for each ship and other ministerial provisions for acceptance. It should be considered that the Regia Marina was fully aware that the indicated data did not correspond to real data of each operational ship (fully fitted out and with equipment corresponding to a displacement close to full load and even higher during the war).

ZARA CLASS

Ship	Date	Displacement (t)	Speed (knots)	Power (hp)	rpm	Fuel (t) Standard/Max	Reserve Feed Water (t)	Range (nautical miles) Maximum Speed	Economical Cruising Speed
Zara	16.05.1931	10,950	34.02	100,200	271.00	1450/2360	260	1953/31.5	5360/16
Fiume	12.11.1932	11,300	32.97	102,702	286.93	1450/2438	260	1560/30	5360/16
Gorizia	01.02.1931	10,860	33.89	106,918	266.80	1450/2291	260	1921/31.5	5184/16
Pola	17.11.1932	11,005	33.88	98,040	264.97	1540/2313	197	1921/31.5	5232/16

Source: Direzione generale delle costruzioni navali e meccaniche (AUSMM).

INITIAL COSTS OF *TRENTO* CLASS CRUISERS

	Trento	*Trieste*	*Bolzano*
Initial cost of ship (lire)*	95,100,000	95,100,000	101,600,000
Value of ship at 30.06.1940 (lire)**	98,001,000	99,876,000	137,152,000

Source: Direzione generale delle costruzioni navali e meccaniche (AUSMM).

* This does not include the cost of armament, fire control equipment and some minor equipment that the Navy purchased directly from other suppliers. On average, for this category of cruiser these costs amounted to about 25% of those listed above, to which must be added at least another 10% of the sum for other items.
** Ship fully fitted out.

INITIAL COSTS OF *ZARA* CLASS CRUISERS

	Zara	*Fiume*	*Gorizia*	*Pola*
Initial cost of ship (lire)*	106,000,000	106,000,000	112,700,000	114,700,000
Value of ship at 30.06.1940 (lire)**	130,769,000	135,557,000	139,940,000	150,837,000

Source: Direzione generale delle costruzioni navali e meccaniche (AUSMM).

* See comments made for *Trento* class and the *Bolzano*
** Ship fully fitted out.

Appendix F

NIGHT GUNFIRE: ITALIAN NIGHT COMBAT READINESS AS PERCEIVED BY THE ITALIAN NAVY IN THE MIDDLE YEARS OF THE WAR

The greatest of the problems encountered by the Italian Navy during the conflict was perhaps its unpreparedness for night combat. The problem became dramatically evident after the wake-up call of the Battle of Cape Passero on 12 October 1940 and, above all, after the tragic night of Matapan on 28 March 1941. It also had a significant impact on the general conduct of operations by the main naval forces, which were conditioned by the need to break contact and move away from the enemy after sunset, only to try resuming operations the following morning when the enemy forces were usually no longer within reach. For a long time – and even today – the Italian deficit in night combat was attributed almost exclusively to the lack of radar. But, in truth, this technical inferiority does not appear to be the decisive factor, especially in the first year of the war – as the most careful historiography has abundantly demonstrated – but it should be placed in the broader context of the prevailing doctrine of the employment of naval forces, their training and organisation and other more conventional technical deficiencies in main armament directors that should have within the capabilities of the national industry to address. This inferiority began to become known as early as 1939, following missions to Germany by officers specialised in the various branches of gunnery technology, with the aim of examining the organisation, means and methods of the German navy, such as: the use of all calibres, even large ones, in night combat at distances of up to 8000m–10,000m, the use of searchlights (which was controversial), gun directors for night firing, the application of luminous 'pigtails' [these were flares attached to the base of the projectiles so that their trajectory could be visually followed at night] to guns of all calibres and the use of illuminating munitions. The different concept and the greater importance that the Germans placed on night actions did not have significant impact in Italy for the time being. With the outbreak of the war and the first hard lessons, exchanges of technical information intensified – including a mission of June 1940 to look at the status of radar in Germany – but it was only from 1941 onwards that the improvement of equipment and employment techniques was accelerated, unfortunately not to the extent necessary to overcome the disadvantage with respect to the British Navy.

At the beginning of 1942 a commission was set up within the Regia Marina to study the causes, scale and nature of the problem and to evaluate the effectiveness of the first measures adopted in training and those of a technical nature. The commission, chaired by Adm. Emilio Brenta produced an extensive report of which, unfortunately, only a draft has been traced: it was sufficient, however, to give an idea of how the problem was perceived during the conflict (and not how it was represented afterwards). The report was divided into the following chapters:

I. superiority of the enemy in technical means for contact and night combat;
II. superiority of the enemy in training for contact and night combat;
III. night training activity in peacetime and in wartime;
IV. reduction in the level of training of our ships due to their being too absorbed by escort and transport services and to the decreasing availability of fuel;
V. conclusions.

Of these, we think it is worth quoting verbatim paragraph 6 of Chapter II, concerning the opinions expressed by German officers regarding Italian night actions before and during the conflict, and Chapter III, indicative of the Regia Marina's level of preparation for night combat, on the eve of and during the war and, in particular, of the major ships, considering that it was precisely the heavy cruisers that were the protagonists of the two most dramatic episodes of the entire Italian naval war in the Mediterranean.

ENEMY SUPERIORITY IN NIGHT CONTACT AND NIGHT COMBAT TRAINING

II/6. – OPINIONS EXPRESSED BY GERMAN OFFICERS (note: all underlining is in the original text)

Below are, in order of time, two very important judgments made by German naval officers concerning night actions

a) Summer 1939 - At the important strategic manoeuvres called 'E.N. [Esercitazioni Navali, ed.] 17' Rear Admiral GRASSMANN and Captain FRANKE (then Director of the Marineakademie, which can be compared to our Maritime Warfare Institute [sic]) had been invited to attend. The latter, who was on board the cruiser *Fiume*, expressed the following opinions:

– it was necessary to provide an anti-aircraft escort for the bulk

of the naval forces by means of units arranged around them at a distance of 8000m [editor's note: as Admiral Angelo Iachino did after the torpedoing of the *Vittorio Veneto* on the evening of 28 March 1941];
- in night navigations with dark weather it is indispensable to keep the destroyers ahead and astern at a great distance (10-15 miles) to avoid dangerous sightings;
- in night navigation with clear weather it is necessary to keep the destroyers in a close position forward;
- increase the efficiency of night-time detection by carefully dividing the lookout service and adopting optical equipment with high magnification and in particular low-light rangefinders and binoculars;
- in Germany, great importance is ascribed to night employment of torpedo boats and to anti-surface defence by larger ships.

The lookout organisation is highly effective: torpedo boats heading out to attack at night are generally spotted at a distance of no less than 5000 metres. Torpedo boats are trained to carry out night attacks at longer distances (6000-7000m). The results of the most recent exercises would have given an average of 4 hits out of 12 torpedoes launched at night at this distance.

These range figures are intended to refer to the type of nights that occur in the North Sea, for the Mediterranean an appropriate reduction should be made but always aimed for the maximum distance.

b) November 1941 - The German Naval Attaché, Rear Admiral [WERNER] LOEWISCH, in a conversation with the Deputy Chief of Staff informed him that:

- the German Navy attributed the Italian Navy's lack of success mainly to the fact that our night training of major and minor ships was absolutely insufficient:
- He was struck by the 'primitiveness' of our night exercises and noted that our equipment and manpower were far inferior not only to that of the German or British navies, but also to that of other less advanced navies.
- During his time in command of the cruiser *Leipzig*, 130 of the 150 exercises she carried out were at night.
- In particular, the German Navy noticed that the large Italian ships lacked rangefinders and night detectors, which had been in use for years in the German Navy; torpedo boats lacked night targeting instruments that would allow firing at distances of over 10,000m (which is common in the German Navy).
- The German Navy is also absolutely convinced that these deficiencies of the Italian Navy were perfectly known to the British Commanders, who have therefore tried to exploit these deficiencies to their advantage by always seeking night combat and generally avoiding daytime combat.

III. NIGHT-TIME TRAINING ACTIVITIES IN PEACETIME AND IN WARTIME

7. – TRAINING ACTIVITY IN TIME OF PEACE (note: all underlining is in the original text)

Training activities were defined by a regulatory publication: vol. IV of MS. 10 S. - *Programme and directives for the training of Naval Forces and fixed and mobile metropolitan defences*, 1937 edition. Annexes 3 and 4 to this publication established the firing exercises to be carried out during the training year (from September to the following September) and the ammunition allocated.

The programme did not include night exercises for large calibre guns, the use of which at night had never been considered. For the medium and small calibre guns (including the 203mm) a small number of night exercises with reduced charges were established: one at 3rd charge for the 203mm; three at 3rd charge for 152mm-135mm [those of the *Duilio* class, ed]. In addition to these exercises, another 'special' one was planned under Ministerial control for a single ship of each type, always with medium and small calibre and always with reduced charge or 'b.r.c.' projectiles for radio-controlled target practice (target ship *San Marco*).

Approximately twice as many exercises were allowed for naval daytime shooting, which averaged six per year for all naval calibres and eight or nine for naval and anti-aircraft [dual purpose, basically the 100/47 gun, ed].

A small contribution to the training activity was made by the conduct on some ships of the Firing Officers' Course (for the attainment of their licence) and of the training courses of specialised personnel. Even in these exercises, the proportion reserved for night shooting was low: ⅓ or ¼ of the total.

The methods used to carry out night firing exercises were very simple: the target was anchored or drifting; when the target was sighted (by the lookouts), direct firing was opened at the same time as the illuminating firing (if necessary); at the end of the session, the searchlight was switched on to check if aim had been correct and to measure the distance from the target of the shots.

As for night firing exercises, the regulatory publication SM. 72 S. prescribed two drills for each cruiser and ten for each destroyer – 50% of the total number of firing exercises, a percentage that could be considered acceptable.

The Commanding Officers of the I and II Squadra have, in their Reports on the training periods 1938–39 and 1939–40 and in particular reports, concluded that:

a) – The direct firing series were good, in general, but very slow; only the *Da Barbiano* in the 1st training period 1939–40 managed to make six salvoes in 40 seconds;

b) – Illuminating fire is very difficult when the deflection of the target is changing rapidly;

c) – In the 2nd training period 1939–40 the 1st Division [the *Zara* class cruisers, ed] performed night firing with 203/53 guns – the flashes created serious disturbances to the rangefinder operator, to the DT [Direttore del Tiro, the officer in charge of Fire direction, ed] and to the Ship's Command itself, as well as to all AA, MG and gun personnel, who were dazzled for several minutes; it is therefore recommended to produce VR (reduced flash) charges.

d) – the lack of night sights on destroyers is complained of (the night detector leads the APG [Apparecchio di Punteria Generale - general sights apparatus, ed]; on these ships firing was very slow due to accentuated rolls (and sometimes due to the permanence of smoke over the ship's superstructure);

e) – the loading times (especially for the 100/47 guns) were longer than in daytime firing, due to lack of training.

It must also be kept in mind that from the beginning of the 1939–40 training period, due to an exaggerated concern for fuel economy in anticipation of our future entry into the war, the ships' departures for exercises were at first suspended and then limited in time and space. This economic criterion was obviously to the detriment of training [an implicit criticism of the then Undersecretary of State and Chief of Naval Staff, Adm. Domenico Cavagnari, ed]. A compromise solution was subsequently adopted, granting each Division a ten-hour exit every ten days and a monthly exit for each Squadra.

8. TRAINING ACTIVITIES DURING WAR (note: all underlining is in the original text)

• 1st training year: September 1940 – September 1941

The outbreak of war made the problem of training even more significant; it appeared to be of increased urgency and importance. The 'maximum' solution to this problem that appeared necessary and possible at the time was to continue to carry out the same training programme during the war as during peacetime, at least as far as firing exercises were concerned. An increase was automatically brought about by the fact that anti-torpedo and anti-aircraft exercises had to be carried out with salvos from both sides (instead of one side only, as in peacetime) as a result of the crews being brought up to full strength.

This programme, which at first appeared almost utopian, was, with great tenacity, almost completely accomplished on the larger ships (despite the difficulties of deployments, war services, and fuel economy), while the same thing was not possible for the destroyers due to the continuous and onerous escort services and the lack of 120/15 illuminating ammunition. On average, the destroyers carried out less than 2/3 of the assigned night exercises; some of them (*Lampo* and *Geniere*) did not manage to carry out any.

It should be noted that the reports were prepared on the basis of a programme drawn up two years earlier. It was evident, therefore, that for the first year of the war, ammunition that had been provided for in peacetime had to be used: the increased training requirements (for anti-torpedo and anti-aircraft guns) could be met with a few reserves set aside and with ammunition assigned to ships by then lost.

The night battle of 28 March 1941 [Matapan] was the first to painfully highlight the inadequacy of our preparation for night combat. In order to remedy the shortcomings of the past, while new weapons and equipment were being studied and provisional backstop arrangements were being worked out, in the field of training for the first time it was ordered to carry out some 1st and 3rd charge exercises for the large calibres and the other calibres had to carry out some 1st charge series, and not only with reduced charges.

However, the ever-increasing difficulties caused by the growing demands of escort and war services in general and the worsening fuel situation, as well as the need to prepare unscheduled ammunition, especially illuminating, made it impossible to give these 'innovations' the necessary development. Especially in the case of large calibre guns, the exercises carried out barely left the 'experimental' phase required by the study and preparation of new weapons or of the provisional solutions adopted.

The evolution of concepts was also reflected in the exercises for the Fire Directors Course held in the second half of 1941: the officers who attended it were assigned an equal number of night, day and anti-aircraft exercises. However, the above mentioned difficulties did not always allow the programme to be carried out in full.

Annex 1 shows a table of the night firing exercises carried out in the 1940-41 training year. It is clear from this document that, in the training year in question, the night firing exercises that were carried out represented 77% of those assigned by the General Staff; *23% were not carried out.*

With regard to night firing exercises, on the other hand, the training activity suffered a drastic setback.

The exercises prescribed by the General Staff for destroyers alone (that had to realistically recognise, when making the concessions, the considerable difficulties in carrying out this type of exercise in wartime) amounted to only 1/3 to 1/4 of those planned for peacetime.

• 2nd training year: 1941–1942

The training guidelines for the 2nd year of the war for night firing decisively abandoned the previously mentioned regulations (S.M. 10 S.) and led to a sharp increase in night exercises. More night firing series are allocated to anti-torpedo calibres than to day firing. For all calibres, approximately one third of the exercises are prescribed for first charge. The amount of illuminating ammunition required to carry them out is also significantly increased.

The difficulties which have been mentioned several times, as will be more fully repeated below, have so far prevented this programme from having the desired prompt start. They have become so serious that the Naval Forces Headquarters has had to devise temporary training courses with ships stationary and anchored behind the protective quays of their bases.

As for night torpedo-launch training, the guidelines are similar to those of the 1940-41 training year: we would indeed consider ourselves fortunate if the various ships could actually carry out the very limited programme prescribed for the previous year. However, there is practically no activity in this field.

Table 1 [complete but simplified, ed.]

DAYTIME FIRING EXERCISES – TRAINING YEAR 1940/1941

Cal.	ship	charge	Assigned by Ministry	Additional	Total	Actual	Difference
381	*LITTORIO*	1^		1	1	1	
		3^		2	2	1	-1
	VITTORIO VENETO	1^		1	1	1	
		3^		2	2	1	-1
320	*DORIA*	1^		1	1	1	
		3^		2	2	2	
	DUILIO	1^		1	1	1	
		3^		2	2	1	-1
	CESARE	1^		1	1	1	
		3^		2	2	2	
203	*GORIZIA*	1^		1	1	1	
		3^	1	2	3	2	-1
	BOLZANO	1^		1	1	1	
		3^	1	2	3	2	-1
	TRENTO	1^		1	1	1	
		3^	1	2	3	2	-1
	TRIESTE	1^		1	1	1	
		3^	1	2	3	2	-1
152	*ABRUZZI*	3^	2		2	1	-1
	GARIBALDI	3^	2		2	1	-1
	AOSTA	3^	2		2	2	
	EUGENIO	3^	2		2	3	+1
	MONTECUCCOLI	3^	2		2	2	
	ATTENDOLO	3^	2		2	2	
	CADORNA	3^	2		2	2	
	BANDE NERE	3^	2		2	1	-1
	LITTORIO	3^	4		4	7	+3
	VITTORIO VENETO	3^	4		4	4	
135	*DORIA*	3^	3	1	4	5	+1
	DUILIO	3^	3	1	4	5	+1
120	*CESARE*	3^	3	1	4	5	+1
	DESTROYERS [total 31]	3^	93		93	57	-36
100	*BOLZANO*	2^	3	1	4	4	
	GORIZIA	2^	3	1	4	4	
	TRENTO	2^	3	1	4	4	
	TRIESTE	2^	3	1	4	4	
90	*LITTORIO*	2^	2	1	3	1	-2
	VITTORIO VENETO	2^	2	1	3	2	-1
	DORIA	2^	2	1	3	3	
	DUILIO	2^	2	1	3	1	-2
TOTAL	ASSIGNED EXERCISES	150 + 38 = 188			ACTUAL 145 = 77%		

NB. In addition to these, a number of series have been carried out by the larger ships (Battleships and Cruisers) for Fire Director courses and training.

Source: AUSMM, fondo Supermarina. Omologazione e apprezzamento danni inflitti al nemico, b. 6: Apprezzamento e promemoria sull'attività operativa del nemico.

SOURCES AND BIBLIOGRAPHY

The following is not a comprehensive list of the documentation and publications on the subject, but includes only the sources and literature actually used by the authors in writing this book.

PRIMARY SOURCES

Archives of the Ufficio Storico della Marina Militare, Rome (USMM)

Raccolta di Base: - b. 1529, f. *Addetto navale italiano a Parigi*; - b. 1568 [miscellanea, fra cui gli studi 'De Lorenzi', n.d.a.]; - b. 1682, f. 2: *Bilanci*; - b. 1684, f. *Quesiti al Comitato degli Ammiragli, Febbraio 1924*; f. *Comitato Ammiragli 1925*; f. *Verbale del Comitato Ammiragli. Adunanze pomeridiane dell'11-12-13 agosto 1925 'Nuove Costruzioni Uff.^{li} per la Direz. Macchine*, f. senza intestazione [ma recante il verbale dell'adunanza del 10 ottobre 1922, n.d.a.]; - b. 2151, f. *R. Nave Fiume*; - b. 2312, f. 3: *Crociera 1^a e 2^a Squadra Navale Spagna e Portogallo 1939*; - b. 2351, f. *Incidente Gorizia a Tangeri*; b. 2352, f. *Incidente di manovra R.I. 'Pola'*; - b. 2373: [Occupazione dell'Albania (5-9 aprile 1939), n.d.a.], f. 11: *Ordini Comando I Squadra Navale*; f. *Ufficio di Stato maggiore della R. Marina. Occupazione Albania aprile 1939 – XVII*; - b. 2516, f. *La nostra politica marittima (Febbraio 1929)*; - b. 2524, f. *R. Nave Trieste*; - b. 2560, f. 2 [Sistemazioni per la condotta del tiro navale e a.a. per gli incrociatori da 10.000 *tons*, n.d.a.]; - b. 3173 [Programmi navali francesi Anni '20, n.d.a.].

Fondo *Comandi Navali Complessi (1940-1946)*: - b. 9, f.13; - b. 11, f. 2, f. *Comando 3^a Divisione Navale*.

Fondo *Commissione d'Inchiesta Speciale. Navi*: - b. 3: *Incrociatori*, f. *Incr. Fiume*; - b. 5: *Incrociatori*, f. *Inchiesta sulla perdita del R. Incrociatore Pola*; - b. 6: *Incrociatori*, f. *Incr. Trento*, f. *Incr. Zara*.

Fondo *Maristat – I.A.M. (Ispettorato artiglierie e munizionamento)*: - b. 3, f. 14.

Fondo *Maristat, I.S.G.N.* [Ispettorato servizi Genio Navale, n.d.a.] *Lavori alle unità di superficie*: - b. B 16 *bis*: *Bolzano*; - b. F 33, f. 17: *Fiume*; - b. G 46, f. 1: *Gorizia*; - b. *P 62*, f. 19: *Pola*; - b. T 78, f. 10: *Trento*; - b. T 79, f. 1: *Trieste*.

Fondo *Maristat. Reparto Naviglio e Addestramento*: - b. 11, f. 112; - b. 18, f. 161, s.f. 1; - b. 28, f. 265; - b. 34, f. 332; - b. 35, f. 342; - b. 62, f. 563/1, 563/2, 563/3.

Fondo *Maristat – Reparto M.D.S.* [Reparto mobilitazione, difese e servizi, n.d.a.]: - b. 216, f. 3055.

Fondo *Maristat. Segreteria generale – 1^a Sezione*: b. 8, f. 58.

Fondo *Naviglio militare*: - b. 5 *bis*, f. *Nave Bolzano*; - b. F 2, f. *Incr. Fiume*; - b. G 4, f. *R.I. Gorizia*; - b. P 9 *bis*, f. *Incrociatore Pola*; - b. T 5: *Trento*; - b. T 6: *Trento*; - b. T 7: *Trieste*.

Fondo *Registri matricolari*: - b. 21: *R.I. Pola*; - b. 24: *R.I. Trento*; - b. 28: *R.I. Gorizia*; - b. 32: *R.I. Trieste*.

Fondo *Santoni* (2^a parte): - b. 63, f. 351.

Fondo *Segreteria Ufficio Storico. Serie senza classifica*: - b. 23, f. 43: Monografia dell'US n. 61: *Evoluzione della Marina militare dal 1920 al 1940*; - b. 34, f. 149: Monografia dell'US n. 309: *L'opera di preparazione della Marina italiana nel campo delle artiglierie, munizionamento e chimica degli esplosivi*; - b.35, f.162: Monografia dell'US n. 322: *Evoluzione nello studio e nella realizzazione dei telemetri ed inclinometri dalla fine della prima guerra mondiale all'inizio della seconda – Studio aggiornato all'inizio del conflitto 1940-45 –Sviluppo durante il conflitto.*

Fondo *Statini dell'attività bellica delle navi*: - bb. 2-6 : *Incrociatori*.

Fondo *Supermarina. Attacchi alle basi*: - b. 1, f. 959 : *Attacco aereo Napoli 15-12-1940*; - b. 7, f. 1035: *Attacco aereo La Maddalena – ore 14.50 – 10 aprile 1943 XXI*.

Fondo *Supermarina. Copia unica*: reg. 34.

Fondo *Supermarina. Omologazioni e apprezzamento danni infitti al nemico*: - b. 6: *Apprezzamenti e promemoria sull'attività operativa del nemico*.

Fondo *Supermarina. Scontri navali e operazioni di guerra*: - 3: *Battaglia di Punta Stilo, 6-9 luglio 1940*, f. A 4; - bb.16 e 16 *bis*: *Scontro navale di Capo Teulada (Forze Navali della I^ e 2^ Sq.)*; - b. 28: *Operazione di Gaudo (28 marzo '41)*; - b. 28 *bis*: *Operazione di Gaudo (28 marzo '41)*; - b. 39: *9 novembre 1941. Convoglio Beta – Scorta 3^a Divisione (Trieste, Trento e cc.tt.) (Fulmine e Libeccio, piroscafi Duisburg, San Marco, Conte di Misurata, Minatitlan, Maria, Sagitta, Rina Corrado)*; - b. 41: *Convoglio Napoli*; - b. 49: [...] *Uscita 7^a Divisione Aosta e 3^a Divisione Gorizia* [...] *Uscita della Forza B e K di Alessandria e Malta per scorta navi mercantili. Attacchi alle unità ed a piroscafi*; - b. 52: *Convoglio rotta Malta – 2° Scontro della Sirte – Uscita Forza 'H' 20-26/3/1942*. - b. 57: *Scontro di Pantelleria – Mezzo Giugno 1942*; - b. 57 *bis*: *Scontro di Pantelleria (1/2.6.1942)*, f. *Grafici schemi*; - b. 62/2: *Battaglia di 1/2 Agosto* [1942, n.d.a.].

Fondo *Supermarina. Squadra Navale*: - b. 1, f. 1, f. 3; - b 2, f. 8, s.f. 18; - b. 3, f. 13; - b. 6, f. 33.

Fondo *Supermarina. Squadra Navale 1* [vecchia collocazione]: - b.10.

USMMLibrary:

Naval Staff History Second World War, *Submarines*, vol. II: *Operations in the Mediterranean*, London, Admiralty - Historical Section, 1955.

Archives of the Army General Staff Historical Office (Archivio dell'Ufficio Storico dello Stato maggiore dell'Esercito)

Fondo I 4: *Carteggio S.M.G.* [Stato Maggiore Generale, n.d.a.] – C.S.[Comando Supremo, n.d.a.] – S.M.D. [Stato Maggiore Difesa, n.d.a.]: racc. 10, f. 4.

Kew National Archives, London (ex Public Record Office)

(ADM) 234/444:

- *H.M. Ships damaged or sunk by enemy action 3rd Sept. 1939 to 2nd Sept. 1945*, 1952.

PRINTED SOURCES

Ministero degli Affari esteri – Commissione per la pubblicazione dei documenti diplomatici, *I documenti diplomatici italiani*, 7a Serie: *1922-1935*, vol. XV: *18 marzo – 27 settembre 1934*, Roma, Istituto poligrafico e Zecca dello Stato, 1990.

Ministero della Marina. Direzione generale del personale e dei servizi militari, *Situazione del Regio Naviglio. Luglio 1936 – XIV*, Roma, Tipografia dell'Ufficio di Stato maggiore della R. Marina, 1936.

Naval Staff Histories Second World War, *The Royal Navy and the Mediterranean*, vol. I: *September 1939 – October 1940* and vol. II: *November 1940 – December 1941*, Frank Cass, London - Portland, 2002.

——, *The Royal Navy and the Mediterranean Convoys*, London - New York, Routledge Taylor & Francis Group, 2007.

——, *Battle Summary no. 44: The Battle of Cape Matapan. 28 March, 1941*, Plymouth (Devon), University of Plymouth, 2012.

Relazione del Direttore generale delle Costruzioni Navali e Meccaniche a S.E. il Ministro della Marina, Esercizio 1928-29, La Spezia, Tipo-lito della Direzione generale costruzioni Navali e Meccaniche, 1930.

Id., *Esercizio 1929-30*, La Spezia, Tipo-lito della Direzione generale costruzioni Navali e Meccaniche, 1930.

Simpson, M. (editor), *The Cunningham Papers*, vol. I: *The Mediterranean Fleet, 1939-1942*, Hants-Brookfield, The Navy Record Society, 1999.

——, *The Somerville Papers*, Hants-Brookfield, The Navy Record Society, 1995.

Ufficio del Capo di Stato Maggiore [della Marina] – Ufficio Informazioni, *Dati sul potere marittimo delle varie nazioni*, Roma, Libreria dello Stato, 1933.

BOOKS

Bagnasco, E., *Le armi delle navi italiane nella Seconda guerra mondiale*, Parma, Albertelli, 1978.

——, *In guerra sul mare. Navi e marinai italiani nel secondo conflitto mondiale*, Parma, Albertelli, 2005.

Bagnasco, E. & Brescia, M., *Il camouflage delle navi italiane 1940–1945*, 'Storia Militare Dossier', September 2017.

Bagnasco, E. & de Toro, A., *Italian Battleships: Conte di Cavour and Duilio Classes 1911-1956*, Barnsley, Seaforth, 2020.

——, *The Littorio Class. Italy's Last and Largest Battleships 1937–1948*, Barnsley, Seaforth, 2018.

Bargoni, F., *Incrociatori pesanti classe Trieste*, Rome, Edizioni dell'Ateneo e Bizzarri, 1977.

——, *Incrociatori pesanti classe Zara*, Rome, Edizioni dell'Ateneo e Bizzarri, 1978.

——, *L'impegno navale italiano durante la Guerra civile spagnola (1936-1939)*, Rome, USMM, 1992.

Bernardi, G., *Il disarmo navale fra le due guerre mondiali (1919–1939)*, Rome, USMM, 1975.

Bernotti, R., *La Guerra sui mari 1939-1941*, Livorno Tirrena, 1950.

Brescia, M., *Mussolini's Navy. A Reference Guide to the Regia Marina 1930–1945*, Barnsley, Seaforth, 2012.

Brescia, M. & de Toro, A., *Incrociatori pesanti classe 'Zara'*, 'Storia Militare Dossier', December 2018.

——, *Incrociatori pesanti* Trento, Trieste *e* Bolzano, 'Storia Militare Dossier', December 2020.

Campbell, J., *Naval Weapons of World War Two*, London, Conway, 1985.

Chiavarelli, E., *L'opera della Marina italiana nella guerra italo-etiopica*, Milan, Giuffrè, 1969.

De Leva, F., *Storia delle Campagne Oceaniche della Marina Militare*, vol. IV, Rome, USMM, 1975.

De Toro, A. & Cicogna, M., *Navi d'Italia a Trieste 1918–1945*, Trieste, Luglio, 2021.

du Ravay, E., *Vingt ans de politique navale (1919-1939)*, Grenoble, Arthaud, 1941.

Ferrante, E., *Il grande ammiraglio Paolo Thaon di Revel*, Rome, Rivista Marittima, 1989.

Fioravanzo, G., *La Marina italiana nel suo primo secolo di vita 1861-1961*, Rome, USMM, 1961.

Friedman, N., *British Cruisers. Two World Wars and After*, Barnsley, Seaforth, 2010.

Gay, F. & Andò, E., *Incrociatori pesanti classe Trento*, parts I & II, Rome, Bizzarri, 1975.

——, *Incrociatori pesanti classe Zara*, parts I & II, Rome, Edizioni dell'Ateneo e Bizzarri, 1977.

Giorgerini, G.& Nani, A., *Gli incrociatori italiani*, Rome, USMM, 1971.

Goldstein, E. & Maurer, J. (editors), *The Washington Conference 1921-1922*, London-Portland, Frank Cass, 2002.

Halpern, P. G., *French and Italian Naval Policy in the Mediterranean 1898-1945*, in Hattendorf, J. B. (editor) *Naval Strategy and Policy in the Mediterranean*, London - Portland, Frank Cass, 2000.

Hinsley, F. H., *British Intelligence in the Second World War*, vol. 2, London, HMSO, 1981.

Hoy-Bezaux, P. & Ducros, P., *La Renaissance de la Marine francaise 1922-1939*, parte 1a: *1922-1930*, parte 2a: *1931-1939*, Lela Press, Outreau, 2011.

Jordan, J.& Moulin, J., *French Cruisers 1922–1956*, Barnsley, Seaforth, 2013.

Kowark, W., *Die Franzoesische Marinepolitik 1919-1924 und die Washingtoner Konferenz*, Stuttgart, Hochschulverlag, 1978.

Masson, P. G., *La 'belle marine' de 1939*, in Corvisier, A. (editor)

Histoire Militaire de la France, vol. III: *De 1871 a 1940*, Paris, Press Universitaires de France, 1997.

Mattesini, F., *L'operazione Gaudo e lo scontro notturno di Capo Matapan*, Rome, USMM, 1998

——, *La battaglia aeronavale di Mezzo Agosto*, Rome, Edizioni dell'Ateneo, 1986.

Maurer, J. & Bell, C. (editors), *At the crossroads between peace and war. The London Naval Conference of 1930*, Annapolis, Naval Institute, 2014.

Minardi, S., *Il disarmo navale italiano (1919-1936)*, Rome, USMM, 1999.

Moulin, J. & Maurand, P., *Le Croiser Algérie*, Nantes, Marines Edition, 1999.

Otter, K., *HMS Gloucester. The Untold Story*, Barnsley, Pen & Sword Maritime, 2001.

Raven, A., *British Cruiser Warfare. The Lessons of the Early War, 1939–1941*, Barnsley, Seaforth, 2019.

Raven, A. & Roberts, J., *British Cruisers of World War Two*, London, Arms and Armour Press, 1980.

Santoni, A., *Il vero traditore. Il ruolo documentato di ULTRA nella guerra del Mediterraneo*, Milan, Mursia, 1981.

Shores, C., Cull, B. & Malizia, N., *Malta. The Spitfire Year 1942, London*, Grub Street, 1992.

Stern, R. C., *Big Gun Battles. Warship Duels of the Second World War*, Barnsley, Seaforth, 2015.

Woodman, R., *Malta Convoys 1940–1943*, London, John Murray, 2000.

Serie *La Marina italiana nella Seconda Guerra Mondiale*:

- vol. IV: Fioravanzo, G., *Le azioni navali in Mediterraneo dal 10 giugno 1940 al 31 marzo 1941*, Rome, USMM, 1970.
- vol. V: Fioravanzo, G., *Le azioni navali in Mediterraneo dal 1° aprile 1941 all'8 settembre 1943*, Rome, USMM, 1970.
- vol. VI: Cocchia, A., *La difesa del traffico con l'Africa Settentrionale dal 10 giugno 1940 al 30 settembre 1941*, USMM, 1978.
- vol.VII: Cocchia, A., *La difesa del traffico con l'Africa Settentrionale dal 1° ottobre 1941 al 30 settembre 1942*, USMM, 1976.

ARTICLES AND ESSAYS

Bagnasco, E., 'I progetti per la trasformazione di unità del tipo 'Di Giussano' in incrociatori a.a. e del *Bolzano* in nave lancia-aerei', *Rivista Marittima*, June 1969.

Bagnasco, E. & Brescia, M., *Il* camouflage *delle navi italiane 1940-1945*, 'Storia Militare Dossier', September 2017.

Bargoni, F., *Lo sbarco e l'occupazione dell'Albania. 1939*, unpublished typescript.

Brauzzi, A., *La Marina italiana il 10 giugno 1940*, suppl. to *Rivista Marittima*, June 1980.

Colliva, G., 'La Marina fa la spesa', *Rivista Marittima*, November 2002.

——, 'Questioni di tiro... e altre', *Bollettino d'Archivio dell'USMM*, September 2003, December 2003, March 2004.

——, 'Il tiro navale italiano', *Storia Militare*, April 2010.

De Toro, A., 'Le incursioni aeree su Napoli nell'inverno 1940-1941', *Storia Militare*, February 2005.

——, 'La Maddalena, 10 aprile 1943', *Storia Militare*, Settembre 2006.

Gabriele, M., 'Leggi navali e sviluppo della Marina, parte II', *Rivista Marittima*, August-September 1981.

Marcon, T., 'Riviste navali a Napoli negli Anni *trenta*', *Bollettino d'Archivio dell'USMM*, June 1995.

Martino, E., 'Gli incrociatori tipo *Washington*', *Storia M*ilitare, n.323 & 324, August-September 2020.

Mattesini, F., 'La battaglia di Punta Stilo', Rome, USMM, no date [1999].

——, 'La battaglia di Capo Teulada (27-28 novembre 1940)', Rome, USMM, 2000.

——, 'L'operazione Gaudo e lo scontro notturno di Capo Matapan', Rome, USMM, 1998.

——, 'Il disastro del 9 novembre 1941. La 3a Divisione Navale e la fine del Convoglio Duisburg', Rome, Società Italiana di Storia Militare, no date.

Paoletti, C., 'Operazione *Oltre Mare Tirana*', *Storia Militare*, August 1995.

Ramoino, P. P., 'La Regia Marina tra le due guerre mondiali', supplement to *Rivista Marittima*, September 2011.

Severi, A., 'Una drammatica vicenda navale – La collisione fra il Pola ed il Lampo', *Bollettino d'Archivio dell'USMM*, June 1990.

INDEX

Page numbers in *italic* refer to illustrations